BUYING A PROPERTY IN
ITALY

THE ULTIMATE GUIDE TO BUYING AND LETTING IN ITALY

Compiled, edited and designed by
Merricks Media Ltd
3 & 4 Riverside Court
Lower Bristol Road
Bath, BA2 3DZ
Tel: 01225 786800
redguides@merricksmedia.co.uk
www.redguides.co.uk

Managing Editor Daphne Razazan
Editor Roz Cooper
Assistant Editor Leaonne Hall
Researchers Helen Hill, Mark Horne
Sub Editors Adam Waring, Mark Wheatley
Art Editor Angela Ashton
Managing Director Lisa Doerr
Publishing Director John Weir
Special Projects Manager Ali Stewart
Creative Director Carole Bohanan
Production Manager Graham Prichard
Sales Director Keith Burnell
Sales Executives Rob Faulkner, Sarah Vokins
Advertisement Design Becky Hamblin
Production Co-ordinator Sarah Dimelow

RED GUIDES is a trademark of Merricks Media Ltd

Cover image © **Alamy**

Regional maps by Jamie Symmonds
© **Merricks Media Ltd** 2005

Italy Touring Map © **Michelin et Cie**

Illustrations by Felix Packer
© **Merricks Media Ltd** 2005

First published 2005

Copyright © **Merricks Media Ltd** 2005

Printed and bound in the UK by St Ives Roche

ISBN 1-905049-17-X
British Library Cataloguing in Publication Data

A catalogue record for this bookazine is available from the British Library

This version of **Buying a Property In Italy** is exclusive to WHSmith

Roz Cooper

Roz Cooper is Editor of *The Italian Magazine*, a travel, lifestyle and property title that showcases the very best of Italy each month. With a varied career as a wine importer, book editor, tour leader and journalist, Roz still pursues a personal passion for wine and food with columns in publications such as *Fresh* magazine. She is a passionate advocate for the Italian way of life.

"The Italians have a unique take on life, which is inspirational and very attractive"

Ciao

THIS BOOK WILL PROBABLY CHANGE YOUR LIFE. YES, I know this is a cliché you've read many times before, but in the case of Italy, life really does change, and for the better, when you take the decision to buy your own home there. If you are seeking an alternative to our stressed, anxious British lifestyle, then the many and varied regions of Italy have much to offer. Even more important is the human dimension. The Italians have a unique take on life, which is inspirational and very attractive. Spend time with them and your pace of life slows, you find yourself chatting for hours over meals, and your eyes are opened to the beauty of the world around you, both natural and man-made, as Italy has a fantastic cultural history.

Of course, the actual move to Italy takes effort. Patience is essential when dealing with officials, everything takes a little longer than predicted, and the Italians have a charming vagueness about dates and deadlines. However, the wait will be worthwhile. And if you think Italy is out of your price range, just turn these pages and prepare to be amazed: look at Puglia, Emilia-Romagna or Le Marche for lovely, affordable property. Even Tuscany and Umbria have homes under €80,000, or consider Sicily or Sardinia for an island retreat. This book is packed with information to make your move as easy as possible, plus up-to-date practical advice and tips from experts and those in the know.

If you want to live in a country that still knows how to make the most of life, Italy is your natural destination.

A presto!

Roz

Roz Cooper, Editor

INTRODUCTION

Contents

OVERVIEW

Learn how to use this guide, meet our experts and get to know Italy with our maps

BUYER'S GUIDE

We give you all the information you need to buy, renovate and let your Italian home

BUYER'S REFERENCE

All the facts, figures and contacts you need in our easy-to-use directory and matrix

REAL-LIFE CASE STUDIES

We did it!...

Our inspirational real-life stories show you how easy it really is to relocate to Italy

CONTENTS

PROPERTY GUIDE

Uncover the delights of Venice **81**

Enjoy the luxury of Italy's riviera **63**

Discover the rural life in Le Marche **127**

Unearth a unique home in Sardinia **171**

Explore the charm of southern Italy **155**

13 in-depth regional guides to property hotspots, typical prices and life in each area

CONTENTS

71
We examine the unique style of Milan, its luxurious shops and fascinating culture

Cultural delights

Our culture guides uncover the history and top attractions of the six hottest regions

99 Tour the treasure trove that is Tuscany

145
Campania offers something for everyone, from Roman villas to Greek temples

How to use this guide

The guide's three sections – the Buyer's Guide, Property Guide and Buyer's Reference – cover every aspect of finding and buying a home in Italy, providing a wealth of expert advice

1. Buyer's Guide

The latest information about the financial and legal processes of buying property in Italy. The guide includes articles on the property and lettings market written by our panel of experts (see page 9), plus a comprehensive Steps to buying section, covering everything from obtaining a survey to completing a purchase.

Property market

The latest facts and up-to-the-minute information about buying and letting property in Italy

■ Informative articles on the economy and property market by our panel of experts

Steps to buying

A comprehensive section takes you through every stage of the financial process and the Italian conveyancing system, from arranging a mortgage to signing the contract

■ A sample bill breaks down the costs of buying a home

Living and working

Expert advice on visas and permits, the Italian healthcare and education systems, connecting utilities and much more

■ Checklists outline all you need to obtain important documents

Restoring a property

Expert advice on how to go about it, with guidelines on costs

■ Top tips on renovating your home

Real life

We did it! Be inspired by our four case studies showing how to turn a dream into reality – buying a *trullo* in Puglia, converting a farm for holiday rentals, renovating a house in Tuscany, and setting up a business in Umbria

■ Invaluable hints and tips based on firsthand experience

■ Q & A format for easy reference

2. Property Guide

Up-to-the-minute information about each region's property market, with detailed profiles of its top hotspots. The guide is divided into 13 regional chapters, from Lombardy and the Lakes to Sicily.

Regional profiles

General information on the region, its geography, economy, population, food and wine

■ Travel factfile

■ Feature boxes on local food and wine

Culture pages

An overview of the region's history and cultural treasures

■ Feature boxes on Italian style

■ Top ten attractions for each area

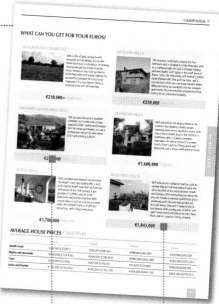

Property price guides

A guide to typical properties in each area, highlighting key architectural features, with sample properties showing you what you can get for your budget. Property price charts give sale prices for two-, three-, four- and five-bedroom properties, with prices averaged from the most recent sales data available

■ Property prices in euros

■ Agents' three-letter codes, listed in Index to agents on page 193

Hotspots

The key 55 places in which to buy a property in Italy, with information on everything from the lettings market and current price trends to the nearest hospitals and schools (in some cases we have been rigorously selective for reasons of space)

■ Regional maps show the main hotspots

■ Detailed hotspot profiles provide cultural information and highlight typical rental and purchase prices

■ Key facts cover everything from population and airports to schools and hospitals

3. Buyer's Reference

Includes three price matrices – for houses, apartments and lettings – to enable you to calculate potential outlay and rental return; a glossary of Italian house-buying and legal terms; a directory of useful contacts for professionals and organisations, from architects to lawyers; plus an index to estate agents specialising in Italy.

■ Price matrices are based on current market prices

Panel of experts

All our contributors are professionally qualified experts in their own field...

Stefano Bellini

Banca Woolwich's Marketing, Products and Remote Channel Director took a degree in Economics in Bocconi University. He has been working in banking and insurance services for 17 years, for companies including Banca Mediolanum, Generali Group, Popolare Commercio e Industria Bank and FreeFinance SpA, an internet marketplace dedicated to banking and insurance services. He started working for Banca Woolwich in November 2002. Stefano wrote our Economy feature.

Linda Stubbs

Linda Stubbs is the Italian-based consultant for Intouch Italia, which provides a tailored property location service. The company also provides relocation services from its offices in Italy and the UK.

Linda wrote our Living and Working and Moving to Italy articles. Contact Linda on +39 0583 97968 or 01908 265309; info@intouchitalia.co.uk; www.intouchitalia.co.uk

Trinidad Passerini

Trinidad Passerini completed her university education in Venice in Business Administration, with a focus on Marketing and Communication in the Luxury Market.

She has several years of experience in the Real Estate industry for the English-speaking market, and is head of Precious Villas, a London-based agency that offers assistance in finding high-end properties in Italy and the Mediterranean area, as well as legal and financial support. Trinidad wrote our Property Market piece.

Alan Tootill

Alan Tootill has lived in Puglia for the past three years, contributing articles to newspapers and magazines about the region and its culture, as well as appearing in television programmes on the Puglia property scene. He wrote the Puglia Property Market section, and works as a housefinder and relocation consultant for Apulia Properties. For details see www.apulia.co.uk; alan@apulia.co.uk

Mark Slaviero

Mark Slaviero is a Director of the leading Italian property sales and holiday rentals company, Homes in Italy. Mark has had articles published in the national press and leading magazines, including *The Italian Magazine*, and he wrote our Restoring a Property, Steps to Buying and The Lettings Market articles. His family originates from the Veneto region, where he owns property. Contact Mark on 01332 341146; mark@homesinitaly.co.uk

© ENIT

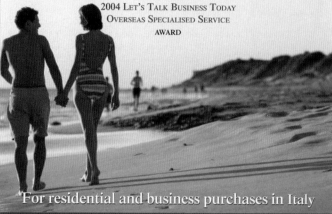

Touring map and facts

POPULATION

- Italy has an estimated population of 58.1 million
- Italy has one of the lowest birth rates in the world, at less than 9 per 1,000, and its 0.07% annual population growth is due to immigration
- Average life expectancy in Italy is 79.68, which is the14th-highest in the world
- Areas in the north contain groups of German, French and Slovene Italians, and areas in the south have small clusters of Greek and Albanian Italians
- From being a country of net emigration for most of the 20th century, Italy is now home to between 1.5 and 2 million immigrants
- 67% of Italy's population lives in urban areas

GEOGRAPHY

- Italy covers 301,230km², including Sardinia and Sicily
- Five of Italy's 20 regions are autonomous: Valle d'Aosta, Trentino-Alto Adige, Sardinia, Sicily and Friuli-Venezia Giulia
- Italy has land borders with Switzerland, France, Austria, Slovenia, San Marino and the Vatican City, measuring 1,932km in total
- Mountainous areas make up 75% of Italy
- The highest point in Italy is Mont Blanc de Courmayeur, a secondary peak of Mont Blanc, at 4,748 metres
- There are six active volcanoes in Italy, which has a fault line running from Sicily up to the Alps in the northeast, and there are frequent minor quakes in the south

CLIMATE

- The far northern reaches of Italy have an alpine climate, with quite severe winters and heavy rainfall, although it is warmer in the valleys
- The northern Italian plain and

TOURING MAP

Po valley have warm summers (average range 24 to 28 degrees Celsius) and cold winters (average range from 2 to 8 degrees Celsius)
- The peninsula has a Mediterranean climate, with mild winters (average temperatures are 11 to 18 degrees Celsius) and hot, dry summers (average temperatures reach 28 or 30 degrees Celsius)
- Occasional Sirocco winds blow in from Africa, bringing hot, suffocating temperatures to

the peninsula, approaching 40 degrees Celsius
- Udine in Friuli-Venezia Giulia is the wettest part of Italy, with 1,520mm of rainfall per year, and the driest is in southern Sicily, with just 460mm a year

ECONOMY

- Unemployment is about 8.6% in Italy, though there is a sharp divide between the north, where there is very high employment, and the south,

where 18 to 20% of people are out of work
- Italian GDP is $27,700 per capita, and is growing at 1.3%
- Over 30% of the population work in manufacturing and industry
- Major exports include clothing, cars, machinery, engineering products and food, of which over 50% go to EU countries
- 30 million people visit the country every year, and at $28.8 billion, Italy has the fourth-largest tourist income in the world

Regional map of Italy

SWITZERLAND

AUSTRIA

HUNGARY

ALTO ADIGE

TRENTINO-ALTO ADIGE

①

FRIULI-VENEZIA GIULIA

④

SLOVENIA

CROATIA

VALLE D'AOSTA

Lake Maggiore

Lake Como

LOMBARDY

Trento

The Dolomites

④

Treviso

Trieste

Aosta

Brescia

VENETO

Lido di Jésolo

Milan

③

Verona

Venice

Turin

Padua

PIEDMONT

Parma

①

Genoa

EMILIA-ROMAGNA

⑤

LIGURIA

②

Cinque Terre

Bologna

Alassio

Levanto

Apennine Ski Resorts

Rimini

FRANCE

Diana Marina

Riviera di Ponente

Lucca

Tuscan Coast

Urbino

Pesaro

Pisa

Florence

Ancona

San Gimignano

Chianti

Arezzo

LE MARCHE

SERBIA

Siena

TUSCANY

Lake Trasimeno

Loreto

Cortona

Perugia

⑦

Assisi

⑧

Montepulciano

UMBRIA

Monti Sibillini

CORSICA

⑥

Lake Bolsena

Todi

Orvieto

Sabine Hills

Adriatic Sea

Viterbo

LAZIO

Pescara

ABRUZZO

Tollo

ROME

KEY

● Hotspots

○ Major towns/cities

66 Road numbers

⑨

MOLISE

Campobasso

REGIONAL MAP

Isola Rossa

Castelsardo

Porto Cervo

CAMPANIA

⑪

Bari

Trulli area

Alghero

⑬

Olbia

⑩

Potenza

Alberobello

SARDINIA

Naples

BASILICATA

PUGLIA

Procida

Amalfi Coast

Matera

Brindisi

Oristano

ISCHIA

CAPRI

⑪

Tyrrhenian Sea

Scalea

Cagliari

Pula

CALABRIA

Chia

Lamezia Terme

Santa Margherita Coastline

Tropea

Catanzaro

AEOLIAN ISLANDS

⑪

Palermo

Cefalù

Reggio di Calabria

Trapani

Taormina

Mediterranean Sea

Castellammare del Golfo

SICILY

⑫

Catania

PANTELLERIA

Ragusa

Syracuse

KEY TO ITALIAN REGIONS

- 1. Piedmont, Valle d'Aosta & Trentino-Alto Adige
- 2. Liguria
- 3. Lombardy & the Lakes
- 4. Venice, the Veneto & Friuli-Venezia Giulia
- 5. Emilia-Romagna
- 6. Tuscany
- 7. Umbria
- 8. Le Marche & Abruzzo
- 9. Rome & Lazio
- 10. Campania
- 11. Puglia, Calabria & Basilicata
- 12. Sicily
- 13. Sardinia

Buyer's guide

Buying property abroad is a big step, so before you rush headlong into the decision, read our expert advice on finding and buying your dream home in Italy

Living la dolce vita

Italy's rich culture, effortless style and fantastic cuisine have been a magnet for the British for decades, but it's living the Italian life that we most desire

© ROZ COOPER

Life in Italy is very relaxed

WHY BUY IN ITALY? MORE THAN ALMOST any other country, Italy draws us to her with the heart as much as the head. That fantastic outpouring of natural exuberance and beauty, plus a wealth of culture, food and wine, is enough to seduce many a Brit to consider a house purchase after just one or two holidays there. Add to this the profusion of books, films and music that all celebrate *la dolce vita* – the sweet life – as lived in Italy, and it seems our choice has been made for us.

Something for everyone

Yet, of course, the purchase of a property is not, and should not be, an impulsive move. Given an initial attraction to Italy, what factors should be considered when taking a serious step to buy? Affordability is a key element for many potential purchasers, and Italy does tend to have a reputation for upmarket, even palatial second homes reserved for wealthy lawyers (Sir John Mortimer has unwittingly played a part in creating this impression) or for those who are blessed with serious cash.

If Tuscany is your sole aim, and it is certainly a region uniquely endowed with superb scenery, historic buildings and fine cuisine and wine, then you will indeed need a fairly full wallet, but even here there are bargains to be found. Take a look

north of Lucca or down into the intriguing Maremma region, which is a complete visual contrast to 'Chiantishire' but has its own expansive charm, and a fine coastline. This contrast within a single region offers in a nutshell the key to why Italy is the right place to buy. For this country, so near by plane, train or automobile, is truly a nation of contrasts, containing every style of life and type of landscape we might seek.

From the alpine grandeur of the north, to the elegance of the Lakes and the classical appeal of great cities, there is a progressive range of lifestyle from 'gentleman wine farmer' in Tuscany or Umbria, to rugged pioneer in the far south. Along the way, you can choose the ultimate sophistication of a Milan lifestyle; the dreamy decadence of Venice; the simplicity of inland Campania or the romance of undiscovered Sicily. For Italy has its islands too, and these are legendary names: apart from Sicily, consider Sardinia, glamorous Capri, tiny volcanic Stromboli, or Pantelleria – so far to the south it is almost part of Africa.

North and south

The divide between north and south is very real here in Italy, and you will probably find yourself drawn to side with one faction or another. The

The dream of relocating to an Italian hill town, deep in the countryside, can become a reality

"That indefinable asset, quality of life, is on offer; people smile, take time to talk, and relish life's pleasures"

© ROZ COOPER

affluent northerners of Turin, Milan or Rome still sneer at the subsistence farmers of Puglia or Calabria, and in recent years there has even been a political movement trying to separate the two halves of the country officially. Italy is, after all, only a loose association of former city states and part of the charm of the place is the powerful individuality found in each region. Despite the best efforts of Garibaldi, Mussolini and now the faceless bureaucrats of the EU, Italy firmly refuses to homogenise. Its diversity is its great asset.

If you are still hesitating over making that move, consider this: a recent American Express survey, which compared the cost of various standard holiday items, demonstrated that, far from being expensive, Italy is the most affordable holiday destination in Western Europe; it was the best-value destination of the six EU nations surveyed and came in at almost half the cost of Ireland.

Despite the famed political muddle that is the Italian government, the economy is remarkably stable, and the essentials of life are not overpriced. Local food and wine are usually available, with ample explanation of how to appreciate their delights, and education for your children is virtually free and of a good standard. The national health service is no worse than that in the UK (and may well be better in the north of Italy), and public transport is efficient and usually inexpensive.

A warm welcome
So there are many factors steering you gently toward the joys of *la dolce vita*, not forgetting the welcoming attitude of most Italians toward foreigners. Pragmatic and tolerant, they will put themselves out to explain, encourage and enlighten

It's the Italians' zest for life that makes moving there such an attractive prospect

the new arrival in their community and show them how to get into the local network. For networking is truly the key to getting on in life in Italy. Speaking the language is a very valuable tool, patience is a great virtue, and learning to make the most of chance contacts is essential. Life in Italy revolves around who you know, and how well; those gifted with charm and social skill will do well here. Alternatively, bring along some children to break the ice for you, as Italians do genuinely adore them. Finding a job is far easier if you simply make enquiries in the neighbourhood.

Similarly, you may discover that estate agents have a very nebulous idea of the value of any house on their books: 'make me an offer' is a real part of Italian culture, and takes some adaptation for the timid British, accustomed to paying full RRP for everything! Even planning consent, building negotiations and utility services are areas for the skilled networker to shine. Persuasive skills and oodles of patience may be more valuable than any amount of internet research.

Life is sweet
That indefinable asset, quality of life, is what's on offer in Italy. Buying a home here will bring you into a world where local people tend to smile at strangers, embrace you on the briefest acquaintance, and take time to talk, explain and relish life and its pleasures. From Mozzarella to Parma ham, Moscato to Prosecco, the range of culinary and vinous pleasures here is too long to list.

We may think we know Italy because its influence is so pervasive, and so benign, worldwide. But real Italian ingredients taste more wonderful than any exported version. And a meal in Italy is a succession of treats, each of which is discussed in loving detail by the assembled company. ●

WHY LIVE IN ITALY?
From the poets and travellers of the 18th century to the romantic films and books of today, this land has lured the sun-starved British away from their chilly, self-conscious island life and into the warmth of an Italian welcome. Though the north of Italy is not by any means warm all year (indeed Tuscany can be dank and chilly in winter), the very real zest for life that the Italians lead is something we can appreciate, envy, and then, eventually, share. This reason alone is enough to take us to Italy.

"This country is truly a nation of contrasts, offering every style of life and landscape we might seek"

LIVING LA DOLCE VITA

17

The economy

While Italy is making slow and steady progress towards economic growth, there is still a lot of work to be done

© MILAN TOURIST BOARD

Italy's economy is growing

ITALY HAS A DIVERSIFIED AND INDUSTRIAL economy, enjoying roughly the same output as England and France. The country has operated a tight fiscal policy in an attempt to meet EU monetary standards, and the benefits have been low interest and inflation rates. The country came out of the 1990s recession in a strong position and has since been on an upward trend. In 2004, the Italian economic growth rate equalled 1.2 per cent, with a 0.4 per cent increase compared with 2003; inflation grew to around 2.7 per cent.

Current economic situation

Over the past 50 years Italy has undergone a massive turnaround, with standards of living rising rapidly, and an average Gross Domestic Product (GDP) growth of six to eight per cent per year. This is largely due to an entrepreneurial bias combined with liberal trade policies. Despite this, current political uncertainty is threatening to impact on this hard-earned economic stability.

The years from 1958 to 1963 were known as '*il miracolo economico*' (the economic miracle), when Italy experienced 10 per cent economic growth, full employment and high levels of investment. Following the 1990s recession, a sweeping privatisation scheme was put in place, and these corrective measures left Italy with a strong fiscal policy, a stable currency and low interest rates, all of

"Areas such as the Veneto, Lazio and Lombardy offer low unemployment and hi-tech opportunities"

THE ECONOMY

COST OF LIVING

Petrol (1l)	€1
Wine (0.75l)	€15
Meal (three-course)	€20.50
Beer (33cl)	€1
Loaf of bread	€2.50
Milk (1l)	€0.77
Mineral water (1l)	€ 0.40

which allowed the country to join the European Monetary Union (EMU) in 1999.

Italian economic recovery and growth are underway but proving slow. Industrial production has dropped by 0.5 per cent, as has GDP. Italy boasts the fourth-highest GDP in Europe, and is regarded as a sophisticated and brand-aware market. With more than 60 million consumers and positioned at the crossroads of the international market, Italy is seen as an excellent investment prospect for foreign businesses. However, although Berlusconi's government partially reduced income taxes, the first quarter of 2005 saw negative economic indicators. GDP, exports, domestic demand and investments all had negative variations, whereas the stock exchange was stable. Italy's labour market is better than the European average, and the employment rate should increase by 0.6 per cent by the end of 2006. The inflation rate should also sit slightly lower than the EU average, only two per cent in 2005 and 1.9 per cent in 2006. In terms of diversity, Italy's economy has a small and rapidly diminishing primary sector, with services generating almost two-thirds of the country's profit. However, manufacturing does remain key, contributing 25 per cent of Italy's GDP.

Regional economies

Italy is strikingly divided between the north and south. The north is industrial and developed, with the northeast being dominated by private companies (of which Italy has very few). The less-developed agricultural south currently experiences 20 per cent unemployment and is heavily reliant on welfare. According to Unione Italiana CCIAA, in 2005 northern regions will have a GDP increase above the national average of 1.3 per cent. Central regions will follow with a 1.1 per cent growth, and southern regions with a 1.0 per cent growth.

Specific regional GDP increases are recorded in Valle d'Aosta (1.6 per cent), Trentino-Alto Adige

Unemployment is highest in the south, where the economy is reliant on agriculture

© ENIT

and Abruzzo (both 1.4 per cent), and Lombardy, Liguria and the Veneto (1.3 per cent). Areas such as the Veneto, Lazio and Lombardy are huge contributors to the country's GDP, offering low unemployment rates and great hi-tech industry opportunities. Liguria is driven by logistics and shipbuilding, as is Campania, while the northern alpine economy benefits from easy access to Northern Europe, with tourism the dominant industry. Similarly Tuscany is buoyant, due to its rampant real estate industry and tourist-driven economy. Areas such as Puglia and Basilicata are also becoming increasingly dependent upon their service industry, although 20 per cent of their economy is still driven by agriculture. Emilia-

"With more than 60 million consumers, Italy is seen as an excellent investment prospect"

Romagna and Umbria offer an excellent quality of life and a good labour pool, with the presence of Bologna and Perugia universities in the respective regions making them good centres for research and development. Finally Sicily and Sardinia are expanding their economies and contributing more to the Italian GDP; however, years of tradition and high unemployment rates are hampering the development of the growing communications and IT industries there.

Future economic growth

Berlusconi's attempts to revitalise the economy with tax cuts in January have had little impact, and this economic uncertainty, coupled with an ageing population, has meant investment has declined. The economy has been dominated by Europe and its markets, and the country has been under political pressure to meet the rigorous measures enforced by the EMU. 2005 and 2006 are expected to see a drop in unemployment; however, productivity has been weak, and although overall the country's debt is reducing, it still exceeds 100 per cent of the GDP.

Political uncertainty and a lack of trust in the Italian government are also damaging economic confidence, with the forecast stating economic growth of 1.4 to 1.9 per cent . This growth may not be achieved, however, as the country continues to deal with the recent financial scandals at the

Tourism plays a large part in Italy's economy, creating jobs throughout the country

Parmalat and Cirio food groups, which have already had an impact on the country's ability to sell exports. Borrowing has increased by 12.2 per cent, mainly due to the high number of house purchases, amounting to 770,000 in 2004 (a one per cent increase on the previous year). The property market has reached a daily average of 2,500 transactions, mainly boosted by favourable rates and over-15-year-term mortgages. This growing trend, both in terms of transactions and in terms of house prices, should stabilise in 2006 as the economy does. ●

REGIONAL GDP (PREDICTED PERCENTAGE GROWTH)

	2004	2005	2006	2007	2008
Piedmont	1.3	1.2	1.4	1.7	1.3
Valle d'Aosta	1.5	1.6	2.2	1.9	3.0
Lombardy	1.2	1.3	1.8	1.6	1.5
Trentino-Alto Adige	1.5	1.4	2.4	2.5	2.2
The Veneto	1.2	1.3	1.8	1.7	1.4
Friuli-Venezia Giulia	1.1	0.8	1.4	1.6	1.2
Liguria	1.1	1.3	1.8	1.6	1.2
Emilia-Romagna	1.4	1.2	1.8	1.8	1.5
Tuscany	1.3	1.1	1.8	1.8	1.5
Umbria	1.7	1.0	2.3	2.3	2.0
Le Marche	1.3	0.9	1.2	2.3	1.2
Lazio	0.9	1.1	1.7	1.7	1.1
Abruzzo	0.7	1.4	2.3	1.8	1.4
Molise	1.1	1.3	2.3	2.1	1.6
Campania	0.9	1.0	2.1	1.7	1.5
Puglia	1.3	1.0	2.0	1.7	1.4
Basilicata	1.0	0.8	1.9	1.8	1.5
Calabria	1.1	0.8	1.9	1.5	1.5
Sicily	0.7	1.0	1.5	1.1	0.7
Sardinia	1.1	1.0	2.0	1.6	1.3
Italy	1.2	1.2	1.8	1.7	1.4

Source: Unioncamere, Scenari di sviluppo delle economie locali italiane 2005–2008

The property market

Property prices have shot up throughout Italy, but there is still good investment potential and there are bargains to be had

Renovation may require work!

PROPERTY MARKET

"With flights costing as little as 99p, it costs less to commute to Forlì than it does, say, from London to Bath"

THE ITALIAN REAL ESTATE MARKET IS growing steadily. Throughout the 1990s the market has experienced strong growth, averaging annual price appreciation of five per cent, and collective growth of 35 per cent since 1999. However, Italy's northern cities, such as Milan and Rome, have appreciated at a rate of 12 to 13 per cent per annum, higher than the national average. With prices reaching an all time high, experts have predicted that they will soon begin to drop slightly as they have hit a natural ceiling.

Italy has always been regarded as a good investment, with coastal resorts traditionally offering cheaper prices than elsewhere in Europe and, despite dramatic price hikes being experienced in some areas, there are still bargains to be found. For those with the money the opportunities are endless, with luxurious Ligurian properties or Venetian apartments available for a cool million euros or so.

Why Italy?

Some trendsetters are also drawing attention to Italian real estate. George Clooney has purchased a villa on Lake Como, and both Sting and Tony Blair own properties in Tuscany. Madonna and Elton John have apartments in Venice, while Sharon Stone is currently looking to buy. However, the biggest draw for overseas buyers remains the Italian countryside, with the 'holy grail' being the rural renovation property surrounded by olive groves and cypress trees. While the price for a renovation property can drop as low as €500 per square metre,

Venice is a unique, but highly expensive, city

bear in mind that after all the work has been carried out you could be looking at a final figure of up to €1,000 per square metre.

Italy has experienced continued demand from overseas buyers due to a fashion that goes back to the 1950s and the desire for 'la dolce vita' lifestyle. The quality of life, the cultural and historical treasures, the food, the mild climate, and the astonishingly beautiful scenery are key factors in the continued demand for Italian property.

The internal demand for new homes is steadily growing at approximately 4.5 per cent, and this is impacting on prices in certain areas of Italy and pushing them higher. The building of new homes is probably the best performing industry in Italy at the moment, one of the major reasons being the offer of low rates of repayment for mortgages – the lowest for 25 years. Banca d'Italia says that mortgages approved for the purchase of homes have grown by 17.4 per cent last year, while the demand for mortgages for investment properties to let has grown by 7.8 per cent.

What are buyers looking for?

The highest demand from foreign buyers is for rural homes to be renovated. Historic old mills, castles, abbeys, farmhouses and *palazzi*, complete with fresco decorations, are much sought after by foreign investors. Often, these types of properties are then

Trulli, found only in Puglia, are distinctive properties that are attracting much interest

© OLI PROPERTIES

Turning your investment into a business takes commitment, but can pay dividends

divided into smaller units and sold separately. Small apartments are still in demand in the big cities, where prices are very high, but they tend to suit those who are interested in being close to cultural attractions. High demand is reflected in the limited supply of historic and renovation properties, which has driven buyers into the recently 'undiscovered' regions of Le Marche and Abruzzo.

Regional trends

The British market and its interest in Italian property has been fuelled by the opening of new routes into regional airports from low-cost airlines. This has encouraged foreign buyers to explore new areas, such as Le Marche, Abruzzo and Puglia, which now offer excellent bargain properties and great investment opportunities, and have seen huge market growth. Puglia is experiencing an average of 20 to 25 per cent price appreciation annually, which makes it great for those seeking a guaranteed profit, while Liguria is still experiencing growth of between 10 and 20 per cent a year.

While Tuscany remains an attractive market, headed by Florence and the Chianti area, it remains the most expensive area of Italy and prices are not expected to decrease. Next to Florence, Venice and Rome are also highly expensive areas, where the price per square metre for a habitable apartment reaches €10,000. While there is a small margin for decrease in these prices, they are unlikely to drop substantially, which is good news for investors. For those seeking a long-term investment, Venice has been earmarked as a reliable earner. Due to the limitations and restrictions on building and the continued demand, prices are unlikely to fall, despite the market hitting an all time high in terms of cost. With over nine million visitors a year, rental income is also guaranteed.

Renovations market

The renovations market has been steadily growing, but has really taken off in the last four or five years, and the government has put financial backing into sustaining renovation projects and developments. High prices and a lack of available properties have made finding a run-down farmhouse in the showcase region of Tuscany all but impossible in recent years. Real estate in lesser-known regions, on the other hand, is another story. In Le Marche, for example, a dilapidated house that needs complete renovation can be purchased for €60,000 to €250,000, depending on the size and location; a fraction of Tuscan prices. While it might seem extravagant to have a weekend house in the Italian countryside, with some flights costing from as little as 99p (plus taxes, of course) it turns out to be much less expensive to commute from Stansted to Forlì than, say, taking the train from London to Bath.

The buy-to-let market

The buy-to-let market is strong in the big cities, such as Venice, Florence and Rome, where it is hard to imagine demand ever reducing. In the countryside, farmhouses offering bed and breakfast are the most popular proposition. Some areas, in particular Tuscany, have seen such demand for holiday accommodation that prices have reached the levels of four or five star hotels for rustic accommodation. However, if you are looking to set up a B&B or rent your farmhouse, you may find it difficult to secure rents in such a saturated market. It is probably more financially worthwhile to look at new regions, such as Puglia, Le Marche, Abruzzo and even Umbria. ●

"Italy has always been regarded as a good investment and, despite price hikes, there are still bargains"

PROPERTY MARKET

ANNUAL PRICE INCREASES

Campania 10%
Emilia-Romagna 10%
Le Marche & Abruzzo up to 100%
Liguria 10–20%
Lombardy & the Lakes 11.2%
Piedmont, Valle d'Aosta & Trentino-Alto Adige 9%
Puglia, Calabria & Basilicata 20–25%
Rome & Lazio 8%
Sardinia 20%
Sicily 20%
Tuscany 10%
Umbria 8%
Venice, the Veneto & Friuli-Venezia Giulia 14%

The lettings market

Italy may not be at the forefront of the overseas buy-to-let market, but more and more people are looking to gain a return from their Italian property

Buy with rental in mind

B UYING-TO-LET IS BECOMING AN increasingly popular activity in Italy, as many people are looking at creating an income to offset mortgage payments and other outgoings, while others view it as an excellent way of creating a nest egg for the future.

Either way, it is imperative, as a potential purchaser, to undertake research from the outset to ensure that it is a viable venture, and that the property will gain the desired rental yields. Italy has been a popular holiday destination for many years and, with the rise of low-cost airlines, many new regions have opened up, allowing people to move away from the traditional package holiday and adopt more tailored vacations. It is estimated that more than 50 per cent of holiday-makers are choosing this alternative. This is good news for the rental market, but if you plan on renting the property regularly, it is important you select the right type of investment.

Choosing the property

You should keep the rental market in mind when buying a property and try to ascertain the target audience and their needs. Are you aiming at young professionals, families or the more mature client? An apartment in Rimini would appeal to families and the young at heart, whereas properties in the Lakes would suit a more mature clientele. The style and

layout of the property are important but the location is key. The sorts of questions you need to ask yourself are as follows: Is the property easy to access? Is it suitable for children? Does it have parking? Would you be happy renting there? Is it within easy access of airports served by low-cost airlines? What are the local amenities?

One-bed apartments will still rent, for example, but if the lounge is large enough to sleep additional guests then this will be a bonus. Pools will boost rentals of countryside properties.

Where to buy

It is worthwhile to research the level of rental income that you can expect in the area. If a property has been rented before, try and obtain details from the estate agent or current vendor. Also, renting before you buy is an excellent way to discover the potential of the area. Finding the next 'undiscovered' area and being the only rental may not be the best strategy, but if there are a few rented properties dotted around, then this is a good sign that someone has tested the market first.

Most holiday-makers prefer to be no more than an hour from an airport, and many potential clients will be deterred if the journey is more than 90 minutes. Make sure that the area is well served by an airport and that it has operated for some time because if the airline pulls out, so will your potential rentals. Also look at the number of regional flights to an airport; Pisa, Rome and Venice have flights from many locations throughout the UK.

Rental returns

Once you have found a suitable property, it is important to be realistic with the rental income – gross rental yields are five to ten per cent of the property value per year and, in some cases, can be as high as 15 per cent. It is unlikely that the property will be occupied all year round, so it is important not to overestimate the income or rely on it totally to pay the mortgage or running costs. Buying this sort of property is a medium to long-term venture if you want to gain real returns. Include agency commissions (which vary from 15 to 35 per cent), advertising costs, furnishing and equipping of the property, specialist insurance (third-party covering injury to guests) and property maintenance.

It is important to be aware of the tax implications of renting – you should take into account income tax, which you are required to pay by law. Income

PREPARE THE PROPERTY FOR RENT

Holiday-makers have high expectations, so ensure that the property is in the best condition, both internally and externally...

■ Make sure that the grounds and pool are well maintained and that the bathroom and kitchen are up to date, fully functional and equipped (crockery, utensils, glassware, pans, etc).

■ Dishwashers and washing machines are a major plus point.

■ Install robust and quality furniture – basic furniture can be false economy.

■ Make sure that the beds are comfortable and that there are ample chairs for eating and relaxing.

■ Adding a few traditional and local touches will enhance the character of the property and impress clients.

■ Don't leave anything of any great importance in the property as items can often be broken (the security deposit may well cover the damage but not replace the item). A lockable chest is always a good idea for personal items.

■ Preparing a welcome pack is always an unexpected surprise and adds a personal touch. Include information on the property, what is available to visit in the area and where to eat, and even include some basic provisions.

■ Finally, don't forget about insurance cover and health and safety regulations.

up to €10,000 is taxed at 18 per cent, €10,000 to €15,000 at 24 per cent, and €15,000 to €30,000 at 32 per cent. You will require a *commercialista* (accountant) to assist you with your return.

The market

Italy is very diverse and research on the location is essential. The season is the longest in the south, where you can rent up to 20 weeks of the year, but in more northern climes, such as Liguria or Piedmont, the average is 10 weeks.

Apartments in major tourist cities have almost year-round letting potential. With budget airlines, people can pop over for a long weekend with ease. Apartments in Venice sleeping up to four can range from €1,000 to €1,300 a week in high season. The average weekly rental for a similar property in Rome or Florence is around €1,000 per week.

Puglia is currently flavour of the month and, with extensive publicity, is attracting a large number of visitors. Especially of interest are the traditional *trulli*, which can rent for an average of €750 per week in high season.

Central Italy

This area continues to be very popular, Tuscany and Umbria in particular. The most popular rentals are rural farmhouses, which range from €2,000 to over €4,500 a week in high season, depending on location and size. Northern Umbria attracts more modest rents, as does the northern Tuscan areas of Bagni di Lucca and Barga, where a typical mountain house sleeping four can fetch between €400 and €700 in high season. The Umbrian hill town of Assisi attracts five million visitors alone, and there will certainly be a tourist market out of season at peak times such as Easter and Christmas.

The lesser known Le Marche and Abruzzo are a good investment in terms of purchase prices, but are not yet fully on the tourist trail, so a greater effort on the marketing front would be required.

A pool is a major plus in rural areas

MAINTAINING YOUR PROPERTY

You'll need to maintain the property and keep it up to the standard that holiday-makers will expect. Some rental agencies offer a full rental service, which will give owners peace of mind knowing that the property is safe and all in order. Don't forget that the property will need cleaning and linen will need to be changed between lets.

If you decide to go down the self-management route, then either being on-site or having a reliable neighbour or local contact is essential. Finding a person whom you can trust is always a problem, but asking neighbours or other English residents will usually lead to the discovery of someone looking for additional work. Make sure that you leave clear instructions and have a back-up contact for emergency call-outs.

Northern Italy

Italy's Lakes have been firmly on the tourist map for years, attracting a mostly northern European clientele and the odd Hollywood film star. Lake Garda leads the field, with colourful resorts such as Riva, Salo and Sirmione, and is very diverse, surrounded by countryside, olive groves and pine trees. Lake Maggiore and Lake Como and their resorts are also popular, and offer stunning scenery and vast expanses of water. The Lakes are within easy access of the key cities in northern Italy (Milan, Bergamo, Verona) and also ski resorts, which will assist with out-of-season rentals. A one-bed apartment in Como can take around €700 – and a two-bed around €1,000 – per week in high season.

Liguria has long been popular and has a mild climate, is easy to access and is connected to the south of France, offering great options for day tripping. Seaside resorts, such as Alassio, San Remo and Diano Marina, attract a large Italian audience, and other highlights include Portovenere and Cinque Terre. The terraced hillsides behind the coast are full of olive groves and lemon trees and offer reasonable purchase prices, with good rental returns. Two-bed apartments to rent in the more popular resorts vary from €1,000 to €1,300 in high season and a small one-bed hill town apartment can even achieve between €350 and €450 per week.

Coastal areas

Sardinia is another great destination for rentals, with turquoise sea and outstanding sandy beaches. Until recently the island has been more difficult to access, and has been regarded as a more expensive and exclusive holiday destination. This has changed with the inclusion of Olbia, Cagliari and Alghero on the low-cost airline schedules. The resorts to the east of Alghero are quite reasonable and easily accessible from the airports. Villas can command from €2,000 a week, depending on size and location.

Until recently, the Amalfi coast has been accessed mostly through package deals, but Naples airport now offers a greater choice of flights. Sorrento, Positano and Amalfi are firmly on the tourist trail. A four-bed property should achieve a weekly rental of at least €600 in high season, and those with exceptional views can achieve as much as €900. ●

Keep property in good order

"Make sure the area is served by an airport that has operated for some time – if an airline pulls out, so will your rentals"

Moving to Italy

Adventurous and challenging, moving abroad is a huge undertaking that promises a dramatic change of lifestyle

Plan ahead for a smooth move

THERE ARE MANY REASONS TO MOVE TO Italy. You could be looking for a holiday idyll or pursuing a job opportunity. Retirement or thoughts of a renovation project may entice you. Whatever the reason, the outcome will be life changing. You'll find a whole new world opening up, and your standard of living improving drastically.

Italy has so much to offer a potential relocator, but the people are probably the country's greatest asset – Italians are helpful, friendly, willing and hard-working. Even the notorious Italian bureaucracy can be conquered with a little patience and the right forms! Relocating can be a challenge, but your reward will be an improved lifestyle in one of Europe's most cultured and sophisticated countries.

Distance from home

Although the end product of your move will be worthwhile, you'll need to take into account practicalities, as well as dreams. If you have very close family links, will you cope being so far away? Of course, with budget airlines and flights from local airports, rapid travel at short notice has become a practical and financial possibility.

The Italian climate

The weather in Italy is a great draw, but if you're going to live there, you do need to think about it. Can you stand consistent temperatures up to 40 degrees for weeks on end? In 2003, it didn't rain for

SHIPPING YOUR BELONGINGS

If you are relocating for work purposes it is more than likely your employer will cover the costs of shipping your belongings. However, most people will be faced with footing the bill themselves. In this case you need to work out what the costs will be and get more than one quote from removals agencies. You also need to find out if you can import your goods into Italy duty-free.

five months! This can be very draining, especially if you're working every day.

Also, Italy experiences a very cold winter, and not just in the north. Southern Italy had snow in 2005, and a number of smaller villages were isolated for days. Many of the northern cities also suffer from fog and smog in the winter, and you must ensure that your property, as well as you and your family, are ready for these conditions.

Learning the language

Italian is constructed very differently from English, but it's not difficult to learn. The younger you start, the easier you'll find it. Consequently, if you're moving with young children, enrol them in a local Italian-speaking school, enabling them to pick up the language much faster. For the rest of us, given a good book and concentration, picking up the basics shouldn't be too hard, and after a few lessons you should be able to hold a basic conversation.

Once you're up and running, it's amazing how helpful your neighbours and acquaintances will be, and with a knowledge of just 100 words or so, you can happily go about daily life. The best means of learning is to actually be in the country. Naturally, if you're coming to Italy to work, more in-depth knowledge will be necessary.

Healthcare

Living in the UK, we tend to take our health and healthcare for granted. However, anybody thinking of retiring abroad should consider the ramifications of possible ill health. If you don't have a good grasp of the language, it may be difficult to explain symptoms or ailments, and just as difficult to understand instructions from a doctor. Consider private health insurance as a matter of importance.

On everyday issues you should try to find an English-speaking doctor to register with. As an EU member, you're entitled to care in the Italian state system and you can register with any doctor you wish, rather than being limited to a certain catchment area. This means you can seek out a doctor who's recommended by acquaintances or by your neighbours, and who speaks English.

Education

There's nowhere in Italian society where the differences between north and south are so exemplified as in the education system. The richer north has the best schools and universities, with

TIMELINE

	6 months	3 months	2 months	1 month	1 week	1 day
BRITAIN	• Contact estate agents about selling your home	• Contact letting agents, seek financial advice and begin organisation • Request information about work permits and visas • Check your passport is valid for your stay and renew it if necessary • Begin to educate yourself about Italy and possibly learn a few useful phrases	• Obtain removal company quotes • Check with vet regarding pets • Make travel arrangements and secure tickets • Inform local authorities and utility companies of your forthcoming move and arrange for utilities to be shut off 24 hours after your departure	• Send out change of address cards • Make an inventory of household items to ship • Ensure you have your house professionally cleaned	• Try to control excitement • Ensure all important items such as passports, tickets, keys and phones are left in a safe place to avoid them being packed or lost	• Give up and go with the flow!
ITALY		• Set up a *codice fiscale* and bank account, and investigate schools		• Ensure utilities are installed or activated (upgrade if needed) • Enrol your child in school • If renting, ensure you have temporary accommodation sorted		

education starting for many as young as three years old. For families, this must be a consideration. All children coming from Britain, an EU member, are entitled to free state education, which is considered as good as any in Europe. The younger children start school – and therefore learn the language – the better. English is the first-choice foreign language in the Italian school system, so your children will be very popular if they can help their friends in class!

Rent or buy?

If you're coming to Italy with a job offer in hand and the contract written and signed, the sensible option is to tailor the type of accommodation to fit the duration of your contract. It may be that your employer has sorted out accommodation for you. If you're planning to stay in your job for only a few years, think about renting rather than buying because the Italian property market is slower than the British market and it can take months, if not years, to sell your property.

Any EU citizen coming to Italy won't need a work permit and your *permesso di soggiorno per lavoro* will allow you to look for work. In the longer term, when you're in full-time employment and settled, purchasing a property is a viable proposition.

Pets

As for your beloved family pet, now that the pet passport has arrived you can easily bring animals into Italy, so there won't be any problems about being separated from them. Some airlines even allow them to travel with you as excess baggage!

Other things to consider

If you're relocating permanently then you need to think about your source of income. Are you planning on working? What qualifications are recognised and what are the growth industries? Similarly, what are the working conditions, benefits and holiday entitlement?

Insurance is also essential. Household insurance and travel insurance will be necessary, as is life insurance. Taxation is something that you need to be aware of too, primarily property tax. However, you also need to think about income tax, which applies to rental income earned, as well as any income you may derive from working in Italy.

Planning ahead

All situations are different when it comes to moving to another country. Whatever your circumstances, a good plan laid out well in advance will make things a lot easier. Assuming the decision is made at least six months before you go, make a written schedule of things that need to be done. If selling a property in the UK, seek advice from estate agents as to how long the property might take to sell. If the property sells quicker than you imagined, then rather than lose the sale, consider renting, or staying with family and friends for the interim.

If you're going to let your property, contact agents at least three months before you go so that they can have a let organised and maximise income from your property. And ensure all certificates are obtained in advance for electrical and gas supplies so that there are no last-minute problems. ●

"The best means of learning Italian is to be in the country"

MOVING TO ITALY

A new life awaits in a country rich in culture and with wonderful food and wine

Meet
THE BUYERS

Name: Stephen Jones & Elaine Barton

Ages: 39 and 49

Jobs: Stephen is a stone mason and Elaine runs a jewellery shop

Nearby Ostuni's friendly locals made integrating easy

Below: *Trulli* are distinctive dwellings found only in Puglia

BUYING A TRULLO

THE AREA

● LOCATION Puglia

Located on Italy's 'heel', Puglia is one of the least-explored regions, but famous for its *trulli* houses

- ● **TRADITIONAL TRULLO**
- ● **ALREADY RENOVATED**
- ● **APPRECIATED IN VALUE**

TRULLI DISTINCTIVE HOMES

Italy has many characterful properties for sale, but none are more striking than the whitewashed *trulli* properties found in Puglia in the south of Italy

FRIENDS STEVE JONES AND ELAINE BARTON, both feeling disenchanted with life in Britain, remortgaged their respective properties in the UK, combined funds and headed to Puglia. They bought a *trullo* in Montalbano near Ostuni.

Q: Puglia is often referred to as 'the new Tuscany', but weren't you put off by the reputation that southern Italy has for organised crime?

A: We had known about Puglia for a long time and knew that it was a good time to buy. Although the area is known for being poor and for having mafia, the only thing we saw on our trips out there were farmers in three-wheeled trucks and locals leaving their cars open with the radio blaring away. It certainly didn't feel poor or dangerous and we have experienced some wonderful hospitality.

Q: Were you at all dubious about buying such an old property?

A: The idea of buying an ancient pile of stones in the middle of the field could seem a little daunting, yes, but ours had been renovated 12 years ago and had all mod cons, such as water and electricity. We were really charmed by the fact that it had a well and olive trees that date back nearly 300 years. As soon as we saw it we knew we wanted to buy it.

Q: Puglia isn't overrun with British people. How did the locals take to you?

A: Fitting in with the locals was the easiest part. The farmer helped us with water supplies, and Donardo, the owner of a local *masseria* (farm), gave us a very warm welcome and took us out for drinks. When we walk around Ostuni, we know the butcher, the greengrocer, and we're regulars at a little bar near the piazza. We have felt at home right from day one. They love British people and even though they don't speak any English, they make communication simple. It's usually helped along by a coffee or a local liqueur!

Q: When you bought the property, were you looking for something that you could also rent out during the holiday season?
A: Yes, that was our intention. The only problem we found was that tourists want a swimming pool. You don't get many pools around here because there's a huge one just ten minutes down the road – it's called the Adriatic and it washes against golden sand. We gave up on the idea of renting it out. To be honest, we're there so often ourselves that it doesn't matter.

Q: How did you find the buying process?
A: It was straightforward really. You just have to be ready to sign your name about 30 times without worrying too much about the small print.

> *"Fitting in was easy. They love the British and make communication simple"*

Q: Are you satisfied with the one *trullo* or are you planning to take full advantage of the low property prices out there?
A: We got into the Puglian market in the nick of time and have almost doubled our money. We've been able to remortgage again and have invested in two further plots of land between Fasano and Locorotondo. Our plan is to build properties on both and, as long as we build traditional-style properties using local materials, there isn't much of a restriction on size. As is typical for the area, negotiations were carried out around a wooden table in a farmer's kitchen. We wouldn't advise that as the way to start, but once you're in with

Above: The insides of *trulli* are just as rustic as their exteriors, but can be made comfortable

the locals you get a feel for it. We bought a *trullo*, but there are also the *lamie*, which look more like villas and are often painted in rich Mediterranean colours. We are quite keen on buying something like that next.

Q: You mentioned that the locals don't speak English. Does that pose any problems?
A: Well, a few, but it's our own fault really. We go abroad and don't learn the local language. What can you expect? For any serious business, such as signing property contracts, the law demands that foreigners employ a translator to read the contract. So, it's more the daily affairs that cause the problems, but even then the worst mishap we have had was when we asked the farmer to trim a tree in the garden. We came back to find that it had been given a 'number one'. It didn't look much like a tree any more!

Q: Have you adapted to Puglian life?
A: The whole approach to life here is so different from Britain – and probably very different from northern Italy. You have to take the rough with the smooth. Although you might find that the bank cashier slips out for a quick smoke whilst you're standing in a queue of 20 people, you also have the advantages of cheap, fresh fruit and vegetables. You can sit in a bar for as long as you like, with no pressure to order a drink. In fact, out here, the more you pester people, the less likely you are to get anything from them. It's a really friendly place to live! ●

Above: Who needs a pool when the Adriatic is a mere ten minutes away?

Left: *Trulli* are built without mortar, and have walls a metre or so thick

trullo
FACTFILE

■ *Trulli* are whitewashed, square buildings with conical roofs that date back to the 15th century.

■ There has been a huge move towards the purchasing of *trulli* in Puglia and it has become a hugely fashionable purchase among foreign buyers. Many *trulli* have been renovated and made into luxurious homes by a number of developers.

■ The downside of *trulli* are that although they are great places to stay in the warm summer months as they keep you cool, during the autumn and winter months they can be very cold and can suffer from damp (unless of course they have been renovated and are heated). They also have tiny windows, or none at all!

■ Prices start from as little as €20,000 for a *trullo* to renovate.

■ You can only find *trulli* in the central Puglia region.

BUYING A TRULLO

top tips
FOR BUYING A TRULLO

■ Don't buy from a picture – you need to view for yourself! What can be described as the perfect renovation project, and is cheap, will usually be very run down and expensive to restore, or in a very poor position.

■ You don't necessarily need to go through a British middle-man as many Italian agents now speak English or have somebody who does. It works out cheaper, as the middle men usually take a bit extra commission off you.

■ Be prepared to be 'patient' with everything! The words 'hurry' and 'quickly' are not recognised!

■ Have a go with the language! The Italians appreciate you having a go, don't mind if you get it wrong and will help you if they can. Plus, it's the best way to learn the language.

Steps to buying…

Italy has long been popular with overseas property buyers, and it's now easier than ever before to purchase your dream home, as our step-by-step guide reveals…

© CASA ITALIA

CHOOSING ITALY AS YOUR DESTINATION TO PURCHASE A PROPERTY MAY NOT *have been the most difficult decision you've ever made. Excellent weather, beautiful surroundings, good food and wine, healthy living, culture, history and friendly people are some of the reasons why Italy is second to none as a destination for overseas homebuyers.*

Italian property sales have risen greatly in recent years due to increased exposure on the television and the emergence of low-cost airlines that have made Italy more accessible. The two most popular reasons for buying a property in Italy are to find a holiday home or to relocate there permanently. Whatever the reason for your purchase, buying in Italy has become increasingly easy and the process can be a pleasurable experience if you make the right decisions from the outset. The more preparation and thought that goes into the buying process at the start, the better the results will be in the long term.

The three main considerations to make when looking to buy are budget, location and the property itself, and it's sensible to take things one step at a time…

1: Establish the budget

Buying property abroad is a big financial commitment and it's very important to be realistic about your limitations. It's essential that you establish a realistic budget from the outset and make sure that you rigidly stick to it. Establishing your budget early on will save both your time and that of your estate agents.

In Italy, you have to allow for a number of extra costs: typical agent fees are three per cent, purchase taxes are ten per cent (three per cent if you're using the property as your main home), and on top of this you have to allow for notary costs and *geometra* (surveyor) fees if required. If you use a UK solicitor, this should also be costed in.

If you propose to take out a mortgage, find out what the limits are, and the repayment terms and costs. Also remember that the costs don't stop at the purchase of the property because you'll also have annual community charges, utility charges and ongoing maintenance charges.

If you're planning to renovate a property, always allow for a contingency sum (at least ten per cent) in case things don't go quite according to plan. Remember to be realistic and don't push yourself to the limit – buying a property in Italy should be a pleasure and an achievement, rather than a financial burden. You need to talk through your financial plan with your solicitor and check that the total cost is going to be achievable, without putting your current home in the UK at risk, or leaving yourself in severe debt.

2: Choose the location

Italy is a large and beautiful country. It's also very varied, and when it comes to location, you'll find yourself spoilt for choice. Italy is blessed with a good climate but the weather varies considerably, so if you're looking for milder winters then it's better to thoroughly check the regional temperatures.

Historical and regional differences are an intrinsic part of life in Italy and this means it's important to establish which region is right for your new life in the country. Among the regions, there are several well-known locations that have been popular for many years, such as the Ligurian Riviera, the northern lakes, the cities of Rome, Florence and Venice, Taormina in Sicily, and the regions of Tuscany and Umbria.

Central Italy is very popular, with its abundance of medieval towns and beautiful countryside, and Tuscany still remains the first choice for many. Those looking for something more affordable in central Italy can opt for the up-and-coming regions of Le Marche and Abruzzo, which share some similarities with their neighbours Tuscany and Umbria.

If you're interested in looking further south, Puglia is now opening up thanks to the introduction of direct flights from the UK, and Sicily is also becoming a serious consideration for many. You'll find that the coastline in the south of Italy can be breathtaking. Sardinia is also a wonderful destination with an excellent coastline, and it's also a good area for investment.

© CASA ITALIA

Rural Italian properties are always popular, but make sure there are adequate transport links

Transport is an important consideration. Flights to northern Italy have always been good (Venice, Milan, Bologna) and central Italy is improving (Pisa, Rome, Florence, Ancona) but the south is still struggling in terms of choice of carrier and availability from the UK. Proximity to the airport must be considered if you're looking at renting your home in Italy – most clients will want to be no more than 90 minutes from the airport. You also have to consider that if this is a holiday home, then you'll travel to the property at least six to eight times a year.

Before you start contacting potential agents, read up on the country. Buy a couple of books or use the internet (try the Italian tourist board – see www.enit.it), familiarise yourself with the different regions and select a couple for your initial search. Always visit a region at least twice before you consider moving there, and preferably visit at least once out of season as some areas can be fairly inhospitable in the winter months.

3: Choose a property

The majority of Italian homes are of a very high standard and Italy does have a lot of options available in terms of types of property, from apartments (both new and old) and townhouses to houses, villas and *casali* (country houses).

Most buyers prefer more rustic properties, but don't discount new-build properties too quickly because they're usually well designed and many blend in very sympathetically with their surrounding environment.

Unlike those in many other European countries, Italy's historic town centres are thriving residential districts where you can buy restored houses and apartments. Many smaller medieval towns are built on hilltops, so make sure that you're fit and able to reach the property on foot.

The idyllic farmhouses found in Tuscany and Umbria, as well as in numerous books,

"Many buyers prefer more rustic properties, but don't discount new-build properties too quickly…"

are many people's idea of a dream property. However, demand has outstripped supply in a lot of areas and you should expect to pay a premium for renovated properties. It's important to realise that many of these buildings are isolated and the reality of having to drive to see another property or person can be daunting for some prospective buyers. Of course, many city dwellers might be more than happy to get lost in their very own corner of Italy.

Italy still has an abundance of farmhouses requiring renovation, and although supplies are now drying up in Tuscany and Umbria, the void has been filled by Le Marche, Abruzzo and Emilia-Romagna. Buying a property requiring renovation can often be

cost effective, but you have to factor in time to obtain planning permission and complete building work before you'll be able to use the property. This could easily amount to more than nine months on top of the purchase process, depending on the state of the property. If you want a hassle-free holiday home, embarking on a renovation may not be the best option for you!

It may be obvious to some, but it's important to establish right from the start who is going to be using the property when deciding on what sort of thing you're looking for. If you're using a property as a holiday home, then a farmhouse may be a suitable option, but remember that you'll have to employ somebody to maintain the property when you aren't there.

If you're planning on moving to Italy, a property in a small town or village may be a better option for integration. Access to transport and the availability of amenities such as shops, restaurants, bars, schools and hospitals are also important factors.

Even though you may amend your search slightly as you visit property in Italy, you'll have saved a considerable amount of time and money by visualising what you're trying to achieve from the outset.

4: New build vs resale

When buying in Italy, one of the major considerations is whether to buy a new-build property or a resale, and there are obviously benefits to both styles of property.

Resales have been a traditional route for the majority of UK buyers because they generally epitomise the traditional dream of buying property in Italy, and most are rustic. As long as the property is purchased at the right market value, money can still be made in the resales market. Prices continue to grow throughout Italy – the average rise is approximately eight per cent per annum, but parts of Italy have risen as sharply as 20 per cent in the past year.

Purchasing a resale property that requires some refurbishment will also provide you with a good investment. Many village properties have been inherited from grandparents and although they may be rustic externally, you're likely to find that the 1960s refurbishment inside simply hasn't stood the test of time!

Renovation projects can also be an excellent return on investments, so long as your budget is adhered to tightly and you don't let the costs spiral out of control.

The new-build market may not be the most obvious choice for buyers but this area has attracted a lot of investment buyers because there's strong potential for capital growth. Costs are similar to resales in terms of taxes, with VAT of ten per cent replacing the Italian purchase taxes of ten per cent for a second homeowner.

The new-build option generally offers the buyer a hassle-free purchase without the vendors, and the growth returns are normally greater than resales, especially if properties are bought off-plan before they're completed. When buying off-plan, it's important to check the credentials of the building company and to use a specialist Italian solicitor to make sure that the sales documentation is watertight.

New-build properties often offer excellent rental potential. A key benefit for choosing a new build is that the property will generally be secure and require limited work, or none at all. The only thing that's usually missing is the kitchen, which isn't normally installed. Fitting can often be arranged separately through the agent or builder though.

An increasingly popular type of new-build development is the renovated *borgo* (hamlet), which offers communal areas, a swimming pool, gated access and other facilities. These have been appearing in Tuscany recently and are now emerging in other areas, such as Umbria and Le Marche. Some developers are even offering lease-back schemes and guaranteed rentals, making these ideal buy-to-let investments.

If you're thinking of reselling at some stage, you should be aware that Italian buyers tend to prefer new-build properties because maintenance tends to be less and they're generally well designed. Consequently, they will be easier to sell and will broaden the market of potential purchasers since you'll be able to sell the property both in the UK and in Italy.

5: Research estate agents

Start your research in the UK either on the internet or in the press, where there are a number of agents advertising. Try the Sunday newspapers or *The Italian Magazine* for a list of agents based in the UK and in Italy.

Firstly, have a look at their website to see the type of properties that they offer and browse to see if there's anything of interest. Be warned – many Italian agents still advertise properties that are no longer on the market. In some cases, this is to give the impression that they have a larger portfolio of properties. In other cases, it's genuinely not their fault because many vendors tend to use multiple agencies to sell a property in Italy, and when it's sold, they may not inform all the agents of this fact.

You can usually complete an online request form on many sites, or you may prefer to give them a call and have a chat directly. If they advertise in the UK then there will be someone who speaks English in their office. A good conversation with them will help them to understand what you're trying to achieve and will also give you a general feeling about their knowledge and competence.

© WWW.FREEIMAGES.COM

Plan your purchase and budget thoroughly

Another way of finding a suitable agent is by visiting an overseas property exhibition in the UK – check out Earls Court, Excel, NEC and other large venues. This will usually give you the opportunity to speak to multiple agents under one roof and also meet people who can offer legal and financial advice. Make sure you contact the exhibition organiser beforehand and check which regions are being covered because many exhibitions only cover certain regions and not all of Italy, as they may claim.

If none of the agents you've found cover a specific town or area that you're interested in, then you'll have no option but to go direct. You can search the National Federation of Estate Agents website (www.fiaip.it) under the section *Agenzie*, try www.casa.it or the online version of the Italian *Yellow Pages*, www.paginegialle.it (type in 'agenzia immobiliare'). However, this is going to be difficult because most Italian agents aren't familiar with working with UK clients, and most won't speak English. Travelling to the destination and walking into the office will be easier.

One significant difference with Italian agents is the property particulars. Don't expect room measurements or pages of details – many will advertise properties without the price or photos, and with only brief summaries. Most UK-based agents are more familiar with working with overseas clients and provide photos and prices.

6: Viewing properties

It's essential to view your potential new home, so make sure that you plan your visit in advance. If you leave everything to the week that you depart, not only are you

INTERNET RESEARCH

With the advent of the internet, many estate agents have chosen to show their wares online. This is a useful way to draw up a list of agents who deal with the particular region you're interested in, and can be the best way to do some preliminary research and background checks before committing yourself to one agent.

The majority of agents will show their portfolio of properties online, and if you're torn between more than one region, this is a useful way to view the price ranges and property styles available.

going to be stressed but you also won't be able to guarantee the availability of the agent. All viewings in Italy are accompanied by an agent, whether the property is vacant or otherwise, and your contact will need to reserve time in their diary, so contact them before you book flights. It's still quite rare for Italians to arrange viewing trips, as happens in Spain, so don't expect to be collected from the airport or put on a coach with other buyers. Most people buying in Italy would hate the thought of that anyway!

The best way to view properties is to hire a car at the airport. Arranging this from the UK in advance can usually save you money. This will give you the flexibility and the freedom to familiarise yourself with the surrounding areas to ensure that this is the right location for you.

It's important to note that nearly all Italian agents are closed on a Sunday and some on a Saturday afternoon. Don't forget to check for public holidays before booking your flights. Most agencies also close for lunch, which can be any time between 1.30pm and 3.30pm. This may be frustrating, but this is Italy and life has a completely different pattern from the UK. Once you have your own place in Italy, you'll appreciate this.

Spring and autumn are good times to visit Italy because the weather will generally be pleasant. The summer months will undoubtedly be hot and busy, and driving around in the soaring heat may not be the best time to look for a property. Believe it or not, August can be a dead month for many agencies. Despite the fact that Italy is full of potential buyers, many agencies choose to close either side of *Ferragosto* (a national holiday on 15 August). During winter, morning viewings are better since there will be limited daylight in the afternoons if the agencies re-open late.

It's always better to make your viewing trip a specific journey, rather than combining it with a holiday. If you're with friends or you have children with you, be realistic about the number of properties that you wish to view.

Many people travel to Italy and try to do too much on their visit by going to multiple destinations and cramming in too many viewings in a short time. This is likely to just leave you tired and confused and will probably be counter-productive. If you're looking for countryside or village property then five viewings a day is really what you should aim for.

> *"The summer months will be hot and busy, and driving around in the soaring heat may not be the best time to look for a property. August can be a dead month for agencies"*

Make sure that you have a map with you, otherwise you are going to get lost, and check distances before you set off. Always be punctual as the agents and vendors will be waiting for you. Also, if you're dealing with more than one agency, allow adequate time between appointments.

Be honest with the person who is showing you around because they won't be able to read your mind and you don't want to waste your time or theirs. Constructive feedback will help them to suggest other suitable alternatives.

A mobile phone, camera and a notebook are essential. If you're visiting lots of different properties, make a list of queries. If you like a property, try to visit both during the day and the evening, and visit shops and restaurants to familiarise yourself with the area.

Many people are lucky enough to find what they're looking for on their first visit, while others require two or three viewing trips. No visit will be wasted since they'll help you to clarify just what you are looking for, and in which particular location. Don't give up or be rushed into making an on-the-spot decision. Finding the perfect home may be an impossibility for some but finding the right property should be easily achievable. Of course, once you've found it, securing it can be another matter.

7: Making an offer

It's often easy to go with your heart and leave your head in the UK. If you find a suitable property, don't make any instant decisions. Go back to your hotel or to a bar and make sure that you've thought the property through carefully. A second viewing will help to clarify any outstanding issues that you may have. Take your time but don't be too complacent because although the

Check out your potential new property several times so you can get a feel for the whole area

© CASA TRAVELLA

SAMPLE BILL FOR A €200,000 PROPERTY

Please note that this is a guide only and the exact fees associated with buying your property may vary and should be outlined to you by your estate agent.

Fee		Cost
Price of property		€200,000
Purchase tax	There are several registration taxes that are combined with the stamp duty. The overall tax is 10% and is calculated on the declared value of the property. It's a good idea to consult with your agent for advice on this*	€20,000 second home
		€8,000 first home
Notary fees	The basic notary fees are fixed by law and are charged according to the price of the property – they range from €1,400 to €3,000, and notaries will also charge for additional expenses	€2,000 approx
Surveyor (Geometra)	Using a *geometra* will ensure that all the paperwork is in order	€1,000
Agency fees	In Italy, both the buyer and seller pay the Italian estate agent fees, which can range from 3 – 6% of the purchase price. The average fee is 3%	€6,000 (based on 3%)
TOTAL		€229,000 (Second home)
		€217,000 (Primary home)

*The purchase tax is 3% if the buyer purchases the property as a first home and applies for residency in the area

ADDITIONAL / OPTIONAL FEES

UK-based Italian-specialist lawyer	A specialist lawyer will ensure that there are no issues with the purchase and provide advice and guidance that isn't available through the notary. Charges can range from £1,500 – £3,000, depending on the level of service required	£1,500
Survey	A local *geometra* will provide a survey of the property upon request. This will vary from the UK and generally won't be in as much depth. It's important to tell the *geometra* the areas that you wish to be covered in the survey. Costs vary from €500 to €1,000, depending upon the amount of work required	€500 approx
Bank charges	There will be charges associated with a bank transfer – please contact your bank for further details. You may also be required to pay for charges at the receiving Italian bank	£40 approx
Translation	Some additional translation may be needed for contracts or the surveyor's report. A UK- based estate agent or specialist lawyer will usually cover this within their services, if you use one	£60 – £100 per 1,000 words
Mortgage fees	Mortgage fees are in the region of 1% for the arrangement fee but vary from bank to bank	1% approx

Italian property market isn't as fast-moving as the UK, it's wise to close the deal before someone else discovers your dream home.

Ask the agent if the price is negotiable because many Italians aren't used to negotiating on property, as is common in the UK. If the property has been on the market for some time or is vacant, then there may be more flexibility on the price. The flexibility of the vendor depends on their need to sell. Bear in mind that many properties in Italy are inherited, so waving your cash may not excite the vendors at all.

Prices are negotiable to a certain extent, though. In recent years, due to the high demand for properties both as homes and as investment opportunities, the negotiation margin has been reduced. It's generally sensible to offer between five to ten per cent less than the asking price to see how the vendor reacts. The Italians are proud people so don't make unrealistic offers because this will insult the vendor and affect the sale.

Other factors to bear in mind when negotiating are the timescale in which you're able to complete and the payment method. Once the offer is accepted, it's advisable to make sure that the funds are in place as soon as possible. Note that if you require a mortgage, this could take up to 12 weeks to be secured, and normally takes a minimum of six weeks.

8: Background checks

It's usually advisable to carry out some sort of survey before signing any official documentation, because it's unusual to have contracts subject to survey in Italy. Ask the agent if there have been any previous surveys and if they can be made available. The agent should also be able to recommend the services of a local *geometra* (surveyor) or architect who will be able to carry out a survey of the property.

Don't expect anything like a UK homebuyer survey – the Italian version is very simple and can often be as short as one page. The basic survey will comment on the roof, ceilings, walls and general structure of the property. A more detailed survey will also include the condition of the property's doors, windows, sewage, heating systems, any registrations at the town planning department and compliance with regulations. You can expect to pay anything from €300 to €1,000 for a survey.

It's important to establish with the *geometra* exactly what will be included in their survey and highlight any areas that you would like to be covered. If the property is a new build or has recently been totally renovated, then you may well be wasting your time and money on organising a survey.

9: Financing the sale

Securing a mortgage for a property in Italy shouldn't be as difficult as it often is, but many Italian lenders are rarely prepared for UK buyers (unlike France and Spain) and are unable to explain the process clearly without the assistance of an agent.

One route to getting a mortgage is by using a UK-based broker. They will liaise with Italian banks and should make your life a lot easier by assisting you throughout the buying process and by giving you checklists and guidelines at each stage.

Make sure that they're knowledgeable about the market and the products they're offering, and that you receive a sample repayment schedule from them. Also, you should always check their fees before signing any documentation – most will be funded by the overseas bank but some will also require an additional fee from clients.

Going direct to an Italian bank is going to be very difficult because in the majority of cases, all documentation relating to their mortgages will be in Italian and you're unlikely to understand what you're committing yourself to. Banks are also likely to be cautious with non-residents. Your agent may be able to assist you through the process of using a local bank, but you should expect to pay a fee for this since there will be a considerable amount of liaising, translation and interpreting involved.

Barclays bank is one of the few lenders to have quickly established itself in the marketplace, with its subsidiary, Banca Woolwich, offering mortgages to UK buyers. Although the bank doesn't have branches throughout Italy, they will provide the mortgage, which can easily be deposited into your local Italian bank. They have a simple qualification form and process, which will quickly give you an answer of whether or not they will be prepared to arrange a

Make sure you have a strict budget so you buy a property that you can comfortably afford

mortgage on your behalf and the maximum amount that will be offered.

In Italy, the maximum borrowing amount for overseas buyers is usually around 70 per cent, so you must be prepared to finance the rest of the sale, in addition to agency and notary fees, plus taxes. Italian loans have a fixed or variable rate of interest, with the fixed rate being higher. Interest rates in Italy have been high for several years and lenders' fees are often the highest in Europe – rates for non-residents can often be even higher.

Make sure that you check the setting up expenses and the penalties for early

> ## "One route to getting a mortgage is by using a UK-based broker who will liaise with Italian banks"

redemption of the mortgage since this varies from bank to bank. It's usually 0.5 per cent to three per cent.

One thing to bear in mind when taking an Italian mortgage is to make sure that all the relevant documentation that's required is in place and on time. Any missing documents will certainly lead to delays and often the rescheduling of the *rogito* (deed of sale). To process a mortgage, you usually require a copy of the *compromesso* (preliminary contract of sale), passports, Italian fiscal codes, recent tax returns, bank statements and all other documents proving

your income. The deposit paid when you sign the *compromesso* will be protected by a clause that will release the buyer from the sale if the mortgage isn't approved. Other documentation relating to the property will be required from your surveyor. Processing an Italian mortgage can take some time but these days it's usually anything from four to eight weeks.

One other element to bear in mind when securing an Italian mortgage is the exchange rate – unless you obtain a favourable rate, you could lose money each time you send money over to Italy to meet the repayments of the mortgage.

A lot of buyers are now remortgaging their properties in the UK in order to pay for the purchase of their Italian property in cash. Whereas in the past this may not have been easy, the mortgage sector in the UK is becoming increasingly flexible, offering homeowners the opportunity to switch for better rates. Obtaining a mortgage through this route can certainly speed up the sales process and is easier to arrange than going through an Italian bank. This is likely to save you both time and costs since it involves less paperwork and fewer legal fees. However, bear in mind that there could be currency fluctuations, which may leave you short of the funds required to complete the sale.

With many lenders, you can borrow up to four times your primary income, plus your secondary income, minus any capital amount borrowed on the mortgage. This is often more than you could borrow from an Italian

STEPS TO BUYING

bank. However, you have to bear in mind that your credit history will be checked to assess whether or not you'll be able to meet the increased payments. The mortgage will also be subject to a valuation of your property in the UK.

10: Managing your euros

There are a number of different ways of transferring funds to Italy and it's important to understand these, both for transactions leading up to the sale and for post-purchase requirements, such as paying utility bills, mortgage repayments and so on.

Bankers' drafts can be organised through your UK bank and they will be treated as cheques in Italy. Always allow a few days in the UK for the preparation of the draft and for it to clear in Italy. Bankers' drafts will be charged through your UK bank and prices vary considerably from bank to bank. Check the exchange rate that's offered because this can often be uncompetitive.

Bank transfers are a simple way of transferring funds from your account in the UK to an Italian bank account. Again, each UK bank has its own pricing structure and types of foreign transfer, which usually revolve around timescales. NatWest, for example, offers a Swift Transfer (24 hours), in addition to a two-day and five-day service. Costs range from £10 to £40.

Although the process is relatively easy, there are lots of numbers and codes required, so make sure you have the full and correct account details in Italy.

Although the UK bank will state that the transfer will take a certain number of days, in reality it can often take longer as the funds are sometimes routed to a head office or regional office of the Italian bank, and then have to be transmitted to the local branch. Italian banks are among the slowest in Europe to process such transfers, so it's always best to ensure that you allow a few extra days for the money to arrive, especially if these funds are part of the sales process and the *rogito* has been arranged. It's also worth checking with your bank what rate they can offer you because this should be better than the rate that's offered for the average tourist transaction.

Currency dealers will often be more competitive than your UK bank and the process of arranging funds through them is also relatively easy. You'll have to open an account with them, which usually just involves the completion of a simple form, and you then transfer the funds from your UK account to their account. They will often hold the funds and release them when the exchange rate is more favourable.

A currency dealer can also offer you a fixed exchange rate for a set period of time, which will save you from any nasty surprises when you're ready to exchange funds.

The savings with a currency dealer can be significant but a number of small operators have emerged on the market in the past couple of years. Although many of these are reputable businesses providing a good service to their clients, it's worthwhile checking their company's details, obtaining testimonials and verifying that your funds are protected.

Always make sure you know who is going to pay the bank charges in Italy because if you're sending funds to an intermediary and the charges aren't met, there will be an inevitable shortfall in funds to complete a transaction. Italian banks often charge significant fees for receiving funds.

11: The contract

The Italian estate agent will draw up the sales agreement between the parties, known as the *compromesso*. Some agents may even suggest a *proposta d'acquisto* (a purchase proposal) beforehand and you'll be expected to leave a small deposit to show your commitment. This document doesn't guarantee your right to buy the property and most agencies now move directly to the *compromesso*. At this stage it's recommended that you engage the services of a *geometra*, who will check that all the necessary documentation is in order and establish the planning status of the property and its boundaries. Expect to pay around €1,000.

Italians are used to signing the *compromesso* very quickly and an agent may ask you to sign this when you're in Italy. Bear in mind that the *compromesso* is a legally binding document – if you withdraw after you've signed it, you'll lose your initial deposit to the vendor (around 20 per cent of the agreed sale price). The *compromesso* will state the names of the buyer and seller, the property details, the date of completion and the agreed price of the property.

If you're working with a UK-based agent, they will usually translate the *compromesso* so you understand exactly what you're signing. The document can either be signed with the vendor in Italy, or signed in the UK and posted or faxed (although it's not binding until received in Italy). You'll be expected to pay the agent for their services at this stage.

In Italy, the *notaio* (notary) performs the role of the solicitor, and once they've

CURRENCY EXCHANGE

Using a currency specialist to transfer funds can be a cheaper and safer option than a bank. Private foreign exchange companies allocate clients an Account Manager, who takes care of the individual's needs, and most currency companies work without fees. A specialist provider establishes the optimum time for purchase and places orders to take advantage of market moves. Currency purchased for immediate delivery is called buying for 'spot'. Alternatively, a 'forward' purchase reserves a guaranteed exchange rate for up to two years ahead, achieved by placing a deposit (invariably 10 per cent of the total), then paying the balance at a later date. This removes the risk and worry that the exchange rate may move against you.

Courtesy of Steffan Jones, SGM-FX Ltd
Tel: 0207 778 0123, www.sgm-fx.com

© TOBY POCOCK

STEPS TO BUYING

FINAL CHECKLIST

✔ Check that the property corresponds with its description

✔ Make sure you're paying market value for the property

✔ Always check the additional costs of the purchase, such as taxes and fees for the notary, agency and *geometra*

✔ Be sure of who is buying the property and going to take ownership

✔ Make sure that planning permission has been granted, if applicable

✔ Always clarify what is and what is not included in the sale

✔ Make sure that the area and property are right for you before you sign the *compromesso*, since this is legally binding

✔ Have the *compromesso* translated into English, either by your agent or a UK-based Italian solicitor

✔ Make sure that there are get-out clauses in the preliminary contract for any areas that have not been fully clarified or which are outstanding

✔ Always have some representation in the UK, either from a UK-based agency or from an Italian solicitor based in the UK. They will be able to assist you though the entire process

✔ Never sign a document unless you know exactly what you're signing

✔ Make sure you have the finances in place to meet the purchase of the property. Also, if you're taking out a mortgage, make sure you can meet the repayments

✔ Be sure what the stage payments are, if applicable

✔ Be sure of any key dates or deadlines and adhere to them

✔ Always use a *geometra* or technical person to check that the paperwork relating to the property is in order

✔ Have a survey done on the property

✔ Always check the exact boundaries of the property

✔ Always clarify rights of way and access to the property

✔ Make sure that all appliances and utilities are in working order

A translator will prove to be a huge help

received the signed *compromesso*, they will conduct all the necessary final checks in order to prepare the *rogito*. The notary works for both parties and is strictly neutral. Italians don't employ the services of a solicitor in addition to the notary, but many English buyers won't understand the differences between English and Italian law.

If you aren't using a UK-based agent to support you through the process, it's best to engage a solicitor based in the UK from the outset. Your regular solicitor won't understand Italian property law, so it's advisable to use a specialist solicitor – try the International Property Law Centre (www.internationalpropertylaw.co.uk).

12: Preparing for the sale

Before the *atto* (signing of the *rogito*), it's important that you've received a fiscal code. This can be obtained through the Italian consulate in the UK (allow up to three weeks), your UK-based specialist solicitor or in person. If you're obtaining it in person, this is a simple process at the local tax office and your agent can usually assist with this.

You'll also require an Italian bank account, which will also be useful after the sale to set up direct debits, and this can be opened from the UK if necessary. You'll need a copy of your passport, your personal details and the address of your future property in Italy to do this. Again, your agent or solicitor should be able to assist you. It's worth noting that although you can open an account and transfer funds, due to EU anti-money-laundering laws, you'll be required to activate the account in person in Italy with your passport. Always allow ample time when transferring funds, and a little extra money to cover Italian bank charges. Some people have arrived at the bank on the day of signing the *rogito* to find that either the funds haven't arrived in time or that there's insufficient to pay all parties. Using a specialist foreign exchange company will usually save you money.

The estate agent should advise you in ample time of the costs involved in the sale. These will include the remainder of the property sale to the vendor, the purchase taxes and fees to the notary. Any fees that are due to the *geometra* will normally be paid at the *atto*.

The signing of the *rogito* is usually conducted in the presence of the vendor, estate agent, notary and mortgage lender, if applicable. If you're signing in person, make sure that there's a translation of the document available and an interpreter present throughout because it's rare for the notary to speak in English. It's also possible to arrange power of attorney through your agent or solicitor if you're unable to attend.

The process usually lasts between one to two hours and you shouldn't be surprised if the meeting is held up due to missing paperwork or documents. The notary will only sign the deed when he's happy that all is in order.

After the signing of the document, the taxes must be paid and the keys are usually made available. The notary will register the property in your name, along with all the relevant documentation. Expect to wait anything from three weeks to three months to receive a copy of the deed of sale.

Buying a property in Italy can often be a complicated and drawn-out affair. However, the more planning and preparation that goes in at the outset, combined with the right support throughout the purchase process, and the easier it will be to locate and secure your dream property. ●

Left: The outbuildings were converted to guest accommodation

Below: A beautiful sunset over the Umbrian countryside

Meet
THE BUYERS

Names: David and Christina Lang
Ages: 31 and 33
Jobs: English teacher and chartered accountant
Contact: +39 075 9414219
www.casasangabriel.com

BUYING TO LET

CONVERTING A FARM FOR HOLIDAY RENTALS

THE AREA

● LOCATION Umbria

Umbria offers spectacular rural scenery, yet is close to towns and accessible by airports

- **● 15TH-CENTURY FARM**
- **● SLEEPS TEN GUESTS**
- **● RURAL LOCATION**

When an Australian and Englishwoman married, they decided to start their new life together in Italy

DAVID AND CHRISTINA LANG BOUGHT and restored a 15th-century farm in Umbria, got married, and started a new life in August 2003. David, 31, is an English teacher hailing from Australia, Chrissie, 33, a chartered accountant from Cambridgeshire. Two years on, they run a successful holiday let business in the green heart of Italy.

Q: What made you give up professional jobs to relocate to Umbria?
A: When we decided to get married, we had to find somewhere to live that would be a fair compromise between our two homes. Chrissie lived on a farm in rural Cambridgeshire and I was from a sheep farm in Victoria, Australia. We thought that the climate in Umbria would be a good compromise. Although our intention was to buy a house with a spare room for me to use for teaching English, we got a bit carried away! The original idea to buy in Italy came to us whilst travelling around South America and we actually named the house after an old house we came across in Mexico, the Hacienda San Gabriel.

Q: Why did you choose Umbria in particular?
A: We wanted to be in easy reach of main airports, but also out in the middle of nowhere. In Umbria, that is possible. The nearest town to us is Umbertide and we are within half-an-hour's drive of Assisi and Cortona. It was really important for us to be out of view of any roads and we didn't want to hear any traffic. Because we also wanted to live in an established community, this valley seemed perfect. All of the other properties were already sold.

"For us, it's about doing the right thing and ensuring guests are looked after"

Q: You bought a 15th-century farmhouse to live in. Do you let out any of the rooms or did you buy extra properties to rent as holiday properties?
A: We were fortunate. In the grounds of the main house, there were three sheds – a hay stable, a

piggery and a *cantina* (a cool house for storing wine). As part of the whole restoration process, we had these three buildings converted into beautiful cottages. One of them has accommodation for a couple and the other two will each sleep up to four guests. We also have a communal room in the house, which has a library, internet access and an open fire.

Q: In this sort of idyllic setting, how easy is it to keep a business head?

A: For us, business is about doing the right thing and ensuring all guests are well looked after. We cater for all their needs – from providing maps and advice for travel, to organising pizza evenings and truffle hunts. The most important thing is that people enjoy themselves and want to keep coming back. In order to encourage people to come back, we make the environment as comfortable as possible. We have a herb garden

"We wanted to be in easy reach of airports, yet also in the middle of nowhere"

for people to sit in and a large pool overlooking the property, which they are also free to use.

Talking of business, this might be an idyllic setting today, but nearby Lake Trasimeno was the site of some very nasty dealings when the Roman Empire came here and saw its greatest defeat at the hands of Hannibal.

Q: Do the holiday cottages earn you enough money to live on?

A: Well, there is also my teaching job. We are developing the business, providing a service for any of our guests who are also looking to buy property. We help them in setting up their bank accounts, fiscal codes and all the other complicated aspects of Italian life.

It's important for us to increase the profits because although we are lucky that Casa San Gabriel is in such a stunning location, looking after 400 square metres of Umbrian stone property surrounded by three acres of olive groves, farmland and wooded hillsides is an expensive business. We spent €300,000 on the property and restoration. There are always things to do and so we are always looking for new business possibilities. ●

BEFORE

Above: A stable, piggery and *cantina* were extensively renovated and made habitable for use as accommodation by up to ten guests

Left: The property feels remote, yet is just half an hour from major towns

Right: Keeping on top of three acres of olive groves and farm is hard work

Below and right: Make guests feel at home and they'll return again and again

top tips
RUNNING HOLIDAY ACCOMMODATION WHILE KEEPING A COOL HEAD

■ When cooking Italian food, especially for a large number of guests, keep it simple.

■ When doing business, be patient; it's often about who you know, but anything is possible.

■ Aim to ensure that you offer something special. That way, your guests will return year after year and so you will spend less on marketing.

■ If possible, involve guests in local life. Don't just offer them bed and breakfast; give them the chance to dabble in cooking or local sports.

■ Make sure you budget for all the expensive notary fees involved in setting up your business, and be sure to employ a professional accountant who understands the Italian system.

BUYING TO LET

Restoring a property

Restoring a property in Italy may sound romantic, but the reality of taking on such a project is often overlooked and can cost more than you bargained for…

"Building in a contingency fund will assist both your bank balance and your blood pressure"

U P UNTIL 60 YEARS AGO MANY ITALIANS lived in very humble homes, some without indoor toilets. Today that has all changed and, to an Italian, their home is just as much a status symbol as their car or their clothes. No longer do the entire family live under one farmhouse roof, rather a luxurious condominium or urban villa. Consequently, many older properties have been left by the wayside, and for the British DIY enthusiast this leaves a swathe of restoration projects to hunt out. There are plenty of renovation properties throughout Italy for the adventurous buyer who isn't afraid to get their hands dirty.

Property costs

Italian properties can still be found at attractive prices in an unrestored condition, and this has enabled many buyers to achieve their dream home at a more competitive price and secure a good return on their investment. However, you have to understand that renovating in Italy differs from the UK. Each region has its own local laws, which can affect your plans to renovate. Also consider that the entire process is going to take place in a foreign country, especially if Italian is an unfamiliar language. Many people go on viewing trips to Italy and leave their minds in the UK, making quick decisions without looking at all the angles.

Establishing your budget

First and foremost, you must establish a budget. Buying property abroad is a big commitment and you must be realistic about your financial limitations. Your new home should be a pleasure and an achievement, rather than a financial burden. It is imperative to find a local *geometra* (surveyor) or architect who can help with the project and give you advice. Your estate agent should be able to suggest someone, or try asking locals for their recommendations. A good UK-based agent may even arrange for an on-site meeting, with technical support, before you make important decisions.

Renovations often run over budget due to unforeseen circumstances and unrealistic initial estimates, so it is important to build in a contingency fund of between 10 to 15 per cent for any unwanted surprises. This will assist both your bank balance and your blood pressure. Bear in mind it may be difficult to obtain a mortgage for your renovation. Banca Woolwich, for example, usually lend 70 per cent when a property is fully renovated, but will only lend renovators money on a 'work in

Large properties with external stairwells can be divided up to provide privacy and greater rental potential

© CASA TRAVELLA

USEFUL WEB ADDRESSES

www.homesinitaly.com
Property agent with hundreds of homes for sale in Tuscany and Umbria, and Italy in general

http://europa.eu.int/citizensrights /index_en.cfm
Part of the EU website. Provides practical information on living and working in Italy

http://www.internationalproperty law.co.uk
Practical advice on buying a property in Italy from a UK solicitor specialising in Italian property law

RESTORATION

Renovating run-down *trulli* is becoming popular

It pays to hire specialist workmen for these projects

The results can be amazing

progress' basis, meaning you will require cash for the initial purchase and renovation.

In Italy, renovation costs are quoted on a price-per-square-metre basis, which varies from province to province. In some northern areas of Tuscany, this can be as low as €700 (£476) per square metre, or as high as €1,000 (£680) in the more popular central areas around Siena. This price quoted is for a fully habitable home, including all external work, windows, doors, plastering, tiles, plumbing, heating and bathroom furniture. It does, however, exclude the kitchen – Italians are very particular about this room, as it is such an important part of their life.

The price per square metre also varies according to the condition of the property, and a good, solid structure could reduce the cost to as little as €450 (£306) per square metre. Consider the building materials, as brick construction can cost a third less than restoring in stone. If you want expensive fixtures and fittings, then expect to pay extra.

Extra costs to consider

One thing to ask yourself when renovating is: do you need to renovate the complete living space of the property? A 400-square-metre farmhouse, for example, is an enormous project to take on, and you could easily leave the attic space and create cellars or store rooms on the ground floor to reduce the overall budget. '*Al Grezzo*' is also an important term; it means that it is possible to have the property restored as a shell. You will then have to install the windows, doors, tiles, plumbing, electricity, and so on, separately. This way you may be able to reduce the costs and manage the finish more accurately.

On top of the building costs, you also need to consider the costs of the architect; there will usually be a charge for initial plans and liaising with the local *comune* (town council). Also bear in mind IVA (Italian VAT), which is normally charged at 20 per cent, and additional charges, such as changing the use of the property from its agricultural classification to a domestic dwelling; this alone can

be between €1,500 (£1,020) and €4,000 (£2,721). It is important to establish whether you are going to pick up this cost, or if the vendor will agree to do so. If so, this can be part of the *compromesso* (sale agreement) and the transaction is usually carried out before the *rogito* (final contract) is signed.

It is imperative to find out exactly what is included in the price that you have been quoted by the builder/architect. Italians can often be vague and will not always give a lot of detail. You should allow for the cost of upgrading access roads, if required. Improving a road can cost €35 (£24) per metre, which may not sound a lot… until you consider a 700-metre access road, cost €24,500 (£16,800)! Landscaping can also be a drain on the budget, and terracing, walls and cypress trees should be factored in. A swimming pool can cost from €10,000 (£6,802) upwards.

Renovating to let

It comes as no surprise that many renovators are looking for some sort of income from the property, and a typical property can be rented out during a five-month period. In sought-after locations, such as the area around Siena, income on a typical three-bedroom property can be more than €1,500 (£1,020) in the height of the season. In addition to renovating outbuildings – if they exist – people are being more creative about the division of the space in the main property. A large farmhouse could be split into different sections, using the front and back to provide privacy from paying guests. Many Tuscan and Umbrian farmhouses have an external staircase, and dividing the property into two apartments – one on each floor – is also fairly popular. Ask again for advice, but it may be possible to build a staircase if it is not currently part of the structure.

Building regulations

Due to the rigid building laws, it is usually only existing buildings that are allowed to be renovated, which means that the views from a property will

TYPICAL FEES

based on a property worth £200,000

Value:
£200,000

Deposit required:
£40,000
(can vary from 20-30%)

Stamp duty:
approximately £20,000
(10% of the declared price if a second home, 3% if a primary residence)

Typical agent's fee:
£6,000
(can vary from 3-6%)

Typical legal fee:
£2,000

RESTORATION

not be ruined by a new-build. You may not always get what you want, but a decent architect can come up with alternatives. A *loggia* (covered terrace) may be restricted in size, or you may not even be able to add one due to size restrictions of the building. You may, however, be able to create one by cutting a section into the building on the first floor. Or you could reduce the space of an outbuilding or annex to increase the size of the main house.

You should always check the plans during the purchase process as many people have discovered additional outbuildings, which no longer exist. If these are listed, then there is no problem rebuilding them or using their volume for other purposes.

Make sure your architect can visualise your ideas

Consider the timescale

It is important to visualise what you are trying to achieve when embarking on a project and translate this to the architect. Problems arise when people lose sight of their initial goals, and changing plans will delay the process (and cost extra). Always be precise, and ask for examples, so that you can choose the specifications, from radiators to tiles and taps.

From the start, you will need to establish how much time you can devote to the project and how hands-on you are prepared to be. A project manager will usually be the best route as it will be difficult to coordinate the contractors if you are not in Italy. Usually there is no better person than the architect to project manage, but expect to pay around 10 per cent of the total build cost for this.

Remember the buying process can take from four to 12 weeks, and you will need to allow up to 16 weeks for planning permission, depending on the location and *comune* that the property falls under. Also be patient; Italy usually comes to a standstill in August, so don't be shocked if you turn up on site to find only a stray dog and not a builder in sight!

DIY

If you are a DIY fan, you may wish to undertake some of the work yourself to reduce costs. But be aware that your dream home may turn into one long working holiday. It is also easy to bite off more than you can chew, so it is important to ask yourself if you are really up to plastering, electrics or plumbing. The work carried out needs to comply with Italian regulations; you will be fined if you try to install your own boiler without using a correctly registered engineer. Using a building company to complete the work will be the easiest option, and your architect should be able to find a reputable builder. Ask for a couple of quotes, with identical briefs, to see how each potential supplier compares.

Payment

Payment is usually in stages, which suits both parties, and the final payment comes when you are

sure that everything works and has gone according to plan. People usually want to include penalties in the contract for not completing on time, but this does not go down well in the Italian building world! Incentives to complete on schedule are often more productive and you can start on a more positive footing with your builders.

Be prepared!

Renovating is not going to be easy; for those seeking a stress-free holiday home quickly, walk away now! However, you do not have to end up on a DIY-disaster TV programme if you follow these simple steps: establish a budget and stick within its boundaries; constantly visualise what you are trying to achieve; be realistic about timescales; source a *geometra* or architect whom you are comfortable with and who understands your vision; and, finally, find a building company with a good reputation and make sure you see examples of their work.

Think about the scale of project that you are prepared to take on. Renovating village properties is starting to become popular. These are generally smaller projects than the typical farmhouse and can be excellent first-time projects for those who are looking for something on a smaller scale. If you are buying with a view to making a profit, then this can be achievable, but make sure that you have analysed prices in the market and the renovation costs carefully as some renovations can prove more costly than buying already finished properties.

If you come through the process without any problems or surprises, then it will be a miracle. The important thing to remember is that many people are carrying out renovation projects every year and are succeeding. Architecturally, Italy is one of the most beautiful countries in the world, and renovated farmhouses and townhouses can be a sound investment. In addition to the hard work, renovating can be a rewarding and pleasurable experience, especially if you enter the project with your head as well as your heart! ●

PRICE FOCUS

Tuscany and Umbria
These two regions are the most popular with buyers seeking a renovation property

■ Property prices here are on average higher than other central and southern areas, especially around Florence and Siena
■ In Tuscany you can expect to pay anything from £300,000 upwards for a renovation project
■ Homes in Cortona start from £200,000
■ Farmhouses in the Casentino, the area north of Arezzo, start from a more affordable £150,000
■ In the Garfagnana area in northern Tuscany it is possible to acquire village properties needing some work from around £40,000
■ In Umbria, prices are cheapest around Lake Trasimeno, from £100,000
■ Smaller village properties can also be found in this area from around £50,000
■ Around Orvieto and Todi, prices range from £200,000

Daily life in Italy

The Italian lifestyle attracts more people every year, be it to take a holiday or start a new life. But how do the Italians really live?

ITALY ONLY BECAME A UNIFIED STATE IN 1861 and, as a result, Italians often feel more loyalty to their region than to the nation as a whole. If there are shared national characteristics, they are to embrace life to the full in the hundreds of local festivals taking place across the country on any given day, the importance of food, the obsession with clothes and image, and the sociable life enjoyed by young and old alike.

The influence of the Catholic church is prevalent, with religious holidays still celebrated with gusto. The Italians are very proud of their country and enjoy sharing it with visitors.

How the Italians live

The stereotype of Italian lifestyle is changing as Italy integrates with the European Union; however, the pace of life is essentially slower and more relaxed than that in Britain. Italians take great pride in their work, illustrated in the wealth of culture, craft and design that defines the country.

The Italian likes his food, he likes his home and most of all he likes his mum! The Italian man has never been one to fly the nest early, but more and more are staying put, and for longer. Many Italian men live with their parents until they are over 30 years old, encouraging the image of the Italian *mammone*: a man who is attached to his mother well into adulthood. The Italians, it seems, don't feel in any hurry to grow up. But to be fair, the

---

Fresh food is of vital importance to the Italian life

© ENIT

A DAY IN THE LIFE OF AN ITALIAN

8:00 Wake up!
8:30 *Dolce* (a small cake) and a *cappuccino* at the lively local bar
9:00 Go to work, often by scooter
1:00 Lunch
2:00 *Siesta* – even though *siestas* are becoming less common, most Italians take time to relax after lunch before returning to work
3:00 Back to work
5:00 An *espresso* at the bar
7:00 Finally the day is over!
8:00 Dinner
9:00 *Passeggiata* (stroll) – as the evenings get warmer, families and friends enjoy a stroll, the perfect occasion to socialise and *fare bella figura* (look good)
10:00 If you are still young and full of energy, this is about the time you want to hit the best bar in town for a drink
12:00 *Discoteca* – the Italian nightlife is fast and furious, with nightclubs open until the early hours, packed with Italians aspiring to *la dolce vita*

---

introduction of the euro has increased the cost of living whilst salaries have remained the same, decreasing the average Italian's spending power on property investment.

Socialising is a big part of Italian culture, so be prepared to interact and respect Italy's code of conduct. Whether an Italian meets someone for the first or the millionth time, he or she always shakes hands. Close family and friends kiss each other on the cheek. At any gathering, no matter how large, Italians are expected to greet each person in the room on arrival and departure, shaking hands or kissing each time. Failure to say hello or goodbye is interpreted as rude.

Italy has so much to offer: a rich cultural heritage, hundreds of kilometres of seashore and mountain peaks to explore, and many beautiful and historic sights, but you need to take time to get to know the people if you really want to understand Italian life.

Eating Italian-style

Food and socialising go hand in hand and many hours can be spent happily at the table. The national diet is based on pasta. However, the excellence of Italian food is also in its vegetables and fruit. Pasta, rice and vegetables are never overcooked and the distinct flavour of Italian food is in the art of cooking! Lunch and dinner are never missed for the sake of a quick pint in the pub, and are shared and enjoyed with family at home or, perhaps slightly later, with friends in a restaurant. ●

A TYPICAL LUNCH OR DINNER MENU

- ■ *Antipasto* (appetiser)
- ■ *Primo* (pasta)
- ■ *Secondo* (meat or fish with vegetables or salad)
- ■ Salad with a light dressing of olive oil
- ■ Cheese
- ■ Fruit
- ■ Sweets and coffee
- ■ *Amazzacaffè* (*grappa* or *amaro*)
- ■ White or red wine, according to the choice of meat or fish

Meet
THE BUYER

Name: Beverley Dewath

Age: 29

Job: Works for a yacht broker

Contact: Topsail Marine Yacht Brokers

01493 751779
www.topsail.co.uk
bev@topsail.co.uk

Inset: A terrace overlooks the countryside

RENOVATING
IN TUSCANY

Above: Set high in the Tuscan hills, the view is worth a million euros...

IN THE HEART OF THE COUNTRY

Having already renovated one property in the UK, Beverley Dewath and Robert Vincent weren't daunted at the prospect of doing the same in Italy

THE AREA

● **LOCATION** Tuscany

Tuscany, with its rich heritage and lush scenery, is the most popular area for renovation properties

● **TWO BEDROOMS**
● **COSMETIC RENOVATION**
● **FANTASTIC VIEWS**

BEVERLEY AND ROB HAD ALREADY FALLEN IN LOVE with Italy and were looking forward to buying a second home there. The fact that they wanted to be able to let the place made them decide on Tuscany, as they knew there would be plenty of holiday-makers keen to rent.

Q: Why did you buy property in Italy?
A: From a financial point of view, we decided that our property would have to be let to help cover the mortgage. It was important that our purchase was a good long-term investment. We relished the prospect of being able to spend time in Italy, enjoying its scenery, culture, art and food.

Tuscany seemed to offer the best of everything Italian, and its location provides a good base from which to explore other parts of Europe. It is also an internationally recognised holiday destination, and as such offers good prospects for letting.

Q: How long did it take and why did you choose to buy a place for renovation?
A: It took approximately eight months to find our property and a further two months to complete the paperwork. We took ownership in December 2003 and spent a very cold, but happy, Christmas there. We had already renovated property in the UK, so the prospect of doing so again did not particularly worry us. However, it would not have been practical without establishing a very trusting relationship with our estate agent, who is managing the project for us.

Q: How did you choose the area?
A: Our first trip took place in May 2003, after extensive research. We were looking for a location with good transport links and that was an hour away or less from a ski resort, the sea and, most importantly, an airport serviced by a

low-cost airline. Our house had to stand a chance of being let for the majority of the summer, and so local tourist attractions were also important.

We knew immediately on arrival that our time surfing the internet had not been in vain. The Bagni di Lucca area was all that we expected, and its location within Tuscany was perfect.

Q: How much did you pay for your property?
A: We paid €65,000 (£45,211), after negotiating a €5,000 reduction from the asking price. While this was more than many properties we had seen, the property required cosmetic, rather than structural, renovation. The price also reflected the location and stunning views.

Q: Can you describe your property and what you will be using it for once it is finished?
A: Our house is in a hill village near Bagni di Lucca. It has a large entrance room, a second reception room and a kitchen on the ground floor, and two bedrooms and a bathroom on the first floor. There is a terrace at the front of the property, which has stunning views of the hills and valleys around Bagni di Lucca and the mountains beyond. We intend to let our property during the summer and use it ourselves for holidays during the rest of the year.

Q: Has it been a good investment so far?
A: We feel that our house has been a very good investment. This is primarily thanks to our estate agent, who has enabled us to restore the property, and therefore add value to it. It would have been difficult – if not impossible – to restore the house by ourselves due to work commitments in the UK and our poor understanding of Italian.

"A two-hour meal in the middle of the day is commonplace in Italy"

Q: Are the locals friendly and welcoming?
A: We have found them to be extremely friendly. We have spent a lot of time enjoying the bars and restaurants in Bagni di Lucca, and have had to purchase many new items for our property. We have done little more than exchange greetings with the people of our village, but hope to become more integrated once our renovation is complete and our Italian has improved.

Q: What's the best thing about life in Italy?
A: Everything! The pace of life in Italy has to be one of the best things. The idea of friends and family having time for a two-hour meal in the middle of the day is incomprehensible in the UK, but in Italy it is commonplace. The lack of crime is incredible, with shops leaving vast arrays of produce out on the streets when they close for lunch. Add to this the scenery, the culture, the language, and of course the food and wine, and who could resist Italy?

Q: What are your plans for the future?
A: We are looking forward to spending time at our house once the renovation is complete and exploring Tuscany and beyond. In time, I think we will consider relocating to Italy, which is a very exciting prospect. In the meantime, we will continue thinking and dreaming about our property as we go about our normal daily lives… and we will keep practising the Italian! ●

Above: The fertile soil provides an abundance of fresh produce

RENOVATING

Above: The house is located in a hill village near Bagni de Lucca

top tips
FOR RENOVATORS

■ Always ensure your budget is larger than the quotes you receive – there's always something that costs more than anticipated!

■ Be realistic; is it going to be cheaper to renovate an old farmhouse or buy a newly restored one?

■ Be prepared for a lot of hard work and to be hands-on with the project. If you try and take a step back and leave it to a hired manager they may not do things the way you want them.

■ It's very helpful to find a reliable and trustworthy estate agent who can recommend a builder and deal with all the paperwork.

■ Be patient! Renovation can be a lengthy process. Beverley and Rob are currently two years into their project and have nearly completed their renovations.

BEFORE

Above: Much work was needed, but it was mainly cosmetic

AFTER

Above and left: Two years' worth of hard work later and the renovations are almost complete

Living and working

Getting to grips with life in a foreign country can be a daunting task, so over the next few pages we give you an insight into life in Italy and what it may hold for you

WHAT IS A *CODICE FISCALE*?

Your *codice fiscale* is a number that's given to you to enable all kinds of purchases and official recognitions. Without it, you can't make any important or substantial purchases and you can't open a bank account, or even buy a mobile phone. To obtain yours, simply visit your local *Ministero Dell'Economia e Delle Finanze* with your passport and proof of your address.

Working in Italy

Visas and residency permits

Moving to Italy from another EU member country means that a visa isn't required for you to travel or work in Italy. However, depending on your intended term and reason to stay, you will need a *permesso*. This is valid for five years and will be tailored for your stay in Italy, whether it's for employment, self-employment, retirement, tourism, family, study and so on. One of your first priorities when arriving in Italy will be to visit the local *questura* (police headquarters) to get your *permesso*, and this should be done within ten days of arrival.

Rules with regard to all aspects of Italian bureaucracy are forever changing so ensure that you take at least one extra copy of all your paperwork with you, especially a couple of extra passport photographs. Italian rules stipulate that for any visit over three days, where you won't be staying in a hotel, you should register with the local police. This technically includes any tourist renting a property and although it isn't generally enforced, be aware.

If and when you eventually decide your move is permanent, you can apply for a residency permit (*certificate di residenza*). Although this isn't obligatory, it has many advantages, such as being able to purchase a car, open a residents' bank account, obtain a residential contract for utilities (which is cheaper) and get an Italian identity card.

SECURING A PERMESSO

■ The paperwork and information required for your *permesso* are relative to the type you require, but are centred on your ability to be self-sufficient and not dependent on state aid.

Requirements include

■ A letter stating that you're either employed in the UK, receiving a pension or are financially self-sufficient

■ Proof you have somewhere to live

■ Proof you have medical insurance, or an E111

■ Four passport-style photos

■ A copy of the photograph page of your passport

■ Your *codice fiscale*

Work permits

With regard to employment for EU members in Italy, your *permesso di soggiorno per lavoro* is all that's required, and it's renewable every five years. If you arrive in Italy with a job already arranged then your employers will organise the formalities and arrange for tax and national insurance payments. However, just how far your employers' help will go with regard to housing, logistics and other formalities will vary. To come to Italy to look for work is a perfectly viable proposition. Having English as a first language can help a lot, but it will be hard to gain any kind of primary employment without your Italian being more than basic.

If you do get a job with a limited grasp of Italian, the work environment is probably the best place to improve it. You can also secure a working holiday visa, or *ricevuta di segnalazione di soggiorno*. Again, this needs to be procured at the *questura*, and application is made in the same way as for any *permesso*.

As an EU resident, your visa will last for as long as you can prove you're looking for work and have a reasonable chance of finding it.

Finding a job

Job opportunities in Italy are still wider in the north of the country. The area from Rome upwards has the majority of the industry and lower unemployment and generates the vast majority of the GNP. The official employment office is known as the *provincia*, with private companies running

A knowledge of the language will be of great use when integrating with the locals

© ROZ COOPER

employment agencies in all of the major cities, and these are the best starting points for those seeking work. August isn't a good time to come to Italy or change jobs because many businesses and industries are shut for the whole month.

In Italy, everybody is entitled to a contract of employment, no matter what the terms of employment may be. However, if you're taken on to cover for prolonged absence or maternity leave, you may have left before it's delivered. The workplace is regulated in Italy under formal collective bargaining agreements, so you should be taken on under the same terms and conditions as the Italians you're working with. Being an EU resident, you have full employment rights and responsibilities in Italy.

Under current legislation, you pay tax and national insurance, and are eligible for state health care and pension rights. Pay will generally be lower than in the UK, especially in rural areas, but the cost of living is also lower, despite the advent of the euro – Italians claim most basic costs rose by up to 100 per cent since its introduction. In major cities, wages are comparable to the UK.

Working conditions

There's a minimum wage in Italy, and a maximum working week. These rules are enforced locally and nationally to ensure fairness throughout the workforce. The majority of employees will receive far in excess of the minimum wage, apart from those in the tourist industry, and trainees or apprentices. Forty hours is currently the maximum working week, spread over five days, with restricted overtime. The working day may start at seven, eight or nine am, with finishing times varying accordingly. A two-hour lunch break is considered the norm, with many companies now using flexi-time so employees can start early or finish late.

Holidays are mostly taken at company-legislated times, with many industries closing for August. There's also a two-week break over the Christmas period, which allows for six weeks of holidays in total. Long-term employees or senior management may get longer holiday periods than this. There are also bonuses paid to employees, normally in the form of an extra month's pay in July or August, or around the Christmas and New Year holiday.

Unemployment and social security benefits

Although you can, by arrangement, continue to be paid unemployment benefit from the UK while you're looking for work in Italy, you won't receive unemployment benefit as an Italian resident. There's no national unemployment scheme in operation in Italy, although payments can be made in specific circumstances.

Life in Italy is more laid back than in the UK, with strict maximum working hours

Living in Italy

Renting a home
If you don't have a property ready for you to move into, it can be beneficial and practical to rent. If your stay is for less than four years then renting would certainly be advisable. The rental market in Italy is substantial, with properties of all kinds available. Rentals can be short-term (six months) to long-term (usually four years). All tenancies are contracted, and you must use a *notaio* (notary) who can translate for you, making sure you understand the agreement, most essentially any restrictions and what notice has to be given to alter the agreement.

When you're initially renting, you may not want to ship all your belongings to Italy, so a short-term furnished let may be your best bet – in other words, properties designed for the holiday or tourist market. You'll find plenty of small ads for rental accommodation, but use a *notaio* recommended to you, making sure you don't fall under the sway of an unscrupulous landlord. You'll be expected to leave the property in as good a condition as you found it, with a deposit held in a bank account to cover any costs or charges when leaving. If using an agent, allow one month's rent as a guide for their charges. Some will require a letter of promise from your accountant or solicitor, proving you're reliable for

"Italians drive on the right (mostly), observe traffic lights rarely, overtake dangerously and toot their horns regularly"

SELF-EMPLOYMENT

To arrive in Italy and become self-employed isn't difficult and can be undertaken in half an hour. However, the use of an accountant is essential in order to fulfil tax and legislative necessities. A visit to the local chamber of commerce to register your business and change the status of your *permesso* to that of self-employed status is all that's necessary. The prospects for self-employment are varied and whatever your skills, there will be opportunities for you. Italy doesn't recognise all professional qualifications from outside its borders so it's advisable to get full translations of any certificates, diplomas or qualifications, and you should seek advice from the local trade organisation or chamber of commerce.

© ROZ COOPER

As an EU citizen, you're entitled to free healthcare, but prescription charges still apply

LIVING AND WORKING

FURNISHED OR UNFURNISHED?

Unfurnished will often mean not only without furniture, but also without a kitchen, bathroom fittings, light fittings and even switches. Contact with the previous tenant is advisable since you can attempt to purchase some of these items from them and gain valuable information about the landlord, the facilities and so on.

Furnished property will come with a kitchen, bathroom fittings and furniture for normal living, but not everyday necessities such as bedding, kitchen utensils or towels.

When renting in Italy, you won't normally be allowed to sub-let, but with your own property, letting in the holiday or tourist market is quite common. Recently, the market seems to be moving into overkill and it's becoming more difficult to find a good agent. This means it's important that your property is of a good specification, with a pool if possible, and that the landlord is properly licensed to rent out property with the local authorities.

the rent payments. If you're employed, a letter from your employer stating your income and the term of your contract is required.

Moving into your home

When it comes to moving into your chosen property, there will be a number of organisational arrangements to be made. Whether renting or buying, you'll be responsible for all utilities and costs relevant to the property.

As soon as you have a moving date, you should contact the utility providers and the commune for refuse disposal to make arrangements for the supplies to be put in your name from that date. If this means the property will be, or has been, disconnected, there will be reconnection fees, as well as the standing charges. Make sure you read the meters when you first arrive and contact the suppliers to ensure the readings match.

Utilities

Most properties will have a supply of mains water and electricity, with telephone services available nationally. However, although gas is widely used in cities, in rural areas it's common for there to be no mains supply, and so bottled gas (*bombola*) is used instead. If your property can have a gas tank installed, it must be at least 25 metres from your property, and any other properties or installations. Otherwise bottled gas is delivered in a variety of sizes suitable for the location it will be stored in.

Southern Italy does occasionally have problems with water supplies, especially in Sicily and on the other islands. Make sure you're aware of the local supply situation before you purchase any property because it can be a serious inconvenience in some of the more remote rural locations.

Electrical equipment

If you want to take any electrical equipment with you to Italy, make sure you have a good supply of adapters for the electrical sockets. All electrical equipment should work correctly in Italy since it's

PROPERTY INSURANCE

■ The bars or grilles on the ground floor of Italian homes aren't for decorative purposes. Ensure that your property is insured, especially if it's empty for some period of the year

■ Property and contents insurance can be taken out for either residential or non-residential accommodation

on a 240-volt system. As long as your TV is a modern multi-system set, it should also work off an Italian electrical system. Sky recently celebrated the first anniversary of the launch of their satellite system in Italy, and upon connection you'll find that there's a varied selection of English language programming to choose from.

Healthcare

As with most things in Italy, the healthcare system is more advanced in the north of the country. The hospitals are better run and doctors tend to prefer to study and work in the north where job prospects and living standards are higher. Generally, the system is good, but as with all organisations, there are problems with supply, demand and costs. As EU citizens, everybody is entitled to free care when carrying an E111. Prescription charges will be made but examinations are free of charge.

Look into private health insurance. This can be extended from your British cover or can originate in Italy, but be sure the broker understands that care is required by English-speaking staff and that cover includes repatriation, should it be required.

Education

Education is the root of your children's future and is something that's taken very seriously by Italian parents. As EU nationals, your children are entitled to free education through to the age of 15 – there are costs for higher education and university places. The Italian state school system is considered to be at least on a par with those of other European nations and improvements are ongoing.

The better schools are found in the large cities of the north, and private schools aren't considered better than the state system, but are used by foreigners and those who prefer a religious or specialised education for their children.

Fees vary enormously but are in the region of €200 – €400 a month, with an enrolment fee of €400 – €600. Once you've decided where you'll be living in Italy, a list of English-speaking schools can be obtained from the European Council of International Schools.

Taxes

Income tax ranges from 23 per cent to 45 per cent. IVA (VAT) is presently at 20 per cent, with reduced rates for foodstuffs, local public transport, books, magazines and some entertainment. You should take professional advice on your personal tax situation as there are many possibilities for reducing your bill. You're normally considered liable for Italian taxation if you're domiciled in Italy or if your business interests or income are initiated in Italy. There are also capital gains taxes and some inheritance tax regulations to be considered too.

Property purchase taxes differ regardless of residency. Currently, upon purchasing a property as a non-resident, you pay ten per cent tax, and this is reduced to three per cent for residents. You also have to pay local taxes, from one to two per cent, which are set by the commune and are paid bi-monthly.

Driving

Driving in Italy is not for the faint-hearted. Italians drive on the right (mostly), observe traffic lights rarely, overtake dangerously and toot their horns regularly. Your driving licence, and therefore test qualification, is valid in Italy and it isn't necessary for you to get an Italian driving licence. However, once you have a residency permit, you can do this if you wish. Lanes are narrower on Italian roads than British, and while the upkeep is good on *autostrada*, or motorways, local roads can be undulating.

Retiring

There are over 30,000 British retirees in Italy, all of whom are entitled to have their pensions paid direct to an Italian bank account. Being an EU member also entitles you to increases in pension payments. For details, see www.thepensionservice.gov.uk, or telephone 0191 218 7777. For private pensions, tax and other investment income, you should consult

your pension provider or independent financial advisor. Some companies will only pay into a British bank account – this doesn't mean you can't get at your money, but it will be more costly to do so. It's important to find out about trust investment for your capital, where tax liability can be minimised, and to allow for exchange rate fluctuations. Until Britain joins the euro, the banks will continue to earn fortunes by changing and transferring funds. However, there are currency companies specialising in the exchange of sterling to euros at lower costs.

Making a will

If you already have a will in the UK, don't assume that it will be recognised in Italy. Italian legislation doesn't allow you to distribute assets as you wish, and there are overriding beneficiaries. In order to ensure that your wishes are carried out, you must make an Italian will. The choice of lawyer is critical, because they must appreciate that you have an existing British will, and so they'll be able to draft a document corresponding to your wishes. This will save money in legal fees and can avoid unfortunate repercussions for those you wish to inherit. ●

MOTORING DO'S AND DON'TS

In Car
- You must carry an emergency breakdown triangle
- You must wear seat belts both in the front and the rear
- You must wear any prescription glasses and carry a spare pair
- You should carry a spare set of bulbs and fuses
- You should carry a first aid kit and a fire extinguisher
- You must not use a mobile phone, except with a hands free kit
- You must carry a high-visibility waistcoat in case of breakdown

On Car
- You must have the new EU number plates with nationality of origin…
- …or a nationality sticker displaying your country of origin
- A valid road tax disc
- Dipped headlights must be used at all times

USEFUL INFORMATION AND TELEPHONE NUMBERS FOR MOTORISTS

- Telephone 113 for general emergency or breakdown help and advice
- Telephone 112 for police (*carabinieri*) in case of an accident or emergency
- Telephone 118 for an ambulance in any circumstance
- Telephone 116 and *Automobili Club d'Italia* (ACI) will send assistance
- Telephone 06-4477 for road reports from *Automobili Club d'Italia*
- Listen to ISO Radio 103.3 and Jiaradio RTL 102.5 for road conditions

You don't need a new driving licence to use your car in Italy – just nerves of steel!

MARRIAGE

Marrying in Italy is popular these days, for financial as well as romantic reasons. Weddings can be organised relatively easily. The waiting period is foreshortened for foreigners, but you will have to be in the country for three or four days before the wedding. You'll also need your original birth certificate, your original passport and one copy of it, and a fee (currently £75). If either party is divorced, you'll need to bring the Decree Absolute, along with a translation. You must also have a translator present if either party doesn't speak Italian. The British consulate will issue a certificate of marriage and send it to the British registry office.

© ROZ COOPER

Meet
THE BUYER

Names: Graham Lane

Age: 56

Occupation: Runs an internet property company and B&B

Contact: www.laportaverde.com

Right: The dramatic Umbrian countryside

Below: The Lanes' new home, Villa Rosa

STARTING A BUSINESS

THE AREA

● **LOCATION** Umbria

Umbria is a beautiful and largely unspoiled area, with rolling countryside dotted with hill towns

● **THREE-STOREY VILLA**
● **REQUIRED RENOVATION**
● **NOW A BED & BREAKFAST**

PROPERTY MARKETING

Graham Lane and his wife, Lin, went to Umbria in search of a retirement investment, but ended up buying a three-storey villa and setting up an internet property business

IN THE EASTER OF 2001 THE LANES DECIDED THAT enough was enough. Conquering their fears of homesickness and worries about acclimatising to life in a foreign country, they made the move to Umbria. Now, four years later, they have a beautiful home, active social life and a thriving internet business.

Q: When you decided to move to Italy, were you already planning to set up a business?
A: Whilst we love England and lived in a beautiful part of Somerset, we were fed up with the rising house prices, endless rain and pressure of work in the UK and often went on holiday to Tuscany and Umbria, staying in self-catering apartments on farms as part of the *Agriturismo* scheme (self-catering apartments on a farm). We didn't really start out with any other plan than to look into buying a house for when we retired.

Q: How did you go about finding a home?
A: We started with the internet and the help of the owner of our holiday apartment. He put us in touch with a local estate agent and we now live in one of the properties shown to us on our first visit. The only problem was that the house we were buying was divided in half and shared a front door. The other half had been empty for 40 years but was not for sale. Somehow we managed to buy rights to the stairs and eventually, when the owners realised they would have to pay half of the restoration costs, they agreed to sell us the other half.

Q: How much work was needed to renovate the property?
A: When we looked around it the first time, four pigs were living on the ground floor. The smell was awful. It's a three-storey villa, but because we

bought it in two stages, I restored the first part myself and left the second section, including the roof, to the experts. The costs weren't prohibitive. We spent about €20,000 rebuilding the roof – complete with chimneys, insulation, waterproof membrane and guttering.

> *"Italian laws are confusing; one tells you something is fine, another says it's illegal"*

Q: What made you set up La Porta Verde, your internet property business?

A: A British woman asked me to find a small holiday home for her in Umbria. I contacted the agent we had worked with and, two days later, she came over and bought a small cottage we had found for her. The agent gave me some commission for finding the client and shortly afterwards, after meeting a Dutch couple at a party and discussing the difficulties involved with finding and restoring properties, she approached us and suggested setting up a business together to help foreign buyers. We now have clients all over the world.

Q: Did you encounter any problems when you were setting up the business?

A: I knew that the internet was the business tool of the future. The actual setting up of the business was straightforward as we are completely internet based. Italian laws can be confusing because they can be conflicting; one law tells you something is possible, but another says it is illegal. Our business strategy had to be flexible enough to accommodate Italian law and the tendency to bend the rules when it suits them. The easiest part of the experience was actually buying the property. The Italian system and all its incumbent bureaucracy is watertight and easy to understand.

Q: How long did the process take?

A: For our own property it took four months, but according to the local notary, as long as all the documents are in order and clients are around to sign them, completion can be achieved in five minutes… It's probably an exaggeration but typically Italian.

Q: What sort of people are your clients?

A: Generally, our clients are in the 50 to 70 age range with high incomes, although we are starting to see more young couples taking the plunge. About 50 per cent of our clients are looking for a permanent residence and the others want holiday homes or something to rent out. Sometimes I have to solve problems, but we've never had a problem after the final contract has been signed.

Q: Do you have any plans for the expansion of your business?

A: Because we work over the internet we tend to go with the flow. We don't have a business plan. I was a Business Advisor back in the UK but I have since thrown my rule book out of the window. We basically look out for good ideas and try to extend the network of services using our site. We also want to create a self-catering apartment in the stables on our ground floor, preferably before Ryanair starts flying to Perugia airport… ●

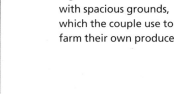

top tips

FOR SETTING UP BUSINESS IN ITALY

■ Keep a good balance between common sense and risk-taking. It's a case of following your heart, but keeping your head.

■ Read plenty of books and websites about making the move. So many people have done it now, there is a wealth of experience to draw on.

■ Learn as much Italian as you can before coming. Once you've got a good grounding in basic grammar, the rest comes with everyday practice. It's not essential but it will help you, especially if you are planning to set up a business.

■ Remember that every business has to be registered and licensed with the *Camera di Commercio* (Chamber of Commerce). Your business will have to fall into an existing category, even if it is a new field. Registering is not cheap and must be done in front of a notary.

■ Registering yourself as an estate agency demands that you pass the relevant exams in Italian. Instead, we registered as a marketing company and work in collaboration with qualified estate agents.

STARTING A BUSINESS

Right: The house came with spacious grounds, which the couple use to farm their own produce

BEFORE

AFTER

Above and right: An old door was transformed into the living room's French window

Left: Their lovingly restored house has a chicken shed in the garden – though thankfully there are no pigs inside any more…

Property guide

Wherever you decide to buy in Italy, you can be sure you will find an abundance of culture, fine food and wine, and traditionally styled properties

Piedmont, Valle d'Aosta & Trentino-Alto Adige

Mountainous and wild, with rice fields and vineyards

© ENIT

FACT BOX

Piedmont
- **Population** 4,231,334
- **Unemployment rate** 5.3%
- **Net migration** 53,136
- **Population growth** 0.43%
- **Average 4-bed house price** €217,000 / £147,619
- **Foreign residents** 53,136

Valle d'Aosta
- **Population** 120,909
- **Unemployment rate** 6.5%
- **Net migration** 1,294
- **Population growth** 1.14%
- **Average 4-bed house price** €218,500 / £148,639
- **Foreign residents** 3,636

Trentino Alto-Adige
- **Population** 950,495
- **Unemployment rate** 2.9%
- **Net migration** 10,203
- **Population growth** 1.06%
- **Average 4-bed house price** €331,000 / £225,170
- **Foreign residents** 42,674

Contents

Area profile

This is a beautiful region that's unspoilt by modern society and has some truly breathtaking countryside and views

GETTING THERE

AIR Turin is served by Caselle airport, 15km from the city. **British Airways** (0870 850 9850, www.britishairways.com) flies daily from Gatwick, **Ryanair** (0871 246 0000, www.ryanair.com) flies from Stansted and **easyjet** (0871 244 2366, www.easyjet.com) flies from Luton. Malpensa airport near Milan is very close to the eastern edge of Piedmont, and is served by flights from a broader range of UK locations than Caselle. See the Lombardy section for further details.

ROAD Cross the channel either by car ferry – try **P&O Ferries** (08705 202 020; www.poferries.com), **SeaFrance** (08705 711 711, www.seafrance.co.uk) or **Hoverspeed** (0870 240 8070, www.hoverspeed.co.uk) – or go through the tunnel (08705 353 535, www.eurotunnel.com) to reach Calais. Next, take the A26 to Reims, briefly take the A4 and then the E17. 170km past Troyes, take the A39, then drive on to the A40 at Bourg-en-Bresse, the N205 just before Le Fayet, through the Mont Blanc tunnel and into Italy. Now take the E25 and, a few miles after Courmayeur, use the A5 to reach Turin and Piedmont.

RAIL From London Waterloo, it's possible to reach Turin in just 10 hours, with a station change in Paris, though many possible routes take in extra changes and add many hours to the journey time. Contact **Rail Europe** (08708 371 371, www.raileurope.co.uk) for more information. For details of connections in Piedmont, go to www.trenitalia.it/en/index.html.

COACH National Express is part of the **Eurolines network** (08705 143 219, www.eurolines.co.uk), which runs coaches that go from London Victoria to Turin in a little over 22 hours, including a two-hour wait and change in Paris. Local coach connections are also available to other cities in the region.

THIS FAR NORTH-WEST CORNER OF ITALY shares similar geographical characteristics with its neighbour, Lombardy. To the north lie the Alps, with their magnificent mountain scenery, lovely alpine villages and Italy's premium national park, aptly named the Gran Paradiso. To the south is the Po River plain, whose vast lowlands are almost entirely under rice fields.

This is essentially a rural area with the exception of Turin, Italy's industrial giant. The city is roughly situated in the centre of the region and acts almost as a frontier between the towering mountains and the flat plains.

Geography

Trentino-Alto Adige, an almost completely mountainous region, is dominated by the higher Alps in the north, which form a natural border between Italy and Austria, and the Dolomites in the south. Most mountains are snow-capped for half the year and provide a stunning backdrop to the many attractive villages and ski resorts. Italy's second-longest river, the Adige, crosses the region from west to south, and the Brenner Pass, one of Europe's

The region is home to spectacular mountain scenery

The Coccia theatre in the elegant town of Novara

busiest roads, divides the region into two before reaching Verona in the south.

Turin is one of Italy's most underrated cities and boasts fine monuments, superb museums, gourmet cuisine and excellent shopping. The city's history is also noteworthy – a key player in Italian unification and the country's capital during the 1860s, Turin later became Italy's economic powerhouse, along with Milan. The city centre is mostly Baroque, with elegant facades and arcades lining many streets and squares, while the Renaissance Duomo houses the famous Turin Shroud.

To the north is the Valle d'Aosta, set in lush mountain valleys replete with icy waterfalls, glaciers

"Much of the area is unspoilt, and it's a paradise for hikers, nature lovers and skiers…"

and dozens of medieval fortresses, whose often austere exteriors hide rich interiors – those at Issogne, Ussel and Verrès being very good examples. Much of the area is unspoilt, and it's a paradise for hikers, nature lovers and skiers. In fact, Courmayeur at the foot of Mont Blanc is often voted Italy's top resort. The main towns include Aosta, with its numerous well-preserved Roman remains; Domodossola; Novara, which boasts a Renaissance elegance; and Varallo, a popular tourist resort.

Alto Adige has a distinctly Tyrolean air to it, which is found in the architecture, language and gastronomy. The region has many attractive towns, including the capital of the region, Bolzano, with its Gothic Duomo; the medieval towns of Bressanone and Brunico; the flower-filled Cavalese; and the spa town of Merano. All are very popular with tourists who flock to the area all year round.

The jagged high peaks of the Dolomites provide ideal slopes for all kinds of skiing along the 650km of runs and are home to some of the world's most spectacular mountain passes, including Sella, Pordoi and Livignalongo. Not surprisingly, there are also several world-class ski resorts here.

Within the three main valleys (Val di Sole, Val di Non and Val Gardena) are many resorts, such as Alpe di Siusi, Canzei (excellent for cross-country skiing), the upmarket Cortina d'Ampezzo, Corvara in the scenic heart of Val Badia, and Ortisei.

Culture

These regions' geographical proximity to France, Switzerland and Austria means that much of their history is speckled with frontier changes and invasions from neighbouring kingdoms. Testimony to this are the numerous castle-fortresses scattered around the countryside, built by noblemen defending their territory from outsiders.

Cultural influences from abroad are very strong, particularly in Alto Adige, which only became part of Italy in 1919. In this area, nearly 70 per cent of the population speak German and the Tyrol culture is much in evidence.

Economy

This is Italy at its wealthiest and this prosperity is reflected in the region's extremely low unemployment figures: in 2004, Trentino-Alto Adige had a mere 2.9 per cent, Valle d'Aosta 3 per cent and Piedmont 5.3 per cent.

© ENIT

The Fondazione Sandretto building in Turin houses works by 58 contemporary artists

Turin is Italy's economic powerhouse and the centre of many household names, such as Lavazza and FIAT – Turin manufactures 40 per cent of Italian cars. Other important industries include aeronautics, telecommunications and home textiles, while Turin is also a major international training centre. Outside Turin, agriculture is the main activity, led by rice cultivation – Verelli produces around 70 per cent of the country's crop.

Trentino-Alto Adige's main industry is tourism, while other important industries include hydro-electricity, metallurgy and agriculture, particularly involving grapes and apples.

Social groups

These areas are generally sparsely populated, particularly Trentino-Alto Adige, and normally experience only small changes in population growth. Piedmont has some 175,000 foreign residents, with German and British residents making up the largest European groups. Valle d'Aosta saw a large increase in relocators in 2003, when the foreign population increased by over 20 per cent to 3,600.

Trentino-Alto Adige also saw a marked increase in foreign residents, and there's a substantial German population in these regions too. ●

FACTS

■ St Bernard mountain rescue dogs are still trained to this day by monks in the valley of Great St Bernard in Valle d'Aosta

■ Ötzi, the mummified 'iceman' from 5,300 years ago, was discovered under the ice in the Dolomites

■ Piedmont tradition claims that "rice is born in water but dies in wine"

FOOD AND DRINK

Turin is one of Italy's culinary capitals and locally grown rice makes a star appearance in the many varieties of risotto. Piedmont is also known for its lake fish with pasta, veal (*vitello tonnato* comes with tuna and caper sauce), *fondata* (a variation of fondue) and exquisite white truffles. Dessert specials include Turin's delicious *San Vittorio* (mint and chocolate pudding) and *spumone piemontese* (a mascarpone mousse with rum).

In Trentino-Alto Adige, expect to find a strong central European influence in the hearty country fare and winter warmers. Beans, game, freshwater fish and strudel feature high on the menu.

Piedmont is Italy's premium wine area and home to internationally renowned names such as Asti Spumante, Barolo, Barbaresco and Malvasia. Vermouth also originated here. Trentino-Alto Adige wines are mostly white and well-known names include Gewürztraminer, Riesling and Terlaner. The region is also a major producer of grappa, Italy's favourite liqueur.

Turin offers many local dessert dishes
© ENIT

TURIN		LONDON
7	Dec	7
11	Nov	10
17	Oct	14
23	Sept	19
26	Aug	21
27	July	22
25	June	20
21	May	17
17	April	13
12	March	10
8	Feb	7
5	Jan	6

Average monthly temperature °C (Celsius)

TURIN		LONDON
49	Dec	81
73	Nov	78
87	Oct	70
72	Sept	65
66	Aug	62
57	July	59
92	June	58
117	May	57
96	April	56
65	March	64
41	Feb	72
40	Jan	77

Average monthly rainfall mm (millimetres)

Property hotspots

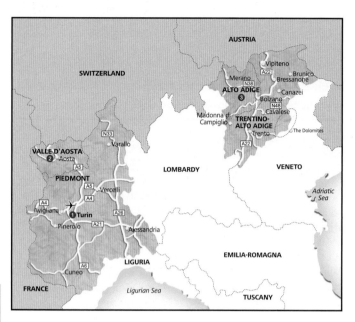

HOTSPOTS

● Hotspot
◔ Major town/city
66 Road numbers

The property market is stable, but currently operating at a slower rate than the average Italian city. City centre property remains in demand, but is certainly cheaper than cities such as Milan and Rome. This trend is set to continue, with prices appreciating at a steady pace. Currently a two-bedroom house retails for €240,000, while a four-bedroom property will sell for €455,000.

KEY FACTS

■ **Population** 864,671
■ **Airport** Turin International Airport, Strada San Maurizio 12, I-10072 Caselle Torinese, Tel: +39 011 567 6361, www.aeroportoditorino.it.
■ **Medical** Ospedale Evangelico Valdese, Via Pellico 19, 10125 Torino, Tel: +39 011 65401
■ **Schools** International School of Turin – ACAT, Vicolo Tiziano 10, 10024 Moncalieri, Tel: +39 011 645 967, www.acat-ist.it
■ **Pros** Turin is heaven for those with a sweet tooth, hosting a three-week chocolate fair in the spring, and with many fine specialist confectionery shops ■ The majestic streets and splendid Baroque architecture are home to an array of exhibits, including galleries of old masters and modern classics, and museums of Egyptian artefacts, cars and warfare ■ As one of the hubs of Italian business, this is a real city, with a thriving nightlife and cultural scene, fashionable boutiques, the biggest market in Europe, and only a moderate level of tourism
■ **Cons** The city is polluted by heavy traffic and industry, which sprawls around the south and west ■ Areas such as Stazione Porta Nuova and the public parks have developed a grim reputation, relating to the large numbers of prostitutes, drug addicts and theft, especially at night.

1. Turin

Set against the backdrop of the river Po and the Alps, Turin is undergoing a major facelift in preparation for the 2006 Winter Olympics. The industrial and economic centre of Piedmont, Turin has always had a strong association with France and is described as the Paris of Italy. Indeed, with its broad boulevards and elegant promenades, it does boast a certain French elegance, yet its industrial heritage cannot be overlooked. Turin is home to the Fiat car company, and it was industrial unrest on the shop floors here that gave birth to the Italian communist party.

For art lovers, Turin has an excellent selection of galleries and museums, such as the Museum of Decorative Arts and the Galleria Sabauda, which houses an outstanding collection of Florentine and Flemish art. The city also boasts a fantastic Egyptian museum, which houses the tomb of Kha Mitir and a statue of Rameses II.

Turin was home to the house and Empire of Savoy, and was

capital of Italy between 1861 and 1865. Evidence of this can be seen throughout the city, with buildings such as the Palazzo Madame and statues such as that of Emanuele Filiberto. No trip to Turin is complete without viewing the Duomo and its world-famous treasure, the Turin Shroud. Turin is also the birthplace of modern chocolate, and a popular local drink is *bicerein*, a liquid chocolate beverage. The region's *nocciole* (hazelnuts) are also famous and are a major ingredient in one of its most famous products, Ferrero Rocher. Another famous 'export' is the Juventus football team. A university city, there is a lively bar and café scene to be found around Via Po.

The rental market is dominated by internal immigrants from the south, who arrive to take advantage of the employment opportunities, and also the student population. Consequently, anyone seeking to invest in a property to let would be looking at a strong rental return, in the region of €920 a week for a two-bedroom property. A four-bedroom house can fetch €1,830 a week.

2. Valle d'Aosta

Covering just 8,500 square kilometres, the Valle d'Aosta is Italy's smallest region, but also one of the wealthiest. Today the domain of skiers and hikers, this autonomous region was once a crossroads between northern and southern Europe, and the crossing point of the Alps for Hannibal and his band of elephants. Littered with Roman artefacts and medieval castles, Valle d'Aosta is an amalgamation of French, Italian and Germanic influences. To the east a Germanic dialect is spoken, while French is on an equal footing with Italian, which was only introduced in 1861.

Aosta, the region's only major city, was founded by the Romans in 25BC. Situated near the confluence of the Buthier and Dora Baltea rivers, and encircled by the Alps, Aosta is linked to France with the Mont Blanc and Gran San Bernardo tunnels. With an attractive medieval centre and narrow cobbled streets, the city has an alpine air. Visit the Roman theatre, forum and bridge, while the Museo Archeologico Regionale is also worth seeing.

Close by is the stunning Parco Nazionale del Gran Paradiso, created in 1922 from part of the royal hunting reserve of the House of Savoy. Unspoilt alpine scenery, wildlife and flora make this a popular destination with walkers in summer and cross-country skiers in winter. Cogne is a traditional mountain village and the main resort of the park. There are a number of ski resorts, the main ones being Courmayeur on Mont Blanc, Cervinia on the Matterhorn and Champoluc on Monte Rosa.

The rentals market is much stronger than the sales market in

The area is an outdoor enthusiast's paradise, with beautiful botanical gardens and stunning scenery

Valle d'Aosta. With thousands of skiers descending on the resorts, there is a lot of income to be had – on average €605 a week for a two-bedroom property. On the other hand, property prices are extremely cheap and there are some real bargains to be had; the average price for a four-bedroom house is €333,000.

KEY FACTS
■ **Population** 119,546
■ **Airport** Turin International Airport, Strada San Maurizio 12, I-10072 Caselle Torinese, Tel: +39 011 567 6361, www.aeroportoditorino.it.
■ **Medical** U.S.L. Valle d'Aosta, Via Rey 1, 11100 Aosta, Tel: +39 0165 5431, www.ausl.vda.it.
■ **Schools** International School of Turin – ACAT, Vicolo Tiziano 10, 10024 Moncalieri, Tel: +39 011 645 967, www.acat-ist.it ■ European School, Via Montello 118, 21100 Varese, Tel: +39 0332 806111
■ **Pros** There are many hiking trails in the area, especially in Gran Paradiso national park ■ Several of the highest mountains in Europe ring the valley and are a magnet for climbers and skiers ■ Villages off the beaten track have retained much of their alpine character
■ **Cons** Due to the local wealth and the levels of tourism, living costs are high ■ The best skiing spots are overrun by ugly tourist developments ■ The main valley becomes clogged with traffic, bringing pollution in its wake ■ Public transport in the valleys is infrequent and irregular ■ High season brings hordes of tourists.

3. Trentino-Alto Adige

Alto Adige, or Südtirol (South Tyrol), as it is known to the Austrians, is a mountainous region, separated from Switzerland and Austria by the Alps. Passing between Austrian and Italian ownership throughout its colourful history, this region offers spectacular views and unspoilt flora and fauna. The Counts of Tyrol, who ruled Alto Adige from the 13th century, built a number of castles in the valleys and mountains, which remain to this day. Offering a very distinct culture, Alto Adige is a centre for walkers, climbers, skiers and those who just want to enjoy the peace and serenity. German is widely spoken and signposts are in both Italian and German. Tyrolean architecture predominates, with Gothic churches displaying onion domes, and lands swathed in vineyards and forests.

Bolzano is the region's capital and the gateway between the overtly Italian Trentino and the decidedly German Alto Adige. Visit the Gothic Duomo, which boasts elaborate carvings reflecting the importance of the wine industry to the regional economy, while the mosaic-covered roof and the spire are highly intricate. The city's Archaeological Museum is home to Alto Adige's most famous ex-resident: 'Ötzi', a 5,000-year-old mummified iceman, found in the Dolomites. The Civic Museum charts the region's Tyrolean history.

The quaint town of Merano, to the north, is overwhelmed by tourists in summer, descending on the town for the thermal spas and mountain ranges. To the north is the Parco Nazionale dello Stelvio, which offers visitors fantastic walks along the peaks and valleys that form the Ortler range. There are a number of alpine valleys scattered throughout the region, including Val Gardena, Val di Solda and Val Martello, most of which offer skiing. Along with Val Badia, Val Gardena is home to the ancient Ladin culture, which is famed for its wooden carvings, and whose legends are populated with witches, dragons, giants and fairies. Alto Adige is also home to Europe's largest plateau at Alpe di Siusi, boasting views across its green pastures to the Sciliar peaks. Finally, across the Dolomites you will find Cortina d'Ampezzo, Italy's most famous, fashionable and expensive ski resort.

The region boasts a strong rentals market, due to the large number of tourists who flock to the ski resorts and national parks. A two-bedroom property commands €650 a week, while a four-bedroom property will average at €875 a week. Property is hard to come by, although once you find it, the traditional wooden cabins can be very cosy. For a three-bedroom property, expect to pay an average of €360,000.

KEY FACTS
■ **Population** 463,207
■ **Airport** ABD Airport Bolzano Dolomiti, Via F. Baracca 1, 39100 Bolzano, Tel: +39 0471 255 255, www.abd-airport.it ■ Aeroporto Valerio Catullo, 37060 Caselle di Sommacapegna, Tel: +39 045 809 5666, www.aeroportoverona.it
■ **Medical** Azienda Speciale U.S.L. Centro Sud Centralino Ospedale, Via Böhler Lorenz 5, 39100 Bolzano, Tel: +39 0471 908111
■ **Schools** Aleardo Aleardi International School, Via Segantini 20, 37138 Verona, Tel: +39 045 578200, www.aleardi.it
■ **Pros** Children are exceedingly well catered for, with family friendly trails, and activities tailored to the little ones ■ All levels of skiers and walkers will find satisfaction, from the craggy peaks of the Catinaccio, to low valleys with breathtaking views ■ Summer activities include hang-gliding, horse-riding, mountaineering, and mountain-biking ■ Merano has restorative baths to relax the muscles after the inevitable aches and pains acquired in the spectacular outdoors
■ **Cons** Public transport is excellent in season, but scarce at other times ■ The high season is terribly busy, whilst off-season some towns are virtually deserted ■ There is little in the way of indoor leisure or cultural activities, other than the après ski bars and the archaeological museum ■ Little work is available outside the tourist industry.

© ENIT

FOR SALE Property guide

With property as varied as its landscape, this region offers excellent appreciation and superb rental return

In the mountainous regions, properties have large, overhanging roofs to protect against snow

GENERALLY SPEAKING, THESE THREE AREAS offer a great investment, being very popular holiday destinations. They are also wealthy areas that are popular with the local market, and this has resulted in prices being pushed up. However, for those seeking an excellent rental return, this is the area to buy in.

The most expensive area in the region is Valle d'Aosta, which is also has the most popular resorts in both summer and winter. The property market is currently buoyant, with Courmayeur the most expensive resort; here a three-bedroom villa can sell for over a million euros.

Piedmont itself is more affordable, with a two-bedroom property selling for €300,000, but rentals are more expensive, especially in areas such as Turin, where a two-bedroom property can fetch €920 a week. Consequently the region makes for a good investment. Langha is Piedmont's most reasonably priced area, although the smaller towns throughout the region also boast reasonably priced homes. Recent trends show that it is fashionable among many foreign buyers to seek out old wine estates, of which Piedmont has an abundance.

Trentino-Alto Adige is dominated by resorts and holiday homes, which may be somewhat overwhelming for those seeking to permanently relocate to the area. However, property is well-built and offers excellent appreciation, with a three-bedroom home letting for €940 a week. Known for its large estates and castles, the region is expensive. Outside Italy's major cities, property in Alto Adige is the dearest in Italy, and property appreciated at a rate of nine per cent in 2002. Homes here are in huge demand, with Bolzano, the most expensive city, leading the way. ●

TYPICAL PROPERTIES

Valle d'Aosta Wood and stone-built chalets, known as *rascards*, are typical of the region. They are sturdily built and fetch a high price.
Piedmont Property styles here are very varied. In mountainous regions you will find small hamlets with grey, stone-built houses, with *ardesia*- (slate) or stone-tiled roofs. On the fertile plains are 18th- and 19th-century villas with red tile roofs. As they are agricultural, they usually come with a package of land. There are also many new developments and modern homes, generally in the wealthy urban areas.
Trentino-Alto Adige In the mountainous areas, chalets of varying sizes, known as *baite* and constructed from wood and white-painted stone, are the norm. They generally have overhanging slate roofs, to protect the property from snow, and dark wood balconies. In hilly terrain you will find large estates and *castelli* (castles), with red roofs and turrets. Town houses generally come with steep roofs, towers and multi-coloured slate.

WHAT CAN YOU GET FOR YOUR EUROS?

HAMLET PROPERTY

Situated near the town of Asti in a peaceful and sunny location, this 250-year-old property is surrounded by vineyards and arable land. South-facing, the farmhouse is in good condition with original features, such as stone stairs and high ceilings, but requires some renovation to render it fully habitable. The grounds would be ideal for vineyards and the construction of a swimming pool.

€140,000 CODE PIE

VILLAGE HOUSE

A 200-year-old detached house with a private courtyard garden, this village property has been partly renovated and is habitable, though it still requires a few finishing touches. It is situated in the village of Nizza Monferrato and all facilities and amenities are nearby. The property is located in the centre of the wine region, and Milan, Turin and Genoa are only an hour's drive away.

€240,000 CODE PIE

RENOVATED HILLSIDE HOUSE

This two-storey farmhouse dates from the 19th century, has been fully renovated, and has a total living area of 200m^2. The grounds cover 2.5 acres, including a patio. Currently split into two separate apartments, the property would suit those looking for joint ownership, or a buy-to-let investment. The property is in a rural location close to the Roman spa town of Acqui Terme.

€359,000 CODE PIE

CHARACTERFUL STONE HOUSE

This 300-year-old, four-bedroom stone house has been lovingly restored to preserve its traditional features, such as the stone fireplace and wood-beamed ceiling. The characterful property is situated on a hillside in a beautiful rural location and boasts stunning views, yet the local town of Santo Stefano Belbo is only 10 minutes away and offers all facilities, including bars and restaurants.

€459,000 CODE PIE

FARMHOUSE IN WINE AREA

Situated in the heart of the Gavi hills, one of Italy's most famous wine regions, this old farmhouse has been traditionally restored. Within its own private grounds of 1.4ha, it comes complete with a swimming pool and a two-car garage. Only an hour's drive from Milan or Genoa, the property is easily accessible from the UK and close to civilisation, while still enjoying a rural location.

€880,000 CODE CIC

VINEYARD ESTATE

This 100-year-old farmhouse is located in a stunning position in the Monferrato wine region. With grounds covering 6.8ha and 360 degree views over the surrounding countryside, it offers huge potential. There are four bedrooms, a wine cellar, a balcony, two courtyards and a spacious garden, ideal for a swimming pool.

€1,180,000 CODE PIE

AVERAGE HOUSE PRICES PIEDMONT, VALLE D'AOSTA & TRENTINO-ALTO ADIGE

	2-bed	3-bed	4-bed	5-bed
Turin	€301,000 (£204,762)	€316,000 (£214,966)	€452,000 (£307,483)	€563,000 (£382,993)
Valle d'Aosta	€128,200 (£87,211)	€209,500 (£142,517)	€251,800 (£171,293)	€361,000 (£245,578)
Trentino-Alto Adige	€253,700 (£172,585)	€357,000 (£242,857)	€335,000 (£227,891)	€398,500 (£271,088)

Liguria

Italy's foremost coastal strip, backed by vine-clad mountains

© ENIT

FACT BOX

- ■ **Population** 1,572,197
- ■ **Population growth** 0.14%
- ■ **Unemployment rate** 6.1%
- ■ **Average 4-bed house price** €423,000 / £287,755
- ■ **Net migration** 16,677
- ■ **Foreign residents** 53,194

Contents

Area profile

Once a maritime power, this region became an aristocratic retreat in the 19th century, and is now a bustling tourist area

GETTING THERE

AIR Ryanair (0871 246 0000; www.ryanair.com) flies from Stansted to Genoa's Cristoforo Colombo airport, though Pisa airport may be better for eastern Liguria (see the Tuscany section for details). For San Remo and western Liguria, Nice airport is only 20km from the border. **British Airways** (0870 850 9850; www.ba.com) flies to Nice from Heathrow, Gatwick, Manchester and Birmingham; **easyJet** (0871 2442 366; www.easyjet.com) flies to Nice from Luton, Gatwick, Stansted, Belfast, Bristol, Liverpool and Newcastle; and **Flyglobespan** (0870 556 1522; www.flyglobespan.com) flies to Nice from Edinburgh and Glasgow Prestwick.

ROAD Fares are cheaper during the evening and through the night on **Eurotunnel** (08705 353535, www.eurotunnel.com), or you could take a ferry to Calais – try **Hoverspeed** (0870 240 8070; www.hoverspeed.co.uk), **SeaFrance** (08705 711 711; www.seafrance.co.uk) or **P&O Ferries** (08705 202 020; www.poferries.com). Once in France, drive south on the A26 to Reims, take the E17 past Troyes, and near Dijon take the A39 to Bourg-en-Bresse. Take the A40 east past Geneva, and after Nancy the A40 becomes part of route E25; follow the E25 until just before Chamonix-Mont-Blanc, then take the N205 to the Mont Blanc tunnel; enter Italy and continue on the E25 southeast to Genoa and Liguria.

RAIL It takes around three hours to reach Paris from Waterloo by Eurostar; change stations and catch the train to Turin, where connections are available to Genoa and beyond. Total travel time to Genoa is about 12 hours. Contact **Raileurope** (08708 371 371; www.raileurope.co.uk) for further information and booking. Italian rail network **Trenitalia** (www.trenitalia.it/en/index/html) has details of connections in Liguria.

COACH Taking a **Eurolines** (08705 143 219; www.eurolines.co.uk) coach from London to Genoa takes 25 hours, with stops and changes at Paris and Milan.

THIS LONG, THIN STRIP OF COAST IS HOME TO some of Europe's smartest tourist resorts, precarious cliffs studded with pastel-coloured villas, the busy historic port of Genoa, and basil-scented olive groves.

Geography

Liguria, one of Italy's smallest regions, is a narrow coastal strip consisting of rolling hills, steep cliffs and mountains. The lush Maritime Alps, with several peaks over 2,000 metres, back the western coast where there are several excellent beaches, while the east has plunging cliffs, making it one of the steepest and most dramatic coastlines in southern Europe. These steep slopes are home to Liguria's most characteristic feature: neatly aligned stone-terraces covered in vineyards.

The coastline known as the Italian Riviera is divided, with Riviera di Ponente in the west, Riviera di Levante in the east, and with the historic maritime city of Genoa conveniently located in the centre of the two. Liguria is home to several elegant resorts, traditionally the playground for Europe's aristocracy, who were attracted to the area by the

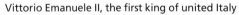

Vittorio Emanuele II, the first king of united Italy

Saint George is the patron saint of Genoa

superb year-round climate – winters are mild and summers refreshingly cool.

Areas

Genoa boasts Italy's largest port, is home to important commercial, industrial and leisure activities, and is a bustling cosmopolitan city packed with history. The world's most famous explorer, Christopher Columbus, was brought up here and is the city's most celebrated inhabitant.

Genoa has several fine palaces concentrated around the Via Garibaldi – the Palazzo Bianco houses a superb collection of European paintings and the Royal Palace boasts lovely gardens overlooking the old harbour. The mainly Gothic Duomo has a striking black and white striped facade and several elaborately decorated chapels. The port oozes history amongst the docks and wharves, and contains a medieval lighthouse and an ultra-modern mast sculpture and conference centre, designed by top Italian architect, Renzo Piano.

East of Genoa is the Riviera di Levante (often referred to as the 'Gulf of Paradise'), mainly steep terrain where towns and villages cling to the rocks above the plunging cliffs. Main resorts here include Portofino, one of Europe's most exclusive resorts, with its perfect natural harbour, pristine marine reserve and elegant waterfront; and Cinque Terre, a collection of five small villages considered to be the jewel in Liguria's crown. Corniglia, Manarola, Monterosso, Riomaggiore and Vernazza, once only accessible by sea, offer beautiful steep, narrow streets flanked by pastel houses and tiny harbours.

To the west of Genoa lies the Riviera di Ponente, a beautiful, but built-up coastline with several

PROFILE

"Liguria is home to several elegant resorts and has a superb year-round climate"

elegant resorts, including the famous San Remo. This smart town, the first to be 'discovered' on the Italian Riviera, has an immaculately groomed beach, several classy hotels and a world-famous casino. Inland are numerous picturesque medieval villages, including Apricale, where the doors on older houses have been painted by artists; Bussana Vecchia, rebuilt after an earthquake in 1887 and home to a large artists' colony; and Dolceacqua, with its medieval bridge and delicious wines.

Economy

Liguria's economy owes most of its prosperity to the port at Genoa, Italy's principal commercial port and home to several important related industries, such as ship-building. The city's university is highly prestigious and boasts one of Italy's main information technology departments – Genoa is also a national centre for technology development.

Outside Genoa, the region's mild year-round climate provides ideal conditions for several

FOOD AND DRINK

While Ligurian cuisine isn't as prolific as that of neighbouring Piedmont, the area is justly famous for the fresh locally caught fish and seafood – an essential part of any Ligurian meal; pesto, made with fragrant local basil; cheese pizza – the ones made in Recco are particularly delicious; and *panettone* (a sweet bread stuffed with raisins), once a staple in any Genovese sailor's diet.

Liguria's wines (mostly whites) are little known outside the region, but are nonetheless excellent and a perfect accompaniment to local dishes, particularly seafood and pasta.

Delicious cheese pizza is a Ligurian treat

The Italian Riviera is home to some of Europe's most fashionable tourist resorts

agricultural activities, including horticulture, fresh flowers (Alassio and Diano Marina have numerous nurseries), olives and vineyards. Tourism is also a major source of income and the main employer in many resort areas. Unemployment is low and figures for 2004 stood at 5.8 per cent.

Culture

Genoa was a strategic trading port centuries ago when the Phoenicians and Greeks settled here. The city later became a major maritime power during the 16th century, when its influence was equalled only by Venice. Invasion by the French in 1668, however, led to Genoa's decline, which lasted until the 19th century, when the area was rediscovered by rich European, British and Russian aristocrats looking for somewhere to escape the cold winters.

Many of the region's towns boast fine churches and palaces built during medieval times and reflecting the new-found prosperity. Most resorts have elegant 19th-century seafront hotels and villas – Villa Hanbury, west of San Remo, with its stunning exotic botanical garden, and San Remo's casino are of particular note – a legacy of the long list of the rich and famous who stayed in the area: Byron, DH Lawrence, Shelley (who drowned near Viareggio), Tchaikovsky and Yeats.

Social groups

Liguria's population grew by some 17 per cent in 2004, and the number of resident foreigners increased by over 53,000, attracted to the area's prosperity and job opportunities. The average age in the region, however, is the oldest in Italy and it also has the highest percentage of residents over 65.

There are pockets of EU residents – the French and Germans make up the largest groups and there are officially around 900 residents from the UK. The resorts, in particular, are growing in popularity with EU nationals, many of whom come here to retire – San Remo's foreign population has grown by nearly 50 per cent in recent years. ●

FACTS

■ Genoa, known throughout Italy for its strong independent character, was the only European city to liberate itself before the Allies arrived in 1945

■ The only route joining the Cinque Terre towns to each other is a cliff-top footpath

■ Slate from the region's Fontanabuona quarries is exported all over the world as billiard tables

	GENOA	LONDON
Dec	12	7
Nov	15	10
Oct	20	14
Sept	24	19
Aug	27	21
July	27	22
June	24	20
May	21	17
April	17	13
March	14	10
Feb	12	7
Jan	10	6

Average monthly temperature °C (Celsius)

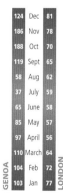

	GENOA	LONDON
Dec	124	81
Nov	186	78
Oct	188	70
Sept	119	65
Aug	58	62
July	37	59
June	65	58
May	85	57
April	97	56
March	110	64
Feb	104	72
Jan	103	77

Average monthly rainfall mm (millimetres)

Property hotspots

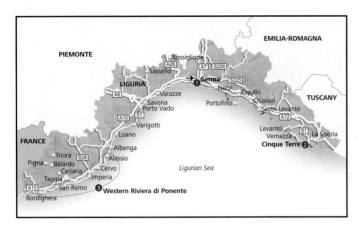

1. Genoa

The long, narrow city of Genoa dates back to pre-Roman times and is steeped in maritime tradition. Once a flourishing commercial port, as trade declined it became a favoured destination for European cruise liners. Nowadays, Caribbean cruises are more popular and it's mainly ferries that stop off here, yet Genoa is still Italy's main port.

Voted cultural capital of the year in 2004, Genoa abounds with interesting things to see and do. From ancient Renaissance buildings and grand palaces to interesting museums and excellent restaurants. The city boasts one of Europe's biggest and best-preserved old towns, and a wander through the narrow streets reveals numerous churches, palaces, galleries, piazzas and intimate cafés. Other attractions include The Genoa Aquarium, the largest in Europe, and the Genoa National Cemetery, an open-air sculpture museum.

City-centre two-bedroom flats have a rental potential of approximately €1,000 per week. At the top end of the property scale, a superb sea-front, seven-bedroom villa on the outskirts of the city costs around €1,800,000.

KEY FACTS
■ **Population**: 609,399
■ **Airport** Genoa (Cristoforo Colombo) Airport, v. Pionieri e Aviatori d'Italia, 16154 Genova, Tel: +39 010 60151, www.airport.genova.it/eng
■ **Medical** Ospedale San Martino di Genova, lg. Benzi 10, 16132 Genova, Tel: +39 010 5551, www.hsanmartino.it
■ **Schools** American International School in Genoa, Via Quarto 13/c, 16148 Genoa, Tel: +39 010 386528, www.aisge.it
■ **Pros** The G8 summit was held here in 2001, which has led to the smartening up of the more run-down districts and the pedestrianisation of some streets ■ Genoa remains off the international tourist trail, avoiding overcrowding from tourists ■ The city has an excellent range of shops ■ This is an excellent family destination and family dining is a major social event
■ **Cons** Trapped between the mountains and the sea, Genoa is a very hilly city, which might prove unsuitable for the less physically able ■ The labyrinth of narrow streets in the old city fills up with disreputable characters and an intimidating atmosphere at night ■ There are few English-speaking inhabitants ■ Genoa is dirty, noisy, and remains, above all, an old port city.

2. Cinque Terre

Cinque Terre, literally the 'five lands' is a group of fishing villages that are linked by a verdant footpath, lush with wild blueberries and apricots.

The villages of Manarola and Vernazza have winding streets, clear seas and pebbly beaches that bustle with visitors during the summer months. Vernazza, the most famous of the villages, was an ancient Roman settlement and a seat of political and economic power over the centuries. Evidence of its colourful history remain today by way of fortification walls, watchtowers and the Castle of the Doria. The ancient seaside village of Monterosso has the best beaches, craft shops, and tourist facilities. The medieval village of Riomaggiore, the most easterly of the five, is famous for its vineyards and excellent white wine. Corniglia offers superb cliff-top views of the Ligurian Sea.

A basic one-bedroom holiday home in the Cinque Terre region can be purchased for around €85,000, whereas the sum of €370,000 could buy a farm with vineyards, olive trees and orchards overlooking Vernazza village.

KEY FACTS
■ **Population** 4,456
■ **Airport** Pisa (Galileo Galilei) Airport, v. dell'Aeroporto, 56121 Pisa, Tel: +39 050 849111, www.pisa-airport.com
■ **Medical** Ospedale San Martino di Genova, lg. Benzi 10, 16132 Genova, Tel: +39 010 5551, www.hsanmartino.it
■ **Schools** International School of Modena, Via Silvio Pellico 9, 41042, Fiorano Modenese, Modena. Tel: +39 0536 832904, www.ismmodena.org ■ American International School in Genoa, Via Quarto 13/c, 16148 Genoa, Tel: +39 010 386528, www.aisge.it
■ **Pros** Cars are not permitted beyond the village entrances, which are hardly road-accessible anyway, so the villages remain a peaceful haven ■ An ideal spot for anyone planning on practising viticulture; locals encourage genuinely committed growers with free leases on vineyards to try and stave off the erosion and collapse of the hillsides ■ Day-to-day living expenses are low by northern Italian standards
■ **Cons** The population of these villages more than doubles in peak season due to tourists, and they lose their tranquil charm ■ Unless planning on working in tourism, fishing or viticulture, it would be necessary to travel quite a distance to work

Colourful buildings line the waterfront in towns all along the Riviera

The Riviera is dotted with abandoned castles, a testament to the maritime importance of the region in medieval times

■ Less mobile people might have some trouble with the motor vehicle ban as the terrain is exceedingly hilly ■ There isn't much of an expatriate community, and non-Italian speakers may find life a little awkward.

3. Riviera di Ponente

The beautiful coastal landscape of the Riviera di Ponente sweeps in an arc from just west of Genoa down to Ventimiglia, right on the French border. This area is also referred to as the Flowering Coastline, because some 20,000 tons of cut flowers, including roses, mimosas and carnations, are exported each year.

Every town and beach along the Riviera has its own particular uniqueness about it. Favourite tourist destinations include: Ventimiglia, San Remo, Riviera delle Palme (between Andora and Varazze), Finale Ligure and Arenzano.

San Remo, or 'City of Flowers', is famous for its Festival of Italian Song, its casino and the Milano–San Remo cycle race. The coastline is scattered with mountain villages and sheltered coves.

This area has been a popular holiday resort since the 19th century and property is pricey. Prices start at about €165,000 for a small one-bedroom flat. Around €200,000 to €300,000 will buy a luxury flat or a two-

to three-bedroom hill-top house. In San Remo, the sum of €650,000 could buy a superb three-bedroom flat in a castle with a swimming pool, tennis courts and stunning sea views. Top-of-the-range villas, with pool and private gardens, sell for upwards of €1.5 million.

KEY FACTS
■ **Population** 356,431
■ **Airport** Genoa (Cristoforo Colombo) Airport, v. Pionieri e Aviatori d'Italia, 16154 Genova
Tel: +39 010 60151,
www.airport.genova.it/eng
■ **Medical** Ospedale Santa Corona, Via XXV Aprile 38, 17027 Pietra Ligure, Tel: +39 01962301,
www.ospedalesantacorona.it
■ **Schools** American International

School in Genoa, Via Quarto 13/c, 16148 Genoa, Tel: +39 010 386528, www.aisge.it
■ **Pros** Amidst this strip of hotels and resorts, many spots have retained their appeal, including the medieval towns of Albengi and Noli ■ The area is only a stone's throw from the French Riviera, with Monaco, Nice and Cannes all within day-tripping distance ■ The area has a wide appeal, from families to hikers keen on exploring the mountains ■ The wide, sandy beaches are amongst the best in Italy
■ **Cons** As almost all of the local population live on the coast, the infrastructure is beginning to groan under the pressure ■ Many towns along the coast are overdeveloped and teem with tourists and apartment blocks ■ Buildings in many areas, such as San Remo, have fallen into disrepair.

FOR SALE Property guide

The Ligurian market has long been established, and the year-round climate and sheltered coastline still draw buyers to the region

Portofino, on the western Riviera, will give an excellent return, but it is an expensive place in which to buy

THE REGION OF LIGURIA IS A LONG-established destination for foreign buyers, and the British have been coming here since the 19th century. Known as the Italian Riviera, Liguria is a continuation of its French counterpart the Côte d'Azur, which has overtaken the Ligurian coastline in popularity in recent decades.

Liguria is an extremely wealthy region and property prices are high, particularly on the coast where property sells at a premium. Apartments with views of Liguria's more popular resorts, such as Portofino, are in particularly high demand, and are consequently very expensive. In 2004 the market peaked with price appreciation of 20 per cent in

some coastal resorts, while the past three years have seen an average increase of 10 per cent annually.

The Ligurian market is divided in terms of prices, Genoa and the western Ligurian coastline being cheaper than the sky-high prices found in the towns dotted along the rocky eastern coastal strip. Here a two-bedroom apartment will set you back €260,000, compared to €244,000 along the western Ligurian coast. A two-bedroom house will cost €285,000 in Genoa, and €251,000 in western Liguria. The most expensive resorts in Liguria are those of Levanto and San Remo, as well as the Cinque Terre fishing villages, which can sell for €4,000 per square metre. Although the market has slowed in recent years, you can still expect to make money from investing in a home here, and can expect appreciation of between seven and 10 per cent per year. Building restrictions have resulted in prices soaring in some areas as demand continues to grow and property becomes more scarce.

As one of the most popular holiday destinations in Italy, Liguria has a booming rentals market. Three-bedroom properties in Genoa and Cinque Terre have an average weekly rent of €1,000 upwards, while those on the western Riviera let for €960 per week. For those who can afford to break into the Portofino and San Remo market, an excellent rental return can be expected. ●

TYPICAL PROPERTIES

- The Italian Riviera has long offered buyers colourfully painted facades, palm tree-lined promenades, and elegant *palazzi*
- The larger resorts offer apartments overlooking the coast, and 19th-century villas dotted along the shore
- Inland you will find stone-built hamlets, while the Cinque Terre villages offer typical fisherman's cottages stacked back up the mountainous slopes, providing a stunning backdrop to the coastline
- In the Riviera di Levante, which stretches east from Genoa, you will find resorts frequented by the wealthy jet-setters, with million-euro villas, mansions and beautifully renovated *palazzi* lining the beaches

WHAT CAN YOU GET FOR YOUR EUROS?

PLOT OF LAND

Situated just above the town of Bordighera, this plot of land offers unparalleled views of the San Martino area. The plot totals 9,500m² and comes complete with an old rustic house requiring complete renovation. It comes with building permission, and this is a unique opportunity for someone to build their dream home in one of Italy's most stunning locations.

€220,000 CODE CIC

RESTORED OLIVE MILL

Situated in the delightful medieval village of Moltedo, just 8km from the Mediterranean, this property comprises two bedrooms and two bathrooms, plus a large living area with a separate kitchen. The garden has a stream running through the bottom, with a mill wheel still in place. This unique property offers a covered terrace and has extra storage space in the cellar.

€330,000 CODE CAT

COUNTRY PROPERTY

This country villa is located in the Imperia area and has a living area of over 250m², comprising a living room, kitchen, four bedrooms, four bathrooms and a huge garage, capable of holding two cars. The spacious garden has a large terrace and offers fabulous coastal views. With a cellar and attic which could be converted to provide more space, this villa would be ideal for a family holiday home.

€580,000 CODE CIC

STONE-BUILT VILLA

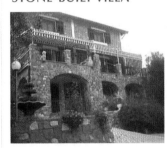

With views over the historic village of Dolceacqua, this property is built of local Badalucco stone. With three bedrooms, two bathrooms and a large living area, it comes with gardens of 2,000m² and has a spacious terrace. Only 2km from the village and all facilities, this is an ideal property for rental.

€800,000 CODE CIC

VILLA OVERLOOKING THE MEDITERRANEAN

This pink villa is situated in one of the Riviera's most sought-after locations, with fantastic views over the coast. The south-facing property has a large veranda and semi-tropical gardens from which to enjoy the copious amount of sun it receives. With three bedrooms and a total living area of 130m², this property offers spacious and luxurious living.

€980,000 CODE CIC

LUXURIOUS VILLA

In excellent condition, this pink-painted elegant villa is extremely luxurious and offers a swimming pool and tropical gardens. With a living area of 245m² and a garage for two-cars, there is also extra storage space ready for development in the 80m² cellar. With four bedrooms and three bathrooms, this property would make an ideal family home.

€1,900,000 CODE CIC

PROPERTY GUIDE

AVERAGE HOUSE PRICES LIGURIA

	2-bed	3-bed	4-bed	5-bed
Genoa	€285,000 (£193,878)	€340,600 (£231,701)	€530,000 (£360,544)	€599,000 (£407,483)
Cinque Terre	€285,000 (£193,878)	€355,000 (£241,497)	€669,000 (£455,102)	€902,000 (£613,605)
Riviera di Ponente	€251,000 (£170,748)	€291,000 (£197,959)	€636,000 (£432,653)	€906,000 (£616,327)

LAKE GARDA

Lake Garda has the best Italy has to offer: good access to airports with low-cost flights, plus golf, skiing, watersports, walking, sun, culture and shopping. Make the most of this affluent, untapped market and buy now!

With Garda Homes, you can see up to 20 properties in two days from dozens of agents, with all transport and translations included. We'll help you find, restore and furnish your home on Lake Garda, taking the stress and pain out of buying in Italy.

We also provide a full letting and management service, so your property can start generating income straight away.

MAKE THIS THE YEAR YOU FIND YOUR HOME IN ITALY – WITH GARDA HOMES

Property to buy:
www.gardahomes.co.uk

Property to rent:
www.gardaholidays.co.uk

Email:
info@gardahomes.co.uk

Telephone:
07005-947-137 (UK)

Home - hunting in Italy

Who are we ?

Global Target deals in the finest real estate and offers an overall high quality consultancy service for the **purchase** and for the **sale** of residential property throughout Italy, guaranteeing rapid, efficient and confidential service from the first contact through to the final legal completion of the negotiation, and beyond. All of this under the management of an English director, Jennifer Hart.

Where do we operate ?

Thanks to reliable and consolidated relationships of collaboration, **Global Target** offers its range of services in all of the most prestigious areas of Italy.

After sales service

Following the purchase, **Global Target** assists in setting up renovation projects and home rentals. When the time comes to sell your Italian home, **Global Target** gives all necessary help at this time too.

Our expertise

Global Target has been dealing in quality real estate for many years, and the proven experience is not only reflected in a high level of know-how, but also guarantees organizational competence and management.

Please call to discuss how we can help you

GLOBAL TARGET
Studio 10, WTC, Milanofiori
20090 Assago (Mi), Italy - tel/fax +39 0257506293
www.globaltarget.org - globaltarget@globaltarget.org

WHY SWIM

WITH SHARKS

WHEN YOU

CAN

RELAX

BY YOUR

POOL?

INTERNATIONAL LAWYERS

A COMPREHENSIVE LEGAL SERVICE TO PRIVATE AND COMMERCIAL CLIENTS WHO REQUIRE LEGAL ADVICE AND ASSISTANCE RELATING TO OVERSEAS PROPERTY CONVEYANCING AND INHERITANCE MATTERS. SPECIALIST AREAS INCLUDE SPAIN, PORTUGAL, FRANCE, ITALY, TURKEY, CARIBBEAN, GREECE, CYPRUS, DUBAI AND CAPE VERDE

144 KNUTSFORD ROAD, WILMSLOW, CHESHIRE, SK9 6JP
TELEPHONE: 01625 586 937 FAX: 01625 585 362
EMAIL: INTERNATIONALLAWYERS@BENNETT-AND-CO.COM
WEBSITE: WWW.BENNETT-AND-CO.COM
Regulated by the Law Society of England and Wales.

Lombardy & the Lakes

Boasting dynamic city living and romantic lake retreats

© ENIT

FACT BOX

- ▦ **Population** 9,108,645
- ▦ **Population growth** 0.8%
- ▦ **Unemployment rate** 3.6%
- ▦ **Average 4-bed house price** €366,000 / £248,980
- ▦ **Net migration** 140,414
- ▦ **Foreign residents** 476,690

Contents

Area profile

This region of contrasts offers towering peaks and peaceful lakes, the bustling hub of Milan and ancient Roman ruins

GETTING THERE

AIR There are a number of services to Milan. **Alitalia** (0870 544 8259; www.alitalia.co.uk) offers services from Heathrow to Milan's Linate airport, as does **British Midlands** (0870 6070 555; www.flybmi.com). **British Airways** (08708 509850; www.britishairways.co.uk) flies to both Linate and Malpensa airports in Milan from Heathrow, Birmingham, Manchester and Edinburgh. **easyJet** (08717 500100; www.easyjet.co.uk) flies to Linate from Gatwick and Stansted, while **Ryanair** (08712 460000; www.ryanair.com) flies to Bergamo from Glasgow, Liverpool, Luton, Newcastle and Stansted.

ROAD Many ferry operators sail to Calais. From Calais the E15 goes to Lyon and then the A32/43 takes you to Turin. From Turin the A4 leads into Milan.

RAIL TGV Trains run regularly from Paris to Milan. Once in Milan it is possible to take a connecting train throughout the Lombardy region. Contact **Rail Europe** (08705 848848; www.raileurope.co.uk).

COACH Eurolines (0870 514 3219; www.eurolines.co.uk) offers services to Milan. Local services are operated throughout Lombardy by **SAB** (+39 035 289000; www.sab-autoservizi.it).

STRETCHING FROM THE SWISS BORDER AND the Alps down to the flatlands of the river Po, Lombardy is home to Europe's style capital Milan, Italy's main industries, and the romantic lakes of Como, Garda and Maggiore. Since the ancient German 'Lombard' tribe invaded nearly 1,500 years ago, Lombardy has been popular with retirees, tourists and foreign property buyers alike.

Geography

Geographically, Lombardy is one of Italy's most contrasting regions: the northern part is essentially mountainous, the heights of which stretch up over 3,000 metres into the Swiss Alps, and is home to the magnificent Stelvio National Park, numerous top-class ski resorts and four large lakes, formed by alpine glaciers and internationally renowned for their romantic and tranquil ambience.

Areas

Lake Maggiore, the furthest west, lies half in Italy and half in Switzerland and is surrounded by gentle slopes, which create an almost tropical micro-climate where azaleas and palms flourish. Dotting the shores are numerous resorts, such as Stresa – the most famous and from where you can get a cable car up to the ski resort of Mottarone – Arona, Baveno and Verbania. The Borromean Islands consist of four large islands, two of which boast some of Europe's most exquisite gardens.

Lake Como, with its curious two-pronged shape, is quieter than Maggiore, although no less beautiful,

The famous wooden speedboats on Lake Como

and for centuries has attracted those in search of tranquillity in beautiful natural surroundings. Lake Como is most famous for its magnificent villas – Villa Carlotta is a particular gem – and many of the rich and famous have properties here. Attractive Como, on the southern shore, is the main town. Other notable resorts include Bellagio – one of the most beautiful lakeside towns with its elegant promenade and café culture – and Menaggio.

"Lombardy accounts for one fifth of the country's GDP, and has very low unemployment"

Lake Garda, Italy's largest lake and situated half in the neighbouring Veneto region, has low-lying shores in the south and dramatic rocky cliffs in the north, from where the snow-capped Alps are clearly visible. Like the other lakes, Garda is home to exquisite villas and gardens, and its most important resorts are Garda, Peschiera – an attractive harbour fortress – and Malcesine.

At the southern tips of the lakes the landscape becomes flatter as it reaches the vast plain formed by the river Po, which provides ideal conditions for two of the region's most important industries: agriculture and manufacturing.

The capital, Milan, lies almost at the dead centre of the region and lays claim to Italy's smartest city as well as its business centre. While Milan doesn't have quite the scale of artistic treasures as Florence or Venice, the city boasts the Teatro alla Scala – one of the world's most prestigious opera houses – the

The Piazza del Duomo in the heart of Milan, Italy's wealthiest city

imposing Gothic Duomo, or cathedral, and several excellent museums, as well as some of the world's best shopping opportunities. Milan is a chic and opulent city – not for nothing is it Italy's most expensive place to live.

Economy

Lombardy, along with Turin, forms the backbone of Italy's industry and is also one of its most important commercial areas as well as the powerhouse behind Italy's economic success – production from Lombardy accounts for one fifth of the country's GDP. A sure sign of this can be found in very low unemployment figures, which in 2004 were four per cent. Main industries include silk and wool, chemical manufacturing, automobile, machinery and plastics, although in recent years there's been a shift towards the services and IT industries.

Milan is Italy's top industrial centre and its financial heartland, home to the stock exchange and numerous international banks. Many major national

The Lakes region, popular with second-home owners, is dotted with attractive towns

FOOD AND DRINK

Lombardy cuisine is based around buckwheat *polenta* and risotto, available in a myriad of variations, not forgetting *risotto alla Milanese* (with saffron) and local beef and pork. In the mountains, hearty country fare is on offer, including *pizzoccheri* – a substantial buckwheat pasta – and freshwater fish from the lakes, such as carp and perch. The area produces fine cheeses such as mascarpone, gorgonzola and *crescenza*, and local sweet specialities include sweet chestnuts, fruit pastries and *sbrisolona*, an almond cake.

Lombardy isn't regarded as one of the country's main wine-producing areas, but nevertheless several notable wines can be found here, including the fine Valtellina Superiore DOC. The Brescia province's wines are particularly good, with excellent whites and some of the best sparkling wines in the country.

Lombardy is particularly notable for its cheeses

firms have their headquarters in Milan as a result, including Pirelli and Breda. The city is also one of the world's fashion capitals, on a par with Paris, London and New York.

Culture

Lombardy's economy has, throughout the centuries, had a direct influence on the region's culture, and many of its fine monuments are a result of the region's prosperity. Numerous rich families, noblemen and dynasties, particularly during the 17th and 18th centuries, became patrons of the arts, commissioning exquisite palaces, churches and artworks. Examples of this rich artistic legacy can be found in Bergamo, home to one of Lombardy's most attractive squares (Piazza Vecchia), with its stunningly elegant Cappella Colleoni, a fine example of the strong Venetian influence in the area; in Cremona, whose Duomo is one of the area's most attractive; Mantova's stunning frescoes in the Palazzo Ducale; and Certosa's fine Renaissance chapter house. Not to mention Leonardo da Vinci's *The Last Supper*, tucked away in the Santa Maria delle Grazie convent in Milan, and the stunning palatial villas that line the shores of the lakes.

Social groups

Lombardy's economic prosperity has long attracted relocators from other regions and countries, and Milan is, today, one of Europe's top job spots for young professionals, drawn to the city's employment opportunities and high standard of living. The city also has a large resident foreign population – some 1,500 British live here. The Lakes are perennial favourites with foreigners – either as retirees or second-home owners, although high property prices here may deter some people. ●

FACTS

▬ Milan's Duomo houses a lift to take you to the roof

▬ Milan's population drops to around 300,000 in August when everyone's on holiday

▬ Como's cathedral took four centuries to build and is widely considered one of the best architectural 'fusions' in Europe

MILAN		LONDON
6	Dec	7
10	Nov	10
17	Oct	14
24	Sept	19
28	Aug	21
29	July	22
27	June	20
23	May	17
18	April	13
13	March	10
8	Feb	7
5	Jan	6

Average monthly temperature °C (Celsius)

MILAN		LONDON
77	Dec	81
122	Nov	78
125	Oct	70
69	Sept	65
91	Aug	62
64	July	59
118	June	58
76	May	57
94	April	56
77	March	64
60	Feb	72
44	Jan	77

Average monthly rainfall mm (millimetres)

Culture

Lombardy is blessed with stunning lake scenery and some of the country's cultural treasures in Milan, Pavia and Bergamo

"Lake Como boasts Villa Carlotta, whose stunning grounds will take even the least-enthusiastic gardener's breath away "

LOMBARDY, FOUNDED BY THE LOMBARDS invading from Germany in the sixth century, has a chequered history of invasions and wars, and the area's strategic position and flat and watered landscape has long provided industrial and commercial prosperity. In the 12th century, influential Lombardians formed a separatist group, known as the Lombard League (precursors of the modern day Lega Nord political party), and together with the region's most powerful and wealthiest families, seized control of the area. Under these families, namely the Visconti and Sforza from Milan, some of Lombardy's finest monuments were built and decorated with magnificent paintings and frescoes. Lombardy is the birthplace of several of Italy's most celebrated citizens, including Virgil, Monteverdi, Stradivarius and Donizetti.

Art and architecture

Milan offers an eclectic mix of architectural styles, all of which add to the city's smart elegance, and many buildings were funded by the city's wealthy benefactors. The huge Duomo – the world's third largest Gothic cathedral – dominates the centre of the old quarter, and the hugely ornate facade (with no less than 135 spires) is only rivalled by the elaborate stained glass and stonework inside. Other religious buildings housing remarkable treasures in the city are the Sant'Ambrogio Romanesque church, with its impressive ninth-century altar, studded with gold and jewels, and exquisite mosaic dome; and the Santa Maria delle Grazie Renaissance convent, home to one of the world's best-known paintings, da Vinci's *The Last Supper*.

Hidden treasures

The Palazzo di Brera art gallery is a treasure trove of the finest in Italian art, and its 38 rooms include gems such as Raphael's *Marriage of the Virgin* and Mantegna's extraordinary *Dead Christ*, as well as the best of some of Italy's more recent artists. The Poldi-Pezzoli museum also houses a magnificent art collection, including works by Botticelli and Piero della Francesca, and a fascinating array of rugs, enamel and porcelain.

Other architectural gems in the region include one of Lombardy's most attractive squares, the Piazza Vecchia in Bergamo, with its stunningly

ITALIAN STYLE

Of all Italian cities, perhaps Milan offers the best in Italian style, the essence of which is understated elegance and simplicity, and the city is home to some of the world's top designers – the very latest in cars, aircraft, furniture, fabrics and fashion are created here.

FASHION WEEK

MILAN is one of the world's top fashion centres and all the best designers are represented here. The height of Italian design is shown off annually during Milan Fashion Week in spring, and most top designers have stores in the Quadrilatero, Milan's smartest quartet of streets formed by the Via Monte Napoleone, Via Sant'Andrea, Via della Spiga and Borgospesso, where Armani, Gucci, Salvatore Ferragamo, Valentino and Versace vie for the already stylishly dressed Milanos' attention.

Further exquisite shopping opportunities present themselves in the incredibly ornate Galleria Vittorio Emanuele II shopping arcade, with its magnificent glass and metal dome, and home to several highly exclusive stores, up-market cafés and restaurants.

The downside to Milan's fabulous shopping are the price tags – take one glance and you see exactly why this is Italy's most expensive city! But window shopping – and the Italians also excel at window dressing – is free, and you can always wait for the sales or visit one of the many discount venues.

ALL PICTURES © ENIT

TOP TEN ATTRACTIONS

Lombardy

1 The Stelvio national park – in winter and summer

2 Lake Como's mountain and water views from one of Bellagio's cafés

3 The villas and gardens lining Lake Garda seen from a steamer as you ride around the water

4 The plunging gorge and dramatic waterfall at Orrido di Sant'Anna just outside Cannobio on Lake Maggiore

5 Mantova's magnificent Palazzo Ducale

Milan

6 The fabulous Galleria Vittorio Emanuele II shopping arcade

7 An opera at the Teatro alla Scala

8 Leonardo da Vinci's *The Last Supper*

9 Any catwalk at the Milan Fashion Week

10 The Duomo, the third-largest Gothic cathedral in the world

"Milan offers an eclectic mix of architectural styles, all of which add to the city's smart elegance"

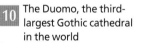

elegant Cappella Colleoni. Cremona offers a richly decorated Duomo, complete with the tallest medieval tower in Italy, and the Palazzo Ducale at Mantova includes some stunning 15th-century frescoes and numerous murals. The Certosa chapterhouse, just north of Pavia, boasts one of the best examples of Renaissance architecture in the country.

On the Lakes

The Lakes are home to their own architectural and botanical gems. Many of the beautiful palaces and villas gracing the shores are works of art in their own right and are well worth a visit, particularly in spring and summer when the gardens are a riot of rich colour. Lake Como boasts the particularly fine Villa Carlotta, an 18th-century summer house, whose stunning gardens will take even the least-enthusiastic gardener's breath away. Lake Maggiore's Borromean Islands include Isola Bella, with the magnificent Baroque Palazzo Borromeo and its beautifully landscaped gardens, complete with fountains, grottoes and peacocks; and Isola Madre, with botanical gardens and Italy's tallest palm trees.

Lake Garda's shoreside resort of Gardone boasts a beautifully planted park and Villa il Vittoriale, an Art Deco treasure once home to the poet Gabriele d'Annunzio and packed with art treasures. ●

CULTURE

Property hotspots

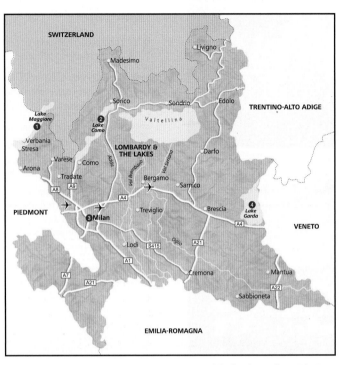

SWITZERLAND
Madesimo
Livigno
Sorico
Sondrio
Edolo
TRENTINO-ALTO ADIGE
Lake Maggiore
Valtellina
Lake Como
Verbania
Stresa
LOMBARDY &
THE LAKES
Darfo
Arona
Varèse
Como
Tradate
A8 A9
Bergamo
Sarnico
A4
Treviglio
Brescia
Lake Garda
PIEDMONT
Milan
A4
VENETO
Lodi
S415
Oglio
A1
A21
A7
A21
Cremona
Mantua
A22
Sabbioneta
EMILIA-ROMAGNA

MAP KEY

● Hotspot
◖ Major town/city
66 Road numbers

The area is excellent in terms of investment as prices continue to rise, so expect appreciation. The rentals market is also extremely healthy, with constant demand for property. If you are looking for a two-bedroom property to rent, then expect to pay €680 (£456) a week. If you are looking to let out a four-bedroom property, then you can charge around €1,310 (£891).

KEY FACTS
■ **Population** Cannobio 4,994
▦ Cannero Riviera 1,060
▦ Stresa 4,862 ▦ Verbania 30,116
■ **Airport** Milan Malpensa Airport, 21010 Varese, Italy, Tel: +39 0274 852 200
■ **Medical** St. Anna Hospital, Como, Italy, Tel: 0039 602 2100
■ **Schools** Sir James Henderson British School, Milan, Italy, Tel: +39 0221 0941
■ **Pros** The climate is sub-tropical, which accounts for the number of gardens and vegetation found around the lakeside ▦ Lake Maggiore is located in a stunning setting, with great views of the Alps ▦ Perfect for nature lovers, with a number of walks and wildlife ▦ There are a number of activities, such a mountain biking and skiing, and there are a number of festivals, such as Jazz, during summer
■ **Cons** During July and August the crowds thicken and the Lake can be overrun ▦ Living costs are expensive.

2. Lake Como

Set against the backdrop of the Alps, this relaxing and peaceful destination is a bolthole of calm compared with the manic nature of nearby Milan. The 'Y'-shaped lake stretches for 51km and is lined by many tiny waterside villages.

Como town itself is the main access point to the lake and has an active café and restaurant scene. It also boasts an attractive cathedral, with a blend of Gothic and Renaissance architecture. Situated in the fork of the lake is Bellagio, described as the 'pearl' of the lake. This attractive little village offers a number of lakeside bars and cafés and is one of the lake's major resorts. Menaggio, on the west bank, is also a popular resort, as is the pretty village of Varenna, with its villas, gardens and castle. Tremezzo has some stunning botanic gardens, full of award-winning rhododendrons and azaleas.

Lake Como has always been a retreat of the wealthy and is a pricey proposition for the average buyer. Lakeside properties come at a premium, and as the region is popular with the Italian market, not just foreign buyers, prices have risen steeply, in some instances more quickly than in parts of Tuscany. Proximity to the Alps pushes costs up. Many Milanese are investing in weekend homes here and demand is huge, with property in limited supply and rarely coming up for sale. Property in the popular Lake Como area usually achieves a healthy resale value, generally due to its scenic location, which draws tourists. Expect to pay upwards of €450,000 for a four-bedroom property. Rentals are high, with a two-bedroom property costing upwards of €600 (£460); good news for those seeking to buy-to-let.

KEY FACTS
■ **Population** Sorico 1,195
▦ Domaso 1,444 ▦ Menaggio 3,141
▦ Tremezzo 1,299 ▦ Bellagio 2,973
■ **Airport** Milan Malpensa Airport, 21010 Varese, Italy, Tel: +39 0274 852 200
■ **Medical** St. Anna Hospital, Como, Italy, Tel: +39 060 22100
■ **Schools** Sir James Henderson British

1. Lake Maggiore

A stunning 65km-long glacial lake, set at the foot of the Alps, Lake Maggiore has been a holiday retreat since Roman times. Originally named Lake Verbano by the Romans due to the presence of the verbana plant on the lake's shore, today Lake Maggiore attracts wealthy jet-setters. Many Milanese own holiday homes and weekend retreats around the lake, and property consists of period villas or modern developments with pools and tennis courts.

There are a number of noteworthy towns lining Lake Maggiore including Arona, an important commercial and tourist town, home to a 13th-century castle whose ruins overlook the lake. Stresa is Lake Maggiore's most important resort, drawing an international crowd. The British first arrived here in the early 19th century, and they continue coming, although now the area attracts a more elderly clientele. With Art Nouveau villas dotted around the town, property is in high demand. Verbania is the original Roman resort, home to the stunning Villa Taranto and its botanical gardens, boasting over 20,000 species of plant. This industrial and commercial centre is also home to the Suna medieval town and Pallanza, a small Roman town. The four Borromean Islands are reached by boat, and are home to the super rich. The Borromeo family of Milan own one island, while the others house splendid gardens, exotic sculptures and sub-tropical vegetation.

The property market here is well established and demand is huge. Properties do come onto the market, but turnover is quick and homes are sold soon after being advertised. Expect to pay handsomely for a piece of lakeside property with a private garden, and given that many homes are period villas, you will be faced with hefty bills. Nevertheless, it is still possible to pick up a two-bedroom property for under €200,000.

Property around Lake Como can be prohibitively expensive

School, Milan, Italy, Tel: +39 0221 0941
■ **Pros** You can go boating along the lake and visit some of the tiny villages, which are only accessible by boat ■ Stunningly beautiful, there are fantastic views of the Alps and the towns of Como and Lecco ■ This is a great area for walkers
■ **Cons** Restaurants are expensive and the food is often only passable ■ For those looking for active nightlife think again; this is an area dominated by the retirement market.

3. Milan

A city for the wealthy and sophisticated, Milan is synonymous with the chic and elegant. Home to the famous Milan Fashion Week, it's a mecca for shoppers and home to two of the most famous shopping streets in the world, the Galleria and Via Montenapoleone. It's also full of stunning monuments, theatres, museums and galleries. The city's Gothic cathedral is the third-largest in Europe, while the world-famous opera house Teatro alla Scala draws visitors from around the globe. Also worth viewing is Castello Sforzesco, built by the ruling Visconti family; the Museo del Duomo, charting the history of the Duomo; and the Civico Museo d'Arte Contemporanea. Some of the city's finest treasures are the religious buildings and monasteries found southwest of the centre.

Italy's stock exchange and most of its major corporations are located in Milan, including Alfa Romeo and Pirelli, as well as telecommunication agencies and Silvio Berlusconi's media empire. The city also contains the country's largest concentration of industry, generating 40 per cent of Italy's entire GDP, and not surprisingly property in Milan is among the

most expensive in the country. With luxurious *palazzi* homes, complete with courtyards, property located in the centre is an unfeasible proposition unless you are exceedingly wealthy; expect to pay anything upwards of €6,000 per square metre. Property in and around Milan is in high demand with foreign purchasers. In 2002, 10 per cent of all property sales went to foreigners, and the city has the highest foreign population in the country. However, demand, high prices and limited supply mean it is sensible to look outside the city. Some small towns, such as Arese, have areas populated mainly by expats and, with the construction of the new motorway, Arona, Baveno, Stresa and Verbania have seen many Milanese buying homes there. Renting is often the best option, and this market is thriving. There are a large number of professionals and students renting, but there is a shortage of top-quality residential apartments in popular areas. Investment is guaranteed to generate a large amount of rental income, with the average two-bedroom property costing €1,450 (£986) a week, which exceeds many London prices.

KEY FACTS
■ **Population** 1.6 million
■ **Airport** Milan Linate International Airport, 20090 Milan Linate, Tel: +39 0274 852 200 ■ Milan Malpensa Airport, 21010 Varese, Italy, Tel: +39 0274 852 200
■ **Medical** Hospital San Raffaele, Milan, Italy, Tel: +39 0226 431
■ **Schools** Sir James Henderson British School, Milan, Italy, Tel: +39 0221 0941
■ **Pros** Extremely efficiently run city ■ Italy's richest city and the marketplace for fashion ■ Plenty of distractions, with a lot of theatres, restaurants and bars
■ **Cons** Smog can become very thick ■ Very hot in August ■ Pickpockets and thieves create problems in the city

centre ■ Overrun with tourists in summer ■ The cost of living is high.

4. Lake Garda

The largest and most popular lake in the Lombardy area, Lake Garda is hemmed in by the mountains and is protected from Italy's cruel northern winds. A popular destination for years, the lake has unfortunately become overdeveloped in recent times. Lying between the Alps and the Po valley, the setting is spectacular. The proximity to the mountains also makes it a great spot for those seeking access to walking routes in the Alps and the ski resorts.

There are a number of large settlements around the lake, but many of these are unattractive. Sirmione, however, retains its charm. This narrow peninsula juts into the lake and is a popular bathing resort, which benefits from a small beach. The islet and castle are worth visiting, as is Castello Scaligero, which offers splendid views over the lake. The Gardone Riviera is located on the western bank of Lake Garda and is hugely popular. It is home to Il Vittoriale, a villa once belonging to an Italian activist, whose grounds house an open-air theatre that holds recitals, ballets, operas and theatre during the summer months. To Lake

Garda's north lies the Riva del Garda, a popular base for walkers venturing into the Alps. With cobbled streets and squares, this is a historic centre, and the Civic museum on the waterfront is certainly worth a visit. A short walk away is Cascata Verone, a picturesque 100ft waterfall.

As the most established and most popular of the lakes, Lake Garda has seen an increase of 5.8 per cent in property value over the past year. Prices for a three-bedroom house average around €318,000, while to rent such a property would cost €835 (£568) a week.

KEY FACTS
■ **Population** Salo 9,982
■ Desenzano del Garda 24,141 ■ Gardone Riviera 2,581 ■ Sirmione 6,749 ■ Riva del Garda 15,037
■ **Airport** Bergamo Orio al Serio Airport, Via Aeroporto 13, 24050, Italy, Tel: +39 035 311269/317375
■ **Schools** Sir James Henderson British School, Milan, Italy, Tel: +39 0221 0941
■ **Medical** Ospedale Generale di Riva, Via Capitelli, 50 38066 Riva del Garda, Italy, Tel: +39 0464 582 222
■ **Pros** This is ideal for those seeking an active holiday, with walking windsurfing, climbing and paragliding all on offer ■ Those seeking a more relaxed holiday can enjoy the stunning scenery while sipping a glass of wine at one of the many waterfront bars
■ **Cons** Lake Garda has become overdeveloped in places, which makes it uncomfortable during summer.

HOTSPOTS

FOR SALE Property guide

Lombardy has some of the most sought-after properties in the whole of the country, with price tags to match…

Demand for property in the region is high, with homes in Milan and those on the Lakes equally popular

L OMBARDY HAS AN ESTABLISHED TRADITION of attracting foreign buyers. Milan has the country's largest proportion of foreigners living in a city, while 10 per cent of properties purchased in 2002 were bought by foreign buyers. The lakes have been holiday destinations and a popular location with second-home buyers since Roman times, when the wealthy citizens used to retreat to their country villas. Today the Milanese have bought in force around the lakes, and the foreign home owners still flock to the region.

Prices for property in this area are often double that of areas such as Piedmont and Puglia; this is due to the continued high demand for homes combined with limited supply. The Lakes are particularly popular with the older end of the market, due to the peaceful nature of the region and the shelter afforded by the surrounding mountains. Property with lakeside views costs a premium, and for a three-bedroom house you will be looking at a sum in excess of €300,000.

Milan is a city full of wealthy buyers and expensive property. Property costs an average of €6,000 per square metre, while a two-bedroom apartment would set you back upwards of €350,000. With the building of a new motorway, access to the centre has been made easier and consequently people are beginning to settle outside Milan. Lombardy has always been well-served by budget flights and, as it offers a well-developed infrastructure and is a centre of business and industry, the property market has thrived from the influx of money and workers.

Buying a property as an investment is a good prospect, with prices still appreciating, albeit more slowly than they were a few years ago. The rentals market is healthy, although it has waned a little with interest from the German market (which has always driven up demand for lettings) slowing due to economic problems. Nevertheless, there are still a large number of British and Americans holidaying here, creating a strong demand for property lets. ●

TYPICAL PROPERTY TYPES

■ Milan boasts luxurious *palazzis* with courtyards, and villas with luscious gardens
■ There are also a number of expensive, modern apartment blocks
■ Lake Maggiore offers many period villas dotted along the shoreline, which have been converted to provide magnificent and elegant apartments with breathtaking views
■ Many properties around the lakes are built in an Art Nouveau or Liberty style
■ Lake Como has a choice of new-build and period properties, as well as modern luxury apartments and glamorous detached villas
■ Many properties in this area are solid and imposing due to the weather conditions, which can be severe

WHAT CAN YOU GET FOR YOUR EUROS?

PERIOD APARTMENT

Only seven minutes' walk from Lake Como, this attractive, traditional-style apartment offers one bedroom, a spacious living area with separate kitchen, a shared garden and a private parking space. Shops and attractions are all within easy reach, making this an excellent proposition for those seeking a villa with buy-to-let potential.

€80,000 CODE CAT

APARTMENT WITH UNSPOILT VIEWS

Located in a luxury development on Lake Maggiore, this modern apartment is located close to the lakefront and watersport activities and enjoys stunning views. There is easy access to the airport and skiing regions, and the beach is only five minutes' walk. For those seeking a luxurious apartment only a short walk from a lakeside restaurant, this is the place for you.

€132,000 CODE UNI

HOUSE IN PALLANZA

Located on the western side of Lake Maggiore, this property offers three bedrooms, a courtyard garden and two garages. Fully renovated, this house is close to the lake and situated in an original Roman town, with picturesque surroundings.

€210,000 CODE HII

TERRACED HOUSE ON LAKE MAGGIORE

Arranged over three floors, this three-bedroom property boasts beautiful views and is close to the town of Stresa. The lounge enjoys a working fireplace, while the bathroom comes complete with a spa bath. There is a four-car garage in the basement. Only minutes from bars, restaurants and amenities, this property represents an excellent investment.

€320,000 CODE HII

MAGNIFICENT VILLA ON LAKE COMO

This affordable apartment comes with a sizeable terrace and splendid views over Lake Como. Recently restored, this 18th-century property has two bedrooms, two bathrooms and a large living area. Outside, it comes complete with a shared swimming pool and tennis courts set in grounds of 50,000m². There is also a private boat mooring.

€100,000 CODE CAT

PERIOD HOUSE IN BREATHTAKING SCENERY

This lovely property has been fully restored and comes with grounds totalling 1,300m². The ground floor boasts a living area of 125m², including a lounge and separate dinning room. On the first floor there are four bedrooms and three bathrooms, while from the balcony you can enjoy the panoramic lake views. There is also a wine cellar and private garage.

€1,170,000 CODE UNI

AVERAGE HOUSE PRICES LOMBARDY & THE LAKES

	2-bed	3-bed	4-bed	5-bed
Lake Maggiore	€207,000 (£140,816)	€308,000 (£209,524)	€448,000 (£304,762)	€738,000 (£502,041)
Lake Como	€173,000 (£117,687)	€337,000 (£229,252)	€798,000 (£542,857)	€906,000 (£616,327)
Milan	€827,000 (£562,585)	€922,000 (£627,211)	€1,180,000 (£802,721)	€1,850,000 (£1,258,503)
Lake Garda	€300,000 (£204,000)	€417,000 (£283,673)	€736,000 (£500,680)	€957,000 (£651,020)

foreign exchange made simple

WARNING!!

Currency movements can increase the price of your property by almost 10% in a year.
Protect your self from this hidden danger!

With a range of over 50 currencies and the facility to send your funds to any bank in the world free of charge Sterling
Exchange is you one stop shop for all your foreign currency needs

When it comes to exchanging your sterling speak to Sterling Exchange

www.sterlingexchange.co.uk   Tel: 0044 (0)20 7329 997

Venice, the Veneto & Friuli-Venezia Giulia

Once a maritime power, now an elegant, sophisticated area

© MARK WHEATLEY

FACT BOX

Venice and the Veneto
- **Population** 4,577,408
- **Population growth** 1.05%
- **Unemployment rate** 3.4%
- **Average 4-bed house price** €359,800 / £244,762
- **Net migration** 65,367
- **Foreign residents** 240,434

Friuli-Venezia Giulia
- **Population** 1,191,588
- **Population growth** 0.67%
- **Unemployment rate** 3.9%
- **Average 4-bed house price** €257,000 / £174,830
- **Net migration** 11,547
- **Foreign residents** 51,889

Contents

Area profile

This corner of Italy has the world's most romantic city, some seriously fashionable resorts, and a rich culture and history

GETTING THERE

AIR Treviso airport, 40km from Venice, is served by charter companies and **Ryanair** (0871 246 0000, www.ryanair.com), which flies from Liverpool, Luton and Stansted. Ryanair also flies from Stansted to Trieste and Brescia airports. The latter serves Verona and is just to the west of the Veneto. There are many direct flights to Marco Polo airport. **BMI** (0870 607 0555, www.flybmi.com) flies from Heathrow, **easyJet** (0871 244 2366, www.easyjet.com) flies from Gatwick, Bristol and Nottingham East Midlands. **British Airways** (0870 850 9850, www.britishairways.com) flies from Manchester and Gatwick, **Jet2** (0871 226 1737, www.jet2.com) flies from Manchester and Leeds Bradford, and **Thomson** (0870 1900 737, www.thomsonfly.com) flies from Coventry. To reach other cities from Marco Polo, catch an **ATVO Fly Bus** (+39 0421 383 672, www.atvo.it/eng/indexen.php) or an **ACTV Number 15** (+39 041 2722 111, www.actv.it) to Mestre-Venice station and catch a train. The **Alilaguna hydrofoil** (www.alilaguna.it) provides a quick link between Marco Polo airport and Venice. **ROAD** Take a ferry or the Channel Tunnel to Calais. From Calais, take the A26 to Reims, then the A4 towards Strasbourg, and the A35 towards Barr, the Swiss border and Basel. Motorway travel in Switzerland requires a motorway licence, which costs under 30 euros and is available from post offices, petrol stations and tourism offices. Once in Switzerland, take the A2 past Lucerne. Follow the Autostrada Dei Laghi/A9 to Milan, and take the A4 to Verona, Padua, Mestre, Venice, or go on to Trieste. **RAIL Rail Europe** (08708 371 371, www.raileurope.co.uk) offers trains from London to Venice, with a change in Paris. For other destinations, contact **Deutsche Bahn** (0870 243 5363, www.deutsche-bahn.co.uk) for routes and timetables. **COACH Eurolines** (08705 143 219, www.eurolines.co.uk) from National Express offers services to Mestre, Verona and Venice, with connections to other towns in the area.

THIS NORTH-EASTERLY AREA OF THE COUNTRY has some of Italy's last undiscovered property markets, and it enjoys a buoyant economy, along with excellent communications.

Venice and the Veneto

Geography

The Veneto region, home to some of Italy's finest cities – Belluno, Padua, Treviso, Verona and Venice – consists of very varied terrain. In the north, on the border with the south Tyrol, are the magnificent and imposing Dolomites, where you'll find Lake Garda and the ski resort of Cortina d'Ampezzo.

In contrast, the remainder of the Veneto is a huge, flat delta whose many rivers meander to the Adriatic and the Gulf of Venice. This is home to several lagoons and numerous seaside resorts, such as Caorle and Jesolo, with its 'Waterfront of Stars', dedicated to Italy's rich and famous. Although flat, the landscape is far from uninteresting, with many hill towns, vineyards, orchards and elegant villas.

Even Venice's sidestreets are elegantly designed

© MARK WHEATLEY

Areas

Considered by many to be the finest jewel in Italy's very glittering crown, the historic merchant port of Venice, with its intricate labyrinth of canals, bridges, squares and thousands of beautiful palaces, is a living museum. Its unique monuments include the Bridge of Sighs, the Doges' Palace and St Mark's Square. The city is an all-time favourite with foreign property buyers, but this is a seller's market – it's very expensive and few homes are ready to move into that don't require extensive restoration.

West of Venice is the university town of Padua, one of the region's oldest cities and a treasure trove

"Venice is an all-time favourite with foreign property buyers, but this is a seller's market..."

of ancient monuments. The vast Della Valle Square is the largest in Europe, and nearby is the magnificent Renaissance Basilica of St Anthony, which is second only to St Peter's in Rome and is a popular destination for pilgrims paying homage to the town's patron saint. Padua is a lively city with excellent shopping and a year-round social scene.

The Veneto's second largest population centre is Verona, a prosperous and lively city that's famous for its beautifully preserved Roman arena. It's perhaps best known as being home to Romeo and Juliet, although it also boasts its own enviable catalogue of fine monuments.

Friuli-Venezia Giulia

Geography

Tucked away in the north-east of Italy, this region is perhaps the least Italian of all, thanks to its strong influences from central Europe (Austria lies to the north) and the Slavs (Slovenia makes up the entire eastern border and almost completely surrounds the city of Trieste). The foothills to the Alps in the north give way to rolling hills and golden beaches in the south, which are home to several attractive resorts, including the stunning Grado.

Areas

Trieste is the region's capital and the main port on the Adriatic. It has an elegant old quarter where there are several fine examples of neo-classical architecture and Art Nouveau. The small city of

The Grand Canal shows off Venice's sophistication

The northern area of the Veneto has more hilly terrain, with numerous small towns

Udine, some 40km north of Trieste, is traditionally one of the area's main trading centres and today it ranks among Italians as being one of the best places in the country to live.

Economy

Tourism is the main engine behind this area's buoyant economy and it's largely responsible for the almost full employment figures – unemployment was only four per cent in 2004. However, other important industries include agriculture (mainly crops, and dairy and meat farming), manufacturing (shoes and clothes), the chemical industry and, in Verona, trade fairs. Tourism figures for the area in 2004 improved on those for the previous year, except for Venice, where figures fell by five per cent.

Culture

Between them, the Veneto's most influential inhabitants, the Romans and the Venetians, left behind a stunning legacy. Some of the country's finest Roman ruins can be found here, alongside a wealth of medieval, Gothic and Renaissance monuments that are almost crammed into all the main cities, not just Venice. Nevertheless, it was the Venetians who were responsible for the region's main attractions, and these can be seen in the many beautiful buildings of the city. This doesn't just include those owned by rich noblemen or the aristocracy, but also those found in 'everyday' villas and palaces, of which Venice has over 5,000!

Social groups

With the exception of Venice, the area has a young, dynamic population, which is attracted to the region by the excellent employment opportunities, high quality of life and reasonable property prices. Property in the area is generally good value and Friuli-Venezia Giulia remains largely undiscovered by foreign buyers.

The slowly sinking city of Venice, however, suffers from a falling population as young people are priced out of the market. In addition, there's the annual invasion of around 15 million tourists and the omnipresent threat of flooding, which is considered by many to be the reason for the lack of major employers and companies located there. The city is essentially for tourists and second home owners, and few Europeans relocate there. ●

FOOD AND DRINK

The Veneto is famous for its rice, freshly caught fish, *polenta* (wheatmeal) dishes, cheeses, cold meats (including prosciutto ham), and locally grown fruit and vegetables. Local sweets include Verona's *pandoro* and Venice's tiramisu. Friuli-Venezia Giulia's cuisine has a strong central European flavour – don't be surprised to find goulash and sauerkraut on the menu.

Nearly a fifth of Italy's wines are produced in the Veneto, including some of the country's best. More than 20 labels have DOC status, the best known being Bardolino, Soave and Valpolicella, although reds, whites and sparkling are equally good. Friuli-Venezia Giulia's wine production – mostly white – is much smaller by comparison, although there are several wines of note, including the Tocai Friuliano.

The area provides a wealth of culinary delights

FACTS

■ Venice is made up of 117 islands, 150 canals and over 400 bridges

■ The Veneto is home to the first school of oenology (the science of wine and wine-making) in Italy, which was founded in 1885

■ A food market has been held at Verona's Piazza Erbe for over 2,000 years

	VENICE		LONDON
Dec	8	7	
Nov	12	10	
Oct	19	14	
Sept	24	19	
Aug	27	21	
July	27	22	
June	25	20	
May	21	17	
April	17	13	
March	12	10	
Feb	8	7	
Jan	6	6	

Average monthly temperature °C (Celsius)

	VENICE		LONDON
Dec	61	81	
Nov	94	78	
Oct	77	70	
Sept	59	65	
Aug	69	62	
July	52	59	
June	69	58	
May	65	57	
April	78	56	
March	61	64	
Feb	48	72	
Jan	37	57	

Average monthly rainfall mm (millimetres)

Culture

Although the Veneto is dominated by the sumptuousness of Venice, architectural delights can be found all across the area

"Take a gondola ride and almost every facade that greets you is an example of fine architecture celebrating exquisite taste"

CULTURE

FOR CENTURIES, THE VENETO HAS MADE THE most of its strategic position as the gateway between Europe and the Orient. For the Romans, the area was a vital frontier, and during the Middle Ages it found itself at the heart of two major trading routes – the Serenissima, linking the prosperous ports of Genoa and Venice, and the Brenner Pass, connecting northern and southern Europe. From the 12th to the 14th centuries, Venice became a world power as it extended its influence around the Mediterranean and as far as Constantinople in the East. The resulting wealth was used to adorn the region, and nowhere more so than in Venice. With a succession of stunning art and architecture, it's a showcase in its own right.

The importance given to the area by the Romans, who virtually ignored Venice, can be best admired in Verona. Here, the Roman ruins are second only to those found in Rome itself. They include the magnificently preserved Arena, capable of seating all those who lived in the city 2,000 years ago, and the huge Roman square, Piazza Erbe.

Later in the Middle Ages, Verona found stability under the Scaligeri family, patrons and benefactors of the imposing Castelvecchio castle – now home to one of Italy's best art collections, exhibiting jewels in Italian art from Roman times to Titian. There's also the beautiful San Zeno Maggiore church, which boasts some extraordinarily ornate bronze door panels depicting biblical scenes, while Padua's exquisite Scrovegni Chapel provides a

© ROZ COOPER

This area is famous for its delicious, fresh food

unique showcase for Giotto's exquisite frescoes, the precursors for a new era in European art. Science and art came together in Padua's Palazzo del Bo, one of Europe's oldest and most prestigious universities, where the medical department set the foundations for modern anatomy.

Venice

Although the Veneto's main towns are all gems in their own right, their sparkle fades somewhat when placed beside the brilliance of one of the world's most beautiful cities – Venice. A major world power during the Middle Ages, Venice is a living museum, and it's a lasting testimony to the vast wealth and opulence enjoyed by the Venetians. Perhaps the most surprising aspect of Venice is its lack of concession to modern life – many districts have barely changed since they were built centuries ago. Take a gondola along any of the canals and almost every facade that greets you is an example of fine architecture celebrating exquisite taste.

The heart of the city is St Mark's Square, Venice's most visited tourist attraction and home to one of the best reflections of the city's powerful links with the Orient. Although there are many magnificent examples of Byzantine art, the best are found in the Basilica of St Mark, which houses dozens of glittering mosaics and panels – the Pala d'Oro altarpiece contains no less than 250 gold panels studded with more than 3,000 precious stones.

Renaissance gems include the Rialto bridge – for several centuries the only way of crossing the Grand Canal on foot – and the Santa Maria dei Miracoli

VENICE STYLE

Venice has an inimitable style and there's little to beat the timeless elegance of a gondola ride along the Grand Canal as your eyes take in the veritable feast of architectural gems at every pull on the oar, or the grandiose extravagance of the February carnival when graceful figures in Renaissance-style masks glide across the city's squares.

More modern style is represented at the annual Film Festival held in late summer, when the Lido positively oozes stylish glamour as the stars cross the red carpet. Also, the Biennale celebrates innovation and creativity in the very best of modern art, with over 70 countries exhibiting their latest creations.

© ROZ COOPER

church, which is a masterpiece in marble and a favourite place with Venetians to get married.

The Gothic style was popular among wealthy Venetians – ornate arches line many of the canals, and are a key part of many palaces. This includes the Doges' Palace, a masterpiece clad in rich, pink Veronese marble and elegant white Istrian stone.

Exquisite artworks almost litter the city: the Accademia shows off the very best from the Venetian school, but most of the main monuments house at least one masterpiece – Bellini, Carpaccio, Tintoretto and Titian are all represented. ●

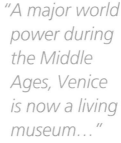

TOP TEN ATTRACTIONS

1. An opera performed in Verona's Arena.
2. The architecture of the Grand Canal in Venice, seen from a gondola.
3. The Sala del Maggior Consiglio in the Doges' Palace (Venice).
4. Verona's beautiful Renaissance garden, Giardino Giusti.
5. Europe's oldest indoor theatre, the Olympic Theatre in Vicenza.
6. The golden Pala d'Oro altarpiece in the Basilica of St Mark (Venice).
7. Galileo's lectern, which is found in Padua's medieval university.
8. The beautiful canal-lined city of Treviso.
9. The carnival, which takes place throughout Venice each February.
10. The Rialto bridge on the Grand Canal in Venice.

CULTURE

"A major world power during the Middle Ages, Venice is now a living museum…"

Property hotspots

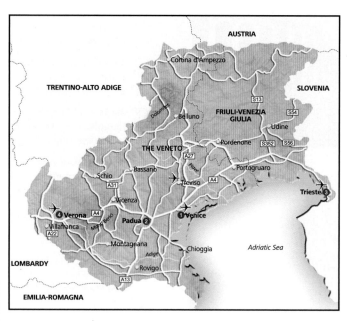

MAP KEY

● Hotspot
○ Major town/city
66 Road numbers

■ **Schools** The English International School of Padua, Via Forcellini 168, 35100 Padova, Tel: +39 049 802 2503, www.eisp01.com
■ **Medical** Ospedale Civile Campo SS Giovanni e Paolo, Venezia, Tel: +39 041 529 4111
■ **Pros** Venice is a unique city ■ There are no cars ■ Many languages are spoken ■ It's easily accessible, with budget flights to two nearby airports ■ Public water transport within the city is frequent and reliable
■ **Cons** Venice has its own style of street numbering, with little apparent logic to it ■ The city can be flooded by high tides ■ This is one of the most expensive places to live in Italy ■ Pollution of the lagoon is causing corrosion of the buildings.

1. Venice

One of the most cultured and romantic destinations in the world, Venice is a heady blend of Byzantine, Gothic and Renaissance art and architecture. Once a wealthy maritime Republic, today it's a slightly shabbier version of its former self, although the city still exudes charm and elegance.

Apart from the Grand Canal, must-sees include St Mark's square, which is the location of the golden mosaics of the Basilica, the stunning Ducal palace and the Bell Tower.

Within the Castello area is the Arsenale, Venice's last remaining symbol of her previous maritime strength; the Scuola di San Giorgio degli Schiavoni, home to Carpaccio's most famous cycle of frescos; and the 16th century Chiesa di San Francesco della Vigna, decorated by some of Pietro Lombardo's stunning reliefs, as well as paintings by Titian and Veronese.

In San Palo is the Frari, a Gothic Franciscan church that's dripping with artistic treasures. Nearby is the Scuola Grande di San Rocco, with Tintoretto's breathtaking cycle of paintings.

Venice's most famous museum is the Accademia, which has 23 rooms crammed with altarpieces, paintings and frescoes from Venetian masters. Moving west along the canal, there's the Peggy Guggenheim collection of modern art.

In property terms, Venice can be summed up in two words – expensive and luxurious. It's almost impossible to find space to build, and even if you do, you're unlikely to get planning permission. If you're seeking to purchase a property here, bear in mind that available homes come up infrequently. Expect to pay upwards of €450,000 for a two-bedroom house. To secure a canal-side pad, you're looking at upwards of €1,000,000.

With over 10 million people visiting annually, demand for accommodation is high, and you can expect to earn in the region of €965 a week through renting.

KEY FACTS
■ **Population** 269,566
■ **Airport** Venice Marco Polo, Viale G. Galilei 30/1, 30030 Tessera, Venezia. Tel: +39 041 260 6400, www.veniceairport.it

2. Padua

An ancient city of art, picturesque Padua is situated on the plains of the Veneto, nestled beside the rolling Euganei Hills and surrounded by the river Bacchiglione. Open spaces, splendid architecture, monumental piazzas full of bicycles, lively cafes and a tangle of narrow cobbled streets characterise this vital city, which is a provincial capital and the economic and communications hub of the Veneto.

The home of Italy's second-oldest university, which was founded in the 13th century, Padua has been the academic heart of the region since the time of the Venetian Republic, and it's still home to a huge student population today.

For those looking for culture, Padua is home to one of Italy's most revered artistic treasures,

namely Giotto's frescoes in the Scrovegni chapel. The Basilica of Il Santo, or Saint Anthony, built in the 13th century and complete with seven domes, is also a major attraction.

Padua has a variety of rental accommodation, and the city is very busy during the summer. Being in close proximity to Venice boosts the number of visitors – many see Padua as a cheaper place to stay.

During the summer, a two-bedroom property will rent for an average of €900 per week, and a four-bedroom property for around €1,600. The large number of students in Padua also ensures a stable long-term rentals market, and properties in the centre and university areas will rent at premium rates.

Padua has a stable property market, which has shown gentle rises in average prices during recent years. Currently, the average price stands at €4,000 per square metre in the city, although this can be higher in central areas.

Home to a large number of enterprises, Padua is popular with young professionals who are snapping up property. A two-bedroom apartment in the city will sell for around €203,000, and a four-bedroom house will fetch around €408,000.

KEY FACTS
■ **Population** 205,645
■ **Airport** Venice Treviso San Angelo Airport, 31100 Treviso, Tel: +39 041 260 6706
■ **Schools** The English International School of Padova, Via Forcellini 168, 35100 Padova, Tel: +39 049 802 2503, www.eisp01.com
■ **Medical** University of Padua Hospital, Via Giustiniani 2, 35128 Padova, Tel: +39 049 821 3515
■ **Pros** Padua is a real Italian city and doesn't suffer from overcrowding by tourists ■ It's a hive of great shops ■ The city has many timeless neighbourhoods ■ There are many

thermal springs in the smaller villages around the city ▪ Padua is a mixture of old-fashioned values integrated with new technology

▪ **Cons** Many tourists stay in Padua but go straight to Venice without seeing any of the city ▪ The restored frescoes in the Scrovegni chapel are difficult to see without an advance booking, and there's a time limit of 15 minutes for each person.

3. Trieste

Perched on a limestone plateau that's lapped by Adriatic, Trieste is handsome and cosmopolitan. Just five miles from Slovenia and ten miles from Croatia, it's a truly European city. In recent years, Trieste has enjoyed a revival due to its proximity to the countries of Eastern Europe, which have become top destinations.

Trieste has many attractions, including a cathedral formed by adjoining churches in a mixture of Venetian, Byzantine and Gothic styles. There's also the main square, Piazza Grande, with its selection of grand cafes; the Palazzo del Governo; and the Palazzo del Commune, with its clock tower and the offices of the Triestino shipping line.

The property market in Trieste is growing steadily and new developments are appearing on the coasts in and around the city. Holiday homes are being snapped up, particularly in Muggia, and coastal properties are expected to be a profitable investment. Towns such as Sgonico and San Pelagio have seen the recent construction of a number of holiday cottages.

San Giacomo is a popular residential area of the city, a self-contained district with excellent amenities. Property is often bought at premium prices here. A four-bedroom house in

Trieste will cost €330,000 (£224,490) on average, while a two-bedroom apartment will cost €149,000 (£101,361).

While there's plenty of accommodation, city centre property will rapidly fill up during the summer months. Expect to pay €820 (£558) per week for a two-bedroom property during the summer, or €1,630 (£1,109) per week for a four-bedroom property.

KEY FACTS
▪ **Population** 209,557
▪ **Airport** Trieste Aeroporto Friuli Venezia Giulia, 34077 Ronchi dei Legionari, Tel: +39 0481 773 224, www.aeroporto.fvg.it
▪ **Schools** International School of Trieste, Via Conconello 16, Opicina 34016, Trieste, Tel: +39 040 211 452, www.istrieste.org
▪ **Medical** Cattinara Hospital, University of Trieste, Strada di Fiume 447, 34149 Trieste, Tel: +39 640 399 1111
▪ **Pros** Trieste is an important port, railway hub and conference centre ▪ The city has a European atmosphere, with mixed aspects of culture that spring from many European countries
▪ **Cons** Trieste almost completely empties in August ▪ Buses are infrequent and not always reliable ▪ Parking is difficult, and some narrow streets can be very difficult to access ▪ The coastal roads are narrow and dangerous if taken at speed.

4. Verona

Encircled by the river Adige, Verona is a truly romantic place where time seems to have stood still. The city is split into four zones: the ancient city with Roman remains; the Citadella zone, which is the economic centre; San Zeno with the impressive cathedral; and the Veronetta, which dates from the early Middle Ages.

Known as Piccola Roma

Waterfront property in Venice sells very rarely, and at a premium

(little Rome) for its importance during the days of the Roman Empire, the medieval palazzi, towers, churches and piazzas provide a testimony to its influence and wealth.

Verona's major attractions include the lively Piazza Brà, which is home to the Arena, or opera house, the third largest Roman amphitheatre. Via Mazzini is home to the choicest shops, while the stylish Piazza dei Signori is the political and administrative heart of Verona.

The 14th-century fortress on the banks of the river Adige commands attention, and the San Zeno Maggiore church is the most atmospheric in the city. The nature parks around Verona also provide a scenic contrast to the city centre.

Property prices in Verona increased by an average of 15-20 per cent between 2001 and 2004, at which point they started to stabilise. Expect to pay €4,500 per square metre for a luxury central apartment, and €3,000 for a suburban detached property. Central properties are thought to be an excellent investment and many have been renovated to a high standard, while still preserving the individual and original features of the architecture.

Suburban properties across the Pietra bridge from the centre also offer good value for money. The average price for a two-bedroom apartment is €208,000

(£141,497), while a four-bedroom house will sell for €445,000 (£302,721).

Verona is a popular tourist destination and short-term rentals can be highly profitable. However, visitors to the city spend an average of only two days there, and tenants for weekly rentals may be hard to find. The average weekly rental for a two-bedroom property is €850 (£578).

KEY FACTS
▪ **Population** 256,110
▪ **Airport** Verona Valerio Catullo Airport, 37060 Casello di Sommacapegna, Tel: +39 045 869 5666, www.aeroportoverona.it
▪ **Schools** Aleardo Aleardi International School, Via Segantini 20, 37138 Verona, Tel:+39 04 557 8200, www.aleardi.it
▪ **Medical** Villa Santa Giuliana Hospital, V. Santa Giuliana 3, 37128 Verona, Tel: +39 045 912 999
▪ **Pros** Verona is close to the beautiful Lake Garda ▪ The city's links to the story of Romeo and Juliet ensure its constant popularity and recognition ▪ Verona is home to a wealth of Roman sites and typical pink-hued medieval buildings ▪ Apart from Venice, it has more sights than anywhere else in the Veneto
▪ **Cons** The balconies around Juliet's house are often filled with tourists and cameras, which has been said to ruin the effect ▪ Parking can be difficult in the city centre ▪ Not ideal for those looking for peace and quiet ▪ The climate is cooler than most of the popular southern towns.

HOTSPOTS

Property guide

FOR SALE

Historically protected and facing strict building regulation, Venice has probably the least flexible property market in the world

Venice is a truly unique city with fantastic potential

THE ACQUA ALTA

■ The winter floods of Venice (*acqua alta*) are threatening many buildings within the city, although some major works are being carried out to reinforce building foundations and pavements. Floods strike in October and November, and generally affect the lower and older areas of Venice

■ The main threat is to *magazzini* (ground floor) properties, and as a consequence ground floors are very seldom used as living spaces, instead being used as halls, with little or no furniture

■ Due to the threat of flooding, the most expensive properties are those on the second floor, also called noble floor, which have the highest ceilings and the widest rooms

■ The top floor was usually used for the servants, therefore they have lower ceilings and no artistic finish, and prices reflect this

■ When buying, bear in mind that every single part of a building, such as doors and windows, has to be made to measure, and it can therefore be more costly than you might expect to renovate an apartment, especially as the facade – and sometimes the interior – is subject to protection orders

THE VENETO IS GENERALLY OVERLOOKED by property buyers, the main focus being on Venice; even then you need a hefty budget to buy there. Venice is Italy's most expensive city, and costs are an average 40 per cent higher than elsewhere. The population has fallen by two-thirds in 20 years, yet an annual nine million tourists visit the city. Consequently, the city is encouraging buyers in an attempt to revitalise the flagging population. Venice is protected by the government due to its historical value, and new builds are almost impossible. Due to this inflexibility prices are either steady or on the increase; either way this means expensive. However, new areas are being uncovered, such as La Giudecca Island, where an old 19th-century mill has been converted into several luxury apartments; the clientele includes Madonna.

The most in-demand areas for homes are within the San Marco and Rialto districts. To buy a renovated apartment in San Marco you are looking at €7,900 to €10,600 per square metre, and prices are steadily rising by three to five per cent per year. Apartments to be renovated are priced from €4,200 to €5,660 per square metre. If you look to the Veneto's other cities, such as Vicenza, Treviso, Padua or Verona, the price drops to €2,000 per square metre. For a one-bedroom apartment in Trieste you will be paying around €108,000, in Padua €147,000, and in Verona €159,000; look to Venice and this jumps to €307,000. Similarly a three-bedroom house in Verona starts at €319,000, while in Venice you are looking at upwards of €450,000.

Within the Veneto, Venice is far and away the best destination for those seeking a financial investment. Rental opportunities are enormous, due to tourist demand. If you can afford to buy in Venice you are certain of generating excellent rental income, with a two-bedroom property earning an average of €965 per week, while four-bedroom apartments can range from around €130 to €150 per day. ●

TYPICAL PROPERTY

Venetian architecture is truly unique and elegant. It is dominated by 15th- to 19th-century *palazzi*, typified by narrow arched windows with balconies and pink Verona or Istrian stone. There are in excess of 5,000 of these buildings in Venice, along with many other *palazzi* with painted pastel facades juxtaposed with dark wooden shutters. Many *palazzi* have been converted into apartments. On the mainland, the countryside is dotted with stately homes and villas.

WHAT CAN YOU GET FOR YOUR EUROS?

BEAUTIFUL VIEWS

This two-bedroom, 5th-floor apartment is situated in the centre of Venice. It has glorious city and canal views, which can be enjoyed from a small terrace. This property is fully renovated and habitable, and is ideal for rental and personal use.

€410,000 CODE HII

OLD FARMHOUSE

Located in the countryside near Mira, this unique farmhouse was built during the 16th century. With four bedrooms, 5,000m² of grounds, and a separate barn perfect for renovation and rental, this property would make an ideal family home.

€450,000 CODE HII

VENETIAN APARTMENT

Situated in the Rialto district, this typical Venetian apartment has been recently renovated and is located on the second floor. With two double bedrooms and two bathrooms, this apartment comes with wood and marble floors, and also enjoys a terrace.

€625,000 CODE PRE

RIALTO APARTMENT

Situated on the Grand Canal in the bustling Rialto district, this spacious two-bedroom property is furnished in a classical Venetian style and overlooks Camp Santa Sofia. With a furnished kitchen plus a balcony, this apartment offers excellent rental potential due to its central location.

€1,000,000 CODE PRE

TOP FLOOR PROPERTY

Located close to the Rialto bridge, this elegant apartment, furnished in typical Venetian style, offers panoramic views of the area and the Campiello below. With a spacious hall, living room, dining room, kitchen, two double bedrooms and one bathroom, this is a unique opportunity for an investor.

€1,100,000 CODE PRE

HOUSE IN CASTELLO

Situated minutes from the St Zaccaria boat stop, this light and airy building is arranged over three floors and is in good condition. With 200m² of living area, the property offers a study, living and dining area, and three bedrooms. With views over the Campo de la Bragora, which can be enjoyed from the terrace, this is the perfect property to be developed into apartments.

€1,200,000 CODE PRE

HOUSE BY THE ACCADEMIA BRIDGE

In good condition and perfect for division into separate apartments, the building has three floors, each of which overlooks a small garden and the canal. The first floor has one bedroom, while the second floor is slightly bigger with two bedrooms. The attic could also be developed into a one-bedroom apartment, and has a roof terrace with views over the Grand Canal.

€2,300,000 CODE PRE

AVERAGE HOUSE PRICES VENICE, THE VENETO & FRIULI-VENEZIA GIULIA

	2-bed	3-bed	4-bed	5-bed
Venice	€369,000 (£251,020)	€453,000 (£308,163)	€1,004,000 (£682,993)	€1,285,000 (£874,150)
Padua	€239,000 (£162,585)	€304,000 (£206,803)	€408,000 (£277,551)	€610,000 (£414,966)
Trieste	€256,000 (£174,150)	€359,000 (£244,218)	€330,000 (£224,490)	€500,000 (£340,136)
Verona	€321,000 (£218,367)	€319,000 (£217,007)	€445,000 (£302,721)	€765,000 (£520,408)

It's your money we're saving

interchange
CURRENCY MATTERS

At Interchange we are experts in foreign currency exchange, which means we pride ourselves on offering the best rates and levels of service available.

We are located at 4 Marble Arch, in the heart of London, and have over 100 years of experience in currency exchange.

Whether it's an international transfer for property purchase, business, regular payments or simply cash or holiday money we can really help you make the most of your money.

If you'd like more information on our services or would simply like a quote please contact us at:

Freephone 0800 197 3994 or Telephone +44 (0) 20 7723 0007
enquiries@interchangefx.co.uk www.interchangefx.co.uk
4 Marble Arch, London W1H 7AP

Emilia-Romagna

Rich in agriculture, a crossroads between north and south

© ENIT

FACT BOX

- ■ **Population** 4,030,220
- ■ **Population growth** 1.15%
- ■ **Unemployment rate** 3.0%
- ■ **Average 4-bed house price** €316,000 / £214,966
- ■ **Net migration** 62,699
- ■ **Foreign residents** 210,397

Contents

Area profile

This wealthy region is largely overlooked, but is home to delightful, cultured cities and some of Italy's best cuisine

GETTING THERE

AIR Bologna's Guglielmo Marconi airport is about 5km from the city. **British Airways** (0870 850 9850; www.britishairways.com) flies to Bologna from Manchester and London Gatwick, and **easyJet** (0871 2442 366; www.easyjet.com) flies from Stansted. The southeast of the region is served by **Ryanair** (0871 246 0000; www.ryanair.com), who operates between Stansted and Forli.

RAIL A train from London Waterloo to Bologna takes around 16 hours, including a station change in Paris. Contact **Rail Europe** (08708 371 371; www.raileurope.co.uk) for booking and further information. To reach other parts of Emilia-Romagna, contact **Trenitalia** (www.trenitalia.it/en/index.html) for details of connecting trains.

ROAD Either catch a ferry – try **SeaFrance** (08705 711 711; www.seafrance.co.uk), **Hoverspeed** (0870 240 8070; www.hoverspeed.co.uk) or **P&O Ferries** (08705 202 020; www.poferries.com) – or use the **Channel Tunnel** (08705 35 35 35; www.eurotunnel.com) to reach Calais. Then take the A26 to Reims, the A4 to Strasbourg, and the A35 to Sélestat, where it becomes the E25; follow this route into Switzerland. You will need to purchase a Swiss motorway tax disc from a petrol station for €27.50 per year. Take the E35 at Basel and drive southeast across Switzerland to Italy. Continue on the E35 to reach Emilia-Romagna. It takes around 11 hours to drive from Calais to Parma.

COACH Eurolines (08705 143 219; www.eurolines.co.uk) travels from London Victoria to Parma (24 hours 45 minutes) and Bologna (26 hours 15 minutes). These include a three-hour wait in Paris.

ALTHOUGH EMILIA-ROMAGNA ISN'T ONE OF Italy's best known areas, this centrally situated region, often cited as the crossroads between northern and southern Italy, is rich in cultural and historic heritage, and offers a high standard of living in small, pleasant cities, as well as some of the country's best gastronomic experiences.

Geography

One of Italy's largest regions, Emilia-Romagna is a rich and fertile land where there are vast stretches of landscape under agriculture, particularly along the Po valley, which runs virtually the entire length of the region's northern border. The wide-spreading Po delta in the northeast, with its maze of marshes, dunes and wetlands, is an area of outstanding natural beauty – it's often known as the 'Italian Camargue' – and a wildlife sanctuary. Emilia-Romagna's Adriatic coastline consists mainly of sandy beaches, much favoured by tourists. In total contrast to this almost completely flat landscape, in the south are the high Apennines, home to many ski resorts.

Areas

Most of the main cities in the region are situated on or near the ancient Roman road, Via Aemilia, connecting Rome and Rimini. Highlights along this route include the attractive cities of Bologna, Fidenza, Modena, Parma and Ravenna, before it finally reaches the coast.

The prosperous city of Bologna, famous as the seat of one of the world's oldest universities (founded in 1088), offers pleasant squares, medieval streets and several fine monuments, including the brick-built San Petronio church, with its beautiful interior and two huge 12th-century towers, both of which lean – Torre Asinelli reaches a height of almost 100 metres!

"The Adriatic coast consists of sandy beaches, while the high Apennines have ski resorts"

The city of Parma is synonymous with fine living and good food, and not surprisingly offers some of Italy's best restaurants, as well as excellent shopping, world-class opera – Verdi lived nearby – and several artistic treasures, including the Romanesque Duomo, with its stunning painted dome and richly decorated baptistry.

Rimini, with its miles of sandy beaches on the Adriatic coast, lays claim to Europe's largest seaside resort, with more than 1,000 hotels, packed beaches – several are private and charge entrance fees – and crowded restaurants to match. The old quarter still retains its original charm and tranquillity, and has pleasant squares and cobbled streets. Although Rimini is very busy in high season, the winter is extremely quiet here.

Rimini is home to Europe's largest seaside resort, but away from the bustle is its charming old quarter

© ENIT

A region of economic prosperity with many small and medium enterprises

The Apennine mountains in the south are home to numerous ski resorts, which, although small, are within easy reach of the main towns in the region and generally offer guaranteed snow in the winter. Abetone, whose skiing grounds have produced several champion skiers, is the largest and boasts 70km of pistes over 30 slopes. Febbio has the highest slopes over its 12km of pistes, and Piandelagotti is a paradise for cross–country skiers.

Economy

Emilia-Romagna is one of Italy's most prosperous regions, and the basis of its economy is agriculture. Not for nothing is the region often called the 'bread basket' of Italy, and cereals and cattle and pig farming are the most important sectors. Salt extraction and fishing are also important in the Comacchio valleys. The area is also highly industrialised, with the emphasis on small and medium enterprises specialising in food processing, engineering, textiles, pharmaceuticals and furniture. Luxury car design and manufacturing is also a main sector – Ferrari and Lamborghini are both based here. Tourism is becoming increasingly important, and the region has one of the highest growth rates in the country.

Unemployment is extremely low, reflecting the region's buoyant economy. Figures for 2004 were just 3.7 per cent.

Culture

Emilia-Romagna's centuries-old prosperity has led to an outstanding cultural heritage, a legacy left by the rich and powerful nobility who ruled the main cities during the Middle Ages and Renaissance. Some of the ruling families were infamous for their despotism and cruelty; the d'Este in Ferrara, Matilda

from Canosa and Rimini's Malatesta were particularly notorious, and poisoning and murder were part of daily life. Nonetheless, they were great patrons of the arts, commissioning both local and national artists and poets. The finest example of this is the d'Este private art collection housed in the Galleria Esteuse in Modena, with paintings by Bernini, Tintoretto and local artists Carracci and Reni, as well as an extensive library containing many rare works, such as a 1488 edition of *The Divine Comedy*. The region is also home to several fine Romanesque Duomos – Ferrara, Fidenza, Modena and Parma all boast stunning examples.

Social groups

The area has Italy's fastest-growing population. In 2003 nearly 42,000 foreigners settled in the region. Emilia-Romagna is also a popular relocation spot with Italians, attracted to the area's plentiful job opportunities and high standard of living. UK nationals represent a small percentage of foreigners (there are fewer than 1,500 officially living here), and most live in Bologna or Parma. ●

FACTS

■ Italy's tricolour flag was first flown in Emilia-Romagna as a symbol of the unified Italy

■ Emilia-Romagna is the birthplace of a long list of illustrious Italians – Armani, Fellini, Ferrari, Pascoli, Pavarotti and Verdi to name but a few

■ The longest cycle route in Italy, part of the pan-European route from Athens to Cadiz, is found here along the River Po

PROFILE

FOOD AND DRINK

Emilia-Romagna is one of Italy's great gastronomical centres and the proud inventor of two of the country's most famous ingredients – Parma ham and Parmesan cheese. The exquisite cured Parma ham (*prosciutto crudo*) and the centuries-old Parmesan are gourmet delicacies the world over. Parma ham should be eaten on its own and Parmesan adds a special touch to many dishes; Parmesan with pears is a particular delicacy. Bologna is famous for the quintessentially Italian pasta sauce, *bolognesa*, now part and parcel of many Europeans' daily diet.

The area's wine is surprisingly different to that produced in neighbouring northern regions and has a distinct flavour. The red Lambrusco from Modena is the region's best known wine and enjoys international fame. Other notable wines include the dry white Albana di Romagna and Sangiovese, a robust red.

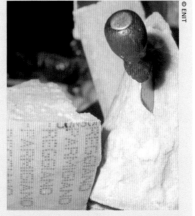

The world-famous Parmesan cheese

BOLOGNA		LONDON
6	Dec	7
11	Nov	10
19	Oct	14
25	Sept	19
29	Aug	21
30	July	22
27	June	20
23	May	17
18	April	13
13	March	10
8	Feb	7
5	Jan	6

Average monthly temperature °C (Celsius)

BOLOGNA		LONDON
61	Dec	81
86	Nov	78
95	Oct	70
70	Sept	65
45	Aug	62
41	July	59
63	June	58
72	May	57
66	April	56
58	March	64
51	Feb	72
49	Jan	77

Average monthly rainfall mm (millimetres)

Property hotspots

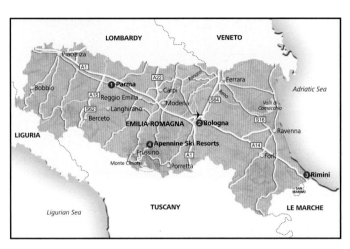

MAP KEY

● Hotspot
◔ Major town/city
66 Road numbers

1. Parma

Regarded as having the highest standard of living in Italy, Parma is an extremely affluent and a very orderly place. Straddling the banks of the Po tributary, the city offers a relaxed and comfortable lifestyle.

Originally an Etruscan city, Parma became an important Roman colony, eventually passing on to the Lombards and the Franks. Parma was brought under Italian ownership following unification, and famously was the only Emilian city that stood against Mussolini.

Parma's turbulent history is reflected in its culture and architecture, which ranges from Roman to Art Nouveau. The cobbled streets and historic centre lead into Parma's two main squares: Piazza Garibaldi, which provides a backdrop to the Palazzo del Governatore; and Piazza Duomo, the location of the 11th-century Duomo. Parma is home to two of Italy's great artists, Correggio and Parmigianino, and many of their works can be seen in the Duomo or one of the city's art galleries. The 17th-century town hall and 12th-century San Giovanni Evangelista are also worth viewing.

Parma isn't hugely popular with the foreign buyer, but the market is strong. Essentially this is a city dominated by Italians who live and work here. Prices start at €205,000 for two-bedroom houses, while a four-bedroom apartment would set you back €393,000. In terms of lettings, the market is extremely buoyant, and you can expect to charge €815 a week for two-bedroom property.

KEY FACTS
■ **Population** 163,786
■ **Airports** G. Marconi Airport, Via Triumvirato 84, 40132 Bologna, Tel: +39 051 6479681, www.bologna-airport.it
■ **Medical** Ospedale Civile Dagnini, Via Matteotti 23, 43010 Zibello, Tel: +39 0524 99365
■ **Schools** International School of Modena, Via Silvio Pellico 9, 41042 Fiorano Modenese, Tel: +39 0536 832904, www.ismmodena.org
■ **Pros** A gastronome's heaven, the city is home to *proscuitto* ham and Parmesan cheese, as well as many specialist food outlets ■ Nightlife is family friendly, with a proliferation of restaurants, theatre and opera ■ An exceptionally orderly, comfortable city to live in ■ Parma is well connected, and Milan, the coast and mountains are all within day-tripping distance
■ **Cons** Cost of living in Parma is high
■ The locals are so affluent and immaculately turned out that some may feel comparatively inadequate!

2. Bologna

The region's most dynamic city, Bologna is the capital of Emilia-Romagna. A striking place, with its red-bricked medieval centre, *palazzi* and porticoed streets and arcades, Bologna is also known as 'Red Bologna' due to its association with left-wing politics. The city was the centre of resistance activity during World War II, and there's a poignant memorial to those who were shot for the cause. Bologna was voted European city of the year in 2000.

Bologna was founded in the 6th century by the Etruscans, but fell into the hands of the Gauls, then the Romans. By the 12th century it was one of Italy's wealthiest cities. Bologna is home to Italy's oldest university, founded in 1088, which attracts a huge number of students, who total a fifth of the population. Gastronomically it is known as *La Grasse*, literally 'the fat one', as the rich cuisine invariably results in the loosening of belts by a few notches!

There is plenty to see here. The two main squares are Piazza Maggiore and Piazza del Nettuno, which is home to the fifth-largest church in the world, the Basilica San Petronio, and the Palazzo dei Notai, where medieval law was laid down. The Museo Civico Archeologico houses many Etruscan reliefs, while the entrance to the lively and dynamic University Quarter is marked by two medieval towers. Within the University Quarter the streets are full of clubs, bars and cafés, and in the university library you will find a number of Rossini's original manuscripts and scores.

Although Bologna is less polished than cities such as Florence and Venice, it has a real charm of its own. The property market has shown continued growth over the past few years, with appreciation of up to 30 per cent in some areas. Property prices are predicted to grow in future years, and the city currently represents a good investment. A two-bedroom house will set you back by €280,000, while a one-bedroom apartment costs an average of €189,000. In terms of rentals, given the nature of the city as a centre of industry and a student hub, the market is strong, particularly long-term. A one-bedroom flat lets for an average of €595 per week, while a four-bedroom property will generate €1,305 per week.

KEY FACTS
■ **Population** 370, 363
■ **Airport** G. Marconi Airport, Via Triumvirato 84, 40132 Bologna, Tel: +39 051 6479681, www.bologna-airport.it
■ **Medical** Bologna Ospedale Malpighi, Via Albertoni Pietro 15, 40138 Bologna, Tel: +39 051 6362111
■ **Schools** International School of Modena, Via Silvio Pellico 9, 41042 Fiorano Modenese, Tel: +39 0536 832904, www.ismmodena.org
■ **Pros** The culinary capital, home to Italy's richest – and arguably finest – cuisine ■ As a centre of industry, there is a wide range of employment in Bologna ■ There is a vibrant arts scene, driven primarily by the vast student population ■ Cultural entertainment is also on offer, catering for the business community
■ **Cons** Living costs in the city are high, especially for accommodation and eating out ■ English is not widely spoken due to the relative paucity of tourists ■ Some areas assume a rather seedy mantle at night.

3. Rimini

Attracting both the hedonistic party seeker and families, Rimini is a typical seaside resort, teeming with holiday-makers during August, and a ghost town, with all restaurants and hotels shut down, during winter. While Rimini's coast is crammed with restaurants, arcades, souvenir shops and hotels, and is home to 100 or so bars and nightclubs, inland you will find the old town, which survives despite heavy bombing during World War II.

Rimini has passed through various hands, from the Romans, Umbrians and Etruscans, to the Byzantines and Papal States. There are a number of Roman remains scattered around the city's outskirts. The Arch of Augustus was built in 27BC and the amphitheatre in the 2nd century AD; the bridge of Tiberius is also worth seeing. From the 13th century, the Malatesta family ruled Rimini and built one of Italy's greatest Renaissance temples, decorated with frescos and art by Giotto and Piero della Francesca. The city also boasts its own castle and town ramparts, while the Piazza Cavour is lined with *palazzi*.

Rimini is renowned for fast-paced nightlife and stunning beaches, but despite its frenetic club scene, Italian families have been coming here for decades. Although you won't find traditional Italy here, Rimini makes for an excellent investment. A two-bedroom property will let for €574 a week, and the rental season is longer than in many cities of Emilia-Romagna. In terms of purchasing property, a three-bedroom house will sell for €339,000, while a four-bedroom apartment sells for an average of €396,000.

Emilia-Romagna is Italy's richest region and home to wealthy cities and towns containing grand buildings

KEY FACTS
■ **Population** 128,226
■ **Airports** L. Ridolfi Airport, Via Seganti 103, 47100 Forli, Tel: +39 0543 474990, www.forli-airport.it
■ **Medical** Ospedale Cervesi, Via Beethoven, 47841 Cattolica, Tel: +39 0541 966111
■ **Schools** International School of Modena, Via Silvio Pellico 9, 41042 Fiorano Modenese, Tel: +39 0536 832904, www.ismmodena.org
■ **Pros** The historic centre has retained much of its charm, despite heavy bombing during World War II ■ With dozens of clubs and bars, the nightlife is superb ■ Popular with all ages, it has many attractions and theme parks
■ **Cons** Whilst the beach is one of the largest in Europe, it is busy, highly regimented and largely privatised ■ Not a suitable spot for those seeking a quiet time by the sea ■ The city is overpriced in summer and virtually shuts down during winter.

4. Apennine mountains

The Apennines are one of Italy's lesser-known ski areas, but offer excellent skiing, despite limited altitude. The peaks act as a natural border between Emilia-Romagna and Tuscany, and the range is the source of the region's rivers, including the Po, Trebbia, Nure, Arda, Taro and Parma. In the centre of these peaks you will find the magnificent sandstone plateau of Bismantova, ideal for adventurous climbers and the backdrop to the town of Castelnovo ne'l Monti.

The Apennines' ski resorts may not be as well known as those in the Alps or Dolomites, but have a charm of their own. Sestola is the largest ski resort and summer holiday centre in the Modenese Apennines, but there is also Fanano, Montecreto and Pian del Falco. Abetone, in Monte Cimono, boasts 70km of pistes, and is the best-equipped resort in the area, offering more than 30 slopes. It is a typical family resort, with good snow conditions, and is close to Tuscany's major cities.

Febbio, in the commune of Villa Minozzo, offers the highest slopes in the Apennines, with 12km of ski runs. Villa Minozzo and La Spezia are also worth a visit. La Spezia spreads across the inside of Golfo dei Poeti (Gulf of Poets) and its wide esplanade makes for a pleasant stroll along the seafront, or you could just relax in one of the lavish parks.

The area is excellent for rentals, as many visit to ski, hike and climb, and the market is generally short term. A two-bedroom property lets for an average of €640 a week, while a larger ski chalet with five bedrooms can be rented out for as much as €1,460. Expect to pay €248,000 for a three-bedroom property.

KEY FACTS
■ **Population** Sestola 2,603
■ Montecreto 928 ■ Pievepelago 2,129 ■ Fanano 2,909 ■ Tizzano Val Parma 2,118 ■ Riolunato 736 ■ Lama Mocogno 3,028
■ **Airports** G. Marconi Airport, Via Triumvirato 84, 40132 Bologna, Tel: +39 051 6479681, www.bologna-airport.it
■ **Medical** Ospedaliera Universitaria Policlinico di Modena, Via Pozzo 71, 41100 Modena, Tel: +39 059 4222111, www.policlinico.mo.it
■ Ospedale Civile Dagnini, Via Matteotti 23, 43010 Zibello, Tel: +39 0524 99365
■ **Schools** International School of Modena, Via Silvio Pellico 9, 41042 Fiorano Modenese, Tel: +39 0536 832904, www.ismmodena.org
■ **Pros** Miles of interconnecting slopes are available year round, thanks in part to artificial snow ■ There are facilities for numerous summer sports, plus walking trails ■ Many towns have picturesque medieval centres ■ There are plenty of museums, archaeological sites, churches and castles to visit
■ **Cons** Public transport is infrequent, so a car is highly desirable ■ Bad weather can easily disrupt travel plans.

FOR
SALE

Property guide

The wealthy region of Emilia-Romagna offers easy access to Tuscany, and while property can be pricey, it's not as expensive as its neighbour

© HOMES IN ITALY

Rural Emilia-Romagna has plenty of desirable properties, although they rarely come onto the market

EMILIA-ROMAGNA IS ESSENTIALLY A RURAL region, dotted with majestic cities, such as Parma and Bologna, and it's also home to the popular seaside resort of Rimini. While the cities offer a range of fantastic and historic apartments and townhouses, inland property is cheaper. Over the past five years Bologna has experienced a 30 per cent appreciation in property prices, and although this is lower than the national average, it is still an excellent prospect for investors. Inland, red-roofed farmhouses and country estates can be found everywhere, but you will find that bargain renovation properties are extremely scarce.

The region offers the highest standard of living in Italy, and the style and luxury afforded by many properties in the area reflect this. Although inland Emilia-Romagna is awash with country properties, those for sale are few and far between. However, prices are cheaper than in Tuscany and Umbria, and a three-bedroom house will cost an average of €300,000 to €400,000.

With Emilia-Romagna proving popular with skiers, hikers, climbers and other adventure-seekers, the rentals market is particularly buoyant, although inland lets are less in demand than those in coastal or city areas, and you will consequentially see a lower return. However, ski areas generate an average of €640 a week for a two-bedroom property. Coastal resorts, such as Rimini, are crawling with holiday-makers during peak season and can generate €770 for a three-bedroom property. City rentals start at €450 to €600 for a one-bedroom property, while a five-bedroom property rents for an average of €1,500. ●

TYPICAL PROPERTIES

- Prestigious estates and country homes are dotted all over the Romagnan landscape
- Typically these are red-roofed farmhouses, many of which are still businesses producing Parmesan and *prosciutto*
- Prices for these properties are high and availability is very low
- External staircases leading to roof terraces are typical of the area
- Properties are built from a grey stone and are isolated in a rustic setting

WHAT CAN YOU GET FOR YOUR EUROS?

TRADITIONAL HOUSE IN A RURAL HAMLET

Stone-built, with exposed wood beams, a stone fireplace and flagstone floors, this property comes with 35ha of land, complete with 100-year-old chestnut trees. The farmhouse is structurally unsound and requires restoration. The hamlet is within easy reach of San Marino and town amenities.

€235,000 CODE IPN

APARTMENT IN FERRARA

This furnished apartment is located in the centre of this delightful walled city. Once a 12th-century *palazzo*, this two-bedroom property comes fully furnished and is fully habitable, having been only recently converted. With high ceilings and restored frescos, this is a unique opportunity to live in a historic city, close to many cultural sites, in a fabulous apartment.

€345,760 CODE IPN

STONE-BUILT ESTATE

Situated on the border with Tuscany, this estate is located on a hillside and offers panoramic views. It boasts 3ha of land and is fully habitable. The airports in Florence and Pisa are within easy reach, and the property itself is within 1km of Selvapiana and all amenities. The property is in habitable condition, with the main house divided into three apartments, plus two annexes.

€385,000 CODE APT

FARMHOUSE IDEAL AS A BUSINESS

Ideal as a rental investment, this partially restored farmhouse is being sold with 1ha of land. Work needs to be focused upon internal renovation, while utilities are all connected. Only 3km from the nearest town and amenities, this house is situated on a hillside and offers great views of the surrounding countryside.

€400,000 CODE APT

HILLSIDE PROPERTY WITH VIEWS

A large farm estate with 70ha of arable land, located close to the Tuscan border. This house is in a rural setting and enjoys panoramic views of the area. Comprising two buildings, the main house and barn, the property requires complete renovation.

€650,000 CODE APT

UNIQUE CASTLE PROPERTY

Within easy reach of major cities and all amenities, this historic castle is encompassed by stone walls and nestles between two rivers in the hills, covering an area of 5.7km². With a courtyard, two towers, a roof garden and a theatre, it is fully restored and is arranged over four floors. There is also a pool and a number of terraces, which enjoy unspoilt views.

€8,500,000 CODE CIT

AVERAGE HOUSE PRICES EMILIA-ROMAGNA

	2-bed	3-bed	4-bed	5-bed
Parma	€227,000 (£154,422)	€340,000 (£231,293)	€449,000 (£305,442)	€753,000 (£512,245)
Bologna	€356,000 (£242,177)	€535,000 (£363,946)	€786,000 (£534,694)	€837,000 (£569,388)
Rimini	€161,000 (£109,524)	€316,000 (£214,966)	€488,000 (£331,973)	€589,000 (£400,680)
Apennine mountains	€170,000 (£115,646)	€248,000 (£168,707)	€305,000 (£207,483)	€412,000 (£280,272)

98

Tuscany

Distinctive rolling hills, cypress trees and lush olive groves

© ENIT

FACT BOX

- ▉ **Population** 3,516,296
- ▉ **Population growth** 0.55%
- ▉ **Unemployment rate** 4.7%
- ▉ **Average 4-bed house price** €460,900 / £313,537
- ▉ **Net migration** 63,029
- ▉ **Foreign residents** 164,800

Contents

Area profile

Tuscany isn't all about the landscape, since it's also the proud owner of some magnificent hill towns and architectural gems

GETTING THERE

AIR The international hub in the region is Pisa's Galileo Galilei airport. From there, regular trains go to Pisa's nearby town centre, and hourly trains go the 80km to Florence. **easyJet** (0871 244 2366, www.easyjet.com) flies direct to Pisa from Bristol, **Ryanair** (0871 246 0000, www.ryanair.com) flies direct from Stansted, Glasgow (Prestwick) and Liverpool to Pisa, **British Airways** (0870 850 9850, www.britishairways.com) flies to Pisa from Gatwick and Manchester, and **Thomson** (0870 1900 737, www.thomsonfly.com) flies from Bournemouth, Coventry and Doncaster/Sheffield to Pisa. **Meridiana** (0845 355 5588, www.meridiana.it) flies to Florence from Gatwick in a little over two hours. **ROAD** Take your car on a ferry – try **SeaFrance** (08705 711 711, www.seafrance.co.uk) or **Hoverspeed** (0870 240 8070, www.hoverspeed.co.uk) – or take the **Channel Tunnel** (08705 353 535, www.eurotunnel.com) to Calais. Once there, take the A26 towards Reims, the E17 to Troyes where it joins the E54 and later the E21 to Dijon. Take the A39 to Bourg-en-Bresse, then the A40 to the N205 Mont Blanc tunnel. Enter Italy and take the E25/A5 towards Genoa. For inland Tuscany, take the A5 turning towards Santhiá, then the A4 to Milan, and continue on the E35/A1 for Florence and beyond. For coastal regions, continue on to Genoa, then follow the E80 along the coast to Livorno and Pisa. **RAIL** From London Waterloo you can reach Florence in under 17 hours, with a 90-minute transfer in Paris. Try **Rail Europe** (08708 371 371, www.raileurope.co.uk). An extensive network links many Tuscan towns (see www.trenitalia.it/en/index.html for details), but regional routes can be slow. **COACH Eurolines** (08705 143 219, www.eurolines.co.uk) from National Express offers services from London Victoria to Florence and Siena, and connections are available to most other Tuscan destinations. It's not a choice for the impatient, though – the journey takes around 28 hours!

O F ALL THE ITALIAN LANDSCAPES, TUSCANY'S is the one that normally springs to mind when we think of Italy. Its evocative rolling hills, graced by centuries-old olive groves and noble cypress trees, have inspired foreigners and Italians alike, and this Etruscan delight is one of the most beautiful places in the world to live.

Geography

Like many Italian regions, Tuscany offers many contrasts, from high mountain ranges to low-lying marshland. The natural park at Maremma boasts one of the country's last stretches of virgin coastline, there's the emblematic Arno river and, more characteristically, thousands of acres of gently rolling hills, criss-crossed with immaculate white roads and home to crops, vineyards and olive groves. The island of Elba, site of Napoleon's 90-day exile, lies just off the south coast.

Areas

The northern Tuscan coast, known as the Versilia coast, has the region's best beaches and some of the most popular resorts – Viareggio is particularly attractive. Further south, the coastline is more rugged and includes the Monte Argentario peninsula with its upmarket resorts of Porto Ercole and Porto Santo Stefano. In the north is Lucca, a pleasant fortress town enclosed by imposing ramparts. Its peaceful streets house many fine monuments, including the Romanesque St Martin's cathedral and the elegant Pfanner Palace.

To the east lies Tuscany's principal prize, Florence, the great Renaissance capital and one of Europe's finest cultural and artistic cities. Divided neatly into two by the Arno, Florence offers the visitor many delights, including the elaborately decorated Duomo, the Gothic Santa Croce, the shop-packed Ponte Vecchio and gallery after gallery of exquisite masterpieces. Visited by millions of tourists every year, Florence is also popular with foreign residents.

South of Florence is the heart of the Tuscan vineyards, concentrated around the area's most popular district with foreign property buyers: the triangle formed by Chianti, Siena and San Gimignano. Chianti, with its quintessential stone villas and farmhouses, is one of the most popular places in Italy to own a home. The noble city of Siena boasts Italy's most beautiful square, Piazza del Campo, plus one of its most stunning cathedrals and a perfectly preserved medieval centre. Nearby is the small town of San Gimignano, with its magnificent

The beautiful landscape of this region is typically Italian, with its gentle rolling hills and old stone buildings

© ENIT

skyline made up of 13 stone towers, a sign of the town's prosperity during the Middle Ages.

Eastern Tuscany is home to one of the most prosperous cities, Arezzo, famous for its thriving jewellery industry and the frescoes painted by Piero della Francesca. Further south is the beautiful town of Cortona. This is one of the area's oldest hillside towns, and it boasts a beautiful medieval old quarter. Montepulciano, famous for its panoramic views stretching far over the surrounding countryside and

> "Chianti, with its stone villas and farmhouses, is one of the most popular places to own a home"

home to one of Italy's best wines, is small and compact, but with a surprising number of Renaissance palaces.

Economy

Although Tuscany doesn't boast industry on the same scale as Lombardy, this is one of the country's most prosperous regions. The backbone of the economy has always been agriculture, mainly cereal, olive and wine production. However, manufacturing industries also play an important part in the area's prosperity, with textiles, chemicals, glass and automobile production being the main contributors. Tourism and related industries are key factors too, as are Florence's many artisans, whose handcrafted goods are famous. Unemployment is low in the area and in 2004 stood at 5.2 per cent.

Culture

Tuscany was an Etruscan stronghold, but is most famous historically as the birthplace of the Renaissance, when this part of Italy pulled Europe out of the ignorance of the Dark Ages and into a

new era of artistic and scientific discovery. The Medici family ruled for almost three centuries in Florence, and during this reign the city was the cradle of the world's intellectual and cultural scene, and the residence of many of Italy's greatest writers, artists and scientists. The city of Pisa was also a major power at this time, dominating the Western Mediterranean for hundreds of years.

Social groups

Tuscany has one of the fastest-growing populations in Italy and the region continues to attract foreign property buyers and relocators drawn to the magnificent natural surroundings and the well-established expatriate community. British and German nationals form the largest groups and many of them are retirees. Florence is a favoured spot – the city's foreign population grew by more than 6,000 in 2003. In spite of the region's high property prices, this trend looks set to continue. ●

Florence is a delightful historic city that's very popular with foreign property buyers

FACTS

▥ The large number of foreign residents around Chianti have led to it being dubbed 'Chianti-shire'.

▥ According to UNESCO figures, nearly a third of the world's art treasures are found in Florence.

▥ Modern-day Italian was first formed in Florence, mostly influenced by Dante's *Divine Comedy*.

PROFILE

FOOD AND DRINK

Essential ingredients in Tuscany's cuisine include the region's excellent olive oil, aromatic herbs, fresh fish (on the coast) and meat, including wild boar (inland). Vegetables and beans form the basis for the region's many delicious soups, while rice or the Tuscan pasta specialities – ravioli and tortelli – feature prominently too. Truffles found in the lush forests are national delicacies.

Although its cuisine is excellent, Tuscany really stars when it comes to wine. The hilly terrain and fertile soil provide perfect growing conditions for many grape varieties, and these are responsible for more than 30 DOC wine labels in the area. Chianti and Chianti Classico are among the most famous wines in the world, but the region also boasts numerous other superb reds and whites.

Tuscany has delicious local cuisine

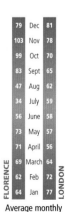

FLORENCE		LONDON
10	Dec	7
12	Nov	10
156	Oct	14
19	Sept	19
23	Aug	21
27	July	22
31	June	20
30	May	17
26	April	13
21	March	10
156	Feb	7
10	Jan	6

Average monthly temperature °C (Celsius)

FLORENCE		LONDON
79	Dec	81
103	Nov	78
99	Oct	70
83	Sept	65
47	Aug	62
34	July	59
56	June	58
73	May	57
71	April	56
69	March	64
62	Feb	72
64	Jan	77

Average monthly rainfall mm (millimetres)

Culture

Tuscany is renowned around the world for its cultured cities, and it has an incredibly rich artistic and historical heritage

"While Florence has plenty to marvel at outside, it's when you go inside that you really get an idea of the treasures in the city"

THE ETRUSCANS WERE THE VERY FIRST settlers in this area, and in Italy. They had a highly cultured civilisation and arrived in the country nearly three millennia ago, where they favoured strategic hilltop locations – the sites of many of Tuscany's main towns today. Some, such as Volterra, still have the original fortified walls. Chiusi was the Etruscan centre of power and the town's fine museum exhibits numerous remains, including friezes, cremation urns and ceramics.

History and growth
Tuscany's most significant historical period began in the Middle Ages when the area was almost a permanent battlefield between warfaring factions vying for power. Witness to the strife between Florentine, Sienan and Pisan armies are the numerous fortified hilltop towns in the region. For instance, Lucca and Monteriggioni both retain their encircling stone ramparts.

During this period, Pisa and its powerful navy were the main centre of power and the city enjoyed great prosperity, reflected in the fine examples of Romanesque architecture, such as the Duomo with its intricately tiered facade, and the Leaning Tower of Pisa. One of Italy's most photographed monuments, this is where Galileo carried out experiments on the velocity of falling objects.

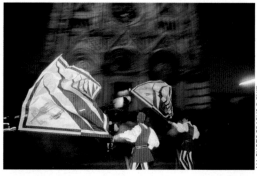

A flag-bearer performing at the Siena *Palio* festival

By the 15th century, Florence had defeated both Siena and Pisa and started its ascent to major world power, as well as its rise to international fame as the birthplace of the Renaissance. Considered by many as the pinnacle of cultural and scientific expression, the Renaissance, which spanned the 15th and 16th centuries, marked a turning point in European civilisation. While several cities patronised the arts during this time, none can match the splendour of Florence, where the ruling Medici family provided much of the economic impetus behind the 'rebirth' of the arts.

A stroll through the streets of Florence today provides living testimony to the richness of the Renaissance. The city is home to a catalogue of work by the world's finest artists: Botticelli, Giotto, Michelangelo, Caravaggio and Titian are all well represented, as are Florentine-born Filippino Lippi and Fra Bartolomeo.

Cultural delights
Architectural delights include St Mark's convent, whose simple but elegant facade is home to several exquisite frescoes. Then there's the highly ornate Duomo. Its burnt-orange tiled dome is considered by many to be Florence's most famous symbol, along with the bell tower designed by Giotto. Europe's fourth largest church, it boasts an extraordinary rich facade, with a unique mix of pink, white and green local marble, plus a highly decorative floor inside. In addition, there's the Gothic church of Santa Croce where one of the finest artists, Michelangelo, is buried, and the Piazza della Signoria, which is the centre of Florentine city life, with its imposing Palazzo Vecchio.

While Florence has plenty to marvel at outside, it's when you go inside that you really get an idea

TUSCAN STYLE

Tuscany's artisans are internationally famous for their exquisite handicrafts – no quintessential Tuscan home would ever be without some beautifully crafted rustic furniture topped with hand-embroidered linen. Leather goods such as stylish handbags and wallets form part of true Italian style, and Florence has several of the world's best leather shops. Other local crafts include decorative ceramics (symmetrical and rustic designs are particular favourites), bookbinding with elaborate Florentine motifs, and perfumes. It's even claimed that the high art of perfumery was born in Renaissance Florence. Arezzo is one of Tuscany's wealthiest cities thanks to its thriving jewellery industry, and some of the world's finest creations are made here by more than 2,000 gold and silversmiths.

BEST BUYS
LEATHER GOODS
DECORATIVE CERAMICS
PERFUMES
SHOES AND JEWELLERY

© MILAN TOURIST BOARD

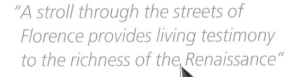

TOP TEN ATTRACTIONS

1 The Central Market, with its hundreds of mouth-watering food stalls

2 A drive round the vineyards of Chianti and a visit to the Maremma natural park

3 The Uffizi art gallery, built in the 16th century

4 Michelangelo's *David*, housed in the Accademia

5 Siena's Duomo. Try to visit the city during the *Palio* festival of medieval pageantries in August

6 The Duomo, Florence. Views from the top of the dome are spectacular

7 The small village of Vinci, Leonardo da Vinci's birthplace, with its fascinating museum complete with models of his many inventions

8 The leaning tower of Pisa, an architectural wonder

9 The fortified village of Monteriggioni, which inspired the abyss in Dante's *Inferno*

10 The Fountain of Neptune in the Palazzo Vecchio

CULTURE

"A stroll through the streets of Florence provides living testimony to the richness of the Renaissance"

of the treasures in the city. The Accademia, Europe's first art school, is home to Michelangelo's *David* – for many, sculpture at its most sublime. There's also Botticelli's *Madonna of the Sea*, as well as numerous other Florentine masterpieces.

The Uffizi, once a Medici palace and now one of the world's top art museums, houses a seemingly endless list of Renaissance gems, such as Botticelli's *The Birth of Venus*, Caravaggio's *Bacchus*, Titian's *The Venus of Urbino*, Leonardo da Vinci's *The Annunciation* and many more. Fabulous frescoes include *The Life of St Peter*, adorning the Brancacci Chapel, and Fra Angelico's *Mocking of Christ*, displayed in St Mark's convent.

Art around the region

If Florence and its millions of visitors get too much, Tuscany offers many other Renaissance jewels. Arezzo's Duomo houses several masterpieces, including Rossellino's *Madonna*, and St Francesco's church boasts Piero della Francesca's unique *Legend of the True Cross*, which is generally considered to be one of the world's finest fresco cycles. Sansepolcro, della Francesca's birthplace, also exhibits several of his finest works. ●

Property hotspots

MAP KEY

● Hotspot
◐ Major town/city
66 Road numbers

■ It boasts an unparalleled selection of art, history and culture ■ Public transport links are very reliable ■ There are over 30 schools, offering a wide range of courses in Italian language and culture
■ **Cons** Summer sees relentless traffic, pollution, stifling heat and crowds
■ The outskirts of the city have been turned into an industrial sprawl
■ Florence has two street numbering systems – one residential and one business – which can be confusing.

2. Arezzo

The lively hillside city of Arezzo has an extremely well-preserved medieval town centre, with many interesting churches and museums. As well as being an established agricultural city, it has many thriving antiques, jewellery and gold businesses, including the largest gold manufacturing plant in the world. One of Italy's most important antiques fair is held in the city centre each month.

Two-bedroom apartments in and around Arezzo can cost from as little as €135,000 to as much as €500,000. Three-bedroom newly built homes just outside Arezzo are currently on the market for €240,000. At the other end of the scale, a six-bedroom restored rustic villa with five bathrooms and a hectare of farmland costs in the region of €900,000.

KEY FACTS
■ **Population** 92,448
■ **Airport** Florence Amerigo Vespucci Airport, Via del Termine 11, 50127 Florence, Tel: +39 0553 0615, www.aeroports.finenae.it

■ **Schools** The International School of Florence, Via del Carota 23/25, 50012 Bagno a Ripoli, Florence, Tel: +39 055 646 1007, www.isfitaly.org
■ **Medical** Ospedale San Donato, Via A de Gasperi, Arezzo, Tel: +39 057 530 5841
■ **Pros** Good transport links ■ The small medieval centre has a host of architectural highlights ■ This is a popular area for relocation and there's a growing expatriate community ■ The climate is warm all year round
■ **Cons** Parts of the city aren't very attractive ■ During the summer there's some overcrowding.

3. Tuscan Coast
(or the Versilian Riviera)

Stretching from Monte Argentario in the south to Viareggio in the north, the Tuscan coast is dominated by sandy beaches and pine woods, with a scattering of fishing ports and small bays. This fabulous coast is characterised by clear seas and long, sandy beaches interspersed with rocky headlands.

La Versilia in the north is a 25km coastline with awesome mountain scenery that includes Viareggio, Camaiore and Forte dei Marmi. Viareggio is easily commutable from Florence and Pisa, and is a popular tourist destination. Its most prestigious area is Zona Mare, where a refurbished two-bedroom loft apartment with a 60-square-metre roof terrace, just a 10-minute walk from the beach, costs around €620,000. Property prices here increase by about 10 per cent per annum.

Residential properties include prestigious and rustic villas, ex-olive presses and apartments. An average new two-bedroom apartment in the centre of town costs around €250,000, while a fully renovated Viareggian-style three-bedroom villa costs €640,000. A luxury five-

1. Florence

The capital of Tuscany, Florence lies on the banks of the River Arno in the heart of the Italian peninsula. The city began life as a Roman settlement in the 1st century BC, and reached the peak of its wealth and power during the 15th century under the rule of the Medici family.

Throughout the centuries, Florence has been home to some of Italy's most prominent and influential artists and intellectuals, including Giotto, Botticelli, Leonardo da Vinci, Michelangelo, Dante and Galileo. Today, with a population of almost half a million, this awe-inspiring metropolis is a thriving centre of industry, commerce, tourism and the arts, and offers a wealth of churches, medieval monuments, Renaissance buildings, galleries and museums, as well as beautiful parks and gardens.

An excellent transport system makes Florence easily accessible by road, rail and air. The airport is only 5km from the city centre and the main motorway, the A1, runs from Florence to Bologna and Milan in the north, and Rome and Naples in the south.

Traditional Florentine-style apartments are a popular choice with tourists and make a viable investment opportunity. Furnished city centre flats in good condition range from €290,000 for one bedroom to €460,000 for two bedrooms. Rental incomes range from €700 to €2,000 per week for one-bedroom flats and €1,500 to €3,500 per week for two-bedroom accommodation.

KEY FACTS
■ **Population** 352,940
■ **Airport** Florence Amerigo Vespucci Airport, Via del Termine 11, 50127 Florence, Tel: +39 0553 0615, www.aeroports.finenae.it
■ **Schools** The International School of Florence, Via del Carota 23/25, 50012 Bagno a Ripoli, Florence, Tel: +39 055 646 1007, www.isfitaly.org
■ **Medical** Ospedali Riuniti di Careggi, Viale Morgagni 85, Firenze 50139, Tel: +39 055 427 7111
■ **Pros** Florence is a captivating city

bedroom sea-view villa set in the wonderful hills of Livorno costs around €850,000.

Alternatively, €454,000 could buy a 70- to 170-square-metre apartment in an 11th-century castle with sea views and a private beach and pool.

KEY FACTS
▓ **Population** Follonica 21,172, Orbetello 14,738
▓ **Airport** Pisa Airport, Via dell Aeroporto 1, 56100 Pisa, Tel: +39 050 58 23 56, www.pisaairport.com
▓ **Schools** The International School Florence, Via del Carota 23/25, 50012 Bagno a Ripoli, Florence, Tel: +39 055 646 1007, www.isfitaly.org
▓ **Medical** Ospedale della Misericordia, Via Senese 161, 58100 Grosseto, Tel: +39 0564 48 51 11
▓ **Pros** Orbetello is a very popular weekend destination ▓ The area boasts a number of attractive beaches ▓ The villages and towns have an excellent selection of restaurants
▓ **Cons** Some of the smaller towns and villages have poor public transport ▓ Accommodation is quite expensive.

4. Siena

This ancient city is brimming with attractions. The 12th-century Duomo is one of the most beautiful Gothic churches and it houses works by Michelangelo, Bernini and Donatello. The 14th-century Palazzo Pubblico and the Archbishop's Palace are magnificent buildings, and the top of Mangia's Tower offers fantastic city-wide views.

Two museums and the National Picture Gallery house important local works of art, while the lively Piazza del Campo is one of Italy's most famous squares.

Top-of-the range property is desirable in Siena, with luxury five-bedroom country villas costing around €2,200,000.

KEY FACTS
▓ **Population** 52,775
▓ **Airport** Florence Amerigo Vespucci Airport, Via del Termine 11, 50127 Florence, Tel: +39 0553 0615, www.aeroports.finenae.it
▓ **Schools** The International School of Florence, Via del Carota 23/25, 50012 Bagno a Ripoli, Florence, Tel: +39 055 646 1007, www.isfitaly.org
▓ **Medical** Ospedale, Viale Bracci 16, Siena 53100, Tel: +39 057 758 5111
▓ **Pros** Siena is one of Italy's most enchanting cities ▓ There's a large expatriate community ▓ No cars are allowed into the centre
▓ **Cons** Budget accommodation is hard to find ▓ During August and the festival of *Il Palio*, it's impossible to find anywhere to stay ▓ The town becomes overrun with tourists during summer.

5. Cortona

The quiet little town of Cortona looks out proudly from its hilltop location. Steep, winding medieval streets lead to numerous interesting churches. The town's museums – the Etruscan and the Museo Diocesano, with its exquisite Fra Angelico *Annunciation* – are well worth a visit. At the top of the town are two monuments: the 14th-century Santuario di S Margherita da Cortona, which houses the saint's tomb, and the Fortezza Medicea, which offers spectacular views over the Val di Chiana and Lake Trasimeno.

A city centre two-bedroom renovated apartment with a roof terrace will cost around €295,000. Alternatively, a fully restored, 19th-century merchant's house within easy walking distance of Cortona, with three bedrooms and bathrooms and about three acres of land, is on the market for €1,100,000. A six-bedroom detached villa in need of some restoration is available for the same price.

Florence's Ponte Vecchio bridge shows off the beauty of the city

KEY FACTS
▓ **Population** 22,279
▓ **Airport** Florence Amerigo Vespucci Airport, Via del Termine 11, 50127 Florence, Tel: +39 055 30615, www.aeroports.finenae.it
▓ **Schools** The International School of Florence, Via del Carota 23/25, 50012 Bagno a Ripoli, Florence, Tel: +39 055 646 1007, www.isfitaly.org
▓ **Medical** Ospedale degli Iferni Santa Maria della Misericordia, Via Maffei 18, 52044 Cortona, Tel: +39 0575 6391
▓ **Pros** Cortona offers stunning views and has changed little since the Middle Ages ▓ It's close to Lake Trasimeno, which has a wide range of sporting opportunities and amenities ▓ There's a large expatriate community ▓ Cortona has a mild and pleasant climate all year round
▓ **Cons** Built on hills and different levels, with stone staircases instead of streets in many cases, Cortona can be difficult to access ▓ The town attracts many more visitors than could be expected for one its size, and overcrowding is a problem in the summer ▓ It doesn't have its own train station, so it's necessary to get a bus from another nearby station in order to enter the town.

6. Lucca

One of Tuscany's most beautiful towns, Lucca's most striking feature is its surrounding 16th-century fortification walls, with 11 bastions of different shapes and sizes. Founded in 180BC, the city layout still adheres largely to the original Roman street plan. Lucca has narrow, winding streets and is built on a flat plain. As a result, the ideal way to get around is by bicycle. Spread across the surrounding hills of Lucca are over 300 15th- to 19th-century villas. These are the former country residences of wealthy Lucchesi merchants.

The town's main historical attractions include the remains of a 1st-century amphitheatre, San Martino Cathedral, Romanesque churches, medieval houses, museums, monuments, and the birthplace of the operatic composer Giacomo Puccini.

Hot on the heels of Chianti, Lucca is quickly becoming a favourite among second-home buyers. Slightly cheaper property prices and the availability of quality homes are key factors in the shift towards Lucca. A new three-bedroom house in Massarosa, 12km from Lucca, is selling for €360,000. A charming Tuscan farmhouse on the hills surrounding Lucca can be purchased for €985,000.

KEY FACTS
▓ **Population** 81,871
▓ **Airport** Pisa Airport, Via dell Aeroporto 1, 56100 Pisa, Tel: +39 050 582 356, www.pisaairport.com
▓ **Schools** The International School of Florence, Via del Carota 23/25, 50012 Bagno a Ripoli, Florence, Tel: +39 055 646 1007, www.isfitaly.org

HOTSPOTS

© ENIT

105

DISCOVER A NEW WAY TO CALL TUSCANY HOME

BORGO DI
COLLEOLI
TOSCANA

You don't have to buy a property outright to enjoy the many pleasures of Tuscany from the comfort of your own home. Fractional Ownership at Borgo di Colleoli gives deeded, freehold interest in a Tuscan apartment for 35 nights each year in perpetuity – meaning you only pay for the time you can actually spend in your Tuscan home. This allows you to share ownership of your apartment with five others for as little as £50,000.

In addition, our management service means you don't have to worry about the upkeep, cleaning, maintenance and security while you are not there. When you are, you'll receive all the services you'd expect from a luxury hotel.

Set amidst 23 acres of ancient olive groves and terraced vineyards, just 30 minutes from Pisa Airport, Borgo di Colleoli boasts an idyllic location, exceptional amenities and easy access to Tuscany's most celebrated attractions.

However, if you are looking for outright freehold ownership, Borgo di Colleoli also offers a range of apartments and villas which are currently available to buy off plan. All are being developed to the very highest of standards and all offer superb buy-to-let opportunities with guaranteed rental income. In addition owners benefit from full concierge service and have the option of having their property fully managed and serviced.

www.viewtuscany.com

ENJOY FOUR DAYS AT FIVE-STAR BORGO DI COLLEOLI

FOR JUST £399 PER COUPLE*

We've made it exceptionally easy to find out more about Fractional Ownership and view our range of properties. Spend four days at the five-star Borgo for just £399 per couple, including flights to Pisa or Florence, airport collection, three nights accommodation with breakfast and a personal tour of the Borgo village – and imagine a lifetime of such pleasures.

homes
overseas
AWARDS *magazine*
2005

Gold Winner

To reserve your stay, simply call us on 0870 243 0314 (quote ref. RG05).

*Terms and conditions apply.
Supplements may be incurred on some air routes.

Medical Ospedale Campo di Marte, Via Campo di Marte, 55100 Lucca, Tel: +39 0583 9701

Pros Lucca is a pretty town that's been almost perfectly preserved ▦ It's close to the popular areas of the Apulane Alps and the Garfagnana ▦ Most cars are banned from the city centre, which has helped to keep pollution levels low

Cons During the summer months, there's a shortage of accommodation ▦ The cost of living is high.

7. Montepulciano

At 605 metres above sea level, Montepulciano is the highest hilltop town in Tuscany. After years of Siena and Florence battling for ownership, Montepulciano finally came under permanent Florentine rule in 1511 when the encircling fortification walls were rebuilt by Cosimo I.

The town's streets are spilling over with well-preserved Renaissance-style palazzi, churches and a cathedral, including the 15th-century Palazzo Communale with its far-reaching views and the beautiful Madonna di San Biagio church on the outskirts.

Montepulciano is the birthplace of the poet Agnolo Ambrogini, but the town is most renowned for its Nobile red wines. There are numerous wine shops scattered throughout the town where you can sample local wines or even try out a traditional Tuscan breakfast of *pecorino* cheese, salami, *crostini* or *bruschetta*.

The Thermal Spa of Montepulciano, located in the neighbouring village of Sant' Albino, is famous for its mud baths and healing waters.

New 100- to 140-square-metre, three-bedroom apartments are selling for the negotiable asking price of €320,000 to €500,000. The sum of €750,000 would buy a 400-square-metre historic villa in need of some restoration, situated in the countryside.

KEY FACTS
▦ **Population** 13,927
▦ **Airport** Florence Amerigo Vespucci Airport, Via del Termine 11, 50127 Florence, Tel: +39 0553 0615, www.aeroports.finenae.it
▦ **Schools** The International School of Florence, Via del Carota 23/25, 50012 Bagno a Ripoli, Florence, Tel: +39 055 646 1007, www.isfitaly.org
▦ **Medical** Ospedale, Viale Bracci 16, Siena 53100, Tel: +39 057 758 5111
▦ **Pros** Montepulciano is famed for the production of quality wines ▦ The town has excellent views ▦ Fewer tourists mean that even during the summer, this is a pleasant place to visit ▦ There's a wide range of palazzos, churches and fine buildings ▦ Montepulciano is well connected to Siena
▦ **Cons** The amenities are more limited than those at most of the other popular Tuscan destinations.

8. Chianti

Set in the heart of Tuscany between Florence and Siena, the hilly landscapes of the Chianti region are among the most gorgeous in Italy. Many places in Chianti are well known because they are the birthplaces of famous people – Boccaccio was from Certaldo, while Leonardo da Vinci's birth home still stands in Vinci. However, the district is most renowned for its vineyards and world-famous red Chianti Classico wine.

The area is littered with villas, castles and stylish farmhouses with their trademark towers, which were originally dovecots. Many of these farmhouses have been lovingly renovated in recent years, often by foreigners.

Some of the most notable places of interest in Chianti are the pretty market town of Greve; Tavernelle Val di Pesa, with its famous abbey; the village of Barberino Val d'Elsa, which has retained its defence walls; and Certaldo, with its brick streets and houses.

Chianti ranks as the top Tuscan location among the British. Greve and Panzano are among the best places to invest, but both are very popular and therefore expensive. Most properties that come onto the market in this region are restored rustic stone houses. A top-notch 19th-century hilltop villa with a swimming pool near Greve, set in 7,000 square metres of magnificent grounds overlooking the Chianti countryside, is selling for around €3,500,000 and would make a very viable rental property.

KEY FACTS
▦ **Population** Greve in Chianti 13,039, Castellina in Chianti 2,737, Radda in Chianti 1,693
▦ **Airport** Florence Amerigo Vespucci Airport, Via del Termine 11, 50127 Florence, Tel: +39 0553 0615, www.aeroports.finenae.it
▦ **Schools** The International School of Florence, Via del Carota 23/25, 50012 Bagno a Ripoli, Florence, Tel: +39 055 646 1007, www.isfitaly.org
▦ **Medical** Ospedale, Viale Bracci 16, Siena 53100, Tel: +39 057 758 5111
▦ **Pros** Home to some of the country's best wines ▦ Ideal for those who are looking for British company
▦ **Cons** In some towns, the number of British outnumber Italians ▦ Public transport is limited ▦ Finding accommodation can be a problem.

9. San Gimignano

The most striking feature of the medieval hilltop town of San Gimignano is the many towers that can be seen from miles around and which offer spectacular views. San Gimignano lies mid-way between Siena and Florence and is called the Town of Towers or 'medieval Manhattan' because it originally had 72 tower houses, built as status symbols and defensive outposts. Only 14 remain standing today.

San Gimignano is now better known for tourism, wine-making and the arts. Places of interest include the stunning Sant' Agostino Gothic Romanesque church, built in 1280, the Museum of Sacred Art, and the Medieval Criminal and Torture Museum.

The San Gimignano area offers a range of farmhouses and traditional stone houses, with prices ranging from €1,500,000 to €3,500,000. For example, just outside San Gimignano, €1,600,000 will buy you an exceptional restored 12th-century stone house with a swimming pool, set in 6,000 square metres of land, with vines, olives and fruit trees. Alternatively, for a farm with its own winery and panoramic views of the medieval towers just 5km away, expect to pay up to €3,200,000.

KEY FACTS
▦ **Population** 7,147
▦ **Airport** Pisa Airport, Via dell Aeroporto 1, 56100 Pisa, Tel: +39 050 582 356, www.pisaairport.com
▦ **Schools** The International School of Florence, Via del Carota 23/25, 50012 Bagno a Ripoli, Florence, Tel: +39 055 646 1007, www.isfitaly.org
▦ **Medical** Ospedale Civile, Borgo S. Lazzaro 5, 56048 Volterra, Tel: +39 058 891 9111
▦ **Pros** The walled town of San Gimignano has 13 towers ▦ It's surrounded by lush and fertile land ▦ There's a growing expatriate community in the region
▦ **Cons** The town is a tourist magnet ▦ Accommodation is very expensive ▦ San Gimignano has no train station.

HOTSPOTS

FOR SALE Property guide

Relocating to Tuscany has always been the epitome of *la dolce vita*, but this popular region has seen property prices rise rapidly in recent years

© KNIGHT FRANK

For many, Tuscany is the most desirable region in all Italy, but it comes at a price

DEMAND FOR PROPERTY IN TUSCANY HAS been continuing at a steady pace over recent years, and 2005 has seen a further rise in demand. There has been roughly ten per cent growth in the Tuscan market from 2004 to 2005 and, as budget flights continue to take off from more and more regional airports throughout the UK, experts say appreciation and demand will proceed at a healthy pace.

Prices are at their highest within a 30km radius of Florence, Pisa and Siena, with the past five years seeing price increases of up to 50 per cent. Consequently, demand has begun to drop off around these cities and pick up along the Tuscan coast and in the areas around Cortona and Arezzo. Most of the region is popular with foreign buyers; for Italians buying second homes, the areas around Cetona and San Casciano dei Bagni are hugely in demand. British buyers have tended to focus on the

RENTALS MARKET

- Tuscany is one of the most in-demand holiday destinations in Italy
- 56% of all visitors to Italy made for Tuscany, with Florence receiving nearly two million visitors per year. Consequently, demand for rental property is high
- Rental income in Tuscany is one of the highest in Italy, with a two-bedroom property in Florence averaging a weekly rent of €1,005 (£684)
- The average property in Florence is yielding between 4.8% and 5.9% from rentals

'Chiantishire' area, but recently overpricing and over-development, the lack of available traditional and rural properties, and Chianti's status as the world's most expensive rural residential area, have resulted in a shift of interest into southern Tuscany.

Properties in this area are generally apartments and townhouses, and consequently you should consider areas further afield, such as northern Lucca and Arezzo, if you are seeking a rural farmhouse or renovation project.

Tuscany is the most expensive region in Italy in terms of property and there is no sign of prices reducing. However, as interest is shifting to neighbouring regions, such as renovation projects in Umbria and Le Marche, the drop in demand could eventually lead to a freeze in prices. ●

TYPICAL PROPERTY

- The stereotypical Tuscan property is the stone-built farmhouse with a tiled terracotta roof, complete with vineyards, olive groves and cypress trees. This is the holy grail for many buyers
- You will also find a number of properties complete with towers and turrets within hilltop towns such as Cortona and San Gimignano
- Within stone-built villages, there are farmworkers' cottages with arched windows and doors
- There are also some fine villas and *palazzi* in the area, painted in the traditional Tuscan red

BORGO DI COLLEOLI TOSCANA

THE VALLEY APARTMENTS

WHAT CAN YOU GET FOR YOUR EUROS?

NEW-BUILD PROPERTY

Located in the Valdera valley, close to Casciana Terme, the Villa San Marco development offers newly built luxury villas. Each villa has three bedrooms and is arranged over two storeys. Situated on the lakeside, they boast stunning countryside views. The grounds, totalling 50 acres, include a swimming pool and palatial Italian gardens. Residents also have access to hotel facilities, which are housed in a former bishop's residence dating to the 9th century.

€588,000+ CODE BOR

CHARACTERISTIC STONE HOUSE

Dating back to the 1700s, this charming property offers chestnut-beamed ceilings and terracotta-tiled floors. Arranged over three floors, the house has two cellars, a terrace and separate balcony, two double bedrooms and a large storage area, which could be converted. Requiring some internal restoration, the property is only 10km from town and all amenities.

€75,000 CODE CAT

TRADITIONAL TUSCAN STONE COTTAGE

Built in the 16th century, this property is in the medieval hamlet of Lanciole in the heart of the Tuscan countryside. The property comprises two cottages, the first of which has been restored and has two bedrooms, while the second requires renovation. Located in an unspoilt area just 50 minutes from the beach, the village offers all basic amenities, including a small bar and restaurants.

€130,000 CODE UNI

CONVERTED MILL

Surrounded by chestnut woods, this stone-built mill has been recently restored. Located in the Teggina valley in the village of Il Mulino di Giacinto, the property comes with two bedrooms. Retaining many of its original features, the living room is built around the original mill wheels. The property also comes with two terraces, from which to enjoy the stunning scenery.

€350,000 CODE CAS

RENOVATION PROJECT

Located near the town of Bagni di Lucca, this semi-detached village cottage is structurally sound but needs fully renovating internally. Arranged over two floors, this property is located on a sunny hillside with panoramic views over the surrounding area. Including a separate stable and barn, which could be used as guest accommodation, this property is full of potential. Located within an hour's drive of the coast and 50 minutes from ski resorts.

€40,000 CODE HII

STUNNING STONE VILLA

Located on a hillside and enjoying panoramic views, this villa is close to a traditional village offering all amenities, including shops and restaurants. The interior has terracotta floors, wooden ceilings and stone fireplaces, the grounds cover 8ha and come with fruit trees, a vineyard and stone terraces. The main property is arranged over three floors and comes with a small tower; there are also three large stone outbuildings which require renovation to make them habitable.

€900,000 CODE APT

AVERAGE HOUSE PRICES TUSCANY

	2-bed	3-bed	4-bed	5-bed
Florence	€331,000 (£225,170)	€624,000 (£424,490)	€1,140,000 (£775,510)	€1,413,000 (£961,224)
Arezzo	€281,000 (£191,156)	€409,000 (£278,231)	€565,000 (£384,354)	€605,000 (£411,565)
Tuscan coast	€310,000 (£210,884)	€580,000 (£394,558)	€816,000 (£555,102)	€1,469,000 (£999,320)
Siena	€371,000 (£252,381)	€548,000 (£372,789)	€666,000 (£453,061)	€857,000 (£582,993)
Cortona	€233,000 (£158,503)	€385,000 (£261,905)	€479,000 (£325,850)	€830,000 (£564,626)
Lucca	€246,000 (£167,347)	€363,000 (£246,939)	€725,000 (£493,197)	€878,000 (£597,279)
Montepulciano	€310,000 (£210,884)	€411,000 (£279,592)	€555,000 (£377,551)	€668,000 (£454,422)
Chianti	€305,000 (£207,483)	€513,000 (£348,980)	€920,000 (£625,850)	€979,000 (£665,986)
San Gimignano	€284,000 (£193,197)	€540,000 (£367,347)	€852,000 (£579,592)	€1,125,000 (£765,306)

PROPERTY GUIDE

€100,000–€500,000
(£68,270–£340,135)

Tuscany still offers some renovation properties in rural locations

€139,000+   CODE CIT
SUBBIANO
Fully restored villa in a private complex, enjoying views over the Tuscan countryside
£94,560+

🛏 1+ ❀ shared gardens and a pool 🏘 situated in the village centre, with all
amenities to hand 🚗 not located on a main road 🅿 private parking

€233,000   CODE CAT
LAJATICO
A partly renovated country house with all traditional features and a 310m² living area
£158,500

🛏 – ❀ 2,000m² 🏘 situated in a rural area, near town 🚗 not located on a main road
🅿 room for parking

€300,000   CODE IPN
SANSEPOLCRO
Located in the Tiber valley, this three-bedroom stone property requires some work
£204,080

🛏 3 ❀ 4,000m² 🏘 situated in a rural hamlet 🚗 access road in good condition
🅿 room for parking

€400,000   CODE HII
CORTONA
18th-century renovated farmhouse with traditional features and close to the airport
£272,108

🛏 – ❀ 3,000m² 🏘 situated in the village centre 🚗 accessible by road
🅿 room for parking

€454,000   CODE PRE
TUSCAN COAST
A unique castle property, divided into 11 apartments, all with terraces and sea views
£308,845

🛏 1+ ❀ shared garden 🏘 situated close to town and amenities
🚗 located on a road and enjoying good access routes 🅿 room for parking

€500,000–€1,000,000
(£340,135–£680,272)

Luxurious and historic rural properties to suit every buyer's tastes

€575,000   CODE APT

ANGHIARI

A well-maintained and fully habitable 19th-century villa with panoramic views
£391,156

🛏 11   ❋ 2,500m²   🏠 situated 2km from town and amenities   🚗 good road access   🚘 room for parking

€588,000+   CODE BOR

CASCIANA TERME

This development offers luxurious three-bedroom properties in rural surroundings
£400,000+

🛏 3   ❋ private garden and grounds of 50 acres   🏠 all amenities on site   🚗 main road access   🚘 room for parking

€725,000   CODE UNI

ANGHIARI

This stone-built country house is in mint condition and boasts a spacious living area
£493,198

🛏 6   ❋ 3,800m²   🏠 situated 2.5km from the town centre   🚗 accessible via a dirt track   🚘 room for parking

€860,000   CODE PRE

FLORENCE

A recently renovated rural home, arranged over two storeys, with a 300m² living area
£585,034

🛏 3   ❋ 3.5ha   🏠 situated close to the city centre   🚗 not located on a main road   🚘 room for parking

€980,000   CODE APT

ANGHIARI

In a secluded rural area, this house boasts timber ceilings and terracotta tiled floors
£667,000

🛏 5   ❋ spacious grounds   🏠 situated close to the village centre   🚗 private drive   🚘 room for parking

€1,000,000+
(£680,272+)

Traditional villas and rambling country estates, all offering excellent facilities

€1,290,000   CODE HII

RAPOLANO

A spacious, renovated farmhouse with traditional features in the Siena countryside,
£877,550

🛏 4 🌼 8.5ha 🏘 5km from the town centre 🛣 easily accessible by road
🚗 room for parking

€1,545,000   CODE PRE

LUCIGNANO

Once owned by the Medici, this unique Renaissance apartment comes fully restored
£1,051,020

🛏 4 🌼 small garden 🏘 situated in the centre of town 🛣 located close to the main
road 🚗 garage

€1,650,000   CODE OLI

CHIANTI

This typical Tuscan country house offers two apartments in an exclusive hillside setting
£1,122,450

🛏 5 🌼 5,000m² plus a swimming pool 🏘 situated 15km from Sienna 🛣 main road
access 🚗 room for parking

€2,990,000   CODE IPN

GREVE, CHIANTI

A luxuriously restored villa, originally a castle, arranged over 3 floors, with 15 rooms
£2,034,013

🛏 6 🌼 5.5ha plus a swimming pool 🏘 3.5km to all shops, restaurants and facilities
🛣 accessible by a road in excellent condition 🚗 room for parking

€3,700,000   CODE CIT

SAN QUIRICO

A restored 18th-century villa with a separate guest annex in the Tuscan countryside
£2,517,005

🛏 12 🌼 6ha plus a swimming pool 🏘 situated 5km from the village centre
🛣 good road access 🚗 room for parking

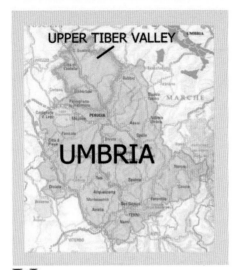

UPPER TIBER VALLEY

UMBRIA

Why Buy in The Upper Tiber Valley of Umbria?

Situated in central Italy, Umbria is probably the country's most gentle and most beautiful region, and the Upper Tiber Valley, between San Sepolcro, and Umbertide. It is 30 minutes north of Perugia and its international airport and centres on Cittá di Castello, with Cortona to the West and Gubbio to the East. The area is served by some eight airports, all within about two hours drive, and a north south motoway links the Tiber Valley to the rest of Italy and Europe. The openess, honesty and friendliness of the population; who use the proverb, "A stranger is a friend as yet unmet"; the climate, the food, the countryside and the ten medieval cities within easy reach on good quality, almost empty roads; allow one to voyage back in time, but with all modern conveniences at just an arm's length.

Visitors have been steadily arriving for twenty years, many have bought an abandoned country house, and with care and patience, have created wonderful homes for modern living, set in medieval shells. The area, by achieving such low key, but high quality popularity has seen prices rising faster than the local, and more expensive area of Cortona in nearby Tuscany. Ville & Casali, the Italian equivalent of Homes & Gardens, ten years ago in its monthly valuations of country properties suggested that the average value of a property around Cittá di Castello was half that of similar properties around Cortona. In the most recent issue, Ville & Casali state that the value of a good quality restored house in the Upper Tiber Valley now commands 78% of the value of its better known neighbours, whilst an unrestored house fetches 91% of Tuscan prices.

On the website propertiesumbria.com John Tunstill has listed some properties that are currently for sale, with details and prices. John was the first foreigner in this area to start buying and developing these beautiful country houses and has sold some two hundred and fifty. He has restored over sixty and is currently working on nine. The site has a list of FAQs which reflect his knowledge and experience gained over the last twenty years. John offers a fully itemised and priced Estimate for all aspects of conversion and restoration work, and also provides an excellent guide to the costs involved for the buying process, and planning applications. For the more adventurous amongst you, John also has a short list of some large and amazing properties that he will be developing in the future.

So, knowing where Umbria's Upper Tiber Valley is, how to get there, and the solid investment returns on property that the area offers, where do you stay when you get there? The obvious answer is with Liliana Richardson de Tunstill, John's wife, at her 11 bedroom, luxurious country guesthouse, La Preghiera, lapreghiera.com. Bought six years ago, an 11th century monastery complex which is a listed building, had been abandoned for forty years and was partially submerged each spring because of poor drainage. The Tunstills gradually repaired and restored the main building, its adjacent chapel and nearby barn. Ideal for a relaxing holiday, special celebrations, a wedding and reception in the grounds, La Preghiera offers a magical setting for an unforgettable experience. Today La Preghiera provides a tranquil atmosphere appreciated by discerning travellers who realise that luxury and sophistication without humanity is quite soulless and who join the increasing number of strangers now met, who have become friends of the Tunstills.

info@lapreghiera.com   info@propertiesumbria.com

+44 207 060 0393   +39 075 930 2428

Umbria

Bustling towns juxtaposed with a mountainous wilderness

© ENIT

FACT BOX

▥ Population 834,210

▥ Population growth 0.97%

▥ Unemployment rate 5.2%

▥ Average 4-bed house price €385,000 / £261,905

▥ Net migration 16,212

▥ Foreign residents 43,151

Contents

Area profile

Overshadowed by its Tuscan neighbour, the landlocked region of Umbria is known as the 'Green Heart of Italy'

GETTING THERE

AIR Alitalia (0870 544 8259, www.alitalia.co.uk) flies from Heathrow to Perugia's tiny airport via Milan, but this is a time-consuming and potentially expensive option. It is usually a better option to fly to Pisa for the northern reaches of Umbria, or to one of Rome's airports for the south. See the Tuscany and Rome & Lazio sections for details of who flies where.

RAIL There are various possible routes to Perugia by train, taking between 18 and 25 hours, and involving between two and six stops. The fastest and simplest routes generally involve Florence as the final transfer. Contact **Rail Europe** (08708 371 371; www.raileurope.co.uk) to book a train to Florence, and **Trenitalia** (www.trenitalia.it/en/index.html) for details of connections in Italy.

ROAD Take a ferry – try **Hoverspeed** (0870 240 8070; www.hoverspeed.co.uk), **P&O Ferries** (08705 202 020; www.poferries.com) or **SeaFrance** (08705 711 711; www.seafrance.co.uk) – or go under the Channel using the **Channel Tunnel** (08705 353535; www.eurotunnel.com). From Calais, take the A26 to Reims, the A4 via Metz to Strasbourg, then take the A35, which joins route E25 at Sélestat. Follow this, and enter Switzerland just before Basel – you will need to buy a €27.50 year-long Swiss motorway tax disc from a petrol station – then take the A2/E35 across Switzerland to Italy. Follow the E35 to Bologna, finally taking the A1/E35 to Umbria. The journey takes approximately 14 hours from Calais.

COACH National Express is part of the **Eurolines** network (www.eurolines.co.uk). Unfortunately it doesn't serve any destinations in the region. However, a coach to Florence takes 28 hours, including a three-hour change in Paris. A daily coach runs from Florence to Perugia and Assisi, and takes between two and two-and-a-half hours. Check with **Sulga** (+39 075 5009641; www.sulga.it) to ensure connection times.

IN RECENT YEARS THIS STUNNINGLY BEAUTIFUL region has justly gained its own place in Italy's list of top destinations. Its rolling hills, awash with flowers and topped with numerous picturesque hill towns, are more than enough to take any visitor's breath away.

Geography

Umbria is essentially hilly and mountainous, with vast areas of lush forests, vineyards and olive groves. The Apennines form the backbone of the region, and much of the south is mountainous, with verdant valleys and numerous waterfalls. Many rivers cross Umbria, including the Tiber (one of Italy's most important and which runs through Rome), Nera, Lopino and Nestore. There are also several attractive lakes, including Alviano, Corbara and Trasimeno, which is Italy's fourth-largest and is situated in the northwest of the region, on the border with Tuscany.

Umbria is home to many stunning hill-top towns

© ENIT

Areas

Umbria's biggest attractions are its lovely medieval towns and cities dotted strategically round the region, some of which count among Italy's jewels. Assisi, in the centre, is one such example, and this picturesque, flower- and fountain-filled town offers fine views over the surrounding countryside. Assisi's main highlight is the Basilica of St Francis, where Italy's patron saint is buried. This beautiful town is one of the most visited pilgrimage spots in the Christian world, with thousands of worshippers flocking here every year.

"Umbria is favoured by EU nationals, drawn by the area's stunning surroundings – and cheaper property than Tuscany"

Orvieto, perched on a cliff-edged plateau with a commanding position over the acres of vineyards below, is no less beautiful. Its striking Duomo is the best example of Romanesque and Gothic architecture in the whole of Italy, and the small town's tranquil medieval streets are flanked with fine examples of local stone architecture. A renowned jazz festival is held here annually.

Perugia, the region's capital, has a perfectly preserved medieval centre, famous for its chocolate, its summer jazz festival and its University for Foreigners – reputedly one of the country's best. The city, with its stone portals, stairways and alleys, boasts several fine monuments, centred around the Corso Vannucci.

The tranquil town of Todi, east of Orvieto, sits overlooking the Tiber valley, and this hill-top position, together with its well-preserved medieval centre, makes it one of the most striking in Italy. This inspirational spot is a favourite with international artists and writers, many of whom have become resident.

The vast stretch of Lake Trasimeno is surrounded by small sandy beaches, flat woodland, sunflower fields and vineyards. This ornithologist's paradise – dozens of species of birds live here – has preserved its scenic tranquillity, even in the light of increased tourism, and remains one of the region's most picturesque spots. Several pleasant small towns lie round the lake, including Castiglione del Lago, Magione and Panicale.

Rich in history and culture, the countryside is dotted with castles and monuments

Piano Grande, a vast plain completely enclosed by mountains, is stunning. This remote area has just one inhabited village, Castelluccio, which is situated on the top of a hill above Piano Grande and has some of Italy's most panoramic views and reportedly Europe's best hang gliding!

Economy

Umbria's economy relies on the region's rich agriculture, based around cattle and pig farming and olive oil production, found mainly in small family enterprises. Hydroelectricity is also a vital part of the economy and there are several plants along the river Nera. Manufacturing, including chemicals, iron and steel, food processing and textiles form the more modern aspects of Umbria's industry, although all are small scale. Tourism is becoming increasingly important, as more and more visitors discover the region's treasures.

Culture

Rich in history, culture and tradition – and with much of it well preserved – the Umbrian landscape boasts a proud legacy of unique monuments and historic cities. Along with Tuscany and Lazio, this was an Etruscan stronghold, a presence that is keenly felt in the landscape, people and traditions. Later conquered by the Romans, Umbria became a key player in the Papal States before becoming part of Italy in the reunification in the 1860s. Many of its historic towns have vital religious significance – Assisi is perhaps the best example – and there are several superb Umbrian churches.

Artisan handicraft is very important in the region, which is home to some of Italy's more beautiful ceramics crafted at Orvieto and Deruta. The ceramics, designed using the *majolica* technique (glazed white enamel with intricate decorations), have been highly prized for centuries and are today among the best in Europe.

Social groups

In 2004, Umbria was Italy's fastest-growing region, and estimates put the population increase at 17 per cent. Along with Emilia-Romagna and Lombardy, Umbria also has one of Italy's fastest-growing foreign populations (up by nearly 12 per cent in 2004) and over 43,000 foreigners are resident here. The area is favoured by EU nationals; the largest groups are Germans followed by British, who are drawn by the area's stunning natural surroundings – and cheaper property than, say, Tuscany. This trend is expected to continue in the near future.

FACTS

■ The writer Henry James reportedly called Umbria "the most beautiful garden in the world"

■ Umbrians are renowned for their hospitable and friendly nature – the inhabitants of Amelia and Narni claim to be Italy's friendliest

■ Umbria is the only Italian region without a coast

PROFILE

FOOD AND DRINK

Local cuisine is essentially country fare and makes liberal use of olive oil. Many claim Umbria produces Italy's best beans, tomatoes and cured meats. The sausages, hams and salamis from Norcia are among Italy's most highly prized. *Mazzafegati* (liver sausages with orange peel, raisins and pine nuts) are a particular delicacy. Suckling pig (*porchetta*), often flavoured with fennel, is another local favourite, as are wood pigeon and fresh carp and trout from the region's many rivers and lakes. Black truffles, found in the Subasio hills, are nationally renowned and add a special touch to many dishes, especially pasta. For dessert, try Perugia's fine chocolate or a *focciata* – sweet pasta with dried fruits and cinnamon.

Umbria's wine production is limited but superb, and includes the internationally renowned white Orvieto, usually dry but also available locally in a delicious semi-sweet version, and Sagrantino di Montefalco, a heavy red whose high alcohol content means it's almost a dessert wine.

Umbria has delicious cured meats

PERUGIA		LONDON	
9	Dec	7	
13	Nov	10	
20	Oct	14	
26	Sept	19	
29	Aug	21	
30	July	22	
26	June	20	
22	May	17	
17	April	13	
14	March	10	
11	Feb	7	
9	Jan	6	

Average monthly temperature °C (Celsius)

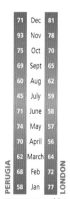

PERUGIA		LONDON	
71	Dec	81	
93	Nov	78	
75	Oct	70	
69	Sept	65	
60	Aug	62	
45	July	59	
71	June	58	
74	May	57	
70	April	56	
62	March	64	
68	Feb	72	
58	Jan	77	

Average monthly rainfall mm (millimetres)

Culture

Although Umbria is more popular than ever, it's still possible to find a quiet corner and some undiscovered cultural treasure…

"A stroll around almost any Umbrian hill town takes you back on a journey through history; they're just as they were centuries ago"

UMBRIA WAS FOR YEARS FAR LESS VISITED than better-known areas such as Tuscany and the Veneto, but the region is one of Italy's best-kept cultural secrets, and its gentle pastoral landscapes are home to a seemingly endless list of beautifully preserved treasures. Umbria enjoys more popularity nowadays, but apart from the pilgrim centre of Assisi, the region breathes peace and quiet much as it has done for centuries.

Early settlers

Its first inhabitants were the Umbrians, a farming tribe who arrived in the 8th century BC, two centuries before the Etruscans, who went on to establish one of their most important strongholds in Italy – most hill-top towns in the area owe their origins to this civilisation. Umbria boasts numerous Etruscan remains, including the necropolis in Orvieto, where the burial chambers are clearly inscribed with the names of the dead inside them, and the temple at Belvedere, a fine example of Etruscan religious architecture. Several local museums contain exhibits, such as ceramics and sculptures, providing excellent insight into this highly civilised people.

The Romans were Umbria's next invaders and legacies of their presence in the region can be found in the amphitheatres at Assisi, Gubbio – today used

There are many architectural gems within Umbria

as a theatre in the annual summer festival – and Terni, which is also close to one of the Romans' top engineering feats, the man-made Marmore waterfalls on the river Nera. One of the country's main Roman roads, Via Flaminia, ran through the region on its way to Rome from Rimini, and it remains a major highway today. On a more macabre note, Trasimeno is the site of one of Italy's largest Roman defeats, the Battle of Lake Trasimeno, where 15,000 Roman centurions were ambushed and slaughtered by General Hannibal in 217BC.

The Renaissance factor

Under Rome in later centuries, Umbria became part of the Papal States, and many of the region's finest monuments were built during the Middle Ages and Renaissance. In common with much of Italy, most of Umbria's architectural jewels owe their presence to religion – St Benedict and St Francis, both highly important religious figures in early Christianity, were born and died here – and several churches are classed among the best in Italy.

The region's Romanesque Duomos are of particular note. Orvieto's is the best example of Romanesque-Gothic architecture in Italy, and many claim it's the country's finest cathedral. The perfectly proportioned church boasts a blue-and-white-striped exterior, fronted by a breathtaking facade composed of bronze and mosaics, with exquisite stone carvings of scenes from the Old and New Testaments. Inside are frescoes vividly portraying the Last Judgement by Luca Signorelli.

The Basilica of St Francis in Assisi is also classed among Italy's most spectacular, and contains superb frescoes by Cimabue, Lorenzetti, Simone Martini and Giotto, whose 28 panels representing the saint's

UMBRIAN FESTIVALS

Umbria is known for its many *feste*, which range from the annual truffle fair in Città di Castello, to celebrations as diverse as the beefsteak, fish and mushroom *festa*. One of the more famous festivals is held in Gubbio; on 15 May the famous Corsa dei Ceri festival, literally meaning 'The race of the candles', takes place. Dating back to the 12th century, its origins are believed to stem from a victorious 12th-century battle. During the celebrations, teams of men race giant wooden candles through the packed streets.

Another famous religious *festa* is La Palombella. Introduced in the 15th century, it is held on Pentecost Sunday, when a dove is tied to a frame encircled with flares. At noon the dove slides down a cable and ignites fireworks and sparklers strapped to a Gothic tabernacle on the Cathedral steps. The ceremony is meant to represent Christ's spirit's entering into the Apostles. Assuming the dove survives, it is then given to the couple last married in the Duomo.

TOP TEN ATTRACTIONS

1. A stroll around the elegant central square in Norcia
2. Exploring the twisting streets of Gubbio, probably the region's most medieval town
3. Giotto's 'Life of St Francis' in the Basilica in Assisi
4. The summer arts festival in Spoleto
5. Santa Maria della Consolazione in Todi
6. The colours gracing the Umbrian countryside in spring and autumn
7. Teatro della Concordia, the smallest theatre in the world, in Montecastello di Vibio
8. Italy's only surviving Etruscan temple, located in Belvedere
9. The Romanesque-Gothic Duomo at Orvieto
10. The amazing views from the village of Montefalco, known as the 'Balcony of Umbria'

life are considered to be some of world's best frescoes. Spoleto's Duomo has eight magnificent rose windows, and the San Pietro church in Perugia boasts a richly decorated bronze interior.

Classic hill towns

A stroll around almost any Umbrian hill town takes you back on a journey through history, with narrow twisting alleyways, stone arches and cobbled streets, just as they were centuries ago. Many towns are universally recognised as medieval gems: Assisi is a World Heritage Site, Orvieto is top of any tourist's list, and Perugia isn't far behind. Even small towns and villages, including Città della Pieve, Montefalco, Norcia, Spello, Trevi – the list is never-ending – are jewels in Umbria's crown.

Other buildings of architectural note include the medieval fortresses found dotted across the region. Those around Lake Trasimeno are particularly good examples: the pentagon-shaped Lion Fortress at Castiglione del Lago and the imposing Castle of the Knights of Malta in Magione give a clear indication of the area's importance during the Middle Ages.

CULTURE

Property hotspots

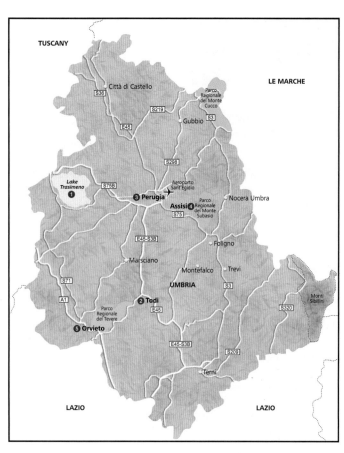

TUSCANY

LE MARCHE

Città di Castello

Parco
Regionale
del Monte
Cucco

Gubbio

Lake
Trasimeno
①

Aeroporto
Sant'Egidio

③ Perugia

Nocera Umbra

Assisi④ Parco
Regionale
del Monte
Subasio

Foligno

Marsciano

Montefalco   Trevi

UMBRIA

Monti
Sibilini

② Todi

Parco
Regionale
del Tevere

⑤ Orvieto

Terni

LAZIO   LAZIO

MAP KEY

● Hotspot
◉ Major town/city
66 Road numbers

KEY FACTS
▥ **Population** 30,219
▥ **Airport** Pisa (Galileo Galilei) Airport, Via dell'Aeroporto, 5612 Pisa, Tel: +39 050 849111, www.pisa-airport.com
▥ **Medical** Azienda Ospedaliera di Perugia, v. Brunamonti 51, 06122 Perugia, Tel: +39 075 5781, www.ospedale.perugia.it
▥ **Schools** International School of Florence, v. del Carota 23/25, 50012 Bagno a Ripoli, Florence, Tel: +39 055 646 1007, www.isfitaly.org
▥ **Pros** The lake is clean and the shallow water warms up quickly in summer, making it ideal for watersports
■ Perugia is only 30km away and is linked by regular buses and trains ▥ Most villages on the shores are secluded and are an ideal place to relax
▥ **Cons** A dual carriageway runs along the northern bank of the lake, which rather spoils the tranquillity in places
▥ Whilst pleasant, the scenery doesn't compare to the wonders available elsewhere in the region.

1. Lake Trasimeno

The biggest lake on the Italian peninsula, Lake Trasimeno, is an area of outstanding natural beauty that has remained largely unspoilt by developers over the years. The surrounding landscape is made up of low-lying hills, lush with vineyards and olive trees, and the banks are swathed with reeds. The lake has three pretty islands: Maggiore, Minore and Polvese, and charming villages are scattered along the shoreline. It is a paradise for nature lovers, watersports enthusiasts and anglers, with a rich and diverse supply of fish, which can be sampled in the local restaurants.

Remains of the Etruscan and Roman settlers that inhabited the lake and its surrounds are particularly visible at the small town of Castiglione del Lago, but the best-preserved historical sites are the medieval castles and fortifications that still stand, almost in their entirety, at Passignano, Monte del Lago and Castiglione del Lago. Also of interest are castle ruins on the islands of Polvese and Maggiore.

This stunning part of Umbria offers investors a variety of properties. A medieval castle, requiring complete restoration, costs in the region of €5 million, while luxury four-bedroom country houses cost between €2.5 and €3.5 million. There is a growing demand for partially restored farmhouses, starting at about €250,000, that can be specifically tailored to a buyer's requirements. Two-bedroom restored stone houses can be picked up for as little as €90,000. Three-bedroom newly built apartments in a small complex sell for €190,000.

2. Todi

The hill-top town of Todi lies 40 kilometres south of Perugia, among some of Umbria's finest scenery. Steep, narrow medieval streets and Renaissance churches are reminders of Todi's long history.

Founded by the Umbrians, Todi later became a part of the Roman Empire and, by the 13th century, was at the height of its power. During this time many great palaces and monuments were erected, such as the Palazzo dei Priori, the Palazzo del Capitano and the cathedral. Other places of interest are the Palazzo del Popolo, in the heart of the town, which is lined with Gothic buildings, San Fortunato and the 16th-century church of Santa Maria della Consolazione.

A two-bedroom renovated apartment with a garden costs around €245,000. Newly built villas with panoramic views sell for about €600,000, as do traditional stone six-bedroom farmhouses. Farmhouses in need of renovation overlooking Todi can be purchased for between €130,000 and €220,000, with reconstruction costs averaging between €20,000 and €80,000. A top-notch luxury villa with pool costs up to €2 million.

KEY FACTS
▥ **Population** 16,692
▥ **Airport** Rome (Leonardo da Vinci) Airport, Via dell'Aeroporto di Fiumicino 320, 00050 Fiumicino, Tel: +39 06 65951, www.adr.it
▥ **Medical** Azienda Ospedaliera di Perugia, Via Brunamonti 51, 06122 Perugia, Tel: +39 075 5781, www.ospedale.perugia.it
▥ **Schools** The New School, v. della Camilluccia 669, 00135 Roma, Tel: +39 06 329 4269, www.newschoolrome.com
▥ Rome International School, Viale Romania 32, 00197 Roma, Tel: +39 06 844 82650/1, www.romeinternationalschool.it
▥ **Pros** Although a small town, Todi has a sizeable foreign population
■ Cultural life in town is more vibrant and varied than its size might suggest, and Todi hosts a ten-day arts festival
▥ **Cons** Set atop a tall, rocky hill, the town is ill-served by public transport
▥ The endless steep inclines won't be suitable for those with ill health.

3. Perugia

The lively city of Perugia has a booming economy and has a population of approximately 150,000. Perugia is rich in history and the arts, and is renowned for its

University for Foreigners, and its international jazz festival.

It was once an important Etruscan city, and many buildings from that era, such as the Etruscan Arch and the Etruscan Well, are still visible. Perugia was conquered by Roman emperor Ottaviano, but became independent after the fall of the Roman Empire. In 1535, the city fell to Pope Paul III and remained in his power until 1860. The medieval old town is located at the top of the hill, and gradually meets with the modern, sprawling lower part of the city. The city's main attractions are the Palazzo dei Priori, the National Gallery of Umbria, the Fontana Maggiore and the cathedral.

Restored period conversions are a popular and profitable choice among investors in this area. A two-bedroom city-centre apartment in a 13th-century building has a monthly earning potential of €550 to €600. Around €450,000 buys an exclusive three-bedroom flat within a medieval stone palace in the centre of Perugia with stunning views across the city. Luxury five- to six-bedroom apartments in the centre can be purchased for around €550,000. Alternatively, if a country location is preferred, around €140,000 could buy the ruins of an old Umbrian stone farmhouse in need of complete restoration and within easy reach of Perugia city centre.

KEY FACTS

▥ **Population** 149,350
▥ **Airport** Rome (Leonardo da Vinci) Airport, Via dell'Aeroporto di Fiumicino 320, 00050 Fiumicino, Tel: +39 06 65951, www.adr.it
▥ **Medical** Azienda Ospedaliera di Perugia, Via Brunamonti 51, 06122 Perugia, Tel: +39 075 5781, www.ospedale.perugia.it
▥ **Schools** International School of Florence, v. del Carota 23/25, 50012

Bagno a Ripoli, Florence, Tel: +39 055 646 1007, www.isfitaly.org
▥ **Pros** Home to the Italian University for Foreigners, the city has a cosmopolitan feel ▥ The city plays host to a range of cultural events, including the Umbria Jazz Festival ▥ Extensive bus and train routes provide easy access to most of the city
▥ **Cons** Drab suburbs and ugly estates surround the medieval centre ▥ The city is the busiest in Umbria, so it's not ideal for those after a relaxing retreat.

4. Assisi

The small medieval town of Assisi, with a population of around 25,000, is perched on a ridge of Monte Subasio. The town's lush surroundings of olive trees and agricultural fields have remained unspoilt for centuries. Assisi is famed the world over as a spiritual centre and the place where St Francis of Assisi founded his religious order. During the spring and summer, Assisi becomes extremely congested as millions of visitors make a pilgrimage.

The town's highlights include: the grand Basilica, built as a monument to St Francis and with world-famous frescoes by some of Italy's finest painters; the Roman Temple of Minerva; Palazzo dei Priori; San Rufino Cathedral; and Rocca Maggiore.

A central one-bedroom flat costs around €115,000. Two-bedroom apartments sell for about €185,000 and generate a weekly rental income of €400 to €700. Renovated farmhouses in the surrounding countryside sell for €500,000 to €775,000.

KEY FACTS

▥ **Population** 25,346
▥ **Airport** Rome (Leonardo da Vinci) Airport, Via dell'Aeroporto di Fiumicino 320, 00050 Fiumicino (RM), Tel: +39 06 65951, www.adr.it

You're spoilt for choice, with many medieval towns to choose from

▥ **Medical** U.s.l. N. 2 Dell'umbria Ospedale, Via Fuori Porta Nuova 10, 06081 Assisi, Tel: +39 075 812824
▥ **Schools** International School of Florence, v. del Carota 23/25, 50012 Bagno a Ripoli, Florence, Tel: +39 055 646 1007, www.isfitaly.org
▥ **Pros** Assisi is full of beautiful architecture and set in a striking position halfway up Monte Subasio ▥ Once the tourists have left for the evening, tranquillity descends on Assisi
▥ **Cons** The town is rife with tacky commercial exploitation ▥ Sightseers and pilgrims saturate Assisi for most of the year ▥ Some living costs are high as tourist demand pushes up prices.

5. Orvieto

Perched high on a rugged volcanic rock, Orvieto dates back as far as the Iron Age. It became an important Etruscan city during the 7th century BC, but was wiped out by the Romans in 256BC. By the Middle Ages the city had grown in stature once more.

21st-century Orvieto retains a medieval flavour, with narrow lanes and the spectacular cathedral dominating the city skyscape. A ban has been imposed on driving in the Old City, but a funicular railway, a series of lifts and escalators, and a minibus transport people up to the Medieval Quarter. Besides Etruscan remains and medieval and Renaissance monuments, a

must-see is the vast 'secret city', a system of underground alleys.

A three-bedroom apartment in a renovated stone building close to the cathedral yields a weekly return of around €750 in high season, while the return on a two-bedroom country apartment in a converted farmhouse can be as much as €1,200 during peak season.

KEY FACTS

▥ **Population** 20,709
▥ **Airport** Rome (Leonardo da Vinci) Airport, Via dell'Aeroporto di Fiumicino 320, 00050 Fiumicino (RM), Tel: +39 06 65951, www.adr.it
▥ **Medical** Azienda U.s.l. N.4 Ospedale Nuovo, Via Sette Martiri, 05019 Orvieto Scalo, Tel: +39 0763 3071
▥ **Schools** The New School v. della Camilluccia 669, 00135 Roma, Tel: +39 06 329 4269, www.newschoolrome.com
▥ Rome International School, Viale Romania 32, 00197 Roma, Tel: +39 06 844 82650/1, www.romeinternationalschool.it
▥ **Pros** Orvieto is home to some of the finest food in Italy, and is renowned for its white wine ▥ The Old City is in a strikingly beautiful location atop a volcanic plateau ▥ It is well-served by a motorway and regular mainline trains ▥ Out of season the town is exceedingly peaceful
▥ **Cons** The funicular railway struggles to cope with demand when the city is swamped with tourists ▥ It could be hard to find employment here, though Rome is only an 80-minute commute.

© ENIT

FOR SALE Property guide

Popular yet still affordable, Umbria offers similar scenery and architecture to Tuscany

PROPERTY GUIDE

Prices have risen sharply in Umbria's beautiful towns, but they still offer good value compared with Tuscany

UMBRIA WAS LONG LOOKED UPON AS A backwater, due to its agriculturally led economy and lack of job opportunities. However, as buyers began to see this region as an unspoilt and undeveloped alternative to Tuscany, foreign investors started to flood the market.

Prices rose by eight per cent in 2002, as British, Dutch and German buyers arrived in force. Today it is Italy's second most popular region, and consequently has become one of the priciest. Property has been doubling in price over the past couple of years, making the region a safe investment. Three-bedroom houses sell for an average of €375,000 in Assisi, or €278,000 in Todi. However, this is still far cheaper than Tuscany, where architecturally similar properties offer the same stunning countryside and surroundings. Here, a three-bedroom house can sell for €624,000 in Florence and €513,000 in Chianti. And unlike Tuscany, it is still possible to find a renovation property for a reasonable price, although some run-down farmhouses can sell for in excess of €200,000.

Demand for property in Umbria continues to strengthen as prices in bordering Tuscany become out of reach for many people. The countryside is dotted with old farms and the ruins of stone houses (*casali*), which can be a perfect investment. *Casali* are often large and can vary a great deal in price, according to their state of repair and the amount of land for sale. In general they are still cheaper than a comparable property in Tuscany. Smaller *rustici* (farm buildings) offer an economic alternative to *casali*, but are not usually sold with a great deal of land.

As Umbria's Etruscan towns and villages become annual tourist attractions, renovated town buildings are regarded as a smart investment for those seeking a tourist business, such as a hotel or B&B. The rentals market is very strong in Umbria and it generally lasts much of the year, with a two-bedroom property earning an income of €625 on Lake Trasimeno and up to €930 in Todi. ●

TYPICAL PROPERTIES

■ There are a lot of similarities between Tuscan and Umbrian architecture, which has enticed many buyers over the border

■ Light-coloured stone, similar to that used in Tuscany, dominates the building materials and gives buildings a warm glow in the setting sun

■ Towers are a typical feature of properties in the region and come in all shapes and sizes, from tall and thin to short and fat

■ Intricate wrought-iron work decorates many houses in the form of balconies, lamp posts, window grilles and door handles

■ Hill-top villages and farming communities offer an array of basic stone cottages and houses

■ Arches are a prominent feature in Umbrian property and are used around windows and door frames. Some properties also come with a *porta della morte* (door of death) on the inside wall of a house, and coffins would once have exited the property through these. Many have been filled in now, but the frames still often remain

PROPERTIESUMBRIA
LILIANA & JOHN TUNSTILL

Their own houses for sale in umbria ... **www.propertiesumbria.com**

WHAT CAN YOU GET FOR YOUR EUROS?

RUINED POST HOUSE

This interesting property is located on a hillside in Città di Castello, and once guarded the road running inland from Fano on the coast. Offering panoramic views of the surrounding woodland and complete with a tower, this unique property comes with 4ha, which could provide space for a garden and swimming pool.

€260,000 CODE IPN

FULLY RESTORED WATER MILL

This working water mill is situated close to Todi and originates from the 12th century. Built in a traditional style, with wood-beamed ceilings, terracotta floor tiles and wooden window and door frames, this property comes with grounds of 1,300m² including an orchard. There are also a couple of outbuildings that would be ideal as apartments for rental.

€550,000 CODE OLI

CLASSIC ITALIAN PROPERTY

This elegant property, constructed of stone and brick, has been fantastically restored and comes complete with hand-made floor and ceiling tiles, exposed beams and three marble-clad ensuite bathrooms. Only 800 metres from shops, bars and restaurants, this three-bedroom house is ready for habitation. The gardens are well established and offer a paved terrace, ideal for barbecues, and a pool.

€750,000 CODE TEC

HILLSIDE VILLA

Located between Città di Castello and Umbertide, this habitable villa has a traditionally designed interior and sits on a hillside, affording stunning views. Arranged over three floors, the property has four bedrooms and a small annex. With 20,000m² of grounds, an entrance gate and tree-lined driveway, this luxurious property would be ideal as a permanent residence.

€980,000 CODE APT

RUIN UNDERGOING RESTORATION

The price of this imposing ruin includes all renovation costs, and restoration is due to be completed over two years. With the option of choosing the finish, from two to three apartments, or as a unique three-bedroom property, this is a fantastic opportunity. Situated in 8,000m² of land and only 15 minutes from the desirable Lake Trasimeno resort, it's perfect as a rental investment.

€1,200,000 CODE UMB

17TH-CENTURY PROPERTY

Situated in the countryside between Cortona and Gubbio, this fully habitable property has 424m² of living space and 1.6ha of land. It comprises a main house, guest house and annex; the main building is arranged over three floors and includes a tower. There are three bedrooms, a jacuzzi, a modern kitchen and study area in the main house, and a further bedroom in the annex. A fabulous property for the more affluent buyer.

€2,300,000 CODE CIT

AVERAGE HOUSE PRICES UMBRIA

	2-bed	3-bed	4-bed	5-bed
Lake Trasimeno	€168,000 (£114,286)	€312,000 (£212,245)	€337,000 (£229,252)	€443,000 (£301,361)
Todi	€175,000 (£119,048)	€278,000 (£189,116)	€443,000 (£301,361)	€644,000 (£438,095)
Perugia	€254,000 (£172,789)	€331,000 (£225,170)	€449,000 (£305,442)	€599,000 (£407,483)
Assisi	€262,000 (£178,231)	€375,000 (£255,102)	€615,000 (£418,367)	€697,000 (£474,150)
Orvieto	€189,000 (£128,571)	€349,000 (£237,415)	€595,000 (£404,762)	€603,000 (£410,204)

PROPERTY GUIDE

€100,000–€700,000
(£68,025–£476,190)

Delightful Umbrian farmhouses and renovation projects dominate the market

€110,000   CODE IPN

CITTÀ DI CASTELLO

In an isolated hill-top village, this house has traditional features, but requires work
£74,830

🛏 5 ❀ 2ha 🏠 situated in the village centre 🚗 access by country road 🅿 room for parking

---

€240,000   CODE TEC

UMBERTIDE

A traditional farmhouse currently being restored in a traditional style, with good views
£163,265

🛏 – ❀ with a large garden 🏠 situated 10 minutes drive from town 🚗 accessible by a main road 🅿 room for parking

---

€395,000   CODE IPN

CITTÀ DI CASTELLO

This restored barn has been converted into a cottage, and enjoys rural surroundings
£268,705

🛏 3 ❀ 1,000m² 🏠 situated 10 minutes from the town centre 🚗 accessible by a tarmacked road 🅿 room for parking

---

€650,000   CODE APT

NEAR PERUGIA

This restored house, set on a hillside, requires some internal work, but it is habitable
£442,175

🛏 – ❀ 7,000m² 🏠 situated 8 minutes from the village centre 🚗 accessible by a main road 🅿 room for parking

---

€700,000   CODE IPN

MONTEPULCIANO

This well-designed and traditionally furnished farmhouse has fantastic rental potential
£476,190

🛏 4 ❀ 5,000m² 🏠 situated 15 minutes from the village centre 🚗 accessible by a main road 🅿 room for parking

€700,000+
(£476,190+)

Outside the ski resorts, there are some truly magnificent modern villas

€750,000 CODE OLI

PASSIGNANO

This refurbished house offers breathtaking views and comes with gardens and a pool

£510,205

– with large gardens and a swimming pool situated in the village centre not located on a main road room for parking

€1,600,000 CODE PRE

UMBERTIDE

This historic restored abbey dates to the Renaissance and offers great rental potential

£1,088,435

10 with expansive grounds situated a short drive from the town centre not located on a main road room for parking

€2,400,000 CODE IPN

MASSA MARTANA

A modern villa with pool, plus a mill and farmhouse to restore, in scenic surroundings

£1,632,653

6 2ha situated 5 minutes from the village centre not located on a main road room for parking

€3,218,000 CODE CIT

CHIUSI

A rare opportunity to buy a complex of 18 apartments, surrounded by woodlands

£2,189,115

– Each apartment has private gardens and shared use of a pool situated 25 minutes from the town centre not located on a main road room for parking

€8,600,000 CODE CIT

CORTONA

A unique old convent offering six apartments, a gym, church and country house

£5,850,340

10 7ha plus a pool situated 20 minutes from Cortona not located on a main road room for parking

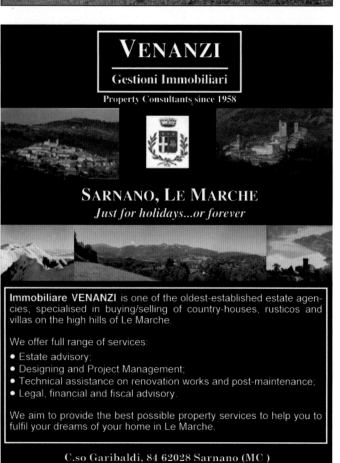

Le Marche & Abruzzo

From Abruzzo's craggy peaks to Le Marche's gentle hills

© ENIT

FACT BOX

Le Marche
- ■ **Population** 1,484,601
- ■ **Population growth** 0.92%
- ■ **Unemployment rate** 4.4%
- ■ **Average 4-bed house price** €315,000 / £214,286
- ■ **Net migration** 23,714
- ■ **Foreign residents** 70,557

Abruzzo
- ■ **Population** 1,273,284
- ■ **Population growth** 0.86%
- ■ **Unemployment rate** 5.4%
- ■ **Average 4-bed house price** €282,000 / £191,837
- ■ **Net migration** 15,313
- ■ **Foreign residents** 32,466

Contents

Area profile

These lesser-known regions form the backbone of central Italy and hide some of the country's best-kept secrets…

GETTING THERE

AIR The regions are served by two small international airports; **Ryanair** (0871 246 0000; www.ryanair.com) flies from Stansted to Pescara and Ancona Falconara airports. Another possibility is to fly to Rome or Rimini – see the Rome & Lazio and Emilia-Romagna sections for details.

RAIL The journey from London Waterloo requires between two and four changes, and takes between 18 and 21 hours. The fastest route involves a change at Paris for Milan, where you should take an intercity along the main east coast line to your destination. For bookings and information contact **Rail Europe** (08708 371 371; www.raileurope.co.uk) and **Trenitalia** (www.trenitalia.it/en/index.html).

ROAD Take a ferry – try **SeaFrance** (08705 711 711; www.seafrance.co.uk), **Hoverspeed** (0870 240 8070; www.hoverspeed.co.uk), or **P&O Ferries** (08705 202 020; www.poferries.com) – or use the **Channel Tunnel** (08705 353535; www.eurotunnel.com) to reach Calais. Then take up the A26 to Reims, the A4 to Strasbourg, the A35 south past Sélestat, and follow route E25 to Switzerland. Ensure you have a Swiss *vignette* (motorway tax disc); they cost 40 Swiss Francs (about £20) and are available from various outlets, including petrol stations and border crossings. Now take the A2/E35 across to Italy, and follow the E35 route past Milan to Bologna. Take the A14/E45, which becomes the A14/E55 after Forlì; this is the east coast road, which runs through the two regions.

COACH It takes 30 hours to travel from London Victoria to Ancona with **Eurolines** (08705 143 219, www.eurolines.co.uk), including a three-hour wait in Paris and a two-and-a-half hour wait in Milan. Once there, private bus companies, such as **Reni** (+39 071 804 6504;www.anconarenibus.it) connect towns in the region, but for Abruzzo, Pescara and destinations in the south the frequent trains are a better option.

L E MARCHE AND ABRUZZO OFFER INVESTORS a cheaper alternative to Tuscany in terms of property prices, yet rival the scenery and rolling countryside found in the Tuscan region. They are still relatively undeveloped, and foreign buyers can discover little-known villages and still find that potential bargain renovation project, which has become a virtual impossibility in Tuscany.

Geography

Situated on the eastern side of central Italy, these two regions enjoy a long stretch of the Adriatic, with over 300 kilometres of steep cliffs, numerous sandy beaches – those at the Conero peninsula are particularly stunning – and attractive resorts.

Inland Abruzzo is a mountainous landscape dominated by the Apennines; their highest peak at Gran Sasso, at nearly 3,000 metres, is found here, as are beautiful beech and maple forests, whose autumnal colours are spectacular. Abruzzo is one of Italy's least-developed areas, and nearly a third of the region is protected countryside.

Le Marche is also elevated away from the coast, but has mainly hilly country, where the lush, verdant landscape, medieval towns and rolling hills are reminiscent of Tuscany.

Areas

Urbino, in the north of Le Marche, is one of Italy's great historic towns, whose small size hides its glorious past – during the Renaissance it was one of Europe's cultural centres, on a par with Florence. This compact medieval town is dominated by the colossal Palazzo Ducale, whose simple but elegant exterior hides a wealth of Renaissance treasures.

On the coast, south of Ancona – the region's capital and an important Adriatic port – the small

"Medieval towns and rolling hills are reminiscent of Tuscany"

town of Loreto is within easy reach of lovely beaches and the Conero peninsula, with its unspoilt headland. Loreto boasts a huge Gothic Basilica, home to Our Lady of Loreto, one of Italy's most revered shrines and a major pilgrimage site.

The magnificent Sibillini mountains in the south, which are snow-capped in winter, are a walkers' and nature lovers' paradise. With peaks rising over 2,000 metres (Monte Vettore is the highest), the area has some of Italy's most beautiful landscapes.

Pescara, in Abruzzo, was once a humble fishing village, but has grown to be the region's principal

The regions are home to splendid medieval hill towns and have a Tuscan feel – but without the price tag

© ENIT

© ENIT

Both regions have long Adriatic coastlines and offer plenty of water-based pursuits

port and largest resort. This modern, dynamic city has two harbours – Pescara Marina and Porto Canale – excellent shopping and nightlife, and lovely beaches.

Inland are several attractive hill towns, whose main architectural characteristics are their brick and stone houses flanking narrow, medieval streets. The small town of Penne is of particular note, with street after street of red brick buildings that 'glow' warmly on the hillside. The smaller town of Tollo, perched on a hilltop with lovely views, is well known for its wine production and lies within close proximity to the sea. The town was almost completely rebuilt after bombing during World War II.

Economy

This area of Italy has traditionally been one of its poorest, but recent state investment in infrastructure and industry has brought new prosperity to the region. Unemployment is below the country's average, and in 2004 was 5.3 per cent in Le Marche and 7.9 per cent in Abruzzo.

Abruzzo's economy is essentially based on agriculture, where wheat, potato, olive and grape production and sheep farming are the most important sectors. Hydroelectric power is becoming

FOOD AND DRINK

The area is noted for its fine food – cheeses, salamis and olives are particularly good – and local specialities include *ascolane* (olives stuffed with meat and herbs), coastal delicacy *brodetto* (fish stew), *vincisgrassi* (lasagne with chicken livers and truffles) and dried cod from Ancona.

This isn't one of Italy's best-known wine-producing regions and few familiar labels are found here, although many of Abruzzo's wines are used for blending in table wines, while Le Marche produces Verdicchio, an excellent white. Wine-growers are now beginning to produce boutique wines, with some success, so this is a region to watch out for in the near future.

© ENIT

The region is home to some of Italy's best salami

increasingly important, and large industrial areas – mainly electronics, food processing, paper and textiles – are found around Pescara and Chieti.

Le Marche, the wealthier of the two regions, has a strong industrial economy with manufacturing, shipbuilding, papermaking and pharmaceutical industries at the forefront. Agriculture – mainly livestock, cereals and olives – is an important sector, but less so than the fishing industry, based at the ports of Ancona, Faro and Pesaro.

Culture

Ancient Apennine tribes first colonised this area, which was later invaded by the Greeks whose fortress town of Ancona marked the northernmost point in Greek territory. Le Marche was later governed by the Holy Roman Empire, and Abruzzo by Naples. The area's golden age was during the Middle Ages and the Renaissance, particularly in Le Marche, when the town of Urbino (the birthplace of Raphael, one of the Renaissance's greatest artists) enjoyed Europe-wide fame as a centre for culture. Urbino's greatest ruler, Duke Federico da Montefeltro, was a keen patron of the arts, and his palace houses several jewels, including Raphael's *La Muta* and Piero della Francesca's *The Flagellation*.

Both regions are scattered with medieval hilltop towns, most of which boast fine churches and monasteries, and the area's golden past is reflected in the many palaces, such as the Palazzo Ducale in Urbania and the Palazzo Malatesta in Fano.

Social groups

Abruzzo and Le Marche both saw increases of over 10 per cent in their populations in 2004 – Abruzzo was particularly popular with relocating Italians – and both regions have relatively young populations. Some 70,550 foreigners are officially resident in Le Marche and around 32,500 in Abruzzo. However, EU nationals are in a distinct minority among foreigners and few relocate here from the UK – just 300 live in Abruzzo and 650 in Le Marche. ●

FACTS

■ Le Marche's Frasassi caves boast some of Europe's most spectacular underground formations, with huge stalagmites and lakes

■ Typical local products include beautifully crafted musical instruments

■ The Abruzzo national park is home to unique fauna, including the Italian brown bear, chamois deer, the golden eagle and a sizeable colony of wolves

PROFILE

	ANCONA	LONDON
Dec	10	7
Nov	14	10
Oct	19	14
Sept	24	19
Aug	28	21
July	28	22
June	25	20
May	21	17
April	17	13
March	13	10
Feb	10	7
Jan	8	6

Average monthly temperature °C (Celsius)

	ANCONA	LONDON
Dec	75	81
Nov	79	78
Oct	74	70
Sept	74	65
Aug	66	62
July	47	59
June	50	58
May	55	57
April	56	56
March	63	64
Feb	57	72
Jan	67	77

Average monthly rainfall mm (millimetres)

Property hotspots

MAP KEY

● Hotspot
◉ Major town/city
66 Road numbers

1. Pescara

The city of Pescara, with a population of around 116,000, lies about halfway down the Adriatic coast and is surrounded by pine trees. It is the most important fishing port in Abruzzo and a popular seaside resort. Pescara is a modern city, with a state-of-the-art railway station, a bustling airport, designer shops, bars and restaurants, and good nightlife.

There is little of historic interest left of Pescara, although the Museum of the Abruzzo People is worth a visit, and there is plenty discover by heading a few kilometres inland. Pescara is the home town of Gabriele d'Annunzio and Ennio Flaiano, two of the 20th century's most important literary figures. Every July, the city hosts an International Jazz Festival.

Property prices in the Abruzzo region are up to 80 per cent cheaper than those in Tuscany and up to 50 per cent

cheaper than in Umbria. One-bedroom recently restored apartments can be purchased for as little as €30,000. A two-bedroom apartment, just a 10-minute drive from Pescara city centre, has a rental potential of €430 to €800 in peak season.

KEY FACTS

■ **Population** 116,226
■ **Airport** Rome (Fiumicino) Airport, Via dell'Aeroporto di Fiumicino 320, 00050 Fiumicino, Tel: +39 06 65951, www.adr.it ■ Abruzzo International Airport, Via Tiburtina Km 229,100, 65131 Pescara Tel: +39 085 4324200, www.abruzzo-airport.it
■ **Medical** Ospedale Di Pescara centralino, Via Paolino Renato 47, 65124 Pescara, Tel: +39 085 4251, www.ausl.pe.it
■ **Schools** Rome International School, Viale Romania 32, 00197 Roma, Tel: +39 06 844 82650/1, www.romeinternationalschool.it ■ CCI – The Renaissance School, Via Cavour 13, Lanciano, Tel: +39 0872 714969, www.ccilanciano.com
■ **Pros** Pescara is on a railway mainline and is served by a motorway and regular buses, making it an

excellent base for exploring and enjoying Abruzzo ■ There are regular flights from London, and regular catamarans run from here to Croatia ■ The city is home to many trendy cafés and boutiques ■ The Pescara International Jazz Festival attracts top performers from across the world
■ **Cons** The heavy development of the resort has drained some of Pescara's appeal ■ Pescara took heavy bomb damage during World War II and is consequently quite unattractive.

2. Urbino

As a World Heritage Site, Urbino is one of the most important towns in Le Marche. Located on the site of an ancient Roman settlement, this Renaissance town sprang up during the 15th century under the reign of Federico da Montefeltro, and practically the whole town dates from this period.

Urbino's most stunning feature is the Royal Palace; its two elegant towers dominate the skyline. Although not much to look at from the outside, its interior is exquisite. Today the Palace houses the National Gallery of Le Marche and the Archaeological Museum. Urbino is the birthplace of the great artist Raphael, several of whose works are on display in the National Gallery. The town's main economies are agriculture and tourism, and it is known for its historic university. The liveliest area of town is the Piazza della Repubblica.

One-bedroom apartments in a converted farmhouse just outside Urbino, with communal

gardens, a pool and panoramic views of the town cost between €85,000 and €135,000, and would make ideal second homes or rental properties. Around €300,000 buys a traditional four-bedroom country house near Urbino, in need of internal restoration. Alternatively, the same amount could buy a four-bedroom town house, split into two flats, in the heart of Urbino, which would make a great rental prospect.

KEY FACTS

■ **Population** 15,270
■ **Airport** Ancona Falconara Airport, pl. Sordoni 1, 60015 Falconara Marittima, Tel: +39 071 28271, www.ancona-airport.com
■ **Medical** Azienda Ospedaliera Ospedale San Salvatore, Via Bonconte da Montefeltro 1, 61029 Urbino, Tel: +39 0722 350521
■ **Schools** International School of Florence, v. del Carota 23/25, 50012 Bagno a Ripoli, Florence, Tel: +39 055 646 1007, www.isfitaly.org
■ **Pros** The town bustles with activity, and there is plenty of live music and nightlife during university term time ■ The Palazzo Ducale is one of the finest Renaissance palaces in Italy ■ Urbino is full of splendid old buildings and is considered the most alluring destination in Le Marche ■ The university offers a language and culture course to foreigners in July and August
■ **Cons** A hill town, Urbino is poorly served by public transport.

3. Monti Sibillini

The awesome Sibillini mountains have been a national park since 1993 and are home to a diversity of wildlife and fauna, including wolves, bears, wild cats, golden eagles, hawks, peregrine falcons, and beech, ash and hornbeam trees. The mountains offer year-round activities for lovers of outdoor pursuits, such as mountain-biking, rambling, and horse-riding, as well as skiing during winter.

Carved out of limestone by ancient glaciers, this wooded mountain range is an area of outstanding natural beauty, and is a haven of peace, tranquillity and fresh air. But civilisation is close at hand, in the form of a number of small, medieval towns and villages, including Amandola, Montefortino and Arquata del Tronto, with its fabulous fortress.

A completely restored two-bedroom house, with stunning views of the Sibillini mountains, can be bought for around €300,000. A six-bedroom farmhouse requiring internal refurbishment close to the Sibillini national park can be purchased for €400,000.

KEY FACTS

 Population Acquacanina 128
 Amandola 3,966 Acquasanta Terme 3,343 Montegallo 619
 Montemonaco 680 Norcia 4,872
 Airport Rome (Fiumicino) Airport, Via dell'Aeroporto di Fiumicino 320, 00050 Fiumicino, Tel: +39 06 65951, www.adr.it
 Medical Unita' Sanitaria Locale N. 24 Ex Sede Ospedale Mazzoni, Viale Della Rimembrenza, 63100 Ascoli Piceno, Tel: +39 736 252550
 Schools Rome International School, Viale Romania 32, 00197 Roma, Tel: +39 06 844 82650/1, www.romeinternationalschool.it
 CCI – The Renaissance School, Via Cavour 13, Lanciano, Tel: +39 0872 714969, www.ccilanciano.com
 Pros The national park is home to 220 species of fauna, and hundreds of species of flora, so would suit nature lovers There is fine architecture to be found in the stone-built, cobbled towns dotted throughout the stunning range
 Horse-riding, hiking, hang-gliding and skiing are popular here
Cons Public transport is scarce, so car ownership is a must Though the barren windswept peaks and the flowery valleys feel like another world,

the area still fills with tourists in the summer months.

4. Loreto

The hill town of Loreto in the Le Marche region is famed world-wide as the site of the Santa Casa (Holy House) and is a holy shrine to the Virgin Mary, with thousands of pilgrims flocking to the town each year. It is claimed that the brick house, believed to have been where Mary lived when in Nazareth, was transported to Loreto by angels in 1294. The Holy House is now surrounded by the Sanctuario della Santa Casa; the church's grand dome is visible from miles away.

With so many prime properties having been snapped up during the recent property boom, the renovation of abandoned buildings in prime locations now offers some of the best investment opportunities in this region. Old stone houses, within a five-minute drive of Loreto and in need of complete renovation, can be picked up for about €25,000, while around €110,000 buys traditional stone farmhouses, also in need of complete restoration.

KEY FACTS

 Population 11,263
 Airport Ancona Falconara Airport, pl. Sordoni 1, 60015 Falconara Marittima, Tel: +39 071 28271, www.ancona-airport.com
 Medical Azienda Usl N.7 Ancona Ospedale Centralino, Via S. Francesco d'Assisi 1, 60025 Loreto, Tel: +39 071 75091
 Schools Rome International School, Viale Romania 32, 00197 Roma, Tel: +39 06 844 82650/1, www.romeinternationalschool.it
 CCI – The Renaissance School, Via Cavour 13, Lanciano, Tel: +39 0872 714969, www.ccilanciano.com
 Pros The shopping, airport and other

Hill towns nestle between the mountains in the area's national parks

facilities at Ancona are a short drive up the motorway, and there are also regular trains to the regional capital
 The town features outstanding religious frescoes and statues
 Cons The influx of visitors is spread throughout the year, as religious pilgrimages are made in all seasons
 On top of the tourists, people come here en-masse in search of cures for a range of ailments between April and October There are few other attractions, aside from the shrine.

5. Tollo

The small town of Tollo is situated in Abruzzo and has a population of approximately 4,000 inhabitants. Its origins date back to Etruscan times, and through the centuries it has fallen under the influence of the Romans, Lombards, Spanish and the French.

Tollo's economy relies on fruit, olives and vineyards, as well as the famous Montepulciano d'Abruzzo and Trebbiano wines. Sadly, the town was all but annihilated by heavy bombing during World War II. It lies about 25 kilometres south of Pescara and six kilometres away from the sea. The nearby beaches are both rocky and sandy. The breathtaking Maiella mountains, 30 kilometres away, are designated as a national park and include the ski resort of Passo Lanciano.

There are good rental prospects in this area, with a three-bedroom house having a weekly rental potential of €375 to €670. A beautiful farmhouse conversion, sleeping up to seven people, yields a weekly rental return of €950.

KEY FACTS

 Population 4,175
 Airport Rome (Fiumicino) Airport, Via dell'Aeroporto di Fiumicino 320, 00050 Fiumicino, Tel: +39 06 65951, www.adr.it Abruzzo International Airport, Via Tiburtina Km 229,100, 65131 Pescara, Tel: +39 085 4324200, www.abruzzo-airport.it
 Medical Ospedale Di Pescara centralino, Via Paolino Renato 47, 65124 Pescara, Tel: +39 085 4251, www.ausl.pe.it
 Schools Rome International School, Viale Romania 32, 00197 Roma, Tel: +39 06 844 82650/1, www.romeinternationalschool.it
 CCI – The Renaissance School, Via Cavour 13, Lanciano, Tel: +39 0872 714969, www.ccilanciano.com
 Pros This agricultural town is within easy reach of the coast and a national park Pescara is a short hop up the motorway, with a range of amenities and the regional airport The town is well known for its excellent Montepulciano and Trebbiano wines
 Tollo is off the main tourist trail
 Cons World War II bombardment left the town in ruins, and there's little of historical interest left There are few tourist attractions here Though there is a small expat population, a working knowledge of Italian is advisable.

FOR SALE

Property guide

On Italy's Adriatic coast, Le Marche and Abruzzo offer hill towns and renovation properties for a fraction of the cost of those in Tuscany

© ENIT

Inland, the hilltop towns offer great value, while the coastal areas tend to be more expensive

WITH SKIING IN THE WINTER, BEACHES IN the summer and the commencement of budget flights to the area, Abruzzo is prime for development. Abruzzo may not be one of the best-known or best-loved regions among foreign buyers, but it does offer an abundance of cheap property and renovation projects.

The region has been overlooked in the past due to its somewhat bleak appearance and problems with accessibility, and the property market has been historically sluggish. Inland, prices for renovation properties are among the cheapest in Italy as the the local population is deserting the area, thus lowering demand and consequently the cost. However, agents have reported that demand is starting to grow for inland properties, especially those that require renovation, as prices are lower and sources dry up elsewhere. It is only along the coast that prices

become anything like comparable with areas such as Umbria and Le Marche, as locals compete with foreigners for homes close to the sea.

With foreign buyers saturating Tuscany and Umbria, many people are turning to Abruzzo for isolated farmsteads. Since last year, some agents have commented that demand has risen by 100 per cent, with prices quoted as being 60 per cent cheaper than in Tuscany.

Le Marche is much more popular than neighbouring Abruzzo and consequently prices are higher. Areas around San Benedetto and in the mountains still represent excellent value, but generally prices have increased hugely as demand rises and supply dwindles. Coastal apartments can be particularly pricey, while inland it is still possible to find some real bargains.

Renovation properties are not as plentiful as in Abruzzo, however, and the few you do find tend to be inaccessible and isolated. The regions of Urbino, Osimo and Camerino do offer cheaper properties for restoration; much cheaper than the regions of Tuscany and Umbria. Coastal prices can be steep, but even then there is the possibility of hunting down a bargain.

Currently Le Marche represents an excellent investment opportunity, with a high demand for rental property and a market that rivals that of Tuscany and Umbria. ●

TYPICAL PROPERTY

Abruzzo Roughly built stone houses grouped together on the hillsides are found throughout the countryside, while in the towns you will find very austere stone *palazzi*. White stone-built cottages, dating back to the 16th century, typify the region around Maiella national park.

Le Marche Small-bricked *palazzi* along picturesque narrow streets dominate the larger towns, while inland white stone farmhouses and cottages are scattered around. There are also a number of uniquely designed villages in the region.

WHAT CAN YOU GET FOR YOUR EUROS?

MAIELLA STONE COTTAGE

This ruined property in Abruzzo needs complete renovation, and is part of an abandoned village. Situated in the Maiella national park, this traditional property offers amazing views and an unspoilt location. Only 10 minutes from ski resorts and 30 minutes from the beach, this is a unique opportunity to create your ideal home in one of Italy's most stunning locations.

€18,000 CODE HAI

HISTORIC PROPERTY

Located in a quaint village with cobbled streets and characterful piazzas, this traditional townhouse overlooks the village square. Only 30 minutes to Urbino and 70km from the beach, the property has original features such as wood-beamed ceilings and stone walls. Habitable but requiring some renovation work, it is only a few minutes' drive from shop, bars and restaurants.

€65,000 CODE APT

MOUNTAIN PROPERTY

This house has two bedrooms, two bathrooms and a spacious living area of 72m². Situated on the edge of the Gran Sasso-Lago National park, this characterful property enjoys stunning views and is a little under 50km from the beach. With no need for restoration, this is a perfect rural retreat for those who love nature and hiking.

€103,000 CODE ABZ

HILLTOP APARTMENT

Soon to be restored, this apartment has maintained all traditional features, with wood-beamed ceilings, terracotta tiles and a stone fireplace. Located in the town of Farneto, this luxurious property is only 20 minutes from Urbino and Pesaro. The apartment also enjoys stunning views over Le Marche's hills.

€200,000 CODE IPN

PROPERTY WITH SEA VIEW

This newly built house has a spacious living area, including three bedrooms and two bathrooms. The property stands in grounds of 20,000m², and has fabulous sea and countryside views. Only 8km from the beach and 2km from town, it is close to all amenities and would make the perfect family holiday home.

€300,000 CODE CIC

LE MARCHE FARMHOUSE

A licensed B&B this spacious farmhouse located in the Sibillini national park is perfect as a business and offers excellent tourist potential. Easily accessible through the picturesque countryside surrounding Sarnano and Amandola, the property boasts one apartment and four separate bedrooms, along with a bar and restaurant.

€650,000 CODE HII

AVERAGE HOUSE PRICES LE MARCHE & ABRUZZO

	2-bed	3-bed	4-bed	5-bed
Pescara	€202,000 (£137,415)	€238,000 (£161,905)	€315,000 (£214,286)	€410,000 (£278,912)
Urbino	€246,000 (£167,347)	€289,000 (£196,599)	€397,000 (£270,068)	€423,000 (£287,755)
Monti Sibillini	€137,000 (£93,197)	€205,000 (£139,456)	€307,000 (£208,844)	€335,000 (£227,891)
Loreto	€187,000 (£127,211)	€204,000 (£138,776)	€253,000 (£172,109)	€297,000 (£202,041)
Tollo	€190,000 (£129,252)	€240,000 (£163,265)	€280,000 (£190,470)	€344,000 (£234,014)

TENUTE SILVIO NARDI

For guided tours of the wine cellar
and wine tastings please call Tenute Silvio Nardi
Tel. +39 075 8583525 or
e-mail: visite@tenutenardi.com

TENUTE SILVIO NARDI

Località Casale del Bosco - 53024 Montalcino Siena Italia
tel. +39 0577 808269 - fax +39 0577 808614 - info@tenutenardi.com

Rome & Lazio

Home to the country's capital and a varied landscape

© ENIT

FACT BOX

- ■ **Population** 5,145,805
- ■ **Population growth** 0.56%
- ■ **Unemployment rate** 8.7%
- ■ **Average 4-bed house price** €395,000 / £268,707
- ■ **Net migration** 59,991
- ■ **Foreign residents** 204,725

Contents

Area profile

Italy's capital city and nearby villages and ports are steeped in history, having been inhabited for around 3,000 years…

GETTING THERE

AIR easyJet (08717 500 100; www.easyjet.com) flies from Bristol, Stansted or the East Midlands to Rome Ciampino. **Ryanair** (08712 460 000; www.ryanair.com) also flies to Rome Ciampino from Glasgow and Stansted. **British Airways** (08708 509 650; www.britishairways.co.uk) flies from Gatwick, Heathrow, Birmingham and Manchester to Rome Fiumicino.

ROAD For those who want to take their time and see the sites, it's possible to drive down to Lazio. If you take a **P&O ferry** (08705 202 020; www.poferries.com) from Dover to Calais, you then take the E15 from Calais to Lyon, and then the A32/43 to Turin. From there, the A6 goes to Genoa and leads into the A12 to Lazio and Rome.

RAIL TGV trains run from Paris to Milan and from there the ES Rail runs to Rome. From Rome, it's possible to get connecting services to the surrounding area. **Rail Europe** (08705 848 848; www.raileurope.co.uk) can offer more details of services and timetables.

COACH Eurolines (08705 143 219; www.eurolines.com) travels to Rome and from there the regional bus service **COTRAL** (0039 0746 256 750; www.cotralspa.it) offers services to the surrounding areas.

ONE OF EUROPE'S TREASURES AND THE SEAT of one of the world's longest-lasting empires, Rome has always been a popular destination because of the wealth of culture and history on show. It doesn't just have museums – it is a museum. At the same time, it's a buzzing, cosmopolitan city with the usual trappings of less-than-glamorous suburbia on the fringes.

The city is divided into districts named after the seven hills on which it was first built, and by the river Tiber. On the left bank of the Tiber are the Vatican City and Castel Sant'Angelo. Most of the famous sites are to be found on the right bank, including the Spanish Steps, Trevi Fountain, the Colosseum, the Pantheon and Trajan's Forum.

The heart of the city is still the ancient Roman centre but the modern urbanisation sprawls outward in all directions. In the centre, thousands of years of history and countless styles of architecture have been mixed together. There are magnificent Roman remains, Renaissance *palazzi* with Roman columns, Romanesque churches with Baroque facelifts and medieval walls built on top of Roman walls, all topped off with some 1930s fascist

monstrosities. The Rome of the 21st century has been carved out of millennia of wars, fires, papal disputes and architectural genius.

Although they're often overlooked, beyond the hills of the ancient kings of Rome lie fascinating destinations on the sunny Tyrrhenian coast. In the hills bordering Umbria, Tuscany and Marche, and throughout the other parts of Lazio, you'll find places like Latina, Frosinone, Viterbo and Rieti.

Lazio has its warm zone, south of Rome, where wild strawberries and myrtle grow. The area around the Alban Hills is home to Frascati wine, beautiful Renaissance villas and the Castelli Romani – small medieval towns that developed during the Middle Ages. Grottaferrata, three kilometres south of Frascati, is famous for its 11th-century abbey; and Nemi, above Lake Nemi, for wild strawberries.

Towards the coast to Ostia, which is currently attracting investment and regeneration, the landscape changes. Although Rome is in central Italy, it's also in southern Europe. Mediterranean scrub, cork woods, white oak and chestnut trees frame the scenery, and in order to escape the summer heat, Romans head for Lido di Ostia,

Rome may be the most famous city in this region, but there are also many unspoilt villages and ports

© ENIT

possibly taking in the archaeological site at Ostia Antica, the 4th-century Roman port located at the mouth of the river Tiber. After Pompeii and Herculaneum, this is one of the best-preserved Roman towns in Italy .

To the north, Lake Bracciano is popular with Romans and foreign tourists alike. The eighth largest lake in Italy, it's situated 302 metres above sea level in the Sabatini Mountains and is perfect for swimming. No activities or motorboats are allowed on the lake because it's Rome's reserve water reservoir, but there's plenty to see with the 12th-century Orsini Odescalchi castle on the shores, along with the medieval town of Trevigna Rome. There are also the remains of countless ancient Roman villas perching on the cliffs above the shore.

Popular with the wealthy classes for centuries because of its fresh air and thermal spas, Tivoli, to

> *"The Rome of the 21st century has been carved out of wars, fires and architectural genius"*

the east of Rome in the Monti Tiburtini hills, has always been an important settlement. Its 4th-century BC town wall is still visible, as are temples from the 2nd century BC. Home to Villa d'Este, the villa built for Cardinal Ippolito d'Este in the 16th century, the gardens are composed almost exclusively of fountains and pools. Tivoli is also where the Emperor Hadrian built a countryside residence, Villa Adriana.

The economy

As the saying goes, all roads lead to Rome. Perhaps that's why it enjoys such a successful and diverse industrial history. A favourite with film directors, Rome has been the setting for 53 of the classic films

In the Piazza della Rotonda, outside the Pantheon, there's a thriving café culture

of all time. In 1936, Cinecittà film studios opened, and the city is now the centre of a huge industry, with its own Hollywood-type district. Industry giants CAR food distribution are based in Rome, along with major steelworks, hydroelectric power plants, knitwear companies and aeronautical engineering companies. Across the rest of the region, agriculture is the prime industry, and in 2005 the Lazio regional council began investing in the regeneration of the tourism trade.

Social groups

As with most capital cities, inflated property prices in Rome guarantee a certain level of wealth among investors. Young people working in the city are renting, but the surrounding countryside is proving popular with 40- to 60-year-old British people who are looking for holiday homes, with a view to retiring in the area. The fact that prices are generally lower than Tuscany and Umbria is also attracting younger purchasers. Rome has a population of four million, 300,000 of whom are immigrants, predominantly Romanian. ●

FACTS

■ Within Rome is the world's smallest country, the Vatican City, with an area of just 0.44km² and a population of 921

■ There are over 900 churches in Rome

■ Palazzo Venezia, a 15th-century building in the centre of Rome, was once Mussolini's headquarters

FOOD AND DRINK

Fresh vegetables are often fried here

In Lazio, there's a tendency to fry foods. *Fritti* may be battered and deep-fried olives, courgette flowers, or even brains. A particular favourite is raw fava beans, eaten with *pecorino romano* cheese and washed down with a crisp white wine, such as Bianco dei Castelli. Alternatively, try *fave col guanciale* (fava beans cooked slowly with pig's cheek – Romans love unusual meat cuts) or *coda alla vaccinara* (braised oxtail and tomato). Local pasta dishes include *pasta amatriciana*, *spaghetti alla carbonara*, *pasta alla gricia* and *pasta e ceci*. Artichokes are given special treatment in Lazio. Try *carciofo alla guidia* or *carciofo romana*. Spinach is usually sautéed (*spinaci alla romana*) with garlic, pine nuts and raisins.

ROME		LONDON
13	Dec	7
16	Nov	10
22	Oct	14
26	Sept	19
30	Aug	21
30	July	22
28	June	20
23	May	17
19	April	13
15	March	10
13	Feb	7
11	Jan	7

Average monthly temperature °C (Celsius)

ROME		LONDON
93	Dec	81
129	Nov	78
99	Oct	70
63	Sept	65
21	Aug	62
15	July	59
37	June	58
46	May	57
51	April	56
57	March	64
62	Feb	72
71	Jan	77

Average monthly rainfall mm (millimetres)

Culture

Home to a veritable treasure trove of stunning architecture and artistic masterpieces, Rome is a living museum

"Few places in the world can match the variety and splendour found in Rome"

FEW OTHER CITIES CAN MATCH THE CULTURAL splendour of Rome, birthplace of one of the greatest empires ever known. Although Rome is best known as the centre of the mighty Roman Empire, the Etruscans first occupied the city in the 6th century BC, when they ruled central Italy for three centuries. Several museums are dedicated to the Etruscan civilisation, notably the National Etruscan Museum, housed in Rome's Villa Giulia, whose highlights include the 'Husband and Wife Sarcophagus', from a Cerveteri tomb, and perfectly preserved ceramics. The Etruscan Museum in the Vatican also contains numerous Etruscan treasures, including exquisite jewellery.

The rise of the Romans
The Etruscans were conquered by the Romans, whose high level of organisation and sophistication eclipsed all other civilisations that went before it. Not for nothing did the Romans go on to become one of the world's greatest empires, stretching far over Europe, Asia Minor and North Africa.

The centre of the Roman world was the Capitol area, in the middle of Rome. Here are the remains of the Forum, several triumphal arches and the imposing Colosseum – an almost intact ampitheatre that once held up to 55,000 spectators and was witness to thousands of gory gladiator combats and wild animal fights. The Palatine, a vast residential complex of palaces and mansions, contains the House of Livia and Domus Flavia, richly decorated with frescoes and mosaics. The Pantheon, one of the city's symbols and now situated in the heart of the financial and political district, is the best-preserved Roman legacy of them all, and this 'temple to all gods' has a magnificent domed interior.

The Renaissance
Even the highly sophisticated Romans couldn't last forever, and Rome fell into centuries of obscurity, ruled by conquering tribes such as the Goths and Lombards, before the Papacy established itself in the city in the late 14th century. Rome was declared the capital of the Papal States. This return to the centre of the world stage brought with it great patronage of the arts, and Rome, along with Florence, became the centre of art and architecture.

Almost all prominent Italian Renaissance artists are represented here, but Bernini, Caravaggio, Michelangelo, Raphael and Titian were the most prolific. The Piazza Navona district, now the centre of the city's café scene, was once the seat of popes and princes, and boasts a wealth of elaborate Baroque fountains and palaces. Numerous churches

ROMAN STYLE

The fashion industry has long been influential on Roman culture, and visitors to Rome are always struck by the elegant and stylish manner with which the city's residents conduct themselves. With boutiques and fashion schools saturating the city, Rome is labelled the '*haute couture*' of the Italian fashion world.

Since the second century AD, the citizens of Rome have been recognised as being well dressed and impeccably turned out, and several of Italy's top fashion houses are based here, including Fendi and Valentino. Many have looked to Milan as Italy's style capital, but while that city caters to the more popular fashion trends, with designers such as Versace, Prada and Armani, Rome is host to classic boutiques and famous names such as Sorelle Fontana, Gattinoni and Renato Balestra.

You will find a number of elegant boutiques in Piazza di Spagna, including Prada, Armani and Gucci, while the flea markets of Rome can provide an equal wealth of retro wear. For those with a mid-range budget, there are a number of chic stores on the via Nazionale and via del Corso.

CULTURE

ALL PICTURES © ENIT

TOP TEN ATTRACTIONS

1. Throwing a coin into the Trevi fountain

2. Villa Giulia's Etruscan treasures, such as the Cerveteri tombs

3. The Trastevere Botanical Gardens, an oasis of tranquillity within the city

4. The Piazza di Spagna and the Spanish Steps

5. St Peter's and Piazza San Pietro

6. Santa Maria sopra Minerva church, with its azure ceilings

7. The view of the Forum from Tarpeian Rock

8. Michelango's frescoes in the Sistine Chapel

9. The Colosseum from its upper storey

10. The ornate Santa Maria Maggiore church

throughout the city are masterpieces: Sant'Ignazio di Loyola church has a richly decorated interior, complete with precious stones and jewels, and the Santa Maria Maggiore church offer fine mosaics. The Spanish Quarter, centred around the Spanish Steps and Piazza di Spagna, has been at the heart of tourist Rome since the 18th century, and offers elegant Baroque hotels and the Trevi fountain.

The Vatican

Nowhere is the Renaissance better represented than in the Vatican, dominated by the colossal Basilica of St Peter, whose lofty dome (136m high) was elaborately decorated by Michelangelo and finished by his disciple, Bernini. St Peter's is home to Michelangelo's most moving sculpture, the Pietà. The Vatican museums contain treasure after treasure: the Borgia

Apartment and its sumptuously gilded frescoes; the Gallery of Maps with precise fresco maps depicting the Papal territories; the Raphael Rooms, exhibiting the painter's talent at his very best; and the sublime Sistine Chapel, whose 32 frescoed panels represent the very best in Renaissance art.

Modern Rome

Few places in the world match the variety and splendour found in Rome, a city destined to remain centre stage in the world arena: the signing of the Treaty of Rome in 1957 laid the foundations for the EU; the city hosted the Olympics in 1960; and several times a year, millions turn their attention to the city for the pope's religious addresses. ●

Property hotspots

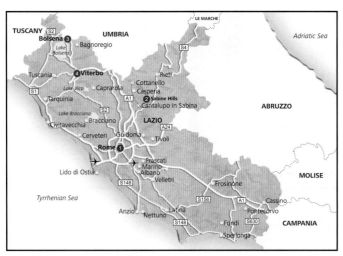

MAP KEY

● Hotspot
◐ Major town/city
66 Road numbers

KEY FACTS

■ **Population** 3.8 million
■ **Airport** Rome Leonardo da Vinci, Tel: +39 06 6595 3640/ +39 06 6595 4455
■ **Schools** St George's British International School, La Storta, Via Cassia km 16, 00123 Rome, Tel: +39 0630 860 021, www.stgeorge.school.it
■ **Medical** Ospedale San Giacomo, Via Canova 29, 00186 Rome, Tel: +39 06 3626 6372
■ **Pros** The city has an excellent public transport network ■ There's a thriving expatriate community ■ The architecture is arguably the most spectacular in Europe ■ Rome is home to a large choice of international schools and has a variety of jobs ■ There are excellent amenities and a sophisticated nightlife
■ **Cons** During the summer months, the heat can become unbearable ■ The cost of living is high ■ Street crime and petty theft are common ■ During the summer, tourists take over the city.

1. Rome

One of the most beguiling and astonishing Italian cities, Rome was founded when Romulus killed his twin Remus. For the next 3,000 years, it survived being sacked, burned, conquered, looted and occupied, and the city's cobbled streets now resound to the march of an army of 12 million annual tourists, here to view the overwhelming wealth of art, architecture and treasures.

Now an astonishingly stylish city with amazingly chic citizens, this bustling, modern capital is a place where scooters and motorbikes swoop past ambling pedestrians, and classical art competes with high fashion.

Rome has a huge cultural heritage that relates not only to the days of the Empire but to the history of the Catholic church, the seat of which lies in the Vatican City at the heart of Rome. The city is awash with churches and temples, the most famous of which are St Peter's Basilica and the Pantheon. There are 67 known underground catacombs, and the ancient forum is embellished with the remains of temples and basilicas.

The list of attractions is endless, from the plundered Colosseum to a huge number of ornate fountains, museums, theatres and piazzas. Rome is also a shopper's paradise, whatever your tastes, and it's heaven for gastronomes.

Being such a cosmopolitan city, Rome tends to appeal to younger investors, and those who are going to work in Italy. It offers a wide choice of central apartments, with larger properties in the suburbs. The past three years have seen significant price rises, and currently 192,000 internationals call the city home.

The most coveted areas are Parioli and Salaria, where an active market has brought prices up to €6,450 per square metre, against an average of €5,600 per square metre. Trastevere and Gianicolo, which offer characteristic dwellings and high standards, are tipped to be the new hotspots and are rising in popularity and price – 2004 saw a price rise of 5.3 per cent.

Rental property in Rome is abundant, but it soon fills up in the summer months when the tourists arrive. Property here is among the most expensive in the country, and while there are good opportunities for short-term tourist lets, long-term lets to students and young professionals would better suit those who don't live locally.

2. Sabine Hills

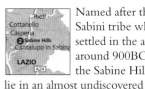

Named after the Sabini tribe who settled in the area around 900BC, the Sabine Hills lie in an almost undiscovered rural corner of Lazio, just south of Tuscany and Umbria. This landscape of rolling, olive-clad foothills is home to a scattering of medieval-structured villages. These offer spectacular views, cool mountain breezes, fields of grapes, olives and sunflowers, and a unique feeling of times gone by. Peppered with papal palaces, ancient churches, castles, abbeys and mountain retreats, they also play host to a selection of traditional festivals to celebrate pasta, wine, olive oil,

polenta and saints days. The olive oil here is considered to be among Italy's finest.

Throughout the 20th century, the villages and towns of the Sabine Hills suffered from depopulation as the inhabitants sought out better work opportunities in Rome and Rieti. This trend is now reversing as a different type of buyer enters the market – those looking for a retreat away from the noise, pollution and tension of city life, particularly those from northern Europe. Low prices in comparison to Rome, Tuscany and Umbria, and the proximity of the area to many attractions, make it very popular with a number of buyers, and village homes in the €100,000 to €200,000 range are selling fast. After spiralling in recent years, there are signs that demand for property is starting to level out, as are the prices.

With year-round active breaks in the area, letting potential remains high even through the winter, although summer is obviously the most popular time for short-term rentals. Properties here are large and so are more suited to family rentals, while the proximity to Rome ensures a stream of visitors.

KEY FACTS

■ **Population** Cantalupo in Sabina 1,629 ■ Casperia 1,093 ■ Cottanello 557 ■ Greccio 1,481 ■ Fara Sabina 11,409 ■ Montopoli de Sabina 3,733
■ **Airport** Rome Leonardo da Vinci, Tel: +39 06 6595 3640/ +39 06 6595 4455
■ **Schools** Rome International School, Viale Romania 32, 00197 Rome, Tel: +39 0684 482 650/1, www.romeinternationalschool.it
■ **Medical** Ospedale San Giacomo, Via Canova 29, 00186 Rome, Tel: +39 06 3626 6372
■ **Pros** Although this is a beautiful rural area, villages in the Sabine Hills are only around an hour from Rome ■ An expatriate community is building

up in the area ■ The climate here is pleasant, and slightly cooler than Rome ■ The area is close to a number of international schools ■ **Cons** Many villages have few or no facilities ■ Public transport to some places is rare ■ The Sabine Hills are becoming more recognised by tourists.

3. Lake Bolsena

The largest lake in Italy, Lake Bolsena is elliptical and boasts two small islands, Bisentina and Martana. Situated close to the rural Lazio-Umbria border, it's also just 100km from Rome. Encircled by low, vineyard-covered hills and beautiful scenery, it's the cleanest lake in Italy.

The main town on the lake is Bolsena, which boasts a pretty medieval quarter and is famous for the feast of Corpus Domini. This is held every June and celebrates a miracle that took place there in 1263.

Montefiascone, a pretty hill town with excellent views of the lake, is famous for its Est! Est!! Est!!! wine. Bisentina is an ex-summer residence of popes and has seven small chapels, some with beautiful frescoes. Oaks, chestnuts, vines, olives and vegetables grow in the fertile shores of the lake, and the economy of the region is largely based on agriculture and tourism. Lake Bolsena is an ideal spot for swimming, surfing and sunbathing, and the towns boast a wide selection of superb fish restaurants, and a good nightlife.

The lake is becoming more popular with foreign investors, particularly those interested in a vacation property. Houses in the local villages are quite often medieval in style, or built in the local *tufa* stone. It's possible to find small or medium properties to restore at reasonable prices, and a large stone house needing restoration near the lake will cost around €100,000.

Lakeside properties attract a premium – a four-bedroom villa overlooking the lake will cost around €470,000, while a slightly smaller villa with a pool on the outskirts of a village will be €180,000. Village apartments start at around €40,000 but prices are rising as the area becomes more popular.

Short-term rentals can be very profitable in this area, and properties overlooking or close to the lake will attract a premium rental rate. It's a popular destination for family holidays, and demand peaks between April and October. A one-bedroom apartment will rent for around €440 per week, while a two-bedroom apartment will be around €660.

KEY FACTS
■ **Population** Bolsena 4,104
■ Montefiascone 12,761
■ **Airport** Rome Leonardo da Vinci, Tel: +39 06 6595 3640/ +39 06 6595 4455
■ **Schools** American Overseas School of Rome, Via Cassia 811, 00189 Rome, Tel: +39 0633 4381
■ **Medical** Ospedale San Giacomo, Via Canova 29, 00186 Rome, Tel: +39 06 3626 6372
■ **Pros** Eating out here is reasonably priced and the local wines are excellent ■ The scenery is some of the most beautiful in Italy ■ There's a good range of watersports and activities ■ **Cons** The towns become busy in the summer as a number of tourists arrive ■ Public transport is infrequent.

4. Viterbo & surrounds

Viterbo is one of the best-preserved medieval towns in Lazio, and this is most obvious in its stunning San Pellegrino quarter. Founded by the Etruscans and taken by Rome, the town was both a papal residence in the 13th century and the site of the first conclave. Located on a low plateau between the sea and the Tiber valley, Viterbo is a haven of atmospheric piazzas, narrow lanes, arches and houses with characteristic *profferli*, or external staircases. The town centre is also home to several impressive palazzi, notably the Palazzo Papale and the Palazzo dei Priori. The survival of ancient artisan traditions has made for a colourful town centre and the regular feasts and folklore events are very entertaining.

The thermal springs around Viterbo are famous and attract many visitors. Surrounding towns include Bagnaia, home to the 16th-century Villa Lante; Caprarola, which has the splendid Palazzo Farnese, an important Italian example of Mannerist architecture; and the spectacular medieval Civita di Bagnoregio, or 'dying town', which is perched high on the edge of a *tufa* ravine.

Viterbo and the surrounding areas have some of the most expensive property in Lazio, outside the city of Rome. Prices are influenced by the proximity of Viterbo and Rome, and the good travel connections between the cities. In addition, there are also the benefits of the rural environment that Viterbo enjoys. Many of the houses within Viterbo are in a beautiful medieval style, while more modern properties can be found outside the town. A two-bedroom villa outside Viterbo can cost €310,000, while a villa with a panoramic view and three bedrooms will cost around €390,000. A four-bedroom townhouse in a medieval style sells for around €620,000.

The rental market is strong and the town is well populated all year round. Vacation rentals during the summer months can be profitable but the winter months are quieter and tenants may be hard to find – long-term lets may be more profitable in the long run. However, in peak summer season and during festivals, rents can double.

KEY FACTS
■ **Population** 60,000
■ **Airport** Rome Leonardo da Vinci, Tel: +39 06 6595 3640/ +39 06 6595 4455
■ **Schools** American Overseas School of Rome, Via Cassia 811, 00189 Rome, Tel: +39 0633 4381
■ **Medical** Ospedale Belcolle, Loc Belcolle, S. Martino al Cimino, Viterbo. Tel: +39 0761 3391
■ **Pros** Viterbo is an easy day trip from Rome and the travel connections are frequent and reliable ■ The architecture here is very attractive ■ Archaeological remains of the ancient Etruscan civilisation have been found here and are on display ■ There are lakes only a short drive away ■ The local cuisine is impressive
■ **Cons** The cost of living here is higher than elsewhere in Lazio ■ Travel to some of the smaller surrounding towns can be difficult without a car.

The hillside town of Caprarola offers traditionally styled properties

© ENIT

HOTSPOTS

FOR SALE Property guide

Lazio's wealthy inhabitants have been building their homes in the countryside since Roman times, and it remains one of Italy's most costly regions

The hill towns in Lazio aren't cheap, but they're not as expensive as neighbouring Tuscany

WHEN IN ROME...EXPECT SMALL apartments and big prices! As you might expect, Italy's capital city is pricey, and costs do not decrease greatly the further you get from the metropolis. Hilltop towns are costly, and coastal resorts are similarly, if not more, expensive. Prices in the Lazio region have risen by 50 per cent since 1996. However prices do fluctuate, and it is possible to hunt down a 400-year old farmhouse for €75,000; on the flip side, a one-bedroom flat in Rome can go for as much as €400,000. Nevertheless, the Lazio countryside has the attention of those looking to invest or buy holiday homes at a cheaper price than neighbouring Tuscany and Umbria.

This central region of Italy is proving particularly popular with people who would like to be in the countryside yet have the option of day trips to Rome. Naturally, being close to the capital, transport links are second to none. Within an hour's drive of the city's two airports, Fiumicino and Ciampino, but also close to Ancona and to Perugia, the towns in the Sabine Hills are attracting a lot of interest. Prices are generally lower than Umbria and there are a lot of affordable properties in the €100,000 to €200,000 price range. Hilltop villages, such as Casperia, are pedestrian only, but trains run from Rome to Poggio Mirteto and a free bus service shuttles visitors to Casperia.

Towns and villages around Lake Bolsena, including Capodimonte and Bolsena, are also beginning to attract increasing interest, particularly with the English and German second home buyers. Lake Bracciano and Vico are also favourites with foreign investors. ●

TYPICAL PROPERTY

- Lazio property is typified by the fortified hilltop towns, such as Frascati and Tivoli
- Property built in Etruscan times is tall and thin, and constructed from local volcanic stone known as *peperino*, which is grey and flecked with black spots, or gold and brown *tufo*, which is a yellow porous volcanic stone. This can be found in the Albani Hills, near Rome
- During Renaissance times, properties were whitewashed and built from calcareous white *travertino* stone
- These typical-style properties can be found in the Castelli area of Lazio, an area popular with those seeking a weekend break from Rome
- Prices for these properties can be as low as €135,000 for a four-bedroom, traditional-style house

WHAT CAN YOU GET FOR YOUR EUROS?

VITERBO FARMHOUSE

Located on a hillside overlooking Viterbo, this property is built from typical materials of the area – *peperino* and *tufo* stone – and requires renovation. Surrounded by nut trees and olive groves and boasting 2,000m² of land, this characterful farmhouse is an ideal proposition for those seeking a romantic hideaway to rebuild.

€80,000 CODE IPN

HOUSE WITH PRIVATE CHAPEL

Located in the heart of the Sabine Hills, this property affords stunning valley views and is only 45 minutes from Rome. It does require restoration work, but offers a total of 18 rooms, including four bedrooms. With a large terrace and garden, this country house is a fantastic prospect at a bargain price.

€150,000 CODE DOP

RUSTIC MOUNTAIN HOME

With three bedrooms, a cellar and eight other rooms arranged over three floors, this property has been recently renovated. Set in an appealing location nestled in the Sabine Hills, it also includes a separate apartment and several outbuildings. Ideal for those seeking a property with rental potential.

€250,000 CODE DOP

VILLA WITH RIVER VIEW

This stunning villa overlooks the Velino river and is close to the ancient Roman baths at Cotilia. Arranged over three floors, this property has five bedrooms, three bathrooms and is fully furnished. With a 150m² terrace set in a 1,180m² garden, this spacious property benefits from a separate storehouse and a garage. Perfect for nature lovers, it enjoys a country setting while remaining close to Rome.

€370,000 CODE DOP

UNRESTORED FARMHOUSE PROPERTY

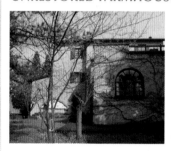

With a well-kept garden and olive groves, this rural farmhouse requires renovation work. With 8,500m² of garden, including pine trees, fruit trees and flowers, this property comes complete with three bedrooms, a sunny terrace, a wine cellar and a separate guesthouse. Only 25 minutes from Orvieto, the property dates back to 1480 and is made from traditional regional materials.

€665,000 CODE IPN

LUXURIOUS MODERN FARMHOUSE

Located in the hills close to Rome and enjoying seven bedrooms, a swimming pool and a 5,000m² garden, this property is ready for habitation and requires no restoration work. It comes with a separate guest wing, and is built from traditional materials, complete with wood beams and a mezzanine floor. As a final flourish, one bedroom is located in the turret!

€1,150,000 CODE CIT

PROPERTY GUIDE

AVERAGE HOUSE PRICES ROME AND LAZIO

	2-bed	3-bed	4-bed	5-bed
Rome	€360,000 (£244,898)	€409,000 (£278,231)	€654,000 (£444,898)	€1,093,000 (£743,537)
Sabine Hills	€180,000 (£124,138)	€291,000 (£197,959)	€356,000 (£242,177)	€468,000 (£318,367)
Lake Bolsena	€143,000 (£97,279)	€186,000 (£126,531)	€256,000 (£174,150)	€372,000 (£253,061)
Viterbo and surrounds	€235,000 (£159,864)	€392,000 (£266,666)	€742,000 (£504,762)	€829,000 (£563,946)

Campania

From chaotic Naples to the glamour of the Amalfi Coast

© ENIT

FACT BOX

- Population 5,725,098
- Population growth 0.42%
- Unemployment rate 21.1%
- Average 4-bed house price €272,600 / £185,442
- Net migration 19,209
- Foreign residents 65,396

Contents

Area profile

Known as *Mezzogiorno*, the 'land of midday sun' is home to a beautiful coast, archaeological remains, pizza and ice cream!

VENTURE FURTHER SOUTH, BEYOND ROME into Campania, and you enter what many regard as the 'real' Italy, with its quintessential character of romance and glamour set alongside decadence and anarchy, as personified in the chaotic regional capital, Naples.

Geography

Campania, roughly at the half-way point between the north and south of Italy, is home to three gulfs along the Tyrrhenian Sea: the Gulf of Gaeta, the Gulf of Naples and the Gulf of Salerno, all of which claim some truly fabulous beaches. The Gulf of Naples is home to three of the world's most beautiful and ultimately romantic islands – Capri, Ischia and Procida.

Inland are the high Lucanian Apennine and Campano Preapennine mountain ranges. The latter includes several active volcanoes, notably Mount Vesuvius (1,280m), responsible for the destruction of Pompeii in Roman times but which hasn't erupted since 1944. Many of the

Tranquil retreats nestle in the hills near Naples

© ROZ COOPER

mountainsides are wooded with chestnut and beech, and the flatter landscape below farmed with crops and vegetables.

Areas

Naples, Italy's third largest city, is a vast sprawling metropolis whose sheer exuberance and colour make it one of the world's most exciting cities. For a unique insight into life in this bustling city, visit Naples' Spaccanapoli and Spanish Quarter, with their labyrinthine alleyways and narrow streets. Once a major Mediterranean port and capital, Naples nowadays offers a wealth of attractive monuments – the Gothic Duomo, the noble royal palace and several museums of note.

The Amalfi Coast is considered by many to be the most beautiful in the world, with exclusive holiday locations and high price tags adorning the many luxury restaurants, hotels and boutiques, not to mention some of the world's most fabulous properties lining the coast. Amalfi, the main town, is a highly popular tourist destination offering lovely

> *"The Amalfi Coast is considered by many to be the most beautiful in the world"*

shops, cafés and a luxury marina. Above Amalfi, and boasting the best views in the area (which is saying something!), is the town of Ravello, with some of Italy's loveliest gardens. Another attractive town, Positano, is the area's most up-market resort.

Sorrento, situated at the Bay of Naples headland and with world-famous panoramic views of the sweeping bay and Mt Vesuvius, has been a long-time favourite with foreigners, particularly the British, and is an ideal base for exploring Campania. The world's reputedly most dangerous drive, along hairpin bends, starts here on the way to Amalfi.

Out in the Bay of Naples are the islands of Capri, Ischia and Procida. Capri, claimed by some as the world's most romantic island, is home to the unique Blue Grotto, the emblematic Faraglioni – three towering rocky pinnacles – and Marina Grande, with excellent shopping along its Via Tragara and one of the world's food meccas. Ischia is the largest and, while it's slightly less glamorous than Capri, it's no less popular. Renowned for its spa and thermal springs, the island offers an attractive capital (also

called Ischia), several beach resorts and panoramic views from its extinct volcanic cone, Monte Epomeo. Procida is tiny in comparison – it measures a mere 3.5km long – and attracts far fewer visitors, particularly in the summer, but has several attractive coves, including Marina Chiaiolella.

Culture

Campania's first inhabitants included the Etruscans, followed by the Greeks, whose legacy includes some fine Doric temples at Paestum, and then the Romans – the region has several stunning remains, including Pompeii.

Many coastal towns, even the smaller ones such as Amalfi, were important maritime powers during the 12th and 13th centuries, when many of the fine monuments were built. Although these towns later lost their power and influence throughout the Mediterranean, they remained popular spots with the nobility and royalty; in the late 18th century Naples and its nearby resorts were considered 'must-sees' in any discerning aristocrat's itinerary around southern Europe.

Economy

Today, Campania is one of Italy's poorest regions – the city of Naples has pockets of slum poverty – due mainly to poor infrastructure and the prevailing influence of the Neapolitan Mafia, the *Camorra*, which has encouraged corruption and crime for decades. Unemployment figures in 2004 for the area as a whole were nearly 16 per cent – rising to 19 per cent in Naples.

Agriculture dominates the region, mainly cereal crops, although these are being replaced with horticultural produce, and grapes, olives and citrus

The well-preserved ancient city of Pompeii offers a glance into Roman life

fruits are also important. Naples and its surroundings are home to southern Italy's major industrial area – manufacturing is the leading sector followed by engineering, metalworking and the petrochemical industry. The fashion industry (mainly shoes and textiles) also plays a vital role in the economy. Service industries employ a mere third of the workforce.

Social groups

Naples has one of the highest population densities in Europe but, in contrast, the area inland has few inhabitants. Despite its many beauty spots and some stunning property, Campania attracts few permanent English-speaking residents; nearly 11,000 foreigners live in Naples but fewer than 150 are from the UK. Fewer than 250 foreigners have made their home in Capri and fewer than 200 in Sorrento. However, the area remains extremely popular with tourists and holiday home owners. ⊕

FACTS

▥ Three times a year, Naples cathedral witnesses a sacred ceremony, when the blood of the city's patron saint, San Gennaro, liquifies

▥ The only inhabitants of Capri's Faraglioni are some extraordinary 'blue lizards'

▥ The island of Ischia boasts some of the world's largest thermal spas, as well as nearly 70 fumaroles and over 100 springs

FOOD AND DRINK

Naples claims the origins to the quintessentially Italian pizza, mozzarella and spaghetti. Neapolitan pizza is simple but delicious, with fresh tomato, basil, mozzarella and possibly a trellis of anchovies on the top. Fresh fish is excellent and the local red sea bream (*pezzogna*) is particularly good. Local desserts are dominated by the world's best ice-cream, but pastries such as *sfogliatelle* (filled with ricotta and candied peel) are just as good.

Campania offers excellent wine and boasts 19 DOC labels, including the world-famous reds Lacrima Christi and Taurasi. The region's pungent lemon liqueur, *limoncello*, has an excellent reputation and is copied throughout Italy, although the Amalfi coast claims to make the best. And on a non-alcoholic note, Neapolitans wash everything down with the world's strongest coffee!

Be sure to try the world's best ice cream

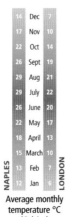

NAPLES		LONDON	
14	Dec	7	
17	Nov	10	
22	Oct	14	
26	Sept	19	
29	Aug	21	
29	July	22	
26	June	20	
22	May	17	
18	April	13	
15	March	10	
13	Feb	7	
12	Jan	6	

Average monthly temperature °C (Celsius)

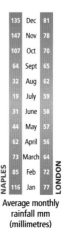

NAPLES		LONDON	
135	Dec	81	
147	Nov	78	
107	Oct	70	
64	Sept	65	
32	Aug	62	
19	July	59	
31	June	58	
44	May	57	
62	April	56	
73	March	64	
85	Feb	72	
116	Jan	77	

Average monthly rainfall mm (millimetres)

Culture

With a number of hidden archaeological splendours to uncover, this is a region rich in history and tradition

"The island of Capri's verdant landscapes have led it to be known as the Garden of Eden"

AMPANIA'S FIRST INHABITANTS WERE THE Etruscans, followed by the Greeks, who established their main city at Poseidonia, now known as Paestum, where visitors flock to admire the three massive and almost intact Doric temples – the Temples of Hera, Neptune and Ceres – dating from 600BC. Herakleia, named after Hercules, was also an important Greek town, which was buried under the ashes like Pompeii.

The region was then invaded by the Romans, who left a legacy of several important monuments, including the white marble Arch of Trajan at Benevento and the perfectly preserved town of Pompeii; buried for centuries under volcanic ash, it is one of the world's greatest historic treasures.

From the ashes

The once-prosperous city of Pompeii, right at the foot of Mt Vesuvius, provides a fascinating insight into the sophisticated Roman lifestyle, frozen in time by the massive eruption of lava and ashes in AD79. Many buildings are almost perfectly preserved and complete with sculptures, paintings and even graffiti!

Later inhabitants in the area brought great prosperity and Naples, in particular, rose to immense power during the Middle Ages. A reflection of this wealth and influence can be seen in the city's many fine monuments, such as several fine Gothic churches, the noble Aragonese Castel Nuovo and the richly decorated Duomo. The Baroque San Gregorio Armeno church has an exquisite interior, with frescoes by Naples' greatest painter, Luca Giordano – Giordano's painting skills were so prodigious he was known as '*Luca Fa Presto*' (Luca the Quick).

Museums and architecture

Naples also boasts a number of excellent museums, notably the National Archaeology Museum, home to many Pompeii finds (including beautiful frescoes, ceramics and casts of humans) but also part of the world-famous Farnese collection, and the Capodimonte Museum, with an excellent range of Italian paintings, including works by Botticelli, Raphael and Titian.

More modern buildings include the Royal Palace (home to Italy's National Library), the glass-domed Galleria Umberto I, and the magnificent auditorium at the Teatro San Carlo. But no tour of Naples would be complete without a stroll round the quintessentially Neapolitan streets found in the bustling Spanish Quarter and Spaccanapoli, with their steps and narrow alleyways decked with lines of laundry and flanked by small shops and bars.

Coastal Campania

Almost all the coastal towns offer fine monuments, legacies of their maritime splendour during the Middle Ages, and even small towns have stunning

CAMPANIAN STYLE

Capri and the Amalfi Coast are synonymous with the very pinnacle of Italian style. The image of a beautiful couple driving round Amalfi's hairpin bends in a sports car is, for many, glamour personified. The coastline, laced with vineyards and citrus groves, studded with cliffs and dotted with picturesque towns and villages, which almost topple into the turquoise waters below, has provided inspiration for countless artists, writers and film directors.

This was the haunt of the international jet-set in the 1950s and 1960s, and was visited by one film star after another; Italian icon Sophia Loren, who was brought up near Naples, made her first films here. The area is still very popular with the rich and famous, and the island of Capri, in particular, caters for the fabulously rich – luxury hotels, sumptuous spas and elegant restaurants all show off the best in Italian opulence.

TOP TEN ATTRACTIONS

1 Naples from its Spanish Quarter

2 The House of the Vettii at Pompeii, with its remarkable frescoes

3 The splendid parks and gardens at the Royal Palace in Caserta

4 The Amalfi Coast and Bay of Naples from the sea

5 A sunset from anywhere around the Bay of Naples

6 Capri's Marina Grande on a summer evening – a place to see and be seen

7 The fascinating National Archaeological Museum in Naples

8 Any village inland in the provinces of Avellino or Benevento, where time has stood still for decades

9 Paestum's three, largely intact, Greek temples

10 The 2nd-century Arch of Trajan at Benevento

"Pompeii, at the foot of Mt Vesuvius, provides a fascinating insight into the sophisticated Roman lifestyle"

Duomos: Ravello's is highly decorated with the local inlaid wood technique (known as *tarsia*); Salerno's has a magnificent 11th-century structure; Amalfi's boasts a highly coloured ornate facade; and the San Michele in Anacapri has an exquisite Renaissance enamel floor depicting Adam and Eve in Paradise.

Proof of the area's long-established reputation as a top holiday spot can be found in its many magnificent villas, both modern and ancient – there are ruins of several Roman villas along the coast, such as those at Minori. Villa Cimbrone and Villa Rufolo in Ravello have particularly beautiful gardens, and concerts are held here in the summer. On the island of Capri, whose verdant landscapes have led it to be known as the Garden of Eden, is Villa di San Michele at Anacapri, home to a world-famous garden and classical statue collection and built on the site of a villa belonging to the Roman emperor Tiberius. But the villa to beat all Campanian villas must be the Royal Palace at Caserta. Built by King Charles III as a holiday home, it has 1,200 rooms containing antiques and treasures comparable only to those in Versailles. ◉

CULTURE

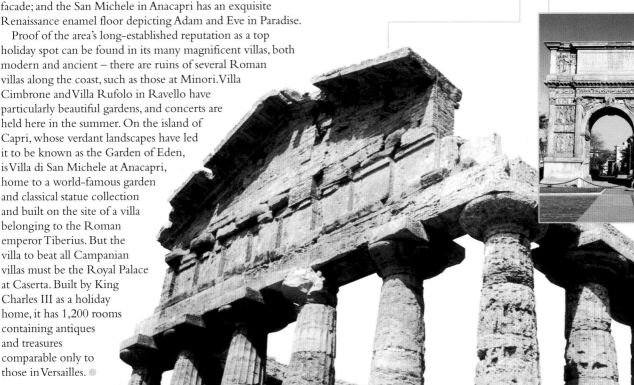

Property hotspots

MAP KEY

● Hotspot
○ Major town/city
66 Road numbers

▒▒▒ **Medical** SM della Misericordia Corso Italia Sorrento, Italy, Tel: +39 0815 331 111
▒▒▒ **Pros** The 50km stretch of coastline is one of Europe's most stunning, with sparkling seas and clean beaches
■ This is a hugely popular area with walkers, with more than 60 cliff-top and village walks in the area ■ This is a cultural area and there are a number of churches, cathedrals and archaeological sites to be viewed ■ The Amalfi Coast is also a haven for nature lovers
■ There are lots of bars and restaurants throughout the area
▒▒▒ **Cons** This is an expensive area, jammed with luxurious properties, and will be above the average buyer's budget ■ This area is overrun with tourists during the summer period.

2. Naples and surrounds

The buzzing, vibrant and sprawling city of Naples is the capital of Campania and one of the largest cities in Italy. Close by are Mt Vesuvius, the ancient cities of Pompeii and Herculaneum, Sorrento, and the islands of Capri, Ischia and Procida.

Naples was first inhabited in the 9th century BC, when the city of Parthenope was built. Parthenope was later abandoned during the 6th century BC, and Neapolis (new city) was built alongside it. In prosperous Roman times, the area attracted holiday-makers from across the Empire. After the Romans came the Byzantines, then the Normans, but the city truly thrived under the reign of Emperor Frederick II. It became a capital again under Anjou rule and the economy flourished.

Naples' cultural highlights, many of which are centrally located, include the National Archaeological Museum, which houses treasures from Pompeii and Herculaneum, the cathedral, the Royal Palace, the Botanical Gardens, the National Gallery, and Napoli Sotteranea – an underground labyrinth of passageways. The main shopping area is in and around Piazza dei Martiri, and the Galleria Umberto arcades at Via San Carlo are worth visiting. Naples also has huge a choice of restaurants, bars and cafés.

Refurbished period apartments in the city centre offer good investment potential. The average weekly rent for a one-bedroom apartment is about €525. A three-bedroom flat in the heart of central Naples, sleeping up to six people, has a weekly rental yield of €1,525.

KEY FACTS
▒▒▒ **Population** 1,050,000
▒▒▒ **Airport** Naples International Airport, Via del Riposo 95, 80144 Naples, Italy, Tel: +39 081 789 6111/789 6259, www.naples-airport.com
▒▒▒ **Medical** Croce Verde, 80136 Napoli (NA) – 111, v. Fontanelle, Tel: +39 081 544 2078
▒▒▒ **Schools** Viale della Liberazione, 1 – 80125 Bagnoli, Tel: +39 081 721 2037, www.intschoolnaples.it
▒▒▒ **Pros** The location on the the Bay of Naples is quite breathtaking ■ The city is overflowing with museums, archaeological remains and churches, and there's the nearby city of Pompeii
■ The city is bustling, with a lots of bars, cafés and restaurants, with raucous markets and a variety of shops
▒▒▒ **Cons** Naples is a polluted and somewhat shabby city ■ The city is hugely disorderly and there is little regard for traffic lights and road regulations ■ This is a tourist destination and the crowds can become quite overwhelming in summer, with petty crime becoming a big problem.

1. Amalfi Coast

The peaceful and pretty Amalfi Coast lies on the peninsula that divides the Bay of Naples from the Gulf of Salerno. The stunning, sun-soaked scenery boasts sandy beaches, sparkling waters and a rocky coastline dotted with precipitous small towns. All of the towns along the coast, such as Amalfi, Positano, Praiano, Ravello, Conca, Atrani, Maiori and Minori, are rich in history and architectural and natural wonders. Each town has its own plethora of outdoor cafés, trattorias, nightclubs and open-air concerts to choose from. Positano is by far the liveliest, and Ravello is the city of music.

For lovers of marine life, there is the Punta Campanella Marine Reserve, which is a 30km stretch of protected coastline. Elsewhere, year-round snorkelling and scuba diving facilities are available.

Not far from Amalfi is the wonderful Emerald Grotto, with its magnificent stalactites, stalagmites and green waters.

There are also many fascinating little museums in the area, dedicated to such subjects as paper and ceramics.

The Amalfi Coast is a popular luxury property location, where the sum of €1,200,000 could buy a 165-square-metre restored villa in a fantastic cliff-side location near Positano that is accessed by a funicular railway line. The rental return on a villa sleeping six persons in the centre of Positano is between €1,700 and €3,700. A luxury pool-side villa in the heart of Sorrento has a weekly rental potential of between €3,365 in low season and €6,390 in high season. Rental potential is excellent, especially during the summer, due to the huge influx of tourists to the area.

KEY FACTS
▒▒▒ **Population** Amalfi 5,600
■ Sorrento 15,659 ■ Salerno 144,078
▒▒▒ **Airport** Naples International Airport, Via del Riposo 95, 80144 Naples, Italy, Tel: +39 081 789 6111/789 6259, www.naples-airport.com
▒▒▒ **Schools** Viale della Liberazione, 1 – 80125 Bagnoli, Tel: +39 081 721 2037, www.intschoolnaples.it

3. Capri

Capri is a small, mountainous island that enjoys year-round sunshine and benefits from rich vegetation, its main produce being fruit, oil and wine. The island is characterised by an extremely steep, rocky coastline that is littered with grottoes and caves. The main town is also called Capri, and the only other sizeable town is Anacapri.

The island has been inhabited since the 8th century BC, when the Greeks and Phoenicians first settled there. Today, its main attraction is the dazzling Blue Grotto, whose enchanting lighting is created as the sun's rays enter the cave via the sea. Also of interest are the ruins of Villa Tiberio (a 45-minute ascent) and the Arco Naturale, a weathered stone arch set in the eastern cliffs. A hike up Monte Solaro (589m), the highest point on the island, is well worth the effort. Capri is easily accessible by water from Sorrento, Positano, Amalfi and Naples.

The expected weekly income from a one-bedroom holiday apartment in Capri town centre is between €450 during low season and €1,500 in high season. A three-bedroom villa with pool and within walking distance of shops and the beach costs approximately €485,000.

KEY FACTS
Population 7,058
Airport Naples International Airport, Via del Riposo 95, 80144 Naples, Italy, Tel: +39 081 789 6111/789 6259, www.naples-airport.com
Schools Viale della Liberazione, 1 – 80125 Bagnoli, Tel: +39 081 721 2037, www.intschoolnaples.it
Medical Croce Verde, 80136 Napoli (NA) – 111, v. Fontanelle, Tel: +39 081 544 2078

Naples is a historical and cultural city that offers many opportunities for the savvy investor

Pros An excellent destination for walkers ▪ Capri is not short of bars and cafés ▪ Despite the huge visitor numbers (up to 5,000 a day) the island remains unspoilt, with its inhabitants leading a traditional life ▪ There are more than a dozen caves set into the rocky Capri coastline to be explored ▪ There are a number of Roman villas and other remains to view on the island
Cons Living costs can be expensive, especially during the summer period ▪ Outside the summer season many hotels and some restaurants shut down ▪ During summer the island can be overrun by tourists.

4. Ischia and Procida

With a circumference of 34km, Ischia is the largest and most developed island in the Gulf of Naples. It is built around a crater lake, and its volcanic slopes are lush with vegetation. The economy is traditionally agriculturally based, and the island experienced something of a boom during the 1960s, when its clear waters and thermal spas first began to attract tourists. Ischia is well catered for with hotels and restaurants, and other entertainments include bathing, sailing and walking.

In contrast to Ischia, Procida, at 3.5km long, is the smallest of the Neapolitan islands. Medieval winding streets lead to flat-roofed, white houses that cling to steep hillsides. The island's main source of income is fishing and vine growing. Up until 1500, most islanders lived in and around the old centre of Terra Murata, the highest point on the island. But, during a period of peace during the 16th century, the population grew and people began to spread out. The first area was beneath Terra Murata, which was inhabited mostly by fishermen. Sailors, on the other hand, gathered in the village of Sancio Cattolico in the north. Both islands are well connected to the mainland by daily ferry and hydrofoil services.

The majority of investment potential on these islands lies in first-class holiday villas. A two-bedroom villa, with sleeping capacity for six people, has an income potential of €660 in low season and €1,075 in high season. A fabulous five-bedroom villa in the tranquil Ischian village of Fiaiano, just a five-minute drive from Maronti beach and surrounded by vineyards and pines trees, costs about €930,000. A six-bedroom villa in Fiaiano with a pool has a weekly earning potential of between €1,200 and €4,500.

KEY FACTS
Population Ischia 18,146 ▪ Procida 10,635
Airport Naples International Airport, Via del Riposo 95, 80144 Naples, Italy, Tel: +39 081 789 6111/789 6259, www.naples-airport.com
Medical Hospital 'Anna Rizzoli', Lacco Ameno, Ischia, Tel: +39 081 994 110
Schools Viale della Liberazione, 1 – 80125 Bagnoli, Tel: +39 081 721 2037, www.intschoolnaples.it
Pros Both islands retain a sense of traditional life and an unspoilt appearance ▪ Both Procida and Ischia are perfect for nature lovers and watersports fanatics ▪ There are a number of attractions, including churches and museums, plus landscaped gardens on Ischia ▪ Both islands have a variety of restaurants, predominantly serving seafood
Cons These are tiny and isolated communities that can be difficult to get to ▪ There are few hotels and restaurants open in winter, and during summer prices are hiked up.

FOR SALE Property guide

Offering everything from luxurious coastal villas to humble hovels inland, Campania is a region of incredible variety

© ENIT

Palazzi are grand properties that have often been converted into apartments and attract hefty price tags

ACQUIRING PROPERTY ALONG THE Campanian coastline – or in Naples itself – will give you a substantial return on your investment. The market here is very buoyant; between 1998 and 2003 prices more than doubled, and in some areas they rose by more than 70 per cent. The Amalfi Coast is home to luxurious property developments, while prices on Capri, Ischia and Procida cater to the higher end of the market and in some cases make it seemingly impossible to buy; there is also a vast shortage of property available, and this shortage precipitates higher prices. Property in Naples offers great rates of appreciation and you can purchase a two-bedroom refurbished apartment here for €293,000. Four-bedroom houses on the Amalfi Coast will set you back an average of €384,000, while inland you can pick up a habitable property for as little as €600 per square metre.

Inland Campania is full of cheap property and potential renovation projects. The further inland

THE PALAZZI

- *Palazzi*, found throughout Campania, are, literally, palaces: old Renaissance (generally) buildings that have been renovated and made into apartments
- You will find *palazzi* along the Amalfi Coast and within Naples itself, along with immaculately painted villas
- The *palazzi* offer fabulous architecture and privacy, usually within walking distance of shops and attractions
- Many *palazzi* in Naples date from the Aragonese and Spanish rule of the 14th and 15th centuries

TYPICAL PROPERTIES

- The Islands of Capri, Ischia and Procida cater to the upper end of the market, with luxurious and modern villas
- Naples offers a number of *palazzi* properties, most of which have been renovated and made into luxury apartments
- The Amalfi Coast has a wide variety of modern homes and colourful villas
- Inland there are basic stone cottages, which could make ideal renovation projects
- There are also a number of old tower blocks, which offer cheap apartments

you travel, the more semi-abandoned villages and houses in disrepair appear. More often than not these properties will need complete renovation and restoration, which may well mean knocking them down and starting from scratch. The dangers of purchasing inland are the earthquake risk the area is prone to, and losing the rental potential you get closer to the coast.

More than a quarter of Campania's population lives around Naples, and consequently this is the hub of the region's activity. However, it can be an overcrowded and decidedly shoddy area to live in, but as an investment it is ideal. Campania is the most visited region in southern Italy so you can charge accordingly. Prime rentals are to be found along the Amalfi Coast, and in Naples itself you can charge €1,260 per week. ●

WHAT CAN YOU GET FOR YOUR EUROS?

RENOVATION FARMHOUSE

With 2.2ha of land, complete with vineyards and woodland, this tumble-down farmhouse is situated in undulating countryside and has lovely mountain views. Permission has been granted to build three villas and a pool, making this an excellent prospect for a buy-to-let investment. It is near Ariano Irpino, a medieval town with all amenities.

€210,000+ CODE UNI

MODERN VILLA

This spacious, newly built property has four bedrooms and is situated in a hilly landscape. Built in a traditional style, the villa is situated halfway between Naples and Foggia, in the small town of Ariano Irpino. The villa comes with land of 2,500m², newly planted with olive and fruit trees, and a veranda from which you can enjoy fantastic views. With potential to be converted into two separate apartments, this is an excellent prospect for those looking for an investment property.

€250,000 CODE UNI

PROPERTY IN ROLLING HILLS

This spacious house is in excellent condition and comes with a living space of 220m². Easily transformable into two large apartments, it is set in picturesque rolling hills and comes with land totalling 2,800m².

€290,000 CODE UNI

SEAFRONT VILLA

With grounds of 1ha sloping down to the seafront, this modern property boasts stunning views and is situated in a very quiet area close to Amalfi. Built in the 1950s in a traditional style, it requires complete renovation. As well as access to a private beach, there is plenty of living space and bedrooms, and a terrace with seafront views.

€1,600,000 CODE IPN

RURAL VILLA

Fully habitable and situated just 4km from the Amalfi Coast, this tasteful villa is built in the typical Amalfi style. With architecture reminiscent of the 16th century, it has grounds of 3,000m², and all three bedrooms overlook the coastline. With unique features such as a library and wine cellar, this fantastic home is bright and welcoming, with a huge living area.

€1,700,000 CODE IPN

RESTORED VILLA

Built with all the traditional touches, such as ceramic tiles and painted external walls, this villa is located on the coast between Amalfi and Positano. With astonishing sea views, the grounds include a separate guesthouse and a swimming pool. The well-kept garden has fruit and lemon trees and a range of plants and flowers. With a living area of 400m² and eight rooms and three bathrooms over three floors, this is a luxurious family property.

€1,843,000 CODE IPN

AVERAGE HOUSE PRICES CAMPANIA

	2-bed	3-bed	4-bed	5-bed
Amalfi Coast	€260,000 (£176,871)	€306,000 (£208,163)	€384,000 (£261,224)	€323,000 (£219,728)
Naples and surrounds	€230,000 (£156,433)	€266,000 (£180,952)	€386,000 (£262,585)	€555,000 (£377,551)
Capri	€194,000 (£131,973)	€262,000 (£178,231)	€310,000 (£210,884)	€395,000 (£268,707)
Ischia and Procida	€195,000 (£132,653)	€256,000 (£174,150)	€359,000 (£244,218)	€409,000 (£278,231)

PROPERTY GUIDE

Inter Italia
Puglia Property Consultants

At **Inter Italia** we make buying a property in Italy's **beautiful Puglia region**, in which we specialise, an easy and trouble free experience. Due to the fact that we are based in the heart of Puglia we can offer our clients the **best advise** in what and where to buy.

WHEN YOU BUY YOUR PUGLIA PROPERTY THROUGH INTER ITALIA, YOU BUY THE EASY WAY

At Inter Italia we make our clients experience of buying a property in Puglia an easy, stress free experience. We dedicate ourselves and our time to looking after your every need from when you first contact us and arrive to Brindisi Airport up until you have purchased the property you love, which hopefully you will find. Even then our service does not end. We look after all pre and post purchase needs of our clients no matter how big or how small.

SO WHAT ADVANTAGES DOES BUYING THOUGH INTER ITALIA OFFER YOU?

- *Full pre-travel advice regarding accommodation with hotels with whom we can offer reduced rates.*

- *Free Airport collection from Brindisi Airport and transfer to your hotel.*

- *Viewing trips where we show you quality properties and at the same time show the region where you would be investing.*

- *Inter Italia deals directly and exclusively with the seller. There are no middle men.*

- *We help arrange a lawyer to give you full legal advice for your property purchase.*

- *We prepare your fiscal codes and open your bank account for you - both necessary for the purchase.*

- *Inter Italia offers its rental division to rent out your property so you ca obtain the best possible return on your investment if you wish.*

- *When you find the property you wish to buy no deposit is payable until all legal searches and a structural survey have been carried out.*

- *After you have returned home Inter Italia can carry out all renovation work and take delivery of any furniture you may have ordered whilst in Puglia. We keep you updated with photos via e-mail and on your return you find your house transformed.*

- *We look after the installation of a swimming pool if you should so wish*

- *Inter Italia will manage your property and manage all your utility bills, etc.*

Inter Italia will help you find your dream home in Italy. Just visit our web site or telephone us and our multilingual staff will send you an extensive information package including property brochures via post.

Please note if you decide to visit us and view properties there are no costs for our services while you are in Puglia, you are under no obligation to purchase and we do not charge you, the purchaser, commission.

So contact Inter Italia today and begin your house hunting adventure in Puglia!!

RYANAIR NOW FLY DIRECTLY TO PUGLIA

INTER ITALIA, VIA DEI GASPERI, 22 73020 UGGIANO LA CHIESA (LE) ITALY Telephone +39 328 744 5847 or +39 320 1187163 Fax +39 0836 485825 Email interitalia@liber

www.interitalia.biz

Puglia, Calabria & Basilicata

Italy's southern regions are far from the madding crowds

© ENIT

Contents

FACT BOX

Puglia
- **Population** 4,023,957
- **Unemployment rate** 13.8%
- **Net migration** 10,904
- **Population growth** 0.11%
- **Average 4-bed house price** €232,000 / £157,823
- **Foreign residents** 42,985

Calabria
- **Population** 2,007,392
- **Unemployment rate** 23.8%
- **Net migration** 3,426
- **Population growth** -0.11%
- **Average 4-bed house price** €207,500 / £141,156
- **Foreign residents** 27,413

Basilicata
- **Population** 596,821
- **Unemployment rate** 16.1%
- **Net migration** 563
- **Population growth** -0.11%
- **Average 4-bed house price** €201,000 / £136,735
- **Foreign residents** 5,154

Area profile

Long considered to be Italy's 'poor south', the regions of Puglia, Basilicata and Calabria are now poised for prosperity

THOUGH A LITTLE LESS POLISHED THAN Tuscany and Umbria, these relatively undiscovered regions offer bargain properties, rich, exotic culture and food to indulge in, and some of the cleanest coastal waters in Italy.

Puglia

Puglia's olive groves feed 80 per cent of Italy's oil production, her fishermen catch most of the country's fish, much of Europe's pasta is made here, and her vineyards are vast. Puglia offers sandy beaches, turquoise waters, hilltop towns, fishing harbours, and elegant towns and cities. Over thousands of years, the region's coasts have suffered countless invasions by Messapians, Greeks and Moors, all leaving their mark on the architecture, cuisine and culture.

In terms of local identity, the region is split into the Gargano, the Itria valley and surrounding towns, and Salento. While the Gargano national park is famed for its sinuous coastal roads and forests, towns such as Vieste, Peschichi, Manfredonia and Rodi di Gargano are established destinations for thousands of Italian sun-worshippers who flock to the beaches

every August. This area rarely features in guides aimed at northern Europeans and so it can be quite barren out of season.

More popular and enjoying current fame is the Itria Valley. British people are moving in and renovating the *trulli*, native conical-roofed dwellings that stood abandoned by farmers for centuries. Today, *trulli* are usually sold with extensive land, their value based on proximity to Martina Franca.

Salento is the name for the southern tip of Puglia. From the beautiful baroque city of Lecce on the Adriatic coast, all the way along the Southern tip and half way up the Ionian coast as far as Pulsano, you'll find shallow, clean and calm seas.

In some towns, a dialect closer to Greek than Italian is still spoken and the local gastronomy is like nowhere else in Italy. Otranto, the most popular destination in Salento, is listed among the 14 most beautiful towns in Italy.

Puglia has something for everyone. Due to the affordable prices, rustic landscape and wonderful cuisine, the area seems to attract a diverse market, not limited to retirement investments or family holiday homes. There's a demand for English

GETTING THERE

AIR Ryanair (08712 460000; www.ryanair.com) offers flights to Bari and Brindisi from Stansted. **British Airways** (0870 850 9850; www.ba.com) offers flights from Gatwick to Bari. **easyJet** (0871 244 2366; www.easyjet.com) flies as far as Naples, and from there it's possible to get a bus or rail link onwards to Puglia, Calabria or Basilicata.

ROAD Travel from Dover to Calais with **P&O Ferries** (08705 202 020; www.poferries.com) and from there the E15 will take you to Lyon, and then you should follow the A32/43 to Turin. Once in Turin, pick up the A4 to Milan and continue on the A1 to Bologna. From here, the A14 will take you into Bari. To reach Calabria, it's best to continue on the A1 from Bologna to Naples and from there take the A3, which runs right down the west coast through Basilicata to Calabria.

RAIL The TGV runs trains from Paris to Milan. From there, the ES rail service operates to Bari, Brindisi, Lecce and Reggio di Calabria. Other stations in Basilicata, Puglia or Calabria require connecting trains. Contact **Rail Europe** (08705 848 848; www.raileurope.co.uk) for more details on timetables and routes.

COACH For those hardy souls who dare sit in a bus all the way to southern Italy, **Eurolines** (0870 514 3219; www.eurolines.com) offers services from various stations in the UK to Bari, Brindisi, Matera and Cosenza. Local coach operators include **SITA** (+39 0881 773 117; www.sita-on-line.it), **CLP** (+39 0815 311 706) and **FC** (+39 0961 896 111; www.ferroviedellacalabria.it).

This Grecian temple in Basilicata shows the influence of invading forces on the culture and architecture

© ENIT

PROFILE

Calabria has many secluded and quiet sandy beaches, like this one at Capo Vaticano

language teaching, and younger people seem to be moving here to work, particularly in towns such as Ostuni, Lecce and Cisternino.

Basilicata

Basilicata is one of Italy's smallest and poorest regions. Its terrain is wild and stark, but it's a region rich in history. Horace, the Latin poet, was born in Venosa, and the capital of Potenza has survived many earthquakes. Although urban and sprawling, it has an elegant centre with fashionable shops and eateries. Matera is also attracting growing interest. It's home to the *Sassi*, caves dug out of *tufa* rock, which housed over 20,000 people. Publicity about poverty and malaria forced the government to rehouse them and it's now a UNESCO world heritage site. Today, visitors come to see the caves,

> "In some towns, a dialect closer to Greek than Italian is spoken"

with their rock churches and Byzantine frescoes, and the town is attracting investors. Much of the art and architecture in Basilicata is 13th century, but many of the castles and ports are even older.

Calabria

Calabria boasts over 800 kilometres of coastline and some of the cleanest beaches in Italy. Mostly mountainous with dense woodland and green countryside, its rugged beauty attracts people for road trips, and its inaccessible paths and vertical summits have made it a popular destination for extreme sports and hiking. This is a land of lush vegetation, ancient monasteries, castles and palaces.

Holidaymakers who prefer to stay on the coast opt for the pretty fishing villages of Bagnara and Scilla. The 9th-century town of Gerace is the ultimate destination for pottery souvenirs, and it's

easy to lose track of time in Calabria's most well-known and largest city, Cosenza.

Until recently, Calabria was untouched by foreign visitors and so property remains affordable, but interest is growing and new villas, apartments and estate agencies are opening up.

The economy

As well as being holiday destinations, all three southernmost regions of Italy have an industrial core. Puglia's industrial triangle of Taranto, Bari and Brindisi have long-established steelworks, ironworks and ship-building areas, but the region's industry is driven mainly by food production. Basilicata only really boasts a giant Fiat plant in Melfi. Nature has dictated the labour of those who work in Calabria, and much of the region's industry is based on agriculture and cereal production.

Since the middle of the 20th century, the Italian government has recognised that tourism is Calabria's best opportunity for industry growth and potential, and this is set to become reality as more British people invest in holiday residences. ●

FACTS

■ Puglia covers an area that's over two-thirds the size of Belgium

■ The area around Bari is renowned for its production of olive oil, with Puglia producing 80 per cent of Italy's oil. Some of Puglia's olive trees are reputedly over 2,000 years old

■ Puglia produces approximately 80 per cent of Europe's entire pasta stock

■ The singer Tony Bennett and actor Steven Seagal are both of Calabrian descent, while the fashion designer Gianni Versace was born in Reggio Calabria

PROFILE

FOOD AND DRINK

Fresh vegetables at a market in Puglia

Puglian cuisine is a fusion between Italian, Greek and Spanish cooking. Meals begin with antipasti, such as roasted chilli peppers in olive oil, calamari, goat's cheese, *polpetti* (meatballs) or *fave* (a purée of broad beans and barley). The dish of the region is *Orecchiette con cime di rape* (fresh pasta with turnip). **Basilicata** has a peasant heritage, and the region's speciality is a type of sausage, the *ucanica*, eaten fresh, cured or preserved in oil. **Calabria**'s regional cuisine is flavoursome and spicy, dominated by seafood and vegetables. With sheep farming a dominant industry, lamb features heavily in dishes, as do chilli peppers. Calabria is also famous for its *caciocavallo* cheese, made from cow's milk.

SOUTHERN ITALY		LONDON
14	Dec	7
18	Nov	10
22	Oct	14
26	Sept	19
29	Aug	21
29	July	22
26	June	20
22	May	17
18	April	13
15	March	10
13	Feb	7
12	Jan	6

Average monthly temperature °C (Celsius)

SOUTHERN ITALY		LONDON
83	Dec	81
96	Nov	78
79	Oct	70
38	Sept	65
30	Aug	62
14	July	59
25	June	58
39	May	57
47	April	56
9	March	64
57	Feb	72
77	Jan	77

Average monthly rainfall mm (millimetres)

Property hotspots

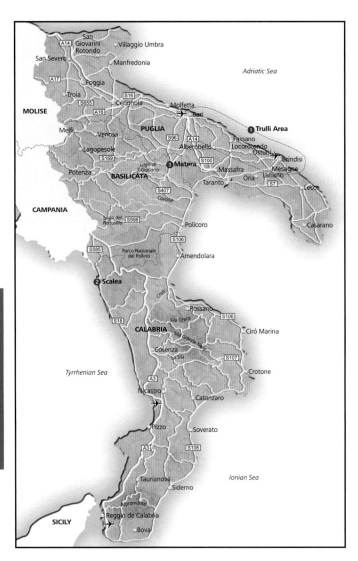

MAP KEY

● Hotspot
◐ Major town/city
66̄ Road numbers

1. The Trulli area

The Trulli area, home to some of the most scenic towns in Italy, extends from the rugged Itria valley to the sparkling Adriatic sea, and is bordered to the north and south by Bari and Brindisi. The quaint circular and conical-roofed white stone dwellings known as *trulli* give the area a unique character, and the local towns all boast unspoilt historical centres.

The variety of attractions and lively atmosphere of the towns in this area contrasts with the natural air of the countryside

forests. The clear blue waters are a paradise for divers, while a journey further inland soon leaves you in a heathland close to rugged limestone ravines.

The range of scenery provides many spectacular backdrops for the towns perched up high, and nature trails and walking opportunities are abundant.

Equidistant from Bari, Brindisi and Taranto, and situated in the Itria valley, the UNESCO world heritage site of Alberobello is considered the capital of the Trulli region.

Ostuni, a radiantly beautiful white city overlooking the Adriatic, is one of the most stunning small towns of

southern Italy. Situated on three hills at the southernmost edge of the Murge, its old centre spreads across the highest of the hills.

Fasano is a serene and popular destination of rustic beauty, and just a few kilometres away lies the smaller Selva di Fasano, a lush area set on a spur of land 450 metres above sea level.

A short distance away is the pleasant summer resort of Laureto-Egnazia. Finally, the small hilltop town of Locorotondo, with its rambling streets and fine restaurants, is developed around a central Gothic church. The town is also famous for its white wines.

The Trulli area is still relatively unknown, and it's thought that the property market here has yet to realise its full potential. Experts in the region expect that house prices will continue to rise steadily in the next few years, perhaps even matching the 25-30 per cent increase that swept the region in 2004-5.

Buyers are attracted to the region by the architecture of the *trulli*, and the amazing views that many properties boast. Anything on the edge of the valley will be considered a great short- or long-term investment.

As well as *trulli*, the area has a good supply of villas, called *lamia*. These are often painted in terracotta, and have extensive land and impressive gates. Alberobello, the best known of the *trulli* towns, is home to the most expatriates and is the most developed and expensive, but plenty of bargains can be found nearby. The outskirts of Locorotondo and Ostuni are ideal locations for low-priced properties, and properties

needing renovation present a particularly good prospect. On the other hand, properties in the historic centre of Ostuni and the popular hilltop town of Selva di Fasano command some of the highest prices in the area.

Prices for the whole region are competitive when compared to areas such as Lecce or Salento, to the south of Brindisi, because traditionally lots of northerners have bought villas there and the market is already developed for Italians.

Trulli are popular with tourists looking for an authentic Italian experience. Properties close to the sea will be especially popular, attracting higher rents. Budget flights to two local airports have increased awareness and attracted more independent travellers who need short-term accommodation.

Rental prices are expected to rise in this area as it becomes more well known, and winter rentals will become more likely.

KEY FACTS

■ **Population** Alberobello 10,913
■ Fasano 38,781 ■ Locorotondo 14,060 ■ Ostuni 32,841
■ **Airport** Bari Palese Airport, 70057 Bari, Tel: +39 080 579 226
■ **Schools** British School, 70124 Bari, 47/0 Via Rosalba Camillo, Tel: +39 080 561 5275
■ **Medical** Casa di Cura Salus, 72100 Brindisi, 366 v. Appia, Tel: +39 083 158 1505
■ **Pros** Both the Adriatic and Ionian coasts are within easy reach of the area ■ It's easily reachable from Bari and Brindisi ■ Ferry connections from Bari are frequent ■ There are many excellent restaurants and hotels
■ **Cons** This is one of the poorer regions of the country and unemployment is high ■ It may be difficult to find a job in this area ■ Although scenic, *trullis* can often be too cold in the winter ■ The Puglia region in general suffers from a shortage of water ■ The cities have high crime rates.

2. Scalea

Scalea, a pretty town on the Tyrrhenian coast of Calabria, has been an Italian summer getaway for decades. The enchanting beaches, sparkling seas and fine sand border a historic and traditional town that's one of the most visited resorts in Italy. During the Swabian, Angevin, Aragonese and Spanish eras, it became an important centre, gradually enriched with monuments and works of art, most of which can still be admired today. Other attractions of the town include operas, plays, music concerts, festivals and many sports facilities.

The Pollino national park, with its amazing scenery, is only 10 minutes away. Towards the beach, the Scalea Marina centre has recently been developed, and there's now a selection of comfortable hotels, splendid villas and fully equipped bathing areas on the beach.

Property in Scalea is very cheap – one-bedroom apartments start from €20,000, and two-bedroom apartments from €25,000. These are usually in a complex with a garden or a pool, and the closer the complex is to the sea, the more expensive the apartment will be.

Apartments further from the town, approaching the hills, often have more space and amazing views, while the historic town centre is the home of some real bargain properties.

Many older buildings will need renovation, but when complete, they will be charming and full of character. Prices here have risen in the last two years as awareness of the town has been raised, and a two-bedroom apartment that would have cost €28,000 in 2003 would now sell for €40,000. Prices are expected

Grape harvesting at a vineyard in the picturesque Calabria region

to continue to rise.

Properties in Scalea have a high rental potential in the summer. Scalea was traditionally a holiday resort for Neapolitan families, but now Italians arrive from all over the country to sample Scalea's delights. They will usually be prepared to pay a premium for a property in August, and it's easy to earn €3,000 in rent over one summer for a small property.

Outside the summer months, it can be hard to find someone to rent your property, but if the number of people visiting Scalea out of season continues to rise as expected, then demand and rents are likely to rise too.

KEY FACTS
■ **Population** 10,094
■ **Airport** Naples Capodichino Airport, 80144 Napoli, Tel: +39 081 751 5055
■ **Schools** The English School di Foote Elizabeth, 87029 Scalea, Via Monticello, Tel: +39 098 521 588
■ **Medical** Ospedale, 87022 Cetraro, Via Reparto, Medicina, Tel: +39 098 297 120
■ **Pros** Scalea is still relatively undiscovered ■ High unemployment means you're more likely to be able to find people to work on your property ■ There are good train connections to the larger cities ■ Outside the summer months, the town still stays relatively busy ■ The climate here is among the best in the Mediterranean, with long, hot summers and very short, mild winters
■ **Cons** Unemployment levels here are

high ■ The closest airports are Rome (four hours) and Naples (two and a half hours) ■ Most people don't speak much English, and it will be necessary to speak at least basic Italian ■ During the summer, the population swells to five times its normal size and the resort can become crowded.

3. Matera

Matera is an elegant and historic town located on a small canyon, and it's the home of the famous and captivating *Sassi*, cave-style dwellings carved from the soft white rock of the hills. Occupied since the early Palaeolithic period, the town is the most intact example of a troglodyte settlement in the Mediterranean region.

This is a town where the ordinary becomes breathtaking. The spontaneous nature of the architecture means that suddenly chimneys pop out of roads and roofs appear as stairways.

The *Sassi* were abandoned in the 1950s after being deemed unsanitary. Now the ancient dwellings are being repopulated by artists and young people, who consider the buildings trendy. Properties here can offer good value for money, and new owners who renovate can claim 50 per cent of the renovation costs back from the state.

However, if you do buy a property in the *Sassi*, part of it

still belongs to the local council and you will hold a type of leasehold. This isn't the case for newer properties. The renewal of the *Sassi* has created new demand for property here, and prices have risen by 20 per cent in the last five years – expect to pay from €1,200 per square metre. A three-bedroom property in the *Sassi* needing renovation will sell for €160,000, while a similar sized apartment in a new block here will sell for around €200,000.

Since Matera was used as the location for the Mel Gibson film *The Passion of the Christ*, awareness of the town as a holiday destination has grown immensely, and coaches arrive at regular intervals. The locals have taken advantage of this and apartments in the *Sassi* have a huge rental potential during the summer, often at premium prices. Properties further from the ancient dwellings and attractions are cheaper, but the large number of pilgrims drawn to the area ensures a constant supply of tenants.

KEY FACTS
■ **Population** 58,256
■ **Airport** Bari Palese Airport, 70057 Bari, Tel: +39 080 579 226
■ **Schools** Centro studi Didattico, 85100 Potenza, 215 via Appia, Tel: +39 0871 470 884
■ **Medical** A.s.l. Mt. 4 Centro di Di Abilitazione, 75100 Matera, 1 Piazza Firenze. Tel: +39 0835 382 101
■ **Pros** Matera is still unspoiled and the atmosphere is magical ■ Budget flights to Bari and Brindisi have made access to the area much easier
■ **Cons** Matera and the surrounding area have long suffered impoverished conditions ■ In recent years, the area has been famous for corruption ■ It's the last provincial capital in Italy to be connected by high-speed trains ■ The cobbled streets aren't practical for parking ■ Some properties get very little light and also suffer from damp ■ The area suffers from earthquakes.

FOR SALE Property guide

The up-and-coming regions of Basilicata, Puglia and Calabria offer traditional and basic homes in a quiet and authentic area of rural Italy

PROPERTY GUIDE

© ALAN TOOTILL

Houses are constructed by linking a series of *trulli*, divided internally by picturesque arches and side alcoves

PUGLIA IS BY FAR THE MOST POPULAR OF THE three regions, with the traditional *trulli* buildings becoming a hugely popular buy in recent years. Thanks to a balmy climate and lifestyle, and the recent introduction of direct flights by Ryanair to both Bari and Brindisi airports in 2004, demand has shot through the roof. Two years ago, British property buyers began focusing on unique rural buildings, and in particular the conical-shaped *trulli*. By 2004, prices of habitable *trulli* in the Itria Valley rose from €80,000 to €130,000 in 18 months. Overall, property prices are increasing by 20 to 25 per cent per year.

Calabria is still in the early stages of development, but Scalea and the Riviera dei Cedri are set to be hugely popular. Many northern Italians and Neapolitan families are swelling the local ranks during summer. Property is selling for an incredibly low €20,000 for a one-bedroom apartment, while a villa outside Scalea in an area such as Tremoli can cost from as little as €65,000. Rental potential in both Scalea and the area between Bari and Brindisi in Puglia is also good as there's a high influx of tourists into these areas. Typical properties include newly built coastal homes, but the traditional village houses are grey stone with terracotta roofs.

Basilicata has also seen growth in demand for property. The revival of the traditional *Sassi* properties of Matera has created new demand and prices have risen by 20 per cent in the last five years. You should now expect to pay upwards of €1,200 per square metre. A three-bedroom renovation *Sassi* will sell for €160,000, while a similar sized new apartment will sell for around €200,000. *Sassi* are rock-hewn structures with undulating stone floors and curved whitewashed walls, and they've been bleached white by the strong sunlight. ●

SASSI

- *Sassi* are literally cave dwellings, which are found in the Barisano and Caveoso regions of Matera
- The *Sassi* are one gigantic sculpture, which were hand carved out of the right-hand side of the ravine
- There are around ten rock-cliff churches, and more than 150 *Sassi* in the whole territory, spread out along the length of the ravine
- Declared a UNESCO world heritage site, the *Sassi* were first inhabited in the Palaeolithic era
- Up until the 1950s, the *Sassi* were inhabited by 20,000 of the city's 24,000 residents, who lived in poor conditions with no utilities
- Times have changed and today the *Sassi* are due to become holiday chalets and second homes

WHAT CAN YOU GET FOR YOUR EUROS?

TRULLO TO RESTORE

This three-cone *trullo*, located only six kilometres from the village of Martina Franca in the Puglia region, is set in 1,000m² of land. A real bargain, this three-room property is ideal for those seeking a DIY project.

€35,000 CODE APP

MODERN APARTMENT

Located in a private complex in the Calabria region, this apartment has three bedrooms, a garden and three balconies. Only 500m from the beach and 100m from the town centre, it also has a shared pool and all mod cons.

€57,000, CODE SCA

CALABRIAN COUNTRY HOUSE

Located in the Pollino national park, this property has 10,000m² of land. Requiring some restoration, the three-bedroom house is in the village of Tremoli. Arranged over two floors, it has a living area of 200m².

€65,000 CODE SCA

CITY LIVING

This city villa has three bedrooms and offers an excellent rental income. Only 20 minutes from the airport, one kilometre from the city of Ostuni and six kilometres from the beach, this is perfect for a retired couple.

€135,000 CODE REN

VILLA COMPLEX

A pretty residential complex located in Metaponto, only one kilometre from the beach. Properties are available with one to three bedrooms and each group of villas has its own pool. The village of Metaponto offers all necessary amenities.

€85,000+ CODE CAT

RURAL VILLA

Located in open countryside, this three-bedroom property requires some decoration work but is fully habitable, with a living area of 240m². The property has a large garden and splendid views. It's only two and a half kilometres from the beach and within easy reach of the town of Belvedere in Calabria.

€135,000 CODE SCA

HABITABLE TRULLO

Fully habitable and with all amenities connected, this *trullo* enjoys 120m² of living space and has two bedrooms. With 5,000m² of gardens, including a paved terrace and olive trees, this three-coned *trullo* is located 15 minutes from the coast and is close to a number of shops and a post office. This property also comes with private parking and has been recently renovated.

€135,000 CODE DOP

HABITABLE TRULLO

Located on a hillside on the edge of the village of Ceglie, this four-bedroom villa has been restored to include central heating. With one hectare of garden, which is full of olive trees and including a patio area, this home is absolutely perfect for outdoor entertaining.

€135,000 CODE DOP

THE TRULLI

- Found in Puglia, *trulli* are the dominant, in-demand property of the region
- The *trullo* gets its name from its strange cone-shaped structure, which is in the antique tradition of the 'maestro trullari'
- A *trullo* consists of a square or round stone-built walled area, topped by a beehive cone made of spirals of local stone without mortar. A small whitewashed peak is topped by a stone pinnacle
- Some *trulli* roofs have a whitewashed sign with a religious, traditional or mystical significance
- Each *trullo* is usually about three metres across and consists of one room
- Some *trulli* are still used as part of working farmsteads

AVERAGE HOUSE PRICES PUGLIA, CALABRIA & BASILICATA

	1-bed	2-bed	3-bed	4-bed
The Trulli area	€134,000 (£91,156)	€167,000 (£113,605)	€237,000 (£161,224)	€315,000 (£214,286)
Scalea	€90,000 (£61,224)	€183,000 (£124,490)	€224,000 (£153,381)	€271,000 (£184,354)
Matera	€140,000 (£95,238)	€147,000 (£100,000)	€274,000 (£186,395)	€276,000 (£187,755)

162

Sicily

A multicultural blend of people, art and architecture

© ENIT

FACT BOX

- ■ **Population** 4,972,124
- ■ **Population growth** 0.13%
- ■ **Unemployment rate** 20.1%
- ■ **Average 4-bed house price** €325,000 / £224,138
- ■ **Net migration** 27,793
- ■ **Foreign residents** 62,900

Contents

Area profile

Known as 'a world within an island', Sicily offers a treasure trove of cultures, stunning scenery and excellent value

GETTING THERE

AIR Ryanair (08712 460 000; www.ryanair.com) flies from Stansted to Palermo. **British Airways** (0870 850 9850; www.britishairways.com) and **Air Malta** (0845 607 3710; www.airmalta.com) fly from London Gatwick to Catania. **Alitalia** (0870 544 8259; www.alitalia.co.uk) offers indirect flights from London to Palermo via Rome or Milan.

ROAD It is possible to drive to Sicily by taking the ferry from Dover to Calais – try **SeaFrance** (08705 711 711; www.seafrance.co.uk), **Hoverspeed** (0870 240 8070; www.hoverspeed.co.uk) or **P&O Ferries** (08705 202 020; www.poferries.com) – or use the **Channel Tunnel** (08705 35 35 35; www.eurotunnel.com) . From Calais take the E15 to Lyon, and then follow the A32/43 to Turin, followed by the A6 to Genoa. From here you can take a ferry to Palermo with **Grimaldi Lines** (+39 081 496111, www.grimaldi.napoli.it)

RAIL TGV trains run from Paris to Milan, and from here ES Rail runs services to Reggio Calabria. Contact **Rail Europe** (08705 848848; www.raileurope.co.uk) for all details and costs. **Grimaldi Lines** (+39 081 496111, www.grimaldi.napoli.it) offers a ferry service from Reggio Calabria to Sicily.

COACH Eurolines (08705 143219; www.eurolines.com) run services to Palermo and Catania.

LYING JUST OFF ITALY'S 'BIG TOE', SICILY IS THE Mediterranean's largest and most densely populated island, which has attracted wave after wave of visitors throughout its coloured history: the Greeks, Carthaginians, Romans, Byzantines, Arabs and Normans, and more recently, the Italian jet-set and foreign property buyers. Palermo, the largest city and an important sea port, is the island's capital and main population centre.

The often snow-capped Mt Etna (3,350m), just north of Catania, dominates the island's landscape and this still-active volcano – eruptions cause numerous earth tremors and destroyed the ski resort in 2002 – is Sicily's main focal point. Rolling hills, home to typically Mediterranean olive and citrus groves and vineyards, make up central Sicily, while the northeastern corner boasts lush forests. Much of the coastline is rugged, but with some excellent beaches, many of them virtually undiscovered – those in Taormina province and in the Gulf of Castellammare are particularly beautiful. The island claims no less than eight UNESCO World Heritage Sites, found in the provinces of Palermo, Ragusa and Syracuse.

Perched high on a hillside awash with bougainvillaea and overlooking the sea is the magnificent town of Taormina, popular with the English aristocracy in the 19th century and still a much-favoured relocation spot. It has several notable monuments, an impressive medieval quarter and some of the best views of Etna's molten heights. Taormina – known as a 'patch of paradise' – offers a lively year-round social scene, excellent cafés and restaurants, great golf and hiking for the active, and a summer film festival.

Syracuse province in the southeast, with its impressive temples and fortresses, provides tangible evidence of the strong Greek influence on the island, and the elegant sandstone cities of Noto, Ortygia and Syracuse offer a wealth of stunning medieval monuments and warm, welcoming people. This corner of Sicily is tipped by foreign

"The picture-postcard town of Cefalù is referred to as one of the Mediterranean's jewels"

home buyers as the 'new Tuscany' – property is equally beautiful, but at a fraction of the price and with views of Africa!

Ragusa province, to the west of Syracuse, is Sicily's smallest province, but probably the most authentically Sicilian, and one of the least known to foreign buyers, although it boasts its fair share of attractive resorts, such as Marina di Ragusa and Marina di Modica, as well as some of the island's quietest and cleanest beaches.

The picture-postcard town of Cefalù, often referred to as one of the Mediterranean's jewels, sits

Beautiful Sicily has been off the foreign property buyer's radar, but that's all set to change

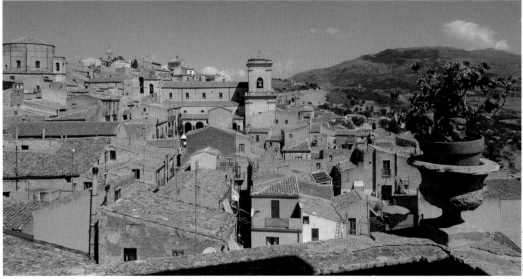

© THINK SICILY

Sicily has some pristine beaches, with views all the way across the Med to Africa

on the central north coast in a stunning setting – perched on a rocky coastline beneath a plunging mountain. The centre, dominated by one of the finest Romanesque cathedrals in Europe, is a unique mix of labyrinthine medieval streets in the west and an ordered elegant 18th-century grid in the east.

Off the north coast, and only accessible by boat, lie the seven Aeolian Islands (literally the 'windy isles'), all sparsely populated but with stunning coves, fascinating Greek ruins and some of the Mediterranean's best snorkelling. Not surprisingly, they're popular tourist spots in the summer months, but quiet out of season. Lipari, the largest, offers the most to do, and the tiny Panarea is home to many wealthy Italians.

Economy

Sicily remains one of Italy's poorest regions and is plagued by the highest unemployment figures in the country (more than 17 per cent in 2004). The mafia is largely responsible for the island's lack of development and infrastructure, the misuse of European funds and a flourishing black economy, and although the mob is less active nowadays it is still influential. Agriculture (mainly wine, olives and fruit and vegetables) and fishing (tuna and sardines) are the island's traditional industries, which have been overtaken in recent years by tourism – now the island's main source of income – and petroleum and gas exploitation.

Culture

The rich collage of Sicilian culture owes its variety to the island's many invaders, whose indelible marks have left a lasting impression on the landscape. Drive just about anywhere and you'll stumble across priceless monuments: superb examples of Greek temples in Agrigento and Segesta; Roman amphitheatres at Catania and Taormina, and Villa Piazza Armerina, whose mosaics are among the best

preserved in the world; Palermo's lavishly decorated Royal Palace designed by the Arabs, who were also responsible for planting the island's vast expanses of olives and date palms; and the many Norman churches and cathedrals, witness to Sicily's finest hour during the 12th century, when it was one of the world's most important centres. Later invaders, namely the French, Aragonese and Bourbons, also left emblematic monuments – such as Catania's many fine palaces – before the island became part of Italy in 1861.

Social groups

The Sicilians are fiercely independent and for years the island was somewhat isolated on the international map, stigmatised by its mafia infamy, while many Sicilians were forced to emigrate from the poverty in their homeland to a better life abroad. The island has, however, been a well-kept property secret among well-to-do Italians for years, and recently improved communications and increased confidence have led to foreigners 'discovering' Sicily. Although property purchases are becoming more common, relatively few foreigners live here and high unemployment means job opportunities are limited for relocators. ●

FACTS

■ DH Lawrence wrote *Lady Chatterley's Lover* during his three-year stay at Taormina

■ Legend says that Cyclops, the one-eyed monster, lives on the slopes of Mt Etna

■ The Aeolian island of Lipari was once the world's talcum powder capital, and had three talcum mines

FOOD AND DRINK

Sicilian food is a unique mix of Arab and Italian cuisine, whose star ingredients are fresh fish and vegetables. *Pasta con le sarde*, with its eclectic mix of sardines, raisins, pine nuts and saffron, is a particular delicacy, as are locally caught tuna and swordfish in late spring. Sicilians excel at desserts: their ice-cream and sorbets, *cassata* (sponge cake with ricotta and glacé fruits) and the sickly-sweet *pignolata* (deep-fried dough covered in honey) are all must-tries.

The fertile soil is ideal for grape production, and Sicily has some of Italy's best wines including Marsala, a heavy fortified dessert wine; several golden whites such as Moscato and Passito; full-bodied reds such as Nero d'Avola, not to mention pungent liqueurs such as *limoncello* (lemon and aniseed), the all-Italian *grappa* and *cynar* (artichoke liqueur – an acquired taste!).

A bustling Sicilian market

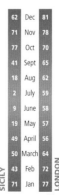

SICILY		LONDON	
18	Dec	7	
21	Nov	10	
25	Oct	14	
28	Sept	19	
30	Aug	21	
30	July	22	
27	June	20	
24	May	17	
20	April	13	
17	March	10	
16	Feb	7	
16	Jan	7	

Average monthly temperature °C (Celsius)

SICILY		LONDON	
62	Dec	81	
71	Nov	78	
77	Oct	70	
41	Sept	65	
18	Aug	62	
2	July	59	
9	June	58	
19	May	57	
49	April	56	
50	March	64	
43	Feb	72	
71	Jan	77	

Average monthly rainfall mm (millimetres)

Property hotspots

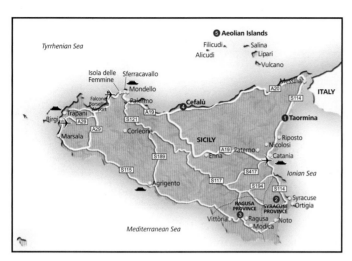

MAP KEY

● Hotspot
◉ Major town/city
66 Road numbers

1. Taormina

Easily Sicily's most picturesque town, Taormina is spectacularly located on a terrace of Monte Tauro, dominating two grand, sweeping bays, and enjoying amazing views of Mt Etna. It is known as a celebrity retreat and has a glitzy lifestyle, although ancient architecture and the traditional culture have been preserved.

Founded by the Siculians, Taormina was a favourite with a long line of conquerors and was a crossroads of the ancient world held by the Greeks, Romans, Arabs, Normans, Aragonese and French, who all contributed to the rich, artistic heritage.

The modern town is well served by amenities, excellent nightlife, impressive museums, numerous shops, medieval *palazzi* and the spectacular Teatro Greco. It's the perfect place to enjoy a leisurely drink at a café in one of the intimate piazzas, which date from as early as the 15th century. Visitors pack the main street, the Corso Umberto I, from April until October, but Taormina is a year-round resort, and is pleasant in the quieter winter months.

Having been discovered by the European jet-set, Taormina is expensive and property prices are comparable with Tuscany. But because of the possibilities for rental income, Taormina proves an excellent investment. As Goethe said in the 18th century, Taormina is 'a patch of paradise on earth' and there are many who share this sentiment.

Taormina is a popular tourist destination and rentals are in demand. A two-bedroom property rents for around €735 per week, higher during the summer festival.

KEY FACTS

■ **Population** 11,000
■ **Airport** Catania-Fontanorossa Airport, Tel: +39 095 7239111, info@aeroporto.catania.it
■ **Schools** Istituto S. Francesco di Sales, Scuole Paritarie, 7 Via Cifali, 95123 Catania, Tel: +39 095 438885, efsisi@pcn.net
■ **Medical** Ospedale Vittorio Emanuele, Tel: +39 095 7435256
■ **Pros** Catania airport has recently been renovated, making access easier ▨ Amenities in the town are excellent ▨ There is a reasonably sized expat community ▨ The climate is agreeable ▨ Making a living here is possible as there is a large tourist industry
■ **Cons** The Sicilian tradition of passing down homes through generations makes buying here a minefield ▨ The cost of living is the highest on the island ▨ The resort becomes overcrowded during summer.

2. Syracuse province

Syracuse is a scenic region with a wonderful selection of towns, a beautiful coastline and a variety of cultural heritages.

The province's capital is also called Syracuse. The name comes from the Greek word *sirako*, meaning swamp, and Syracuse was once a powerful city to rival Athens. Over the centuries the Romans, Arabs, Normans, Swabians, French and Spaniards all left their mark. The oldest part of town is the island Ortiga, characterised by medieval architecture and Baroque palaces and churches.

The picturesque town of Noto, which was flattened by an earthquake in 1693, was rebuilt in a Grand Baroque style. The warm hues of the golden local stone contrast with the detailed palaces and churches.

In terms of investment, Syracuse is one of the biggest growth regions in Sicily. Small British communities have sprung up in historic Ortiga and Noto, which has pushed up prices. Properties closer to the beach are more expensive than those in the towns, and rural properties, which often have a large amount of land, are cheap and plentiful. A small property for renovation with 44,000 square metres of land outside Noto can be found for €44,000.

For letting, accommodation in Syracuse's old town is rare and attracts premium rents. There is a shortage of rental property in Noto. Properties close to the sea are profitable for short-term lets.

KEY FACTS

■ **Population** Syracuse 122,896
▨ Noto 23,139
■ **Airport** Catania-Fontanorossa Airport, Tel: +39 095 7239111, info@aeroporto.catania.it
■ **Schools** Istituto S. Francesco di Sales, Scuole Paritarie, 7 Via Cifali, 95123 Catania, Tel: +39 095 438885, efsisi@pcn.net
■ **Medical** Azienda Ospedaliera Umberto I, 96100 Siracusa, 1 v. Testaferrata, Tel: +39 0931 66132
■ **Pros** Catania airport is close by, and BA, Ryanair and Air Malta operate direct flights ▨ The area has a great combination of art, history, sea, nature and food ▨ Expat communities are growing in the area ▨ Amenities in Syracuse and Noto are excellent ▨ Tourism sustains the economy and seasonal jobs are easy to find
■ **Cons** Prejudice about mafia activity has held back many from moving to the area ▨ Syracuse province has one of the highest population densities on the island ▨ Many buildings in Noto have fallen into disrepair because of neglect and minor earth tremors.

3. Ragusa province

One of the most tranquil regions, Ragusa has some of the cleanest and quietest beaches on the island and some real architectural treasures.

The provincial capital, also called Ragusa, is set on a hill and split by the Valley of the Bridges. One side is Ragusa Ibla, the old town, a cocktail of medieval and Baroque architecture. The new town, on the other side, was built in the 18th century. Ragusa is famous for *caciocavallo* cheese.

A short distance from the capital is Modica, the 'town of a hundred churches'. It has a Baroque style, with blond buildings, a maze of narrow streets and many gorgeous *palazzi*, and it is famed for its restaurants. Its heritage shows signs of Greek, Roman, Arab,

Norman and Spanish rule.

House prices in Ragusa have risen 40 per cent in the past three years, but it's still one of the cheapest provinces in Sicily. Rental accommodation is scarce as it has not traditionally been a tourist area, though this is changing. Properties in Ragusa's old town and those close to the sea attract a premium. A two-bedroom apartment takes €700.

KEY FACTS
■ **Population** Ragusa 69,686
▨ Modica 52,867
■ **Airport** Catania-Fontanorossa Airport, Tel: +39 095 7239111, info@aeroporto.catania.it
■ **Schools** Istituto S. Francesco di Sales, Scuole Paritarie, 7 Via Cifali, 95123 Catania, Tel: +39 095 438885, efsisi@pcn.net
■ **Medical** Ospedale Civile, Ragusa, Tel: +39 0932 623946
■ **Pros** Buses run regularly to Catania, Palermo and Syracuse ▨ Ragusa has the lowest crime rate in Italy ▨ The idyllic landscape around the town is a UNESCO World Heritage Site ▨ Oil on Ragusa territory represents a major reserve for the economy
■ **Cons** Accommodation in Ragusa can be expensive ▨ Trains from Syracuse, Noto and Agrigento, although reliable, are few and far between.

4. Cefalù

Anchored between the sea and a craggy limestone promontory, Cefalù is a town of winding medieval streets, intimate squares and delightful restaurants. The attractive beach and rocky coastline also attract visitors, and Cefalù is the premier Tyrrhenian destination. In ancient times it was known as Kephaloidon, derived from the Greek word for head, *kefale*, a reference to the rock overlooking the town.

Cefalù was under Roman control between 254BC and AD853, when it was conquered by the Arabs. Their rule lasted until 1063. Cefalù has been well preserved, and many examples of ancient architecture exist in the unspoiled medieval streets. The Romanesque cathedral is particularly impressive.

Cefalù's economy is based on tourism and agriculture, and the area around the town is ideal for growing olives, grapes and citrus fruit, staples of the local diet. Restaurants are often family-run and feature many fish dishes.

Properties in Cefalù are often large. The proximity to both the capital, Palermo, and the beach has meant a rise in prices in recent years. Properties in the centre of town or with a sea view carry a premium; a central three-bedroom apartment sells for €450,000, and a six-bedroom seaside villa for €530,000. A four-bedroom villa on the outskirts of town, however, is as little as €180,000, and the average price for a four-bedroom house is €261,000.

Cefalù's popularity as a tourist destination ensures a strong summer rentals market with profitable short-term lets. High-end accommodation is particularly in demand; a four-bedroom villa will take €1,680.

KEY FACTS
■ **Population** 13,800
■ **Airport** Palermo Airport, I90139 Punta Raisi, Sicilia, Tel: +39 091 7020111
■ **Schools** Euro School, 24 vl. Amedeo d'Aosta, 90123 Palermo, Tel: +39 091 6218268
■ **Medical** Cefalù hospital, Via Aldo Moro, Cefalù, Tel: +39 0921 920111
■ **Pros** Cefalù is conveniently located on the train line between Palermo and Messina ▨ Cefalù was featured in the Oscar-winning film *Cinema Paradiso*, which attracted many visitors
■ **Cons** Tourists arrive in huge numbers during the summer season ▨ Prices of food and everyday goods are very high ▨ Parking is almost impossible in the summer.

The medieval town of Cefalù has attracted many buyers

5. Aeolian Islands

An archipelago situated off the northern coast of Sicily, the seven Aeolian Islands have been inhabited for 3,000 years. Photogenic black beaches and rocky outcrops lead to sparsely populated villages and an amazing variety of scenery.

Lipari, situated on a plateau of red volcanic rock, is the most developed island, the most volcanically active is Stromboli, and rugged Vulcano is home to bubbling therapeutic mud baths. To a lesser extent, the other islands have also become holiday destinations. Panarea is a chic jet-set resort, and even the remote Alicudi and Filicudi have their share of visitors. Salina, home to fertile vineyards, is perhaps the quietest.

Ancient Greek sailors believed that these islands were the home of Aeolus, god of the winds. Characterised by the rich colours and crystalline waters, these coastlines are at times lashed by fierce winds.

Most homes are in a traditional Mediterranean style, with a characteristic Aeolian shape – a flat house with a large external 'L'-shaped patio, supported by *pulere* columns and surrounded by a rocky garden. A three-bedroom villa in central Vulcano is sells for around €280,000, whilst a one-bedroom apartment in the same location is around €70,000.

There is a severe lack of rental accommodation during the summer months, which makes bookings essential and sees prices treble; a one-bedroom apartment will fetch €700, up from €200 in winter, while a two-bedroom apartment will earn €1,000, up from €350 during winter.

KEY FACTS
■ **Population** Lipari 10,554 ▨ Salina 870 ▨ Stromboli 500 ▨ Vulcano 500 ▨ Panarea 315 ▨ Filicudi 300 ▨ Alicudi 100
■ **Airport** Palermo Airport, I90139 Punta Raisi, Sicilia, Tel: +39 091 7020111
■ **Schools** Euro School, 24 vl. Amedeo d'Aosta, 90123 Palermo, Tel: +39 091 6218268
■ **Medical** Azienda Unita Sanitaria Locale N.5, 98124 Messina, 263 v. La Farina, Tel: +39 090 3651
■ **Pros** The larger islands have a frequent hydrofoil service from the mainland ▨ The peaceful lifestyle is perfect for those looking for a getaway ▨ There are opportunities for active holidays, such as walking, climbing, swimming, snorkelling and spearfishing
■ **Cons** Many businesses close down in winter ▨ The smell of the sulphurous mud baths can be unpleasant at first ▨ During storms, which can be violent, boats stop running and it is possible to become stranded.

Property guide

A melting pot of architectural influences, today Sicily is a blend of the modern and the ancient, jumbled together across the island

Classic cube-shaped Sicilian houses are dotted over the hillsides, and are constructed seemingly at random

MANY PEOPLE HAVE BEEN PUT OFF from investing in Sicily due to the perceived mafia connection with property throughout the island. However, recent years have seen something of a stabilisation and now Sicily is tipped to become Italy's most popular region with foreign investors. The market is described as constantly expanding, with demand growing, yet the inevitable boom has yet to hit, due to these old prejudices and fears of mafia control.

Up until recently the property market was dominated by northern Italian buyers, but this has changed as access to Sicily has been made easier for the British due to direct flights from British Airways and Ryanair. Taormina remains the most popular area with the foreign market; however property is in limited supply and prices have skyrocketed – nowadays it is not unusual to pay upwards of a

TYPICAL PROPERTIES

- Sicilian properties have a large amount of Arabic influence due to Palmero once being an Arab Emirate
- Houses are traditionally cube shaped and have flat roofs, and are arranged chaotically over the hillsides. Many of these are weatherbeaten older properties, which are full of character
- In recent years there has been an increase in the number of flimsy, modern buildings and concrete resorts being constructed

million euros for a villa. Cefalù, Noto, and the Ragusa and Syracuse provinces are also incredibly popular, and prices here range from €40,000 to €1,200,000, making Sicily even more expensive than Tuscany in many areas. The Aeolian Islands offer exclusive properties, but once again prices are very high and supply is limited.

Sicily currently remains something of a niche market, partly due to the cost of property and partly due to access being so restricted until recent times. Nevertheless, as an investment, property in the area offers a potential gold mine, as demand from both the Italian and foreign market for holiday lets remains high. However, with property in such limited supply, especially around the coast where building restrictions apply, you will have to be prepared to move quickly. ●

BUYER BEWARE!

- Many modern buildings along the coast have been constructed illegally and are under threat of demolition. In 1967 a law was passed which outlawed the construction of any building within 250m of the beachfront, yet many developers ignored this
- The situation is improving, but many buildings and developments still maintain links with organised crime. Be extra vigilant; it should become clear during negotiations if there are any mafia links
- Open protests against mafia control in Palermo have led to a clamp down on the mob's activity. Prices have started rising rapidly as a result, so it is advisable to move quickly if you are seeking a bargain property

WHAT CAN YOU GET FOR YOUR EUROS?

ARABIC-STYLE HOUSE

Located in the historic town of Noto, this property offers two bedrooms and a comfortable living area. Situated in the Arabic quarter, this traditional property is close to the centre and all amenities. Complete with a balcony with a stunning view of the valley below, this habitable property is a real bargain.

€28,500 CODE FON

RENOVATED PROPERTY

Arranged over two storeys, this fully renovated and furnished house has two spacious bedrooms, a large living area and plenty of storage space. Situated in the historic centre of Noto, it house comes complete with a balcony and is great for watching the world go by.

€65,000 CODE FON

RURAL PROPERTY WITH OLIVE GROVES

Only 5km from the historic town of Noto, this farmhouse has a living area of 450m². It currently requires complete renovation, but there is an electricity and water supply. With grounds of 67,370m² including almond and olive groves, this is an ideal property for a rural business or tourist enterprise.

€148,000 CODE FON

MODERN FAMILY HOME

With four bedrooms, four bathrooms and two kitchens, this spacious and luxurious property is ideal as a family holiday home. Located in the centre of Campofelice di Roccella, near Cefalù, this property offers garage parking for two cars and comes complete with a spacious terrace.

€200,000 CODE IIS

18TH-CENTURY FARMHOUSE

In a rural setting only 12km from Noto, this traditional farmhouse property does require some renovation work to be carried out, but is connected to water and electricity supplies. With a spacious living area of 1,000m², this house offers excellent potential and plenty of space. Boasting 2.7ha of land with stunning views over Noto, Rosolini, Ipsica and the coast, it's a fabulous buy.

€800,000 CODE FON

MAGNIFICENT VILLA

Composed of two separate properties, this four-bedroom, five-bathroom, two-kitchen property is extremely luxurious. Situated in a village near Lipari, it offers spectacular country views from its numerous terraces. With a large garden complete with swimming pool, this home would be ideal as a buy-to-let investment or for permanent relocators looking for a peaceful rural retreat.

€1,500,000 CODE IIS

AVERAGE HOUSE PRICES SICILY

	2-bed	3-bed	4-bed	5-bed
Taormina	€320,000 (£217,687)	€317,000 (£215,646)	€559,000 (£380,272)	€741,000 (£504,082)
Syracuse province	€107,000 (£72,789)	€214,000 (£145,578)	€339,000 (£230,612)	€372,000 (£253,061)
Ragusa province	€135,000 (£91,837)	€179,000 (£121,769)	€262,000 (£178,231)	€256,000 (£174,150)
Cefalù	€143,000 (£97,279)	€169,000 (£114,966)	€261,000 (£177,551)	€408,000 (£277,551)
Aeolian Islands	€165,000 (£112,245)	€220,000 (£149,660)	€218,000 (£148,299)	€283,000 (£192,517)

PROPERTY GUIDE

Sardinia

Sandy beaches, a rugged interior and a rich tradition

© ENIT

FACT BOX

- **Population** 1,637,639
- **Population growth** 0.42%
- **Unemployment rate** 16.9%
- **Average 4-bed house price** €290,000 / £197,279
- **Net migration** 6,498
- **Foreign residents** 14,371

Contents

Area profile

The beautiful Mediterranean island of Sardinia offers a cultural blend that you won't find on the mainland

GETTING THERE

AIR Ryanair (0871 246 0000; www.ryanair.com) flies to Alghero from Stansted. **easyJet** (08717 500 100; www.easyjet.com) offers flights to Olbia from Gatwick, and Cagliari from Luton. **British Airways** (08708 509 850; www.britishairways.co.uk) offers flights from Gatwick to Cagliari.

ROAD Travel to Calais with **SeaFrance** (08705 711 711, www.seafrance.co.uk), **Hoverspeed** (0870 240 8070, www.hoverspeed.co.uk) or **P&O Ferries** (08705 202 020; www.poferries.com) – or take the **Channel Tunnel** (08705 353 535, www.eurotunnel.com). From there take the E15 to Lyon, then follow the A32/43 to Turin. Continue on the A21 to Genoa. From Genoa you can travel to Porto Torres with **Tirrenia** (0039 81 317 2999; www.tirrenia.it).

RAIL TGV offers services from Paris to Turin. From there, ES Rail offers services to Genoa, and once in Genoa you can take a ferry to Porto Torres. Contact **Rail Europe** (08705 848848; www.raileurope.co.uk).

COACH Eurolines (0870 514 3219; www.eurolines.com) offers services to Genoa, and from there you can get a ferry to Porto Torres. Contact Eurolines for more details on timetables and prices.

THE QUINTESSENTIALLY MEDITERRANEAN island of Sardinia – the second largest after Sicily – is a melting pot of cultures and a reflection of the many invaders who claimed the island as their own, leaving a legacy of great hospitality and many different dialects. Perhaps the least 'Italian' of all the regions, Sardinia, bathed in turquoise waters and with pristine white shores, is one of the last relatively unspoilt places in Europe.

Geography

Sardinia lies off the west coast of Italy – the nearest Italian port is Civitavecchia, north of Rome – and French Corsica sits just 7km across the Straits of Bonifacio. This elongated island is essentially rugged, and most of the coastline consists of sheer cliffs, home to many caves and grottoes, including the extraordinary Bue Marino at Cala Gonone. Nestling within the rocky cliffs are dozens of beautiful beaches, mostly white sand, some of which stretch for several kilometres.

Inland the landscape is typically Mediterranean with grassland and scrub (known locally as *macchia*) where gorse, prickly pear, myrtle and thyme flourish, as well as olives and holm oaks, whose dense bark provides cork. The *macchia* is grazed by Sardinia's numerous sheep and goat herds.

The forbidding Gennargentu mountains, running north-south along the eastern side, are made up of thick forests – so dense that they're impenetrable in some parts – and home to a wealth of wildlife, including the unique Sardinian fallow deer. On the opposite, westerly, side of the island are vast rolling plains. This is Sardinia's 'bread basket', where the majority of the island's crops are grown.

Areas

Due to the rugged inland terrain, most settlements are on the coast, where there's a contrast between the ultimate in luxury – Costa Smeralda in the northeast corner is one of the world's most exclusive and expensive resort areas – and some almost 'undiscovered' tranquil coves, whose only inhabitants are seals.

To the south of the island, in the Gulf of Cagliari, is Sardinia's capital, Cagliari, a bustling harbour city with plenty to do and see. The main monuments include the well-preserved Roman amphitheatre, several interesting museums and its Pisan-Romanesque Duomo. Its busy port makes the most

> *"Sardinia, bathed in turquoise waters and with pristine white shores, is relatively unspoilt"*

of Sardinia's strategic position and provides a main stopping point on maritime routes across the Mediterranean. Cagliari boasts one of Italy's longest beaches at Poetto, with a small marina offering plenty of opportunities for water sports.

Further south is the small resort of Pula, home to the island's largest golf course and stunning stretches of white sand and coves. Nearby resorts include Porto d'Agumu and Santa Margherita di Pula, both of which offer lovely beaches. The town of Nora, to the north, has a beautiful Roman amphitheatre, which is used as the site of the annual summer music festival.

Still further south, on the very tip of Sardinia, is Chia, often referred to as 'Europe's Caribbean'. Its silky-white sand and crystal-clear azure waters provide some of the world's best snorkelling grounds. Chia is also home to magnificent pristine sand dunes, some of which rise up several metres. Dolphins are often seen here, as are flamingoes on the inland lagoons. Set in some of the island's most beautiful countryside, Is Cannoneris nature reserve is particularly stunning.

Economy

Sardinia has traditionally been one of Italy's poorest and least-developed areas, but international

The bustling regional capital, Cagliari, has plenty to offer and a fantastic setting

© ENIT

Sardinia's blend of cultures sets it apart from Italy

Sardinia is a rocky island, with hundreds of kilometres of white beaches and azure seas

investment in Cagliari, where several multinationals are based, and the advent of tourism have improved the island's economy.

Agriculture – particularly sheep and goat farming, and crops – has always been the traditional backbone of the Sardinian way of life, and much of the island's economy still relies on farming. Coal-, lead- and zinc-mining remain important, and modern industries include chemicals and the all-important tourism.

Unemployment has traditionally been among the country's highest and was nearly 14 per cent in 2004 – considerably higher than the national average, but lower than some southern regions.

Culture

Located strategically in the middle of the Mediterranean, Sardinia was a convenient stopping-off point for invaders, which included the Phoenicians, Carthaginians, Romans, Arabs, Spanish and, finally, the Italians. But the island's first visitors were the Nuragh (1500 to 800BC), whose origins constitute one of the world's unsolved mysteries. A highly civilised people, the Nuragh left an extraordinary legacy of some 7,000 round stone towers known as *nuraghe*, Sardinia's symbol. Many of the towers are exceptionally well-preserved – the one at Santu Antine has three storeys and the site at Su Nuraxi forms part of Italy's UNESCO heritage.

Later visitors left many fine monuments, such as Alghero's Duomo (Catalan-Gothic) and the medieval streets at Bosa, containing Aragonese and Romanesque buildings. But Sardinia's greatest heritage from its invaders comes in the assortment of dialects spoken and the wealth of colourful festivals held even in the smallest village.

Social groups

For its size, Sardinia is very sparsely populated and the inhabitants are mostly concentrated in the coastal towns. The island has a large young population – nearly 45 per cent of Sardinians are under 35 – and relatively few foreign residents. The largest EU groups among the nearly 15,000 foreigners are German, French and British. While the island is increasingly popular with foreign property buyers, few relocate here, mainly because of the lack of job opportunities and amenities outside the summer tourist season. ●

FACTS

■ More than 2,000 different festivals are celebrated on the island over the year

■ Sardinia has its own language, Sardu, although Italian is widely spoken and used for all official purposes

■ One of the island's seafood delicacies is fried sea anemone!

FOOD AND DRINK

Sardinia's cuisine is based around fish, seafood and meat, particularly locally farmed lamb, goat and pork. Spit-roasted suckling pig or kid goat are part and parcel of many festivals. *Suppa quata*, an oven-baked hearty broth with bread and cheese, is an inland staple, and other specialities include *culingioni*, which is ravioli filled with spinach and *pecorino* cheese – considered by many to be the world's best sheep's cheese. Typical desserts are *rujoli* (sweet cheese fritters) and almond-based sweets, such as nougat.

Sardinia is home to many fine wines, characterised by their strong and aromatic flavour. Cannonau and Nebbiolo are renowned reds, while the white Vermentino di Gallura is one of only four in Italy with the highly prized DOCG label. Dessert wines are particularly good.

Nougat is a delicacy in Sardinia

SARDINIA		LONDON
16	Dec	7
19	Nov	10
23	Oct	14
27	Sept	19
30	Aug	21
30	July	22
27	June	20
23	May	17
19	April	13
17	March	10
15	Feb	7
14	Jan	6

Average monthly temperature °C (Celsius)

SARDINIA		LONDON
67	Dec	81
72	Nov	78
54	Oct	70
32	Sept	65
10	Aug	62
1	July	59
13	June	58
26	May	57
31	April	56
45	March	64
50	Feb	72
50	Jan	77

Average monthly rainfall mm (millimetres)

PROFILE

Property hotspots

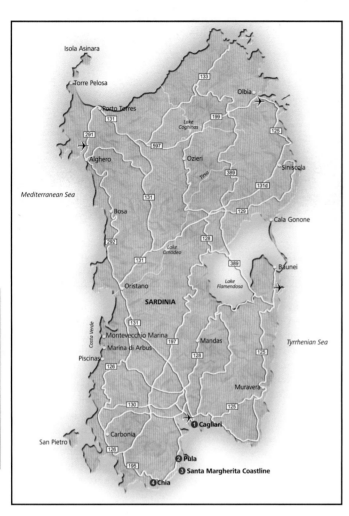

MAP KEY

● Hotspot
◉ Major town/city
66 Road numbers

Just outside Cagliari lies Il Poetto beach, the liveliest on the island, which is very popular with the locals. New daily flights from London were launched in April 2005, making Cagliari more accessible than ever.

One-bedroom apartments in the popular Quartu suburb, a 10-minute drive from the city centre and Poetto beach, cost around €110,000. Alternatively, in the same area just €145,000 could buy a traditional three-bedroom villa with 900 square metres of land and countryside views. If you're looking to buy in the heart of the bohemian quarter, Castello, expect to pay around €160,000 for a characterful one-bedroom, renovated flat. Around €180,000 buys a newly refurbished, two-bedroom apartment in the smart suburb of Selargius, a 15-minute drive from Cagliari centre.

KEY FACTS
■ **Population** 250,000
■ **Airport** Cagliari/Elmas Airport, 09030, Sardinia, Italy, Tel: +39 0702 10531
■ **Medical** Samed sas di USALA & C., 09121 Cagliari (CA) – 42/a, v. Is Mirrionis, Tel; +39 0702 75074
■ **Schools** Contact the Sardinian Ministry of Education for more information; Urp della Pubblica Istruzione, Beni Culturali, Informazione, Spettacolo e Sport, Viale Trieste, 186 – 09123 Cagliari, Tel: +39 070 6067040; www.regione.sardegna.it/tematiche/istruzione
■ **Pros** This is the island's capital and an attractive city with many amenities ▦ There are a number of historical and cultural attractions to be enjoyed, including Roman remains and medieval architecture ■ Nature lovers can enjoy the numerous bird species found in the

city's wetlands and the botanical gardens ■ The city's National Museum is well worth visiting
■ **Cons** The city can become overrun with tourists and is expensive in summer months.

2. Pula

Just a half-an-hour's drive west from Cagliari is the delightful, laid-back town of Pula. On summer evenings, the town square throngs with music and dancing, and there are plenty of agreeable restaurants to choose from.

The coasts, coves and caves in and around Pula are among the most gorgeous in Sardinia. Local beaches offer a range of watersports, including windsurfing and sailing, and one of Europe's most stunning golf courses (Is Molas) is just a few minute's drive away. Nearby natural beauty spots include the stunning Chia Dunes and the sandy beaches at the Bay of Nora. Nora is a large Roman amphitheatre, which lies on a small headland jutting into the sea, and is the site of an annual summer music festival.

A one-bedroom furnished apartment with private parking in the centre of Pula, a little over one kilometre from the beach, costs in the region of €75,000, while €85,000 could buy a spacious two-bedroom apartment in a peaceful countryside setting just five kilometres outside Pula. You can expect to pay as much as €240,000 for a top-end, two-bedroom central apartment. New developments, such as luxury four-bedroom villas within the exclusive Is Molas Golf Club, just a few kilometres from Pula and the sandy beaches of Santa Margherita, typically sell for €400,000. In terms of rentals, Pula is popular with

1. Cagliari

Cagliari, an industrial port and the capital of Sardinia, is also the island's largest city. It offers a wonderful mix of old and new, with medieval features blending comfortably with more modern structures into the attractive cityscape.

Founded in the 7th century BC, Cagliari was a thriving Carthaginian city before falling to the Romans in 238BC. The city suffered from repeated Arab invasions during the 8th and 9th centuries, and was a Pisan stronghold during the wars with Genoa (from the 11th to 14th centuries). Cagliari was used as a submarine base during World

War II, and was heavily bombed by the Allies.

The grand castle, which looms high above the city, is now home to a fascinating museum. Other buildings that are of particular architectural interest are a large Roman amphitheatre, the 5th-century Basilica of San Saturnino, the 13th-century Romanesque-Gothic cathedral, and the huge 14th-century tower of St Pancras. The Marina district, nestling between the castle and the harbour, is a surprisingly vibrant spot, especially Via Sardinia, with its diverse range of eateries. The old city is the place to head to for an amble and to explore the shops. The main shopping streets are Via Roma and Via Manu.

holiday-makers, due to its stunning location and proximity to the capital. Rental income is good, and a two-bedroom apartment can rent for an average of €890 per week.

KEY FACTS
■ **Population** 6,533
■ **Airport** Cagliari/Elmas Airport, 09030, Sardinia, Italy, Tel: +39 0702 10531
■ **Medical** Samed sas di USALA & C., 09121 Cagliari (CA) – 42/a, v. Is Mirrionis, Tel: +39 0702 75074
■ **Schools** Contact the Sardinian Ministry of Education for more information; Urp della Pubblica Istruzione, Beni Culturali, Informazione, Spettacolo e Sport, Viale Trieste, 186 – 09123 Cagliari, Tel: +39 070 6067040; www.regione.sardegna.it/ tematiche/istruzione
■ **Pros** This is one of the loveliest and most unspoilt stretches of coast in Sardinia ■ There is a mix of Roman and Phoenician remains, including those at Nora ■ This is a relatively affordable destination ■ There are lots of activities to indulge in such as walking, windsurfing and golf
■ **Cons** There is a lot of tourist activity in the area which could lead to overcrowding ■ It is possible that potential future development may damage the environment.

3. Santa Margherita coastline

Thirty kilometres south of Cagliari lies the upmarket coastal resort of Santa Margherita di Pula. This lush strip overlooks the Bay of Gabriele and stretches all the way from Pula to Chia.

Clean, child-friendly white-sand beaches make Santa Margherita an ideal family destination. The sparkling aquamarine waters and varied wooded coastal landscape at Santa Margherita di Pula are the perfect setting for enjoying

leisurely strolls along the beach. At the centre sits the isolated chapel of Santa Margherita, after which the resort is named. Shopping and dining out are very much restricted to local hotels or trips further afield. It is possible to take boat trips to caves and the tiny islands that litter the coast. Other entertainments include golf, tennis, water sports, and horse riding. The local bus service is somewhat irregular.

There are many purpose-built holiday complexes available. For example, €120,000 will buy a one-bedroom apartment in the Abamar residence, just 150m from the beach, beside the exclusive Forte Village Resort and 12 kilometres from the nearest town of Pula. New three-bedroom villas, within a kilometre of the beach and with stunning panoramic views over the Santa Margherita coastline, can be picked up for around €155,000. A five-bedroom, three-bathroom villa in Santa Margherita di Pula costs in the region of €400,000.

KEY FACTS
■ **Population** 6,474
■ **Airport** Cagliari/Elmas Airport, 09030, Sardinia, Italy, Tel: +39 0702 10531
■ **Medical** Samed sas di USALA & C., 09121 Cagliari (CA) – 42/a, v. Is Mirrionis, Tel: +39 0702 75074
■ **Schools** Contact the Sardinian Ministry of Education for more information; Urp della Pubblica Istruzione, Beni Culturali, Informazione, Spettacolo e Sport, Viale Trieste, 186 – 09123 Cagliari, Tel: +39 070 6067040; www.regione.sardegna.it/ tematiche/istruzione
■ **Pros** The unspoilt coastline, which runs for several kilometres, is a series of sandy bays backed by pine forests, dotted discreetly with hotels and the exclusive Forte Village resort ■ There are a number of activities, including the Fralomar diving centre, Is Molas golf course, and the Ranch Is Morus stables

Sardinia's rugged interior landscape is softened by wildflowers

■ **Cons** Shopping and dining is largely restricted to local hotels ■ The area gets very busy because day-trippers from Cagliari come to enjoy the resorts and beaches.

4. Chia

The tiny southern coastal village of Chia nestles among orchards and fig trees, and is a popular choice with tourists. The Torre di Chia, a 17th-century watch tower, looks out proudly from its summit; the wonderful views of Baia Chia (Chia Bay) and the Costa del Sud are well worth the 10-minute climb to the top up a rocky footpath. At the base of the tower lie the ancient ruins of the Phoenician settlement of Bithia, which for centuries was submerged by the sea.

Chia is an area of outstanding natural beauty, with an unspoilt mountainous landscape, white sandy beaches and lagoons, which are home to colonies of flamingoes. Along the road is the bay of Chia, which is renowned for its juniper-clad sand dunes, measuring up to 30 metres high in places, and its enticing, azure-blue waters. The sheltered beaches offer perfect weather conditions for windsurfers, and the reefs at neighbouring Cala

Cipolla are a great attraction for scuba divers.

A luxury detached villa with private pool and up to six bedrooms costs anything from €700,000 to €3,000,000. A villa that sleeps up to six people can yield a weekly income of between €340 in the low season to €1,600 during high season.

KEY FACTS
■ **Population** 9,865
■ **Airport** Cagliari/Elmas Airport, 09030, Sardinia, Italy, Tel: +39 0702 10531
■ **Medical** Samed sas di USALA & C., 09121 Cagliari (CA) – 42/a, v. Is Mirrionis, Tel: +39 0702 75074
■ **Schools** Contact the Sardinian Ministry of Education for more information; Urp della Pubblica Istruzione, Beni Culturali, Informazione, Spettacolo e Sport, Viale Trieste, 186 – 09123 Cagliari, Tel: +39 070 6067040; www.regione.sardegna.it/ tematiche/istruzione
■ **Pros** This is part of the stunning stretch of coastline, known as the Costa del Sud, with attractive beaches ■ There are a number of caves along the coast, making this a haven for walkers and nature lovers ■ There are a number of interesting historical sites, including the Monte Siri city, boasting ancient remains ■ Building is restricted here, which is helping protect the area from overdevelopment
■ **Cons** Some hotel complexes are a blight on the area.

HOTSPOTS

FOR SALE

Property guide

Sardinia is a relatively unspoilt island, offering a wide variety of villas and apartments to suit all tastes and price ranges, yet it still remains undiscovered by British buyers…

Sardinia is sparsely populated and many properties are near the coast with stunning settings

APPEALING TO THE FOREIGN BUYER DUE TO its rocky and mountainous terrain, sandy white beaches and great food, Sardinia first became a tourist destination in the 1960s. It was in the northeast that resorts first sprang up, causing the area to be renamed as the Costa Smeralda. However, this is a destination for jet-setting millionaires, with elegant and luxurious villas selling for extortionate prices. Alghero is Sardinia's other long-established resort, and although still expensive, prices are nothing compared with Costa Smeralda.

It is in southern Sardinia that the real bargains are to be found. With direct flights recently launched to the southern capital, Cagliari, the prospect of purchasing a second home there has become a reality. Cagliari is a popular destination which offers

TYPICAL PROPERTIES

- Sardinia lacks much of the dynamism and charisma of mainland Italy, with many towns lacking a central *piazza*, and houses that often appear bland and characterless
- While most second homes are relatively new, they are usually built from traditional materials and tend to look dated. Materials used include terracotta, white travertine stone, ceramic tiles and chestnut beams
- Elsewhere architecture can be basic, with stone-built shepherds' crofts and coastal fishermans' houses typically available

a good return on your investment. A two-bedroom apartment here would set you back roughly €268,000 (£182,313). Just down the coast are the resorts of Pula and Chia, two of the cheapest areas in Italy for property purchase. It is predicted that Sardinia will soon become one of Italy's most popular destinations with overseas buyers.

In terms of rentals, Sardinia has primarily been a destination with holiday-makers, rather than second home buyers or relocators. The tourist industry is long established in Sardinia, and consequently purchasing property as a buy-to-let investment will result in excellent returns. Again with budget flights opening up, it is expected that the market here will soon take off. Currently, a two-bedroom property in Cagliari rents for €600 (£408) a week, while Chia averages €1,400 (£952) a week ●

THE COSTA SMERALDA

- Costa Smeralda translates as the 'Emerald Coast', due to its 50km of sandy beaches and coves bordering an emerald-green sea
- The area was purchased in 1962 by a group of international investors, headed by Prince Karim Aga Khan, who developed the area from scratch
- Before the Aga Khan purchased the 5,000ha of land, wealthy yacht owners used to moor up here during summer months
- Costa Smeralda offers elegant and expensive villas situated on the coast, complete with swimming pools, and close to golf resorts
- The Costa Smeralda has become a millionaires' retreat, but has avoided the condo blitz that often arrives hand-in-hand with new developments. Today it is a place for celebrities – and celebrity wannabies – to be seen

WHAT CAN YOU GET FOR YOUR EUROS?

SEASIDE VILLA

This one-bedroom property has splendid beach views and would make an ideal holiday home. Recently built, this modern villa has a spacious living area and will be perfect for a family. Situated in Santa Maria Coghinas, it is close to all amenities.

€65,000 CODE CHU

COMPLEX ON THE MARINA

Fully furnished and air conditioned, this property comes with one bedroom, a veranda with a stunning views, and a kitchenette. Located within a new residential complex, this private development is only a short walk from the town centre of Santa Teresa Gallura and is situated right by the marina. The property comes with access to a shared swimming pool.

€150,000+ CODE EUS

COASTAL PROPERTY

Only 8km from the town of Sassari and all amenities, this two-bedroom house is just 5km from the beach. Complete with a spacious garden full of fruit and olive trees, the property also comes with a garage, and a veranda, from which you can enjoy the delightful views.

€240,000 CODE EUS

VILLA WITH VIEWS

This three-bedroom villa has two bathrooms and two reception rooms. It is situated on a large plot of land that overlooks the coast, with staggering views. The property is detached and would be ideal as either a permanent residence or as a holiday home. Located in the village of Punta Tramontana, it is within a short drive of all amenities.

€370,000 CODE CHU

TRADITIONAL SARDINIAN VILLA

Located in a residential complex, this modern villa comes complete with all mod cons, yet enjoys a traditional interior design. With all amenities located on site, it is only a short walk from the coast, while the town of Porto Cervo is just a 10-minute drive away. With a small garden and shared swimming pool, this is a perfect holiday retreat.

€700,000 CODE EUS

LUXURIOUS ESTATE HOME

Situated in one of Costa Smeralda's most exclusive resorts, and only a short walk from La Celvia beach, this estate has a fantastic atmosphere and offers a great deal of privacy. With three bedrooms, three bathrooms and a veranda, the property is perfect for open-air dining. Complete with a swimming pool and 1,000m² garden, this well-designed, modern villa is a wonderful residence.

€1,550,000 CODE PRE

AVERAGE HOUSE PRICES SARDINIA

	2-bed	3-bed	4-bed	5-bed
Cagliari	€226,000 (£153,741)	€292,000 (£198,639)	€360,000 (£244,898)	€400,000 (£272,109)
Pula	€181,000 (£123,129)	€227,000 (£154,422)	€317,000 (£215,646)	€375,000 (£255,102)
Santa Margherita coastline	€141,000 (£95,918)	€253,000 (£172,109)	€282,000 (£191,837)	€332,000 (£225,850)
Chia	€150,000 (£102,040)	€201,000 (£136,735)	€235,000 (£159,864)	€295,000 (£200,680)

PROPERTY GUIDE

BUYER'S REFERENCE

Buyer's reference

You'll find all the resources you need in our reference section, from at-a-glance house and letting prices to useful contacts

House price matrix

	2-bed house	3-bed house	4-bed house	5-bed house
Piedmont, Valle d'Aosta & Trentino-Alto Adige				
Turin	€301,000 (£204,762)	€316,000 (£214,966)	€452,000 (£307,483)	€563,000 (£382,993)
Valle d'Aosta	€128,200 (£87,211)	€209,500 (£142,517)	€251,800 (£171,293)	€361,000 (£245,578)
Trentino-Alto Adige	€253,700 (£172,585)	€357,000 (£242,857)	€335,000 (£227,891)	€398,500 (£271,088)
Liguria				
Genoa	€285,000 (£193,878)	€340,600 (£231,701)	€530,000 (£360,544)	€599,000 (£407,483)
Cinque Terre	€285,000 (£193,878)	€355,000 (£241,497)	€669,000 (£455,102)	€902,000 (£613,605)
Riviera di Ponente	€251,000 (£170,748)	€291,000 (£197,959)	€636,000 (£432,653)	€906,000 (£616,327)
Lombardy & the Lakes				
Lake Maggiore	€207,000 (£140,816)	€308,000 (£209,524)	€448,000 (£304,762)	€738,000 (£502,041)
Lake Como	€173,000 (£117,687)	€337,000 (£229,252)	€798,000 (£542,857)	€906,000 (£616,327)
Milan	€827,000 (£562,585)	€922,000 (£627,211)	€1,180,000 (£802,721)	€1,850,000 (£1,258,503)
Lake Garda	€300,000 (£204,000)	€417,000 (£283,673)	€736,000 (£500,680)	€957,000 (£651,020)
Venice, the Veneto & Friuli-Venezia Giulia				
Venice	€369,000 (£251,020)	€453,000 (£308,163)	€1,004,000 (£682,993)	€1,285,000 (£874,150)
Padua	€239,000 (£162,585)	€304,000 (£206,803)	€408,000 (£277,551)	€610,000 (£414,966)
Trieste	€256,000 (£174,150)	€359,000 (£244,218)	€330,000 (£224,490)	€500,000 (£340,136)
Verona	€321,000 (£218,367)	€319,000 (£217,007)	€445,000 (£302,721)	€765,000 (£520,408)
Emilia-Romagna				
Parma	€227,000 (£154,422)	€340,000 (£231,293)	€449,000 (£305,442)	€753,000 (£512,245)
Bologna	€356,000 (£242,177)	€535,000 (£363,946)	€786,000 (£534,694)	€837,000 (£569,388)
Rimini	€161,000 (£109,524)	€316,000 (£214,966)	€488,000 (£331,973)	€589,000 (£400,680)
Apennine mountains	€170,000 (£115,646)	€248,000 (£168,707)	€305,000 (£207,483)	€412,000 (£280,272)
Tuscany				
Florence	€331,000 (£225,170)	€624,000 (£424,490)	€1,140,000 (£775,510)	€1,413,000 (£961,224)
Arezzo	€281,000 (£191,156)	€409,000 (£278,231)	€565,000 (£384,354)	€605,000 (£411,565)
Tuscan coast	€310,000 (£210,884)	€580,000 (£394,558)	€816,000 (£555,102)	€1,469,000 (£999,320)
Siena	€371,000 (£252,381)	€548,000 (£372,789)	€666,000 (£453,061)	€857,000 (£582,993)
Cortona	€233,000 (£158,503)	€385,000 (£261,905)	€479,000 (£325,850)	€830,000 (£564,626)
Lucca	€246,000 (£167,347)	€363,000 (£246,939)	€725,000 (£493,197)	€878,000 (£597,279)
Montepulciano	€310,000 (£210,884)	€411,000 (£279,592)	€555,000 (£377,551)	€668,000 (£454,422)
Chianti	€305,000 (£207,483)	€513,000 (£348,980)	€920,000 (£625,850)	€979,000 (£665,986)
San Gimignano	€284,000 (£193,197)	€540,000 (£367,347)	€852,000 (£579,592)	€1,125,000 (£765,306)
Umbria				
Lake Trasimeno	€168,000 (£114,286)	€312,000 (£212,245)	€337,000 (£229,252)	€443,000 (£301,361)
Todi	€175,000 (£119,048)	€278,000 (£189,116)	€443,000 (£301,361)	€644,000 (£438,095)
Perugia	€254,000 (£172,789)	€331,000 (£225,170)	€449,000 (£305,442)	€599,000 (£407,483)
Assisi	€262,000 (£178,231)	€375,000 (£255,102)	€615,000 (£418,367)	€697,000 (£474,150)
Orvieto	€189,000 (£128,571)	€349,000 (£237,415)	€595,000 (£404,762)	€603,000 (£410,204)
Le Marche & Abruzzo				
Pescara	€202,000 (£137,415)	€238,000 (£161,905)	€315,000 (£214,286)	€410,000 (£278,912)
Urbino	€246,000 (£167,347)	€289,000 (£196,599)	€397,000 (£270,068)	€423,000 (£287,755)
Monti Sibillini	€137,000 (£93,197)	€205,000 (£139,456)	€307,000 (£208,844)	€335,000 (£227,891)
Loreto	€187,000 (£127,211)	€204,000 (£138,776)	€253,000 (£172,109)	€297,000 (£202,041)
Tollo	€190,000 (£129,252)	€240,000 (£163,265)	€280,000 (£190,470)	€344,000 (£234,014)
Rome & Lazio				
Rome	€360,000 (£244,898)	€409,000 (£278,231)	€654,000 (£444,898)	€1,093,000 (£743,537)
Sabine Hills	€180,000 (£124,138)	€291,000 (£197,959)	€356,000 (£242,177)	€468,000 (£318,367)
Lake Bolsena	€143,000 (£97,279)	€186,000 (£126,531)	€256,000 (£174,150)	€372,000 (£253,061)
Viterbo and surrounds	€235,000 (£159,864)	€392,000 (£266,666)	€742,000 (£504,762)	€829,000 (£563,946)
Campania				
Amalfi Coast	€260,000 (£176,871)	€306,000 (£208,163)	€384,000 (£261,224)	€323,000 (£219,728)
Naples and surrounds	€230,000 (£156,433)	€266,000 (£180,952)	€386,000 (£262,585)	€555,000 (£377,551)
Capri	€194,000 (£131,973)	€262,000 (£178,231)	€310,000 (£210,884)	€395,000 (£268,707)
Ischia and Procida	€195,000 (£132,653)	€256,000 (£174,150)	€359,000 (£244,218)	€409,000 (£278,231)
Puglia, Calabria & Basilicata				
The Trulli area	€134,000 (£91,156)	€167,000 (£113,605)	€237,000 (£161,224)	€315,000 (£214,286)
Scalea	€90,000 (£61,224)	€183,000 (£124,490)	€224,000 (£153,381)	€271,000 (£184,354)
Matera	€140,000 (£95,238)	€147,000 (£100,000)	€274,000 (£186,395)	€276,000 (£187,755)
Sicily				
Taormina	€320,000 (£217,687)	€317,000 (£215,646)	€559,000 (£380,272)	€741,000 (£504,082)
Syracuse province	€107,000 (£72,789)	€214,000 (£145,578)	€339,000 (£230,612)	€372,000 (£253,061)
Ragusa province	€135,000 (£91,837)	€179,000 (£121,769)	€262,000 (£178,231)	€256,000 (£174,150)
Cefalù	€143,000 (£97,279)	€169,000 (£114,966)	€261,000 (£177,551)	€408,000 (£277,551)
Aeolian Islands	€165,000 (£112,245)	€220,000 (£149,660)	€218,000 (£148,299)	€283,000 (£192,517)
Sardinia				
Cagliari	€226,000 (£153,741)	€292,000 (£198,639)	€360,000 (£244,898)	€400,000 (£272,109)
Pula	€181,000 (£123,129)	€227,000 (£154,422)	€317,000 (£215,646)	€375,000 (£255,102)
Santa Margherita coastline	€141,000 (£95,918)	€253,000 (£172,109)	€282,000 (£191,837)	€332,000 (£225,850)
Chia	€150,000 (£102,040)	€201,000 (£136,735)	€235,000 (£159,864)	€295,000 (£200,680)

Apartment price matrix

	1-bed apartment	2-bed apartment	3-bed apartment	4-bed apartment
Piedmont, Valle d'Aosta & Trentino-Alto Adige				
Turin	€133,000 (£90,476)	€240,000 (£163,265)	€360,000 (£244,898)	€455,000 (£309,524)
Valle d'Aosta	€158,000 (£107,483)	€187,000 (£127,211)	€271,000 (£184,354)	€333,000 (£226,531)
Trentino-Alto Adige	€188,000 (£127,891)	€239,000 (£162,585)	€360,000 (£244,898)	€471,000 (£320,408)
Liguria				
Genoa	€173,000 (£117,687)	€253,000 (£172,109)	€269,000 (£182,993)	€391,000 (£265,986)
Cinque Terre	€262,000 (£178,231)	€333,000 (£226,531)	€527,000 (£358,503)	€567,000 (£385,714)
Riviera di Ponente	€167,000 (£113,605)	€244,000 (£165,986)	€304,000 (£206,803)	€378,000 (£257,143)
Lombardy & the Lakes				
Lake Maggiore	€149,000 (£101,361)	€193,000 (£131,293)	€269,000 (£182,993)	€341,000 (£231,973)
Lake Como	€131,000 (£89,116)	€209,000 (£142,177)	€379,000 (£257,823)	€449,000 (£305,442)
Milan	€219,000 (£148,980)	€342,000 (£232,653)	€437,000 (£297,279)	€628,000 (£427,211)
Lake Garda	€196,000 (£133,333)	€284,000 (£193,197)	€319,000 (£217,007)	€385,000 (£261,905)
Venice, the Veneto & Friuli-Venezia Giulia				
Venice	€307,000 (£208,844)	€431,000 (£293,197)	€572,000 (£389,116)	€992,000 (£674,830)
Padua	€147,000 (£100,000)	€203,000 (£138,095)	€340,000 (£231,293)	€413,000 (£280,952)
Trieste	€108,000 (£73,469)	€149,000 (£101,361)	€243,000 (£165,306)	€389,000 (£264,626)
Verona	€159,000 (£108,163)	€208,000 (£141,497)	€313,000 (£212,925)	€416,000 (£282,993)
Emilia-Romagna				
Parma	€147,000 (£100,000)	€205,000 (£139,456)	€315,000 (£214,286)	€393,000 (£267,347)
Bologna	€189,000 (£128,571)	€280,000 (£190,476)	€405,000 (£275,510)	€534,000 (£363,265)
Rimini	€167,000 (£113,605)	€216,000 (£146,939)	€339,000 (£230,612)	€396,000 (£269,388)
Apennine mountains	€103,000 (£70,068)	€158,000 (£107,483)	€185,000 (£125,850)	€199,000 (£135,374)
Tuscany				
Florence	€231,000 (£157,143)	€363,000 (£246,939)	€486,000 (£330,612)	€633,000 (£430,612)
Arezzo	€133,000 (£90,476)	€184,000 (£125,170)	€220,000 (£149,660)	€303,000 (£206,122)
Tuscan coast	€165,000 (£112,245)	€228,000 (£155,102)	€310,000 (£210,884)	€465,000 (£316,327)
Siena	€286,000 (£194,558)	€371,000 (£252,381)	€455,000 (£309,524)	€547,000 (£372,109)
Cortona	€184,000 (£125,170)	€205,000 (£139,456)	€249,000 (£169,388)	€440,000 (£299,320)
Lucca	€142,000 (£96,599)	€226,000 (£153,741)	€317,000 (£215,646)	€376,000 (£255,782)
Montepulciano	€142,000 (£96,599)	€172,000 (£117,007)	€240,000 (£163,265)	€284,000 (£193,197)
Chianti	€245,000 (£166,667)	€238,000 (£161,905)	€357,000 (£242,857)	€409,000 (£278,231)
San Gimignano	€227,000 (£154,422)	€278,000 (£189,116)	€355,000 (£241,497)	€444,000 (£302,041)
Umbria				
Lake Trasimeno	€100,000 (£68,027)	€131,000 (£89,116)	€199,000 (£135,374)	€231,000 (£157,143)
Todi	€128,000 (£87,075)	€166,000 (£112,925)	€179,000 (£121,769)	€320,000 (£217,687)
Perugia	€98,000 (£66,667)	€179,000 (£121,769)	€272,000 (£185,034)	€509,000 (£346,259)
Assisi	€162,000 (£110,204)	€205,000 (£139,456)	€256,000 (£174,150)	€302,000 (£205,442)
Orvieto	€77,000 (£52,381)	€133,000 (£90,476)	€180,000 (£122,449)	€233,000 (£158,503)
Le Marche & Abruzzo				
Pescara	€152,000 (£103,401)	€177,000 (£120,408)	€233,000 (£158,503)	€341,000 (£231,973)
Urbino	€155,000 (£105,442)	€151,000 (£102,721)	€239,000 (£162,585)	€380,000 (£258,503)
Monti Sibillini	€118,000 (£80,272)	€142,000 (£96,599)	€209,000 (£142,177)	€317,000 (£215,646)
Loreto	€116,000 (£78,912)	€122,000 (£82,993)	€205,000 (£139,456)	€231,000 (£157,143)
Tollo	€93,000 (£63,265)	€115,000 (£78,231)	€130,000 (£88,435)	€163,000 (£110,884)
Rome & Lazio				
Rome	€500,000 (£340,136)	€582,000 (£395,918)	€615,000 (£418,367)	€1,120,000 (£761,905)
Sabine Hills	€115,000 (£78,231)	€137,000 (£93,197)	€170,000 (£115,646)	€181,000 (£123,129)
Lake Bolsena	€71,000 (£48,299)	€98,000 (£66,667)	€124,000 (£84,354)	€164,000 (£111,565)
Viterbo and surrounds	€156,000 (£106,122)	€160,000 (£108,844)	€259,000 (£176,190)	€265,000 (£180,272)
Campania				
Amalfi Coast	€185,000 (£125,850)	€415,000 (£282,313)	€400,000 (£272,109)	€615,000 (£418,367)
Naples and surrounds	€202,000 (£137,415)	€293,000 (£199,320)	€352,000 (£239,456)	€610,000 (£414,966)
Capri	€252,000 (£171,429)	€401,000 (£272,789)	€478,000 (£325,170)	€610,000 (£414,966)
Ischia and Procida	€299,000 (£203,401)	€381,000 (£259,184)	€437,000 (£297,279)	€458,000 (£311,565)
Puglia, Calabria & Basilicata				
The Trulli area	€83,000 (£56,463)	€143,000 (£97,279)	€214,000 (£145,578)	€237,000 (£161,224)
Scalea	€32,000 (£21,769)	€48,000 (£32,653)	€84,000 (£57,143)	€115,000 (£78,231)
Matera	€130,000 (£88,435)	€160,000 (£108,844)	€201,000 (£136,735)	€257,000 (£174,830)
Sicily				
Taormina	€178,000 (£121,088)	€265,000 (£180,272)	€478,000 (£325,170)	€609,000 (£414,286)
Syracuse province	€72,000 (£48,980)	€140,000 (£95,238)	€170,000 (£115,646)	€294,000 (£200,000)
Ragusa province	€88,000 (£59,864)	€95,000 (£64,626)	€172,000 (£117,007)	€231,000 (£157,143)
Cefalù	€112,000 (£76,190)	€157,000 (£166,803)	€205,000 (£139,456)	€293,000 (£199,320)
Aeolian Islands	€136,000 (£92,517)	€178,000 (£121,088)	€212,000 (£144,218)	€238,000 (£161,905)
Sardinia				
Cagliari	€205,000 (£139,456)	€268,000 (£182,313)	€286,000 (£194,558)	€418,000 (£284,354)
Pula	€121,000 (£82,313)	€122,000 (£82,993)	€174,000 (£118,367)	€202,000 (£137,415)
Santa Margherita coastline	€94,000 (£63,946)	€127,000 (£86,395)	€173,000 (£117,687)	€211,000 (£143,537)
Chia	€92,000 (£62,585)	€118,000 (£80,272)	€154,000 (£104,762)	€293,000 (£199,320)

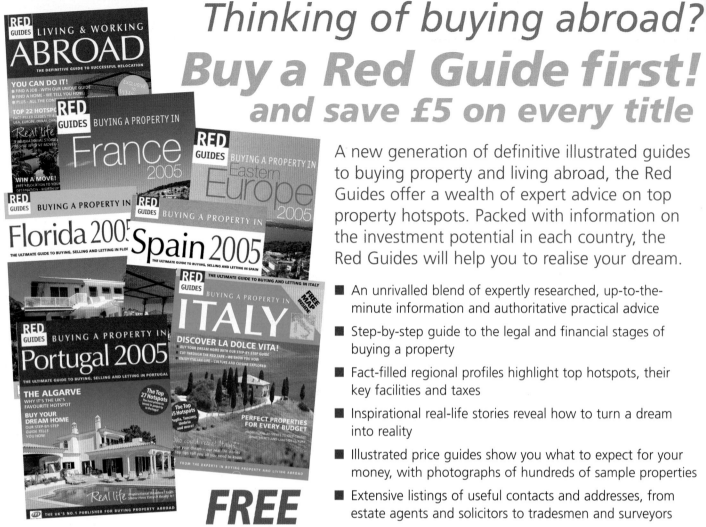

Thinking of buying abroad?
Buy a Red Guide first!
and save £5 on every title

A new generation of definitive illustrated guides to buying property and living abroad, the Red Guides offer a wealth of expert advice on top property hotspots. Packed with information on the investment potential in each country, the Red Guides will help you to realise your dream.

- An unrivalled blend of expertly researched, up-to-the-minute information and authoritative practical advice
- Step-by-step guide to the legal and financial stages of buying a property
- Fact-filled regional profiles highlight top hotspots, their key facilities and taxes
- Inspirational real-life stories reveal how to turn a dream into reality
- Illustrated price guides show you what to expect for your money, with photographs of hundreds of sample properties
- Extensive listings of useful contacts and addresses, from estate agents and solicitors to tradesmen and surveyors
- Detailed analysis of each country's economy and property market from our panel of experts

FREE POSTAGE & PACKAGING!

CALL OUR ORDER HOTLINE TODAY ON 01225 786850
Please quote order code IPBG05 when ordering

☐ **YES!** I would like to buy a copy of *Buying a Property in France 2005* at £11.95 **SAVE £5!**

☐ **YES!** I would like to buy a copy of *Buying a Property in Eastern Europe 2005* at £11.95 **SAVE £5!**

☐ **YES!** I would like to buy a copy of *Buying a Property in Spain 2005* at £11.95 **SAVE £5!**

☐ **YES!** I would like to buy a copy of *Buying a Property in Florida 2005* at £11.95 **SAVE £5!**

☐ **YES!** I would like to buy a copy of *Buying a Property in Portugal 2005* at £6.99 **SAVE £5!**

☐ **YES!** I would like to buy a copy of *Buying a Property in Italy 2005* at £9.99 **SAVE £5!**

☐ **YES!** I would like to buy a copy of *Living and Working Abroad* at £9.99 **SAVE £5!**

Title ☐ Initial ☐ Surname _____

Address _____

Postcode _____ Telephone _____

Quantity _____ TOTAL _____

ORDER CODE G14

CREDIT CARD

☐ VISA ☐ MASTERCARD ☐ SWITCH ☐ AMERICAN EXPRESS

Card no. ▢▢▢▢ ▢▢▢▢ ▢▢▢▢ ▢▢▢▢ ▢▢▢▢

Expiry Date ☐ / ☐ Issue/Valid Date ☐ / ☐

Signature _____

CHEQUE

☐ I enclose a cheque/postal order payable to *Merricks Media Ltd*

Please return this form with payment to:

£5 off Property Buying Guide Offer
Merricks Media Ltd
FREEPOST
(SWB 10668)
Bath
BA1 2ZZ
UK

Please allow up to 14 days for delivery

☐ Merricks Media Ltd may pass on your details to carefully selected companies whose products and services may interest you. Please tick here if you would prefer not to receive such offers.

Letting price matrix (weekly income)

	1-bed	2-bed	3-bed	4-bed	5-bed
Piedmont, Valle d'Aosta & Trentino-Alto Adige					
Turin	€640 (£435)	€920 (£626)	€1,320 (£898)	€1,830 (£1,245)	€2,090 (£1,422)
Valle d'Aosta	€450 (£306)	€605 (£412)	€880 (£599)	€1,040 (£707)	€1,600 (£1,088)
Trentino-Alto Adige	€590 (£401)	€650 (£442)	€940 (£639)	€875 (£595)	€945 (£643)
Liguria					
Genoa	€770 (£524)	€860 (£585)	€1,230 (£837)	€1,630 (£1,109)	€2,100 (£1,429)
Cinque Terre	€510 (£347)	€770 (£524)	€1,050 (£714)	€1,600 (£1,088)	€2,150 (£1,463)
Riviera di Ponente	€480 (£327)	€750 (£510)	€960 (£653)	€1,360 (£925)	€1,980 (£1,347)
Lombardy & the Lakes					
Lake Maggiore	€670 (£456)	€680 (£463)	€1,110 (£755)	€1,310 (£891)	€2,200 (£1,497)
Lake Como	€430 (£293)	€610 (£415)	€1,140 (£776)	€1,560 (£1,061)	€1,950 (£1,327)
Milan	€890 (£605)	€1,450 (£986)	€1,860 (£1,265)	€2,425 (£1,650)	€2,600 (£1,769)
Lake Garda	€580 (£395)	€715 (£486)	€835 (£568)	€1,470 (£1,000)	€1,870 (£1,272)
Venice, the Veneto & Friuli-Venezia Giulia					
Venice	€640 (£435)	€965 (£656)	€1,100 (£748)	€2,090 (£1,422)	€2,850 (£1,939)
Padua	€800 (£544)	€910 (£619)	€1,160 (£789)	€1,660 (£1,129)	€1,750 (£1,190)
Trieste	€695 (£473)	€820 (£558)	€1,020 (£694)	€1,630 (£1,109)	€1,580 (£1,075)
Verona	€550 (£374)	€850 (£578)	€1,070 (£728)	€1,300 (£884)	€1,900 (£1,293)
Emilia-Romagna					
Parma	€490 (£333)	€585 (£398)	€720 (£490)	€1,240 (£844)	€1,450 (£986)
Bologna	€595 (£405)	€815 (£554)	€890 (£605)	€1,305 (£888)	€1,550 (£1,054)
Rimini	€490 (£333)	€575 (£391)	€770 (£524)	€990 (£673)	€1,240 (£844)
Apennine mountains	€580 (£395)	€640 (£435)	€860 (£585)	€1,050 (£714)	€1,460 (£993)
Tuscany					
Florence	€725 (£493)	€1,005 (£684)	€1,105 (£752)	€2,140 (£1,456)	€2,530 (£1,721)
Arezzo	€600 (£408)	€780 (£531)	€1,250 (£850)	€1,810 (£1,231)	€1,970 (£1,340)
Tuscan coast	€580 (£395)	€740 (£503)	€1,070 (£728)	€1,370 (£932)	€1,890 (£1,286)
Siena	€550 (£374)	€770 (£524)	€905 (£616)	€1,520 (£1,034)	€2,050 (£1,395)
Cortona	€770 (£524)	€925 (£629)	€1,220 (£830)	€1,530 (£1,041)	€1,910 (£1,229)
Lucca	€600 (£408)	€680 (£463)	€1,210 (£823)	€1,880 (£1,279)	€2,180 (£1,483)
Montepulciano	€725 (£493)	€830 (£565)	€930 (£633)	€1,275 (£867)	€2,080 (£1,415)
Chianti	€625 (£425)	€910 (£619)	€1,630 (£1,109)	€1,740 (£1,184)	€2,825 (£1,922)
San Gimignano	€620 (£422)	€980 (£667)	€1,240 (£844)	€1,580 (£1,075)	€2,260 (£1,537)
Umbria					
Lake Trasimeno	€500 (£340)	€625 (£425)	€930 (£633)	€1,490 (£1,014)	€1,730 (£1,177)
Todi	€625 (£425)	€930 (£633)	€1,580 (£1,075)	€1,610 (£1,095)	€2,050 (£1,395)
Perugia	€715 (£486)	€850 (£578)	€1,260 (£857)	€1,390 (£946)	€1,800 (£1,224)
Assisi	€510 (£347)	€725 (£493)	€1,140 (£776)	€1,670 (£1,136)	€2,020 (£1,374)
Orvieto	€485 (£330)	€690 (£469)	€870 (£592)	€1,275 (£867)	€1,620 (£1,102)
Le Marche & Abruzzo					
Pescara	€620 (£422)	€725 (£493)	€840 (£571)	€1,190 (£810)	€1,660 (£1,129)
Urbino	€680 (£463)	€860 (£585)	€1,080 (£735)	€1,280 (£871)	€1,790 (£1,128)
Monti Sibillini	€530 (£361)	€595 (£405)	€820 (£558)	€1,020 (£694)	€1,580 (£1,075)
Loreto	€625 (£425)	€730 (£497)	€880 (£599)	€1,120 (£762)	€1,800 (£1,224)
Tollo	€440 (£299)	€520 (£354)	€750 (£510)	€990 (£673)	€1,180 (£803)
Rome & Lazio					
Rome	€760 (£517)	€960 (£653)	€1,385 (£942)	€2,380 (£1,619)	€2,750 (£1,871)
Sabine Hills	€660 (£449)	€760 (£517)	€1,150 (£782)	€1,420 (£966)	€1,790 (£1,218)
Lake Bolsena	€680 (£463)	€720 (£490)	€1,110 (£755)	€1,560 (£1,061)	€1,840 (£1,252)
Viterbo and surrounds	€460 (£313)	€610 (£415)	€840 (£571)	€1,210 (£823)	€1,420 (£966)
Campania					
Amalfi Coast	€605 (£412)	€670 (£456)	€930 (£633)	€2,140 (£1,456)	€2,310 (£1,571)
Naples and surrounds	€720 (£490)	€1,260 (£857)	€2,120 (£1,442)	€2,580 (£1,755)	€2,390 (£1,626)
Capri	€880 (£599)	€1,130 (£769)	€1,960 (£1,333)	€2,190 (£1,490)	€3,130 (£2,129)
Ischia and Procida	€450 (£306)	€850 (£578)	€1,870 (£1,272)	€1,920 (£2,822)	€2,150 (£1,463)
Puglia, Calabria & Basilicata					
The Trulli area	€515 (£350)	€525 (£357)	€800 (£544)	€1,170 (£796)	€1,510 (£1,027)
Scalea	€320 (£218)	€395 (£269)	€615 (£418)	€780 (£531)	€900 (£612)
Matera	€400 (£272)	€440 (£299)	€670 (£456)	€830 (£565)	€1,050 (£714)
Sicily					
Taormina	€940 (£639)	€1,300 (£884)	€2,080 (£1,415)	€2,460 (£1,673)	€2,950 (£2,007)
Syracuse province	€610 (£415)	€605 (£412)	€1,095 (£745)	€1,255 (£854)	€1,460 (£993)
Ragusa province	€580 (£395)	€700 (£476)	€1,060 (£721)	€1,330 (£905)	€1,625 (£1,105)
Cefalù	€525 (£357)	€750 (£510)	€1,220 (£830)	€1,680 (£1,143)	€2,360 (£1,605)
Aeolian Islands	€740 (£503)	€1,070 (£728)	€1,380 (£939)	€1,550 (£1,054)	€1,850 (£1,259)
Sardinia					
Cagliari	€600 (£408)	€600 (£408)	€1,050 (£714)	€1,440 (£980)	€1,530 (£1,041)
Pula	€705 (£480)	€890 (£605)	€905 (£616)	€1,680 (£1,143)	€1,660 (£1,129)
Santa Margherita coastline	€650 (£442)	€970 (£660)	€1,240 (£844)	€1,570 (£1,068)	€1,630 (£1,109)
Chia	€645 (£439)	€1,330 (£905)	€1,400 (£952)	€1,700 (£1,156)	€1,910 (£1,299)

PRICE MATRIX

Glossary

A

Affittasi
To let, for rent

Agenzia immobiliare
Estate agency

Appartamento
Flat or apartment

Appezzamento di terreno
Plot (of land)

Architetto
Architect

Assegno circolare
Banker's draft

Assicurazione
Insurance

Atto
Act (of signing the 'rogito')

Atto notarile
The final conveyance document

Autostrada
Motorway

Avvocato
Lawyer

B

Bifamiliare
Semi-detached house

Bilocale
Two-room apartment

Bollo
Tax stamp

Bollo auto
Car tax

Bombola
Bottled gas. Literally: cylinder or bottle

Borgo
Hamlet or village. Also a suburb or district when used in reference to a city

C

Camera di commercio
Chamber of commerce

Canone RAI
TV tax; similar to the television licence fee in the UK

Caparra
Deposit

Carabinieri
Police officers

Carta d'identita
Identity card; all residents are required to carry one

Casa
House or home

Casa colonica
Farmhouse

Casa gemella
Semi-detached house

Casale
Country house. Plural: Casali

Casetta
Small house

Castello
Castle

Catasta
Land registry office

Certificato di residenza
Residence permit

Clausola
Clause, as in a contract

Codice fiscale
Tax code, akin to a NI number, for personal identification. Required for employment, house buying and opening a bank account

Commercialista
Accountant or book-keeper (specialising in tax returns)

Compromesso (di vendita)
Preliminary contract (of sale) that is legally binding. Also known as 'contratto preliminare di vendita'

Comune
Town hall. Also a town, city or county council, and an administrative area

Concessione edilizia
Planning permission

Condominio
Apartment building, block of flats

Consegna
Exchange of contracts

Conto bancario
Bank account

Contratti di affitto
Rental contract or lease

Conveyance
The transfer of title to a property from one person to another by means of a written instrument

Costruttore
Builder

D

Deposito di garanzia
Deposit

Dichiarazione dei redditi
Tax declaration, income tax return

F

Falegname
Carpenter

Fisco
Tax office

G

Geometra
Surveyor

I

Imposta
Tax

Imposta comunale sugli immobili (ICI)
Property tax based on the 'valore catastale'

Imposta di registro
Registration tax

Imposta regionale sulle attività produttive (IRAP)
Regional production tax levied on businesses

Imposta sui Redditi delle Persone Fisiche (IRPEF)
The old name for income tax, still widely used

Imposta sul Reddito delle Persone Giuridiche (IRPEG)
Corporate income tax, replaced by the IRES in 2004

Imposta sul valore aggiunto (IVA)
Value added tax (VAT)

Imposta sul Reddito delle Società (IRES)
Corporate income tax which replaced the old IRPEG in 2004, still often referred to as IRPEG

Imposta sulle successioni
Inheritance tax

Intendenza di finanzia
Local tax office

Ipoteca
Mortgage

IRE
Income tax, replaced the old IRPEF in 2005

L

Libretto di lavoro
Worker's registration card

M

Medico convenzionato
Health service doctor; GP

Monolocale
Studio flat or bedsit

Municipio
Town hall

Mutuo
Mortgage, loan

N

Notaio
Public notary. Draws up the deeds, ensures the arrangements are legal and registers the transfer of ownership

P

Palazzo
Large building, mansion or palace. Plural: Palazzi

Perito agronomo
Land surveyor

Permesso
A permit or licence granting authorisation to stay in Italy for a stated reason, renewable after five years

Permesso di soggiorno per lavoro
Permit to stay in Italy for work purposes

Piano
Floor (i.e. of an apartment)

Piscina
Swimming pool

Pozzo
Well

Pozzo nero
Cesspit

Prestito
Loan

Preventivo
Estimate or quotation

Prezzo effettivo
Actual price

Prezzo di domanda
Asking price

Procura
Power of attorney

Proposta d'acquisto
Proposal of purchase. Not legally binding

Proprietario
Landlord

Provvigione
Commission

Q

Questura
Police headquarters

R

Ragioniere
Accountant

Ricevuta di segnalazione di soggiorno
Temporary residence permit, entitles the holder to stay for three months looking for a job

Rilevamento
Land survey

Rinnovare
Renovation

Rogito
Final deed of sale or contract. Signed in the presence of the *notaio*

Rustico
Dilapidated rustic or rural house. Literally: peasant

S

Scrittura privato
Simplified version of the final contract

Società a responsabilità limitata (S.r.l.)
Limited liability company

Società in Accomandita Semplice (S.A.S.)
Limited liability partnership

Società in nome collettivo (s.n.c.)
General partnership

Società per Azioni (S.p.A.)
Public limited company

Società semplice (s.s.)
Ordinary partnership (no commercial activity permitted; used for professional activities, and small-scale agriculture and property management)

Spese
Expenses

Stima
Valuation, estimate, assessment

T

Tassa communale dei rifiuti
Refuse collection tax. Also known as the 'Tassa sui refuti solidi urbani' (TARSU)

Tassa di bollo
Stamp duty

Terreno coltivable
Farmland

Titolo di proprietà
Title deed

Traduttore
Translator

Trattabile
Negotiable

Trullo
Small house with conical roof found in southern Italy. Plural: Trulli

U

Ufficio anagrafe
Registry office that holds records, such as births, marriages and residence

Ufficio delle imposte direct
Tax office

Ufficio di Collocamento Manodopera
Local employment office

Unità Sanitaria Locale (USL)
Local health authority

V

Valore catastale
The official tax value of a property

Vendesi
For sale

Vigile urbano
Municipal police, traffic police

Villa
Detached house or mansion, usually with garden, yard or other grounds

Villetta
Detached house

Villetta a schiera
Terraced house

Villino
A small villa or cottage with a garden or yard

Z

Zona tranquilla
Quiet area

Useful contacts

Note: when dialling Italian phone numbers, the area code must always be dialled in full, even when calling from the same area. It is also necessary to dial the leading zero, even when calling from abroad

Accountants

La Rosa & Associates, Piazza Luigi di Savoia 28, 20124 Milano, Tel: +39 02 669 3086, www.studiolarosa.com,

Nicolina Madonia, Via Torino 63, 95128 Catania, +39 0954 36834

PriceWaterhouseCoopers, Piazza Dante 7, 16121 Genova, Tel: +39 010 570 2013, www.pwcglobal.com

Studio Associato de Luca, Galleria Passerella 2, 20122 Milano, Tel: +39 02 365 5651, www.studiodeluca.it,

Studio Capaccioli, Via San Gallo 76, Firenze 50129, Tel: +39 055 474945, www.studiolegalecapaccioli.com

Studio Tributario Celli & Associati, Via Michele Mercati 51, 00197 Roma, Tel: +39 06 808 5594, www.studiocelli.com

Air Conditioning

Aesse Impianti Montaggio Impianti Aria Condizionata, Piazzale Cosulich A. 1, 34074 Monfalcone, Tel: +39 0481 486583

Benedetti Renzo Impianti Frigoriferi Aria Condizionata, Via Delle Catene 40, 56017 Madonna Dell'acqua, Tel: +39 050 869114

I.m.a.c. Refrigerazione Impianti Aria Condizionata, Piazza Della Libertà 12, 16033 Lavagna, Tel: +39 0185 395349

Krios Aria Condizionata, Via Santi Fratellli 25, 10024 Moncalieri, Tel: +39 011 647 3580

Rimer, Via Bligny 35, 70011 Alberobello, Tel: +39 080 432 3863, rimer.srl@libero.it

Tecnoservizi impianti Aria Condizionata, Via Mazzacurati 31, 40013 Castel Maggiore, Tel: +39 051 712881

Architects

Acta Architettura, Via Cavour 256, 00184, Tel: +39 06 474 3723, www.actaarchitettura.it

Arch Caprioglio, www.caprioglio.com

Bisi & Merkus Studio Associato, Vicolo Trivelli 6, 42100 Reggio Emilia, Tel: +39 0522 337447, www.bisimerkus.it

Lucadello & Stocco Architetti Associati, Via Vaccari 1a, 36061 Bassano Del Grappa, Tel: +39 0424 523009, lucadello.stocco@tin.it

Martello Arch. Damiano, Via Lorenzo Il Magnifico 54, 50129 Firenze, Tel: +39 055 480968, d.martella@archiword.it

Massimo Rella Architect Studio di Architettura, Corso Italia 11, 20122 Milano, Tel: +39 02 8969 7403

Miyagima Harucki Landscape Architect, Via Dante Alighieri 30, 22040 Lurago d'Erba, Tel: +39 031 696081

Rava Elena – Architetto, Via Luigi Lagrange 29, 10123 Torino, Tel: +39 011 531 944, elena.rava@tiscali.it

Studio Archemi, Via Cappuccino 16, 20122 Milano, Tel: +39 02 7602 3732, mailbox@studioarchemi.it

Studio DA. MA., Via G Matteotti 31, 36012 Asiago, Tel: +39 0424 462031, arch.giomarcato@infinito.it

Studio Tecnico Immobiliare A. Bergamaschi, Via Garibaldi 16, 54027 Pontremoli, Tel: +39 0187 831224, www.studiobergamaschi.it

Tage Architect Tauber Gerhard, Via Bruno 5, 39042 Bressanone, Tel: +39 0472 838128

Banks

ABN Amro Bank Spa, Via Ludovisi 16, 00187 Roma, Tel: +39 06 324761, www.abnamro.com

Banca Fideuram, Via Incoronata 3, 80133 Napoli, Tel: +39 081 971 1311, www.bancafideuram.it

Banca Intesa, Via Monte di Pietà 8, 20121 Milano, Tel: +39 02 87911

Banca Mediolanum, Via Logudoro 48, 09127 Cagliari, Tel: +39 070 659814

Banca Popolare di Verona, Piazza Nogara, 37121 Verona, Tel: +39 045 820 2599, www.bpv.it

Banca Popolare Sant'Angelo, Corso Vittorio Emanuele 10, 92027 Licata, Tel: +39 0922 86011, www.bancasantangelo.com

Banca Woolwich, Piazza Dante 49, 16121 Genova, Tel: +39 010 576 3811, www.bancawoolwich.it

Barclays Bank, Piazza Dante 49, 16121 Genova, Tel: +39 010 572371

Citibank, Foro Buonoparte, 20121 Milano, Tel: +39 02 864741, www.citibank.com

HSBC, Piazzetta Bossi Maurilio 1, 20121 Milano, Tel: +39 02 724371, www.hsbc.com

The Royal Bank of Scotland, Via Po 25, 00198 Roma, Tel: +39 06 853 7851, www.rbs.com

Builders and Decorators

Anteprima, 13045 Gattinara, Tel: +39 0163 827487, anteprima_srl@libero.it

Art Casa – de Lucci Giuseppe, 20159 Milano, Tel: +39 02 688 3156, artcasa@tiscalinet.it

Art In Colour Di Zanni Stefano decoratori Stuccatori, Via Radici in Piano 16, 42014 Castellarano, Tel: +39 0536 857900

Bertarello Remo – Ditta Decoratori Riuniti, Fraz. Crotache 2, 11027 Saint-vincent, Tel: +39 328 227 4523, decoratori_riuniti@virgilio.it

Brilli Interni, Via Lisbona 17, 50065 Pontassieve, Tel: +39 55 8367240, brilliinterni@libero.it

Decoratori ADF di Errichetti Daniele & Co, Viale Gorizia 152, 47100 Forli, Tel: +39 0543 720079

Edilcolor, Via Certaldese 31, 50026 San Casciano In Val Di Pesa, Tel: +39 055 822 8485

Elena Lisa Colombo decoratori, Via Forlanini Carlo, 21052 Busto Arsizio, Tel: +39 0331 685020

Equipe Casa di Federico Cuscianna, Piazza San Lorenzo 5, 20090 Trezzano Sul Naviglio, Tel: +39 02 445 9930, federico@tele2.it

Di Gennaro Costruzioni, Via Sirena - Tortoreto Lido 11a, 64018 Tortoreto, Tel: +39 0861 787008, www.digennarocostruzioni.com

Impresa Edile Ristrutturazioni, Via Teodorica 26, 00162 Roma, Tel: +39 06 440 2825, crisedilizia@virgilio.it

Iniziative Edili bi Zeta, Via Manna 16, 34134 Trieste, Tel: +39 040 282 0014, iebizeta@catea.com

L'artelier decoratori, Via Sforza Cesarini 54, 00186 Roma, Tel: +39 06 687 9424

MG Eco Engineering di Giuseppe Marinelli, Via Cibrario 6, 10144 Torino, Tel: +39 011 473 1753, www.ecobuilding.it

De Pace Ivan – Impresa Edile, Via Prete 106a, 50127 Firenze, Tel: +39 055 428 9139, depace@virgilio.it

Project Immobiliare, Via Negri, 00042 Anzio, Tel: +39 339 300 1740

Pulvirenti Antonio, Piazza Pitagora, 88100 Catanzaro, Tel: +39 340 746 4172

Rossi Vasco Snc Rossi Vasco E Luciano decoratori, Località Astronome 222, 53042 Chianciano Terme, Tel: +39 0578 62692

Società Decoratori Forlivesi di Cappelli, Via Rolandini Grisignano 6a, 47100 Forli, Tel: +39 0543 86423, soc.dec.forlivesi@tiscali.it

Builders Supplies

Angelozzi, Via Prato Cornelio, 00125 Roma, Tel: +39 06 5235 5945, info@angelozzi.com, www.angelozzi.it

Bellamoli Granulati, Via Betteloni 4a, 37023 Grezzana, Tel: +39 045 865 0355, info@bellamoli.it, www.bellamoli.it

Botti Sperandio, Via Bagozzi 41, 25069 Villa Carcina, Tel: +39 030 881754, botti.sperandio@tiscalinet.it

Calevo Nestore & F. sas, Via Provenciale 386, 19021 Arcola, Tel: +39 0187 988010, calevo@libero.it

Garden House, Viale Michelangelo 2499, 90135 Palermo, Tel: +39 091 222072, www.gardenhousepalermo.com

Haro-Bau, Via Vecchia 17, 39040 Ora, Tel: +39 0471 802388, www.hara-bau.com

Idrosanitaria di Rinaldi Vincenzo, Via Brodolini 73, 58017 Pitigliano, Tel: +39 0564 616147

MAT.ED. di Centi Laura, Via G B Vico 33 (La Rosa), 57100 Livorno, Tel: +39 0586 812335, mat.ed@tiscali.it

Sola Graziella, Str. Collegara 27 – Loc. San Damaso, 41100 Modena, Tel: +39 059 469313, cer.solagraziella@libero.it

Ve-Va, Via Fornace Verni 153, 47842 San Giovanni In Marignano, Tel: +39 0541 955130, ve-va@ve-va.it, www.ve-va.it

Business Advice

British Chamber of Commerce for Italy, Via Dante 12, 20121 Milano, Tel: +39 02 877798, www.britchamitaly.com

Logos Studio Professional, VIa Ancona 17, 30172 Venezia Mestre, Tel: +39 041 532 2600, www.logostudi.it

Car Hire

Avis Autonoleggio, Via della Giuliana 25 (S. Pietro), 00195 Roma, Tel: +39 06 3974 2375, www.avis.com

easyCar, www.easycar.com

Europcar Italia, Via Cesare Giulio Viola 48, 00148 Roma, Tel: +39 06 967091, www.europcar.com

Hertz Italiana, Viale Leonardo da Vinci 421, 00145 Roma, Tel: +39 06 542941, www.hertz.com

Maggiore, Via di Tor Cervara 225, 00155 Roma, Tel: +39 06 229351, www.maggiore.it

Pinna Autonoleggio, Zona Industriale, 07026 Olbia, Tel: +39 0199 180180, www.autonoleggiopinna.com

Sardinya Rent A Car, Viale Caprera 8a, 07100 Sassari, Tel: +39 079 291113, www.autonoleggiosardinya.it

Win Rent Sixt Franchisee, Via Corona Boreale 86, 00050 Fiumicino, Tel: +39 06 659651, www.e-sixt.it

Carpenters

Antonio Caputo, Via Delle Betulle 14, 20040 Busnago, Tel: +39 039 695 9139

Armando Amoretti, Via San Sisino 4, 00068 Rignano Flaminio, Tel: +39 0761 507133

Bruno Tresca, Via Pone S. Giovanni, 67019 Scoppito, Tel: +39 0862 717381

Franco Baroni, Via Peloda 2, 24021 Albino, Tel: +39 035 753273

Mauro Massi, Via Flaminia, 61030 Cartoceto, Tel: +39 0721 897563

Mirando Lombardi, Via Puccini 19, 51018 Pieve A Nievole, Tel: +39 0572 80187

Salvatore Drago, Via Nazario Sauro 25, 21020 Taino, Tel: +39 0331 956322

Cleaning Services

Cooperativa Traslochi Fossolo, Via Due Madonne 51/3, 40138 Bologna, Tel: +39 051 534911, www.traslochifossolo.com

CPM Servizi, Via Gregorio VII 80, 00165 Roma, Tel: +39 06 3938 8081, www.cipiemmeservizi.it

Complimentary Therapy

Carla Bastianelli (Homeopathy), Via Benedetto Croce 62, 00142 Roma, Tel: +39 06 594 3794, c.bastianelli@jumpy.it

Centro San Sebastiano (Acupuncture), Via Catalani 11, 09128 Cagliari, Tel: +39 070 490408

Dott. Jianmin Zhang (Traditional Chinese), Via. E. Giovenale 4, 00176 Roma, Tel: +39 06 214 7746, j_zhang@tin.it

Dott. Yuanrang Zheng (Acupuncture), Corso Buenos Aires 92, 20124 Milano, Tel: +39 02 2951 1121, zhengyuanrang@hotmail.com

Erboristeria Virya (Herbalist), Via Galliera 60b, 40121 Bologna, Tel: +39 051 240986, www.virya.com

Farmacia Caronna Dr. Fabio (Herbalist), Piazzetta Porta Guccia 9, 90134 Palermo, Tel: +39 091 320072, farmaciacaronna@tin.it

Terme Luigiane (Health Spa), Via Frugiuele 2, 87100 Cosenza, Tel: +39 0984 27440, www.termeluigiane.it

Computer Services

A.B. Computer, Via XX Settembre 14, 24047 Treviglio, Tel: +39 0363 302740, info@ab-computer.it

Assice Assistenza Informatica Caserta, Via Mazzocchi 15, 81100 Caserta, Tel: +39 0823 216528, info@assice.it, www.assice.it

Computer On, Via I Maggio 27, 96010 Sortino, Tel: +39 0931 952000, www.computeron.it

Eco Store, Viale Premuda 27, 20129 Milano, Tel: +39 02 7600 0008, ecostore@serviziocliente.it

HAL 9000 PC di Callai Ramona, Via Tommaseo 8, 09131 Cagliari, Tel: +39 070 495767, info@hal9000pc.com

Iceberg Technology, Vicolo Verdi 69c, Castrette, 31050 Villorba, Tel: +39 0422 9171, www.icebergtechnology.it

JPC, Via Gasperina 147, 00173 Roma, Tel: +39 06 9761 1055, informazioni@jpc.it, www.jpc.it

Prink, Via Emilia Ponente 355, 48014 Castel Bolognese, Tel: +39 0546 50077, info@prink.it, www.prink.it

Re-Charge, Via don Minzoni 23, 54033 Carrara, Tel: +39 0585 779030, re-charge@inwind.it

Studio di Informatica, Via Stufa Secca 16, 53100 Siena, Tel: +39 0577 288045, sassetti@sdisiena.it

V&GA Sistemi, Via Sanbro Pertini 47, Loc. Montarioso, 53035 Monteriggioni, Tel: +39 0577 344005

Culture

British-Italian Society, The Offices of Venice in Peril Fund, Hurlingham Studios (Unit 4), Ranalagh Gardens, London, SW6 3PA, jo.t@british-italian.org

Italian Cultural Institute, 39 Belgrave Square, London, SW1X 8NT, Tel: 0207 235 1461, www.italcultur.org.uk

Italian Tourist Board, 1 Princess Street, London, W1B 2AY, Tel: 0207 408 1254, www.italiantouristboard.co.uk

Currency Services

Caxton FX, 2 Motcomb Street, London, SW1X 8JU, Tel: 0845 658 2223, www.caxtonfx.com

Currencies Direct, Hanover House, 73/74 High Holborn, London, WC1V 6LR, Tel: 0207 813 0332, www.currenciesdirect.com

Currency Solutions, 10-12 Arcade Chambers, High Street Eltham, London, Tel: 0208 850 2266, www.currencysolutions.co.uk

Currency UK, 1 Battersea Square, London, SW11 3RA, Tel: 0207 738 0777, www.currencyuk.co.uk

Escape Currency, Escape House, 45 Buckingham Street, Aylesbury, Bucks, HP20 2NQ, Tel: 0800 032 1109, www.escapecurrency.com

Foreign Currency Direct, The Old Malt House, Currencies Court, Old Amersham, Bucks, HP7 0HL, Tel: 0800 328 5884, www.ukcurrencies.co.uk

FX Solutions, FX Solutions House, Fairway, Petts Wood, Kent, BR5 1EG, Tel: 01689 601 111, www.fxsolutions.co.uk

HIFX, 59-60 Thames Street, Windsor, Berkshire, SL4 1EP, Tel: 01753 859159, info@hifx.co.uk, www.hifx.co.uk

ISX FX, 107-111 Fleet Street, London, EC4A 2AB, Tel: 0207 936 9562, info@isxfx.com, www.isxfx.com

Migrate4Less, 160 Brompton Road, Knightsbridge, London, SW3 1HW, Tel: 0207 594 0570, www.migrate4less.com

Moneycorp, 100 Brompton Road, Knightsbridge, London, SW3 1ER, Tel: 0207 589 3000, www.moneycorp.com

SGM-FX, Prince Rupert House, 64 Queen Street, London, EC4R 1AD, Tel: 0207 778 0123, www.sgm-fx.com

Dentists

Centro Odontoiatrico Odontobi, Via XXV Aprile 38, 28053 Castelletto Sopra Ticino, Tel: +39 0331 962405, odontobi@dente.it, www.dente.it

Eurodont Day Hospital Odontoiatrico, Via Matteotti 101, 20041 Agrate Brianza, Tel: +39 039 651938, eurodont@eurodont.com

Garau Piero, Via Dante 77, Tel: 09128 Cagliari, Tel: +39 070 498313

Dr. Roland Michael Marrek, Laser Dental Treatment, Via Legnano 16, 20121 Milano, Tel: +39 02 869 3938, info@studio-marrek.it

Studio Odontoiatrico Associato Casagni, Piazza Attias 37, 57125 Livorno, Tel: +39 0586 895548, studiodrcasagni@inlinea.net

Studio Odontoiatrico Podda & Sorci, Via Villa Lucina 78, 00145 Roma, Tel: +39 06 540 5761, info@podda-sorci.it

Disability & Special Needs

Ortopedia ASOR Sanitari (Orthopaedic), Via Casarini 4d, 40131 Bologna, Tel: +39 051 556409, info@asor.com

Bibiana Autoscuola (Disabled Driving School), Via Principe Amadeo 28, 10123 Torino, Tel: +39 011 812 6828

Pasteur (Wheelchairs), Via Antiochia 2a, 16129 Genova, Tel: +39 010 540676

SVA Ascensori (Lifts), Via Natta 16, Settimo, 37026 Pescantina, Tel: +39 045 715 2877, info@svaascensori.it

Tecnorehab di Giorgio Contini (Orthopaedic), Viale Croce Rossa 114-116, 90146 Palermo, Tel: +39 091 682 1220, tecnorahab@virgilio.it

Thermomat (Bathroom Accessories), Via M. Curie 3, Cerese, 46030 Virgilio, Tel: +39 0376 448428, www.thermomat.com

Domestic Staff & Nurses

Famiglia Assistenza, Via Castagnole 4, 31100 Treviso, Tel: +39 340 342 3402

Jolli Express, Via Monte Grappa 64, 67051 Avezzano, Tel: +39 0863 412351, jollyexpress@tiscali.it

Milano Work Service, Via Fratelli Bronzetti, 20129 Milano, Tel: +39 02 715820, www.milanoworkservice.it

Torres Victoria Liliana, Via Maestri Campionesi 26, 20135 Milano, Tel: +39 02 5410 1727

Driving Schools

Autoscuola Lucarelli Alvaro, Via Cimabue 20-22, 51039 Quarrata, Tel: +39 0573 775350, autoscuolamontalbano@lucarelli.it

Autoscuola Velox, Via Gazzani 28, 53100 Siena, Tel: +39 0577 40282

Automobile Club Bari, Via Serena 26, 70126 Bari, Tel: +39 080 553 0187, acibari@acibari.it, www.acibari.it

Galletti, Via Emilia Ovest 475, 41100 Modena, Tel: +39 059 828403

Immobiliare 2000, Via Bellini 85, Oriago, 30034 Mira, Tel: +39 041 429288, imm2000@duemilauno.com

Electrical Appliances

Chiale Centrocasa Expert, Via Nazionale 117a, 10064 Pinerolo, Tel: +39 0121 201200, chiale@chiale.it

FAE, Via Ferraris 11, 43036 Fidenza, Tel: +39 0524 518611, fae@faesrl.it

Tricarico Elettrodomestico, Corso Roma 40, 73014 Gallipoli, Tel: +39 0833 266016

Toffoli Elettrodomestici, Centre Commerciale Serenissima 1, 33077 Sacile, Tel: +39 0434 781240, commerciale@toffoligroup.it

Electrical Repairs

3T Elettrodomestici, Via Repubblica 45, 28053 Castelletto Sopra Ticino, Tel: +39 0331 962080, tropy@interfree.it

Home Service, Via Rasponi 19, 00162 Roma, info@home-service.it

Megahertz, Via Messina 14, 09126 Cagliari, Tel: +39 070 343051

Electricians

Angelo Ardori, Via Leone XIII 24, 46023 Gonzaga, Tel: +39 0376 58425

Bertolli Fratelli, Via Gustavo Modena 60, 38065 Mori, Tel: +39 0464 918345

Elio Crosetta, Via Po X 98, 35010 Loreggia, Tel: +39 049 935 5050

Mario Barracu, Piazza Gramsci 8, 58043 Castiglione Della Pescaia, Tel: +39 0564 934091

Pietro Accossato, Via Morbelli 9, 10040 Pralormo, Tel: +39 011 948 1165

Embassies

British Embassy in Rome, Via XX Settembre 80, 00187 Roma, Tel: +39 06 4220 0001, www.britain.it

Embassy of Italy, 14 Three Kings Yard, London, W1K 4EH, Tel: 0207 312 2200, ambasciata.londra@esteri.it

Exporters & Importers

BEL & S, Via San Zaccaria 6, 34125 Trieste, Tel: +39 040 370 2200, m.kujbus@xnet.it

Euriisko Import Export, Via Ridolfi 108, 50053 Empoli, Tel: +39 0571 447013, www.eurisko99.com

FM, Via Roma 17, 31023 Resana, Tel: +39 0423 715948, info@fmexport.it

ITS International Trade Service, Via Gen. Cantore 2, 34170 Gorizia, Tel: +39 0481 530559, its.go@tin.it

Financial Services

The 4Less Group, 160 Brompton Road, Knightsbridge, London, SW3 1HW, Tel: 0207 594 0594, info@the4lessgroup.com

Ashley Law, 30-32 Staines Road, Hounslow, Middlesex, TW3 3LZ, Tel: 0500 104106, www.ashleylaw.co.uk,

Banca d'Italia, 39 King Street, London, EC2V 8JJ, Tel: 0207 606 4201, www.bancaditalia.it

Chase de Vere Financial Solutions, 1 King Street, Manchester, M2 6AW, Tel: 0845 600 0900, www.chasedevere.co.uk

Jayga, PO Box 5854, Wimborne, BH21 3ZS, Tel: 01202 692529, www.jaygaltd.co.uk

The Pension Service, The International Pension Centre, Tyneview Park, Newcastle Upon Tyne, NE98 1BA, Tel: 0191 218 7777, www.thepensionservice.gov.uk

Florists

Ampezzan Fiori, Via Marconi 14, 32043 Cortina d'Ampezzo, Tel: +39 0436 862358, info@fiori.it, www.fiori.it

Fiori Labardi Silvano, Via Doni 20, 50144 Firenze, Tel: +39 055 364105, www.labardifiori.com

Meschi, Via Nuova Cappelletti 17/19, 55018 Segromigno In Monte, Tel: +39 0583 920091, meschisrl@libero.it

Funerals

Barreca Enzo, Via Catania 72, 98124 Messina, Tel: +39 090 293 1490

Onoranze Funebri Fratelli Medea, Via A L Moro 25, 33078 San Vito Al Tagliamento, Tel: +39 0434 81456, medea.of@libero.it

Palmas & Ruggeri, Via Redentore 164, 09042 Monserrato, Tel: +39 070 523385

SER. O.F., Viale O. Flacco, 70124 Bari, Tel: +39 080 500 2588, serof@libero.it

Gardens

Alex Cappelli (Gardener), Via Strada Bagnola 12a, 47014 Meldola, Tel: +39 0543 497166

AM Verde 2000 (Outdoor Pest Control), Via Casalnoceto 63, 00166 Roma, Tel: +39 06 6159 7444

Boletti Ennio (Pools & Fountains), Via Vantini 153, 25011 Calcinato, Tel:+39 030 996 4983, info@enbo.it, www.enbo.it

Genova Garden (Gardening & Plant Sales), Via Somalia 14, 16146 Genova, Tel: +39 010 362 9622

La Franca Vincenzo (Nursery), Corso Mille 1171, 90122 Palermo, Tel: +39 091 476615

Limpia (Gardener), Riviera di Chiaia 276, 80121 Napoli, Tel: +39 081 240 0376

Re di Fiori (Gardening), Via San Sebastiano 6, 34121 Trieste, Tel: +39 040 305621, redifiorimarcovich@tiscali.it

Pulizie Tergi di Bova Teresa (Gardening), Via Fontanassa 15/3, 17100 Savona, Tel: +39 019 820805

Glaziers

Artigiani Marco & Associati, Via Mameli 44, 20129 Milano, Tel: +39 02 7611 0088

Futur Glass, Via di Vittorio 12, 41011 Campogalliano, Tel: +39 059 527047

MI.RO. Glass di Rossi Mirko, Via Torino 25, 22063 Cantù, Tel: +39 031 714973, miroglass@libero.it

Vetreria Pini Giuliano & C., P.te San Marco 51, 25011 Calcinato, Tel: +39 030 996 9933

Heating

Bencistà Giuseppe di Bencistà Cesare & C., Via Livorno 8/20, 50142 Firenze, Tel: +39 055 732 7138, bencistagi@virgilio.it

BF Impianti, Via Cesare Battisti 2, 21040 Lozza, Tel: +39 0332 812383, bf-impianti@libero.it

Centra Cristian, Corso Amendola 43, 60123 Ancona, Tel: +39 071 205520

Clima Center, Via Tuscolana 892, 00174 Roma, Tel: +39 06 7696 7933, www.climacenter.it

Domotecnica Italiana, Viale Venezia 59, 31020 San Vendemiano, Tel: +39 0438 3644, www.domotecnica.it

Electra, Via del Mare 97, 20142 Milano, Tel: +39 02 8950 0212, www.electraonline.it

Fiorin Impianti, Via del Lavoro 13, 31013 Codognè, Tel: +39 0438 470062, info@fiorinimpianti.it

Termo Sanitari di Zolezzi Luigi & C., Corso Dante 117, 16043 Chiavari, Tel: +39 0185 309619

Home Furnishings

Area, Piazza Libertà 10, 37014 Castelnuovo Del Garda, Tel: +39 045 715 0201, area.sas@tin.it

Avant Garde Arredamenti, Via Pian di Guido 8, 52036 Pieve Santo Stefano, Tel: +39 0575 799070, arredamenti@avantgardebynasini.com

Centro del Mobile di Sereno Fratellli, Via Marconi 54, 12044 Centallo, Tel: +39 0171 211333

Chiarugi, Via P. Valdera 140-144, 56038 Ponsacco, Tel: +39 0587 731133

Giglio Ceramiche, Via Nazionale 45/47, 98079 Tusa, Tel: +39 347 810 3836

Guazzolini Mobili, Via San Apollaria 2, 00039 Zagarolo, Tel: +39 06 687 7145, www.guazzolini.it

El Marangon, Via Marini 84, 31020 San Zenone Degli Ezzelini, Tel: +39 0423 968778, www.elmarangon.com

Mobilart Sardo Rustico, Zona Industriale Sett. 4, 07026 Olbia, Tel: +39 0789 58629, mobilarts@tiscalinet.it

Nasini Arredamenti, Via Tiberina 61, 52036 Pieve Santo Stefano, Tel: +39 0575 799028

Nuovarredo, Via per Grottaglie, 72021 Francavilla Fontana, Tel: +39 0831 819881, www.nuovarredo.it

La Permanente Mobili Cantù, Piazza Garibaldi 9, 22063 Cantù, Tel: +39 031 712539, info@permanentemobilicantu.it

Peroni Arredamenti, Via Tuscolana 1197, 00173 Roma, Tel: +39 06 723 4026, www.peronimobili.it

Insurance

Andrew Copeland Insurance Consultants, 230 Portland Rd, London, SE25 4SL, Tel: 0208 656 2544

Bernese Assicurazioni, Via G. Guattani 6/a, 00161 Roma, Tel: +39 06 441641

Ergo Italia, Via Pampuri 13, 20100 Milano, Tel: +39 02 57441

Genialloyd, Viale Monze 2, 20127 Milano, Tel: +39 02 28351, www.genialloyd.it

Gruppo Filo Diretto, Via Paracelso 14, 20041 Agrate Brianza, Tel: +39 039 605 6804, www.filodiretto.it

London & European Title Insurance Services, 5th floor, Minerva House, Valpy St, Reading, Berks, RG1 1AQ, Tel: 0118 957 5000

Ocaso Insurance Services, 3rd floor, 110 Middlesex St, London, E1 7HY, Tel: 0207 377 6465

Sharpley & Regent Insurance Services, 38 Alexandra Road, Lowestoft, NR32 1PW, Tel: 0845 130 0202, sri@srins.co.uk, www.srins.co.uk

Zurich Italia, Piazza Erba 6, 20129 Milano, Tel: +39 02 59661

Interior Designers

A.B.I. di Rivella A. & C., Via Cento Croci 4, 10025 Pino Torinese, Tel: +39 011 842477, t-agnese@virgilio.it

Abitare Design, Via Giovanni Prati 18, 38100 Trento, Tel: +39 0461 232103, abitare.design@virgilio.it

Amlor Design, Via Gattorno 9, 29100 Piacenza, Tel: +39 333 412 7082, info.amlor@libero.it

Arkimede Multiservizi, Via Ghibellina 14/r/b, 50122 Firenze, Tel: +39 055 246 6211, info@arkimedeservice.it

Marchini Marco Studio d'Arte, Via Venosa 19, 20137 Milano, Tel: +39 02 546 6337, marcomarchini@usa.net

Language Schools (Italy)

Cultura Italiana, Via Castiglione 4, 40124 Bologna, Tel: +39 051 228011, www.culturaitaliana.it

Il Centro, Via Brera 11, 20121 Milano, Tel: +39 02 869 0554, www.ilcentro.net

International House Language Centre, Via Quintino Sella 70, 90139 Palermo, Tel: +39 091 584954, www.ihpalermo.it

Istituto Venezia, Campo Santa Margherita 3116a, Dorsoduro, 30123 Venezia, Tel: +39 041 5224331, www.istitutovenezia.com

Rimini Academy, Via Q. Sella 31, 47900 Rimini, Tel: +39 0541 26665, www.riminiacademy.it

StudioItalia, Via dei Gracchi 71, 00192 Roma, Tel: +39 06 3600 3865, www.studioitalia-italy.it

Language Schools (UK)

Anglo Italian Teaching & Translation, 34 St. Marys Lane, Louth, Lincolnshire, LN11 0DT, Tel: 01507 609328

Babble Language School, 72 Union Street, Farnborough, Hampshire, GU14 7QA, Tel: 01252 691474

Italian Language & Culture Diffusion Centre, Rodwell Tower, 111 Piccadilly, Manchester, Lancashire, M1 2HY, Tel: 0161 236 1938

Italian Tuition, 55 Dean Street, London, W1D 6AF, Tel: 07774 703686

Language Upon Thames, 53a George St, Richmond, Surrey, TW9 1HJ, Tel: 020 8940 5400, info@languageuponthames.co.uk, www.languageuponthames.co.uk

Leigh Languages, Bedford House, 4 Westbury Rd, Buckhurst Hill, Essex, IG9 5NW, Tel: 020 8504 3652

Legal

Bennett & Co, 144 Knutsford Road, Wilmslow, Cheshire, SK9 6JP, Tel: 01625 586937, www.bennett-and-co.com

Chiomenti Studio Legale, 20 Berkeley Square, London, W1J 6HF, Tel: 0207 569 1500, www.chiomenti.net, london@chiomenti.net

CMS Adonnino Ascoli & Cavasola Scamoni, Via Agostino Depretis 86, 00184 Roma, Tel: +39 06 478151, info@aacs.it, www.aacs.it

De Pinna Notaries, 35 Piccadilly, London, W1J 0LJ, Tel: 0207 208 2900, info@depinna.co.uk, www.depinna.co.uk

Gianni, Origoni, Grippo & Partners, Via delle Quattro Fontane, 00184 Roma, Tel: +39 06 478751, rome@gop.it, www.gop.it

International Property Law Centre, Unit 2, Acorn Business Centre, Waterside Park, Livingstone Road, Hessle, HU13 0EG, Tel: 0870 800 4591, www.internationalpropertylaw.com

LCA Legal and Tax Advisors, 16 Old Bailey, London EC4M 7EG, Tel: 0207 597 6491, www.studio-lca.com

MB Law, King Charles House, King Charles Croft, Leeds, LS1 6LA, Tel: 0113 242 4444, www.mb-law.co.uk

Sammatrice, Via Cola di Rienzo 162, 00192 Roma, Tel: +39 06 689 6272, www.sammatrice.com

Studio Legale Sutti, 19 Princess Street, London, W1R 7RE, Tel: 0207 409 1384, www.sutti.com

Medical Services

BUPA International, Russell House, Russell Mews, Brighton, East Sussex, BN12NR, Tel: 01273 208181, www.bupa-intl.com

Ministry of Health (Italian), Lungotevere Ripa 1, 00153 Rome, Tel: +39 06 59941

Morgan Price International Healthcare, 11a Forge Business Centre, Upper Rose Lane, Palgrave, Diss, Norfolk, IP22 1AP, Tel: 01379 646730

Mortgages

Alexander Hall, 30-32 Lombard Street, London, EC3 9BQ, Tel: 0800 038 3736, www.alexanderhall.co.uk

Balla Brokers, 29 Victoria Street, Douglas, Isle of Man, IM1 2LG, Tel: 0800 652 4410, www.ballabrokers.com

Conti Financial Services, 204 Church Road, Hove, East Sussex, BN3 2DJ, Tel: 01273 772811, www.mortgagesoverseas.com

International Mortgage Plans, Blandings, Cobbetts Hill, Weybridge, Surrey, KT13 0UA, Tel: 01932 830660, www.international-mortgage-plans.com

International Mortgages, Elan House, PO Box 118, Berwick Upon Tweed, TD15 1XA, Tel: 0870 787 5100, www.internationalmortgages.net

Kevin Sewell Mortgages, 7A Bath Road Business Centre, Devizes, Wiltshire, SN10 1XA, Tel: 01380 739198, www.internationalmortgages.org

Mutui Online, www.mutuionline.it

Property Finance 4Less, 160 Brompton Road, Knightsbridge, London, SW3 1HW, Tel: 0207 594 0555 www.propertyfinance4less.com

Notaries

Dr. Alberto Nessi, Via Garibaldi 30, 22100 Como, Tel: +39 031 279270

Dr. Antonio Garau, Via Marconi 73, 09045 Quartu Sant'Elena, Tel: +39 070 880 5435, notaiogarau@tiscali.it

Dr. Luciano Pellegrini, Via San Spiridione 12, 34121 Trieste, Tel: +39 040 634815

Dr. Livia Coco, Piazza Duomo 1/c, 90018 Termini Imerese, Tel: +39 091 811 1151

Rita Merone, Via del Monte 8, 40126 Bologna, Tel: +39 051 270490, merone@tin.it

Opticians

Blu Ottica by Made in Italy, Via Nazionale 44, 31010 Godega Di Sant'Urbano, Tel: +39 0438 388576

Carlo La Barbera, Via Battisti 136a, 00187 Roma, Tel: +39 06 679 4487

Davide Borghesi, Via Marconi 43c, 25069 Villa Carcina, Tel: +39 030 8982078

Francesco Boschetti, Via Cavallotti 6, 25018 Montichiari, Tel: +39 030 964721

Giuseppe Guglielmo, Via Cairoli 9, 00041 Albano Laziale, Tel: +39 06 932 4609

Ottica Gasperini in Piazza, Piazza Garibaldi 42, 09127 Cagliari, Tel: +39 070 659710, web.tiscali.it/otticagasperini

Ottica Gherardi, Via Machiavelli 23, 50026 San Casciano In Val Di Pesa, Tel: +39 055 820176, gherottica@inwind.it

Ottica Torinese di Maura Teppati, Via San Sebastiano 9/10, 54100 Massa, Tel: +39 0585 840480, otticatorinese@ooeyes.com

Pet Transportation

Animal Airlines, Mill Lane Cottage, Mill Lane, Adlington, Macclesfield, Cheshire, SK10 4LF, Tel: 01625 827414

The Animal Inn, Dover Rd, Ringwould, Deal, Kent, CT14 8HH, Tel: 01304 373597

Chilworth Pet Export, Lordswood Lane, Chilworth, Southampton, Hants, SO16 7JG, Tel: 023 8076 6876

Pet Travel Services, 24 Couston St, Dunfermline, Fife, KY12 7QW, Tel: 01383 722819, www.chilworthkennels.com

Skymaster Air Cargo, Room 15, Building 305, Cargo Centre, Manchester Airport, Manchester, Lancashire, M90 5PY, Tel: 0161 436 2190

Trans-Fur, 19 Dene Close, Sarisbury Green, Southampton, Hampshire, SO31 7TT, Tel: 01489 588072, paws2doorpets@trans-fur-animals.com

Plumbers

ACA Idraulica, Via Pitagora 25, 20052 Monza, Tel: +39 039 747435, l.capaldo@tiscali.it

Assistenza Gas Idraulica di Caputo Giovanni, Via Fratelli Macario 5, 10098 Rivoli, Tel: +39 011 959 1510

Euroservice, Via Carducci 30, 20123 Milano, Tel: +39 333 2192026

Idraulica C.M.G., Via Manzoni 2, 21019 Somma Lombardo, Tel: +39 0331 259476, idraulicacmg@libero.it

M. Taiti, Via Bocci 31/35, 50141 Firenze, Tel: +39 055 422 0211, m.taiti@virgilio.it

Novo Impianti di Novo Ugo & C., Corso Torino 38, 10014 Caluso, Tel: +39 011 983 2873

Roland Pfraumer & Co, Via Hans Feuer 18, 39040 Termeno Sulla Strada Del Vino, Tel: +39 0471 861014, pfraumer@dnet.it

Plumbing Supplies

DI EMME BI, Via Tolstoi 79, 20098 San Giuliano Milanese, Tel: +39 02 984 0703, info@diemmebisrl.it

Incea, IS A7 Centro Direzionale, 80143 Napoli, Tel: +39 081 562 5192, info@incea.it, www.incea.it

Pishiutta Renato, Via Idrovore della Maglaine 55, 00148 Roma, Tel: +39 06 655901

Romana Cermiche, Via Appia Nuova km 17,400, 00100 Roma, Tel: +39 06 7934 0203, www.romanaceramiche.it

Property Consultants

Brian A French & Associates, The Nook, Sowerby Street, Sowerby Bridge, West Yorkshire, HX6 3AJ, Tel: 0870 730 1910, www.brianfrench.com

Carol Baker, Via Vittorio Veneto 4, 61010 Fratte di Sassofeltrio, Tel: +39 0541 857602, alesorty@libero.it

Casa Tuscany, 205 St Matthew's Gardens, Cambridge, CB1 2PS, Tel: 01223 360523, info@casatuscany.com, www.casatuscany.com

Inter Italia, Via de Gasperi 22, 73020 Uggiano la Chiesa, Tel: +39 328 744 5847, interitalia@libero.it, www.interitalia.biz

Intouch Italia, 3 The Willows, Mill Farm Courtyard, Beachampton, Milton Keynes, Buckinghamshire, MK19 6DS, Tel: 01908 265309, info@intouchitalia.co.uk, www.intouchitalia.co.uk

Liliana Pivato – Le Marche Property Sales, Sant Ippolito 8, Amandola 63021, Tel: +39 0736 854001

Villaman, Via di Tiglio 433, 55100 Lucca, Tel: +39 0583 464591, villaman@tin.it, www.villaman.it

Property Management

Agenzia Aurora Immobiliare, Piazza Aurora 1, 30017 Jesolo Lido, Tel: +39 0421 972118, agenzia.aurora@libero.it

Agenzia Immobiliare Daniela Fumagalli, Via Tripoli 35, 50122 Firenze, Tel: +39 055 244963, daniela@immobiliarefumagalli.it, www.immobiliarefumagalli.it

Giorgio Mazzantini, Corso Roma 11, 19015 Levanto, Tel: +39 0187 801616

HolidayLets.net, Cranfield Innovation Centre, Cranfield, Bedfordshire, MK43 0BT, Tel: 01234 757281, www.holidaylets.net

Pimar Immobiliare, Via Giacomo Leopaldi 34, 63013 Grottammare, Tel: +39 0735 735700, pimarimm@infinito.it, www.pimarimm.3000.it

Properties Umbria, Tel: +39 075 930 2428, www.propertiesumbria.com

Studio Alfa, Via Orazio 59, 39100 Bolzano, Tel: +39 0471 285111, info@studioalfa.info

Relocation

Lore Living Services, Via Santa Monica 2, 50124 Firenze, Tel: +39 055 265 4089, www.loreliving.com

Mercurius Relocations, Via Roma Libera 16, Roma, Tel: +39 333 825 6354, info@mercuriusrelocations.com, www.mercuriusrelocations.com

Relocation Council Italy, www.relo-council-italy.net

Relocation Enterprises, Via Francesco d'Ovidio 35, 00137 Roma, Tel: +39 06 824060, www.relocationenterprises.com

Relocation Support Group, 72 St Mark's Road, Maidenhead, Berkshire, SL6 6DW, Tel: 01628 631111, www.relocationsupport.co.uk

Removals

AGS London, 43-49 Minerva Road Park Royal, London, NW10 6HJ, Tel: 0208 961 7595, www.ags-worldwide-movers.com

A & M Removals, 16 Clayfield Rd, Pocklington, York, North Yorkshire, YO42 2RG, Tel: 01759 301020, nick.davies@tiscali.co.uk

Crown Worldwide, Crown House, Unit 1, Ninian Way, Tame Valley Industrial Estate, Tamworth, Wilnecote, Staffs, B77 5ES, Tel: 01827 264100, www.crownworldwide.com

Excess International Movers, 4 Hannah Close, Great Central Way, London, NW10 0UX, Tel: 0800 783 1085, sales@excess-baggage.com, www.international-movers.com

Grayline Overseas Direct, Unit B1, Lower Farm, Wrotham Road, Meopham, Gravesend, Kent, DA13 0AN, Tel: 07803 014955, www.graylineoverseasdirect.com

Lawlers, Dronfield Storage Centre, Wreakes Lane, Dronfield, Derbyshire, S18 1PN, Tel: 0800 542 3249, www.lawlersremovals.co.uk

Rosenkavalier Removals & Storage, 3 Clifton Arcade, 1a Boyces Avenue, Bristol, BS8 4AA, Tel: 0117 973 0500, bengraves@hotmail.co.uk

Scottish Removal Services, 3 Carsegate Road North, Inverness, IV3 8DU, Tel: 0800 195 9173, www.scottish-removals.com

Walkers International Movers, 33-34 Lilliput Road, Brackmills Industrial Estate, Northampton, Notts, NN4 7DT, Tel: 01604 704030, www.walkersremovals.co.uk

Security

Cooperativa V.O.L.P.E. (Personnel), Via Stufa Secca 24, 53100 Siena, Tel: +39 0577 44300

E.L.G.A. Sycursistem (Technology), Via Necropoli Grotticelle 26/c, 96100 Siracusa, Tel: +39 0931 44118, elgasicursystemss@virgilio.it

E.R.H. di Sambellini Ottavio (Technology), Via Baracca 43, 20017 Rho, Tel: +39 02 930 2125

L'Investigatore (Personnel), Centro direzionale, isole G2, 80143 Napoli, Tel: +39 081 787 9288

Professional Security (Technology), Via Mastri 12, 50135 Firenze, Tel: +39 055 600609, www.profess-sec.it

Ultrak a Honeywell Company (Technology), Via Treviso 2/4, 31020 San Vendemiano, Tel: +39 0438 3651, info@ultrak-italy.com

V.C.M. Vigilanza Città di Milano (Personnel), Via Monte Generoso 37, 20155 Milano, Tel: +39 02 326 6583

Travelling through Europe?

Make sure Michelin is with you all the way!

Surveyors

Ag Associati Architetto Zurli Andrea & Geometra Parati Giampaolo, Via Tresimeno 7, 52100 Arezzo, Tel: +39 0575 182 2164

Agostinelli Catherine geometra, Via Federici Marco 46, 19122 La Spezia, Tel: +39 0187 704023

Agp Compas Del Geometra Pizzano Alfonso, Via Pasolini 14, 09010 Villa San Pietro, Tel: +39 070 907581

Alborno Studio Associato A 2, Via Lagazzi 12, 18012 Bordighera, Tel: +39 0184 262529

Geometra Angelo Nicotra, Via Umberto 65, 98030 Gaggi, Tel: +39 0942 47081

Immobiliare 'Il Borgo', Via Francesco da Barberino 20, 50021 Barberino Val d'Elsa, Tel: +39 055 807 9124, www.immobiliareilborgo.it

Maurizio Sangalli Maurizio geometra, Via Ferrini Contardo 11, 20135 Milano, Tel: +39 02 55184581

Pirelli RE Agency, Via del Fiumicello 7, Napoli 80142, Tel: +39 081 694 8111, residenza@pirellire.com

Salvatore Caico Studio Tecnico Geometra, Via Vittorio Emanuele 333, 92024 Canicattì, Tel: +39 0922 831174

Studio Tecnico Salatino, Via Girasoli 17/e, 00172 Roma, Tel: +39 06 3550 0355, a.salatino@email.it

Swimming Pools

Aquaform Piscine e Benessere, Via Cascina Croce 190, 20010 Cornaredo, Tel: +39 02 9356 2087, www.aquaform.it

Big Blu, Via dell'Artigianato, 53011 Castellina In Chianti, Tel: +39 0577 740280, www.bigblu.it

Centro Italia, Via Silvio Giovaninetti 37, 00123 Roma, Tel: +39 06 3089 5183, www.centroitalia.it

Olympic Italia, Via de Gasperi, 92024 Canicattì, Tel: +39 0922 855955, olyital@tin.it

Pinna Fratelli, Zona industriale - Settore 7, 07026 Olbia, Tel: +39 0789 53870, www.fratellipinna.it

Tax

Ex-Pat Tax Consultants, Suite 2, 2nd Floor, Shakespeare House, 18 Shakespeare Street, Newcastle Upon Tyne, NE1 6AQ, Tel: 0191 230 3141, www.expattax.co.uk

Expatriate Tax Solutions, Global Tax Network Ltd, No 1 Poultry, London, EC2R 8JR, Tel: 0207 415 4009, www.expatriatetaxsolutions.com

The Fry Group, Crescent House, Crescent Road, Worthing, West Sussex, BN11 1RN, Tel: 01903 231545, www.thefrygroup.co.uk

HM Revenue and Customs, Centre for Non Residents, Fitzroy House, PO Box 46, Nottingham, NG2 1BD, Tel: 0845 070 0040, www.hmrc.gov.uk/cnr/index.html

Telecommunications

MCI Worldcom, Corso Garibaldi 86, 20121 Milano, Tel: +39 02 360011, info_it@lists.mci.com, global.mci.com/it

Phone Center, Via Sciascia 30, 95030 Gravina Di Catania, Tel: +39 095 725 5191, info@phonecenter.it

Telecom Italia Group, Tel: +39 339 9119, www.privati.tim.it/eng

Translation (Italy)

AG. Speakeasy, Via Lanzarini 8, 40127 Bologna, Tel: +39 051 363677, speakeasygroup@libero.it

Alba del Prof. Edmond Maksuti, Via B Bernardini 120, 00156 Roma, Tel: +39 06 411 5794, albatraduzioni@virgilio.it

Global Target, Corso Palestro 5, 10122 Torino, Tel: +39 011 1970 4450, p.palmesano@globaltarget.it

Language Centre, Via Sella 70, 90139 Palermo, Tel: +39 091 584954, www.ihpalermo.it

Simultanea di Manuela Ravetta, Stefania Marzani & C., Via Pontaccio 12/a, 20121 Milano, Tel: +39 02 72001266

TDR, Via Pordenone 13, 20132 Milano, Tel: +39 02 2159 7210

Translation (UK)

Domenico Hill German & Italian Translation, 18 Sydenham Rd, Knowle, Bristol, BS4 3DF, Tel: 0117 971 5722

Italeng, Kinver House, 22 Barbrook Drive, Brierley Hill, West Midlands, DY5 3PZ, Tel: 07957 860777

Italian & French Translation Services, 18 Nappin Close, Aylesbury, Bucks, HP20 1LY, Tel: 01296 487634

Italia Translating & Interpreting, 38 Woodhead Rd, Read, Burnley, Lancs, BB12 7PH, Tel: 01282 773183

Italian Translating Service, 26 Arran Rd, London, SE6 2NL, Tel: 020 8695 6751

Travel – Air

Air One, Via Cesare Giulio Viola 27, 00148 Roma, Tel: +39 06 4888 0069, www.flyairone.it/en

Alitalia, 2a Cains Lane, Bedfont, Middlesex, TW14 9RL, Tel: 0870 544 8259, www.alitalia.co.uk

British Airways, Waterside, PO Box 365, Harmondsworth, UB7 0GB, Tel: 0870 850 9850, www.ba.com

British Midland, Castle Donnington, Derby, DE74 2SB, Tel: 0870 607 0555, www.flybmi.com

BMI Baby, PO BOX 737, Castle Donington, Derby, DE74 2XP, Tel: 0870 264 2229, www.bmibaby.com

easyJet, easyLand, London Luton Airport, Bedfordshire, LU2 9LS, Tel: 0871 244 2366, www.easyjet.com

Excel Airways, Explorer House, Fleming Way, Crawley, West Sussex, RH10 9GT, Tel: 0870 169 0169, www.xl.com

Jet2, PO Box 6190, Christchurch, BH23 9AY, Tel: 0871 226 1737, www.jet2.com

KLM, Plesman House, Cains Lane, Feltham, Middlesex, TW14 9RL, Tel: 0870 507 4074, www.klm.com

Meridiana, Via Barberini 67, 00187 Roma, Tel: +39 0199 111333, www.meridiana.it

Monarch, Prospect House, Prospect Way, London Luton Airport, Bedfordshire, LU2 9NU, Tel: 0870 040 5040, www.flymonarch.com

Ryanair, Corporate Head Office, Dublin Airport, Co. Dublin, Ireland, Tel: 0871 246 0000, www.ryanair.com

Thomsonflights.com, Balmoral House, Hollins Brook Way, Bury, BL9 8RR, Tel: 0800 107 1517, www.thomsonflights.com

Travel – Coach

ATVO, Piazza IV Novembre 8, 30027 San Dona' di Piave, Tel: +39 0421 594508, noleggi@atvo.it, www.atvo.it

Autolinee Reni, Via Albertini 18, 60020 Ancona, Tel: +39 071 804 6504, www.anconarenibus.it

Autoservizimereu, Piazza Giovanni XXIII 37, 09128 Cagliari, Tel: +39 070 494345, www.autoservizi.com

Eurolines, Unit 6/7 Colonnades Walk, London, SW1W 9SH, Tel: 0870 514 3219, www.eurolines.co.uk

Interbus, Via Roma 353, 94100 Enna, Tel: +39 0935 503141, www.interbus.it

SITA, Viale dei Cadorna 105, 50129 Firenze, Tel: +39 055 47821, www.sita-on-line.it

Sulga, Strada dei Cappuccinelli 2, 06125 Perugia, Tel: +39 075 5009641, www.sulga.it

Travel – Ferry

Brittany Ferries, Millbay Docks, Plymouth, Devon, PL1 3EW, Tel: 0870 901 0500, www.brittany-ferries.com

Condor Ferries, Condor House, New Harbour Road South, Hamworthy, Poole, Dorset, BH15 4AJ, Tel: 0845 641 0240, www.condorferries.co.uk

Hoverspeed, International Hoverport, Dover, Kent, CT17 9TG, Tel: 0870 240 8070, www.hoverspeed.co.uk

Norfolk Line, Norfolk House, Eastern Docks, Dover, Kent, CT16 1JA, Tel: 0870 870 1020, www.norfolkline.com

P&O Ferries, Channel House, Channel View Rd, Dover, Kent, CT17 9TJ, Tel: 0870 520 2020, www.poferries.com

SeaFrance, Whitfield Close, Whitfield, Dover, Kent, CT16 3PX, Tel: 0870 571 1711, www.seafrance.co.uk

Sem Marina, 00385 021 352 533, www.sem-marina.hr

Tirrenia Navigazione, Tel: +39 081 317 2999, www.tirrenia.it

Venezia Lines, Santa Croce 518/A, 30135 Venezia, Tel: +39 041 242 4000, www.venezialines.com

Travel – Rail

Deutsche Bahn UK, Tel: 0870 243 5363, www.deutsche-bahn.co.uk

Eurostar, Waterloo Station, London, SE1 7LT, Tel: 0870 518 6186, www.eurostar.com

Eurotunnel, St. Martins Plain, Cheriton High Street, Cheriton, Folkestone, Kent, CT19 4QD, Tel: 0870 535 3535, www.eurotunnel.com

Rail Europe, 178 Piccadilly, London, W1, Tel: 0870 837 1371, www.raileurope.co.uk

Trenitalia, Tel: 89 20 21 (only from within Italy), www.trenitalia.it

Television & Satellite

Alessandro Elettrodomestici, Via Medici 1a, 98076 Sant'Agata Di Militello, Tel: +39 0941 722790, alessandro.fg@tin.it

Benali & Antolini – Bang & Olufsen, Via Fincato 154, 37131 Verona, Tel: +39 045 526717

New Electronics, Via Nazionale 53-54, 80143 Napoli, Tel: +39 081 261051, www.newelectronics.org

Telerent, Via Pellegrino Rossi 14, 20161 Milano, Tel: +39 02 6620 1530, info@telerent.it

Tricarico Elettrodomestici, Corso Roma 40, 73014 Gallipoli, Tel: +39 0833 266016

Utilities

Edison, Foro Buonaparte 31, 20121 Milano, Tel: +39 02 62221, www.edison.it

Italgas, Via XX Settembre 41, 10121 Torino, Tel: +39 011 23941, www.italgas.it

Vets

Ambulatorio Veterinario Associato, 90044 Carini, Tel: +39 091 867 4832

Anubi, Strada Genova 299/a, 10024 Moncalieri, Tel: +39 011 681 3033, info@anubi.it, www.anubi.it

Bruno Laterza, Via Arenaccia 121, 80143 Napoli, Tel: +39 081 780 1400, laterza.b@tin.it

Clinica Veterinaria 24 Hour, Via Senese 259/b, 50124 Firenze, Tel: +39 055 232 2025

Clinica Veterinaria Berica, Via Fratelli Rosselli 28, 36100 Vicenza, Tel: +39 0444 241070, veterinariaberica@libero.it

Clinica Veterinaria San Antonio, Via Montale 2, 25087 Salò, Tel: +39 0365 21596

Diamoci la Zampa, Via Parco 8a, 32043 Cortina d'Ampezzo, Tel: +39 0436 860584, fabiodlz@libero.it

Federico Coccia, Via S. Bandini 16/corner Piazza Carli, 00191Roma, Tel: +39 06 3630 4219, mesotelioma@libero.it

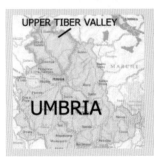

Index to agents

code	Name, address and contact details
ABZ	Abruzzo Houses, Tel: +39 085 291327 Corso Vittorio Emanuele, 78b, 65121 Pescara, www.abruzzohouses.com, info@abruzzohouses.com
AIH	Andiamo Italian Homes, Tel: 01825 723996 Fletchling, East Sussex, TN22 3TD, www.andiamo-homes.com, annie@andiamo-homes.com
APP	Apulia Properties, Tel: 01634 324794 50 Birch Drive, Chatham, Kent, ME5 8YU, www.apulia.co.uk, info@apulia.co.uk
APT	AptaDomus, Tel: 01628 474513 Via Aggiunti 88, Geom. Bruno Coleschi, Sansepolero, www.aptadomus.com, barbara@aptadomus.com
BOR	Borgo de Colleoli, Tel: 0870 243 0314 www.viewtuscany.com/info, info@viewtuscany.com
BUY	Buy a House Italy, Tel: +39 328 093 0519 www.buyahouse-italy.com, info@buyahouse-italy.com
CAS	Casa Tuscany, Tel: 01223 360523 205 St Matthews Gardens, Cambridge, CB1 2PS, www.casatuscany.com, info@casatuscany.com
CAT	Casa Travella, Tel: 01322 660988 65 Birchwood Road, Wilmington, Kent, DA2 7HF, www.casatravella.com, casa@travella.f9.co.uk
CHU	Churchill Overseas, Tel: 01983 550400 Office Suite H, Innovation Centre, St Cross Business Park, Monks Brook, Newport, Isle of Wight, PO30 5WB, www.churchilloverseas.com, info@churchilloverseas.com
CIC	Cicol Italia, Tel: 0208 358 3555 www.cicolitalia.com, info@cicolitalia.com
CIN	Case in Italia, Tel: +39 335 832 9779 Via Romagna 26, 00187 Roma, www.caseinitalia.net, pietro@caseinitalia.net
CIT	Casa Italia, Tel: +39 0743 220122 Piazza della Vittoria 26, 06049 Spoleto, www.casait.it, info@casait.it
DOP	Dionisi Ovington Property Search, Tel: 0208 674 5675 41 Rosebery Road, London, SW2 4DQ, www.dopropertysearch.it, info@dopropertysearch.co.uk
EUS	EuroSarda, Tel: +39 0789 751911 La Fileta 07028, Santa Teresa Gallura, Sardinia, www.eurosarda.it, info@eurosarda.it
FON	La Fonte Immobiliare, Tel: +39 0931 836103 Ronco Leanti n.1, 96017 Noto, www.lafontenoto.it, info@lafontenoto.it
GAR	Garda Homes, Tel: 0800 011 2127 Withybrook, Lockfield, Monmouthshire, NP2S 5QA, gardahomes.co.uk, sarah@gardahomes.co.uk
GTA	Global Target, Tel: +39 025 750 6293 Palazzo Congressi Studio 10, Milanfiori, Assago, 20090 Milan, globaltarget@infinito.it
HAI	House around Italy, Tel: +39 0854 305 318 Pescara Airport, Via Tiburtina, Pescara, www.housearounditaly.com, enquiries1@housearounditaly.com
HII	Homes in Italy, Tel: 01332 341146 22 Irongate, Derby, DE1 3GP, www.homesinitaly.co.uk, mark@homesinitaly.co.uk
HIT	Houses in Tuscany, Tel: +39 0583 644027 Via Garibaldi 18, Castelnuovo Garf, 55032 Lucca, bcasci@libero.it
IBF	Immobiliari Brian French Italia, Tel: +39 075 829 9630 Viale Roma 17, 06065 Passignano Sul Lago, www.brianfrench.com, sales@brianfrench.com
IHS	Italian Houses for Sale, Tel: +39 071 54094 Via Gentiloni 3, Ancona 60128, www.italianhousesforsale.com, info@italianhousesforsale.com
IIS	Invest in Sicily, Tel: 0191 209 9379 www.investsicily.com, info@investsicily.com
INI	Inter Italia, Tel: +39 328 744 5847 Via del Gasperi 22, 73020 Uggiano la Chiesa, www.interitalia.biz, interitalia@libero.it
IPN	Italian Property Network, Tel: 01425 655654 71 High Street, Fordingbridge, Hants, SP6 1AS, www.ipncastello.com, sales@ipncastello.com
ITI	Homes in Italy, Tel: +39 0742 98987 Via Collazzone 11/1, 06058 San Terenziano, www.itili.com, mail@itili.com
IVE	Immobiliare Venanzi, +39 0733 657171 C.so Garibaldi 84, 62028 Sarnano, www.immobiliarevenanzi.it, nicola.venanzi@de.bosch.com
KEC	Kennedy Chilton, Tel: 01572 823315 Leamington House, Uppingham, Rutland, LE15 9TH, kennedychilton@aol.com
LAR	L'Architrave, Tel: +39 0187 475543 Via Montebello 20, Licciana Naroi, 54016 Toscana, www.larchitrave.com, info@larchitrave.com
MAR	Marche Property Network, Tel: +39 0733 694 352 www.marchepropertynet.com, robert@marchepropertynet.com
MHO	Marche Homes, Tel: +39 0733 559268 Cda. Prati 16, 62010 Mogliano, www.marchehomes.com, info@marchehomes.com
MIF	Marken-Immo-Fewo, Tel: +39 0721 981251 Via B. Pozzaccia 30, 61038 Orciano di Pesaro, www.marken-immo-fewo.it, info@marken-immo-fewo.it
MPC	Marche Property Consultancy, Tel: +39 0733 667091 Piazza V. Emanuele No. 1, Palazzo Del Cassero, 62020 Gualdo di Macerata, www.marchepropertyconsultancy.com, info@marchepropertyconsultancy.com
OLI	Oli Properties, www.olipropertiesitaly.com, italy@oliproperties.com
PLC	Property Click, Tel: +39 338 868 4841 www.propertyclick.com, info@propertyclick.com
PIE	Piedmont Properties, Tel: 01344 624096 www.smithgcb.demon.co.uk, info@piedmont.co.uk
PPP	A Place in Puglia, Tel: 01733 394955 www.aplaceinpuglia.co.uk, info@aplaceinpuglia.co.uk
PRE	Precious Villas, Tel: 0870 446 3086 Suite 32-35, London Fruit Exchange, Brushfield Street, London, E1 6EU, www.preciousvillas.com, passerini@preciousvillas.com
REN	Renna Immobiliare, Tel: +39 0831 333289 www.italiarennavacanze.com, ostuni@ostinirennavacanze.com
RIN	Real Invest, Tel: 0207 376 7919" Unit 1, 437 Fulham Road, London, SW10 9TY, www.realinvest.co.uk, info@realinvest.co.uk
SCA	Scalea Property, Tel: 07092 192979 Scalea Property services, 37 Margaret Avenue, Nottingham, NG10 5JW, www.scalea-property.com, info@scalea-property.com
SCH	Sicilian Homes Ltd, Tel: +39 0942 716941 www.sicilianhomes.com, mail@sicilianhomes.com
TRU	Trullishire, Tel: 01444 454886 59 The Hollow, Lindfield, Haywards Heath, West Sussex, RH16 2SX, www.trullishire.com, billl@trullishire.com
UMB/TEC	Properties Umbria, Tel: 01905 381327 www.propertiesumbria.com, properties@tunstill.it
UNI	Unicasa, Tel: 0207 924 3302 Suite 6, Sherwood Court, Riverside Plaza, London, SW11 3UY, www.unicasa-italy.co.uk, info@unicasa-italy.co.uk
VAI	Voltaia Agenzia Immobiliare, Tel: +39 0578 757714 Via Voltaia nel Corso 32, 53045 Montepulciano, www.immobiliare-voltaia.it, voltaia@immobiliare-voltaia.it
VAO	Verde Abitare di Oggero, Tel: +39 0141 955109 Piazza Unione Europea 3, 14047 Mombercelli, www.verdeabitare.it, info@verdeabitare.it

Index to advertisers

Acknowledgements

Contributors

Stefano Bellini
Banca Woolwich

Trinidad Passerini
Precious Villas

Alan Toothill
Apulia Properties

Mark Slaviero
Homes In Italy

Linda Stubbs
Intouch Italia

Images

Micaela Maguolo, Italian Tourist Board

Regional information

Abruzzo
Nikki Di Girolamo, Houses Around Italy Srl
Pier Luca Di Ciccio, Abruzzo Houses

Calabria
David Thorpe, Scalea Property Services

Puglia
A Place in Puglia
Ben Ovington, DO Property Search
Kamran, Apulia Properties

Sicily
Ayan Gorhan, Sicilian Homes
Roger Lewis, Island Breeze
Valeria, Invest Sicily

Tuscany
Diana Levins Moore, Tuscany Inside Out
Karen Roos, Casa Tuscany
Miriam, Casaltalia International
Philippa Tuscia, Retreats/Rural-Retreats-Italy

Umbria
John Tunstill, Properties Umbria
Marc Wisbey, Itili